EL ALAMEIN

The Battle that Turned the Tide of the Second World War

BRYN HAMMOND

First published in Great Britain in 2012 by Osprey Publishing,
Midland House, West Way, Botley, Oxford, OX2 0PH, UK
44-02 23rd Street, Suite 219, Long Island City, NY 11101, USA

E-mail: info@ospreypublishing.com

OSPREY PUBLISHING IS PART OF THE OSPREY GROUP

A CIP catalogue record for this book is available from the British Library.

Print ISBN: 978 1 84908 640 0
PDF e-book ISBN 978
EPUB e-book ISBN 978

Page design by Myriam Bell Design, UK
Index by Mike Parkin
Typeset in Rockwell Condensed and Cambria
Originated by PDQ Digital Media Solutions
Printed in China through Worldprint Ltd

12 13 14 15 16 17   10 9 8 7 6 5 4 3 2 1

Osprey Publishing is supporting the Woodland Trust, the UK's leading woodland conservation
charity, by funding the dedication of trees.

www.ospreypublishing.com

Front Cover: British infantry on patrol near the German lines. (Imperial War Museum, E 14582)

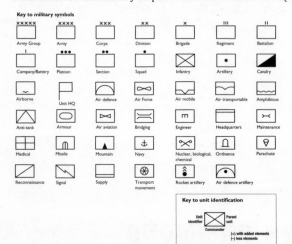

CONTENTS

ACKNOWLEDGEMENTS

In *Cambrai 1917: The Myth of the First Great Tank Battle*, I made full and proper reference to the support and encouragement of friends and family in the preparation and completion of that book during difficult times. The same people have continued to support me and I must offer once more my thanks for their innumerable kindnesses and generosity.

First and foremost, I must thank Abby, Holly and Bryn. Their patience with me during the writing of this book and their pride in their dad's achievements is rewarded by a second 'mention'. This means they are now twice as famous as they were before.

I would also like to thank my wonderful family especially my mum, Margaret, for practical help as well as huge amounts of love, and my brother and sister, Dave and Sarah and their families and loved ones. Dad would be so proud of us all for what we all continue to achieve.

Amongst my fantastic friends, Alan Jeffreys, Philip Dutton, Chris McCarthy and Lee Murrell all generously supported me in practical ways with book loans, advice and encouragement. Alan – a fine historian in his own right – also read early drafts of the text and commented on my Great War perspective on the Second World War. The indomitable Peter Hart found time in his punishing work programme to read draft material and offered comments on my work, none of which can be printed. John Paylor, George Webster and Laurie Milner also gave great help by reading drafts and providing helpful comment. Had they been given more time, they would have made even more valuable contributions than the great help they did offer. Tim Roberts deserves a special mention for the opinions he shared on the relative strengths and weaknesses of British and German armour. Steve Grace and Donald Hislop were especially good at tolerating the idiosyncratic ways of an author with a deadline.

At the Imperial War Museum I was greatly assisted by many members of staff including Julie Robertshaw, Marius Gasior, Sarah Paterson, Tony Richards, Simon Offord, Richard McDonough, Richard Hughes, Sabrina Rowlett, Victoria Rogers, Jane Rosen, Alison Duffield, Alan Wakefield and Ian Proctor. Staff at the Durham County Records Office and National Army Museum were also extremely helpful. A particular thank you goes to Pam and the ladies of Balderton Library and to Nottinghamshire County Council's Library Service who found me many obscure volumes on the Desert War from the Basement Library in Nottingham. Use your local library – you'll be amazed by what you can find there!

I must thank everyone at Osprey but especially Kate Moore, Marcus Cowper and Emily Holmes for patience and encouragement throughout the period in which this book came into being. I hope they will all be proud of the end product. They all worked very hard and were extremely tolerant of my faults.

Two historians, Corelli Barnett and Niall Barr, deserve mention for producing excellent books which considered Alamein but who, between them, left a sufficiently large opportunity for a book of this type to make an additional contribution. I urge all readers of this book to read *The Desert Generals* and *Pendulum of War* as well, if they have not already done so.

Particular thanks must go to all those individuals who gave me permission to quote from the sources for which they hold copyright. Similar thanks must go to the publishers of the various books from which I have quoted for allowing me to do so. I am grateful to The New Zealand Electronic Text Centre, Victoria University of Wellington Library and the New Zealand Ministry of Culture and Heritage for kind permission to publish extracts from *Infantry Brigadier* by Howard Kippenberger and various volumes of the *Official History of New Zealand in the Second World War* series. I hope all those I have been unable to contact or trace, despite my best endeavours, will grant me their forbearance.

The quotations from letters, diaries, personal accounts and oral history interviews used in this book have occasionally, where necessary, been lightly edited for overall readability. Punctuation and spellings have been largely standardised, material has occasionally been re-ordered and irrelevant material has been omitted, usually without any indication in the text. Nevertheless, changes in the actual words used in the original sources have been avoided wherever possible.

Bryn Hammond
December 2011

PREFACE

The desert was the novel element. Despite a twenty-five-year gap, many of the difficulties faced by those fighting in North Africa between late June and early November 1942 were reminiscent of those encountered by the British and Germans in the Great War. The manner in which memoirists, other writers and historians have approached the three 'headline' battles – First and Second Alamein and, sandwiched between them, the battle of Alam Halfa – raises a number of familiar issues. Many of these centre on the cult of the personality that surrounds two of the three chief protagonists, Montgomery and Rommel, but others have contributed to the mythology that surrounds the battle: a misapprehension of events, the ready acceptance of some accounts of participants without consideration for the context in which they were prepared and the motivations in producing them, and a failure to connect with the wider strategic context. This is all familiar ground, in many ways – but the desert remains unique.

There was no single 'Battle of El Alamein' nor, strictly speaking, can the fighting be simply split into 'First' and 'Second Alamein'. These names are convenient devices imposed by historians to provide structure to the events of the period. Each of these chronological periods of fighting comprised many different attacks and counter-attacks. Many were interconnected. Quite often they were not. The British gave many of their attacks the status of 'Operation', but much of the fighting featured Eighth Army in defence and was not so easily labelled. This was like the desert. Vague areas of seemingly featureless sand and gravel given 'labels' in attempts to make sense of something otherwise incomprehensible – a practice reminiscent of the naming of British trenches in the Great War where many struggled to make sense of a bleak and alien landscape – the 'empty battlefield'.

The origins of this book lie in a decision to research and describe the important events of a period of conflict in the Second World War using techniques already proved in looking at a crucial battle of the Great War – the 1917 battle of Cambrai. The personal accounts of participants have once again been used to support and enhance a narrative of the military operations and strategic background and to make a vitally important connection between the decisions of politicians and generals and their very real 'life or death' consequences for men in battle. This has allowed the narrative to develop and explore important tactical and technological contributions by individuals who frequently get ignored in accounts of warfare that focus solely on the senior commanders.

This book, I hope, goes beyond the 'Rommel versus Monty' approach, which sees 'Rommel' as a cipher for the Deutsch–Italienische Panzerarmee and 'Monty' as an odd, but successful chap who fought 'Rommel' and won. The senior commanders feature in this account for their importance in leading and organizing the men who did the fighting and the dying. Montgomery, Rommel and Auchinleck defined the broad framework for military operations, with their decisions being especially connected to the wider strategic situation. This was never more clearly demonstrated than in regard to Rommel's decision to continue his offensive drive into Egypt which provoked the fighting at Alamein, or in Auchinleck's assumption of command of only one of the armies (albeit the crucial one) that made up his enormous Middle East Command.

As this narrative is intended to show, there are other ways to make sense of the battle than solely through the consideration of the actions of the three main generals involved. In support of this approach, the narrative steers away from general use of 'Monty', 'the Auk' and 'the Desert Fox', although all three terms were in currency during the period under consideration. A biographer might consistently refer to his subject, as indeed he does, as 'Monty' but an army commander is no one's 'mate' and such terminology is, therefore, unhelpful to an approach that does feature 'mates' in combat.

In the final stages of preparation of this book, two reminders arrived that the events described here are connected to men alive still today. A local newspaper article regarding the return of a ninety-three year-old veteran to the battlefield with his family was one. This followed the sudden and unexpected contact from the son of Major Tom Bird, who commanded 2nd Battalion, The Rifle Brigade's Anti-Tank Company in the action at 'Snipe' and who is very much alive today. An opportunity to meet a man who added a DSO to his MC and Bar in the fighting was the outcome. I hope all survivors of the battle will feel that this book does justice to the hugely important events in which they participated.

CHAPTER ONE

THE ROAD

A photograph capturing a moment in time, and hinting at a dramatic story. In it, a line of vehicles travelling along a long, straight road watched by a solitary soldier, dressed in shorts with long socks and wearing no hat, without obvious signs of rank on his well-worn tunic. The photograph was taken at El Daba in Egypt on 28 June 1942. The road was the coastal highway from Tobruk in Libya to Alexandria. The vehicles carried the retreating units of the British Eighth Army, comprehensively defeated in recent fighting by their German and Italian opponents and now falling back to defensive positions around the railway halt at El Alamein. Here it was hoped they might stop their opponents' seemingly inexorable advance. The man watching with paternal concern was General Sir Claude Auchinleck, Commander-in-Chief of all British forces in the Middle East, who in time of great crisis had recently assumed command of Eighth Army, and was now preparing for its greatest test of the war. The road stretched back to the horizon suggesting the long road travelled in the Desert War that had finally led to this critical moment.

––––––––––

With the fall of France and Italy's entry into the war on 10 June 1940, British expectations that Italy would ally itself with Nazi Germany were realized. New theatres of operations became a definite concern for the British as territorial possessions, dominions and protectorates came under threat from a new enemy which saw British forces and territories overseas as its primary targets.

The Italian Duce, Benito Mussolini, fearful that the war might end without his Fascist empire becoming a reality, hoped to occupy and annex French and British colonies and Egypt, which was a British protectorate. This would give him control of the Suez Canal and considerable influence on world trade, allowing Italy to dominate the central and eastern Mediterranean.

Their nation's entry into the war was both surprising and unwelcome to many Italians. The most senior commanders knew just how ill-prepared the country was. The reaction of many was one of surprise and despondency – indeed, as Tenente Paolo Colacicchi of the Granatieri di Sardegna recalled:

> In fact, of no enthusiasm at all. Marshal Balbo, who was the governor of Libya and one of the four Fascists – the *Quadrumvirs* of Italy – was apparently playing billiards when the news came through Italy had declared war and he was so angry that he picked up the billiard balls and smashed all the glasses in this billiard room. He was absolutely furious because he knew the position there and he had a lot of friends in Egypt among the British.[1]

Italo Balbo was dead less than a month later, killed when his plane was shot down by Italian anti-aircraft fire whilst over Tobruk harbour, but Maresciallo d'Italia Pietro Badoglio, of the Italian Comando Supremo, continued to counsel against Mussolini's annexationist ambitions. There was little military ardour amongst the Italian troops in Tripolitania and Cyrenaica either, as Paolo Colacicchi confirmed:

> I was commanding a platoon then in a machine-gun battalion on the Tunisian front and I was told to call my men and tell them we were at war now with France (this was a few days before France gave up) and Britain. And the main reaction amongst my men was 'What about our mail? Aren't we going to hear from home anymore?' Which is symptomatic, I think, of the type of man we had there. These were not all young; they were not even good troops. There were some recruits, but there were very few and they were tired and wanted to be home. They were thinking of home, they were thinking of leave and they were thinking of their fields left unattended. They certainly had no imperial or aggressive dream about them. This was one of the problems.[2]

Despite this lack of will amongst many of his subjects, the Duce was not to be denied. In August 1940, Italian forces occupied the British protectorate known as British Somaliland, and Mussolini turned his attention to Egypt, defended by a small, but relatively modern (by comparison with its opponent), Western Desert Force. This consisted of 7th Armoured and 4th Indian Divisions with elements of 6th Division from Palestine. Commanded by Lieutenant-General Richard O'Connor, it comprised approximately 36,000 men. On 9 September 1940, Maresciallo d'Italia Rodolfo Graziani, who had replaced Balbo as commander of Italy's North African forces, was finally persuaded to invade Egypt with the X Armata (Italian Tenth Army) of 80,000 men. After an advance of sixty miles, the Italian force (chiefly composed of unmotorized infantry formations) stopped at Sidi Barrani and set up fortified camps. This was disappointing for O'Connor who had plans to annihilate them if they moved on Mersa Matruh.[3] The Commander-in-Chief Middle East, Lieutenant-General Sir Archibald Wavell, resisted pressure from Prime Minister Winston Churchill to launch an immediate counter-attack. Instead, he and O'Connor began planning an unconventional all-arms surprise attack on the Italian camps.

The plan depended on co-operation from the aircraft of Air Headquarters Western Desert and especially from Air Commodore Raymond Collishaw's No. 202 Group. Despite his aircraft chiefly being obsolete Gloster Gladiators and increasingly obsolescent Bristol Blenheims operating with no radar and an unreliable signals network, Collishaw's guiding principle was that obtaining and retaining air superiority were essential before any other task, even close support for troops in an advance or retreat, could be attempted with any reasonable hope of success. Nevertheless, he and O'Connor forged excellent relations. Chiefly, aircraft were to ensure that the initial advance of almost seventy miles by O'Connor's force was not detected and reported by Italian reconnaissance planes.

Although O'Connor was not a tank officer and had never worked with large armoured forces, this was not a barrier to his successful use of the tanks available to him. There was considerable experience in his command of military exercises in desert conditions, which the British had acknowledged for many years as ideal for armoured warfare. In the inter-war years several formations trained there and, in 1938, Major-General Percy Hobart had trained the 'Mobile Division' (7th Armoured Division's predecessor) in modern armoured warfare theory. Although Hobart was no longer in command by late 1940, 7th Armoured's training put it in good stead for the role envisaged by O'Connor, as O'Connor himself explained:

The 'Infantry' tanks from their name were there to assist the infantry's advance and help them in every possible way and they were obviously used for that. The 7th Armoured Division with its much larger radius of action could be used in a way – especially in this fine desert country – for getting behind and cutting off troops – in fact in the way strategic cavalry used to be used.[4]

O'Connor's unsophisticated approach to the operation was based rather more on common sense than military theory:

It's quite true I had read most of [Basil] Liddell Hart's ideas in his books but at that time the ordinary officer of my 'height' in the army didn't really have any great reason for adopting his point of view. We had our own regulations, our own instructions and I don't think that I considered very greatly Liddell Hart's any more than I considered our own Field Service Regulations. In our very small operation, I can't think I said to myself, 'Now, what would Liddell Hart have done?'[5]

On 9 December 1940, after a long and difficult approach march, shielded by the light reconnaissance units of 7th Armoured and Collishaw's aircraft, O'Connor's infantry with Matilda heavy tanks in close co-operation attacked and routed the Italians. Within two days, 38,000 prisoners, seventy-three tanks and 237 guns had been captured.[6] Soon Bardia and Tobruk had fallen. The Italian forces fell back into Libya but were harried all the way and eventually outflanked and trapped. This culminated in a further heavy Italian defeat on 5 February 1941 at Beda Fomm and the surrender of X Armata with the loss of 130,000 prisoners, 400 tanks and 1,200 guns during the campaign. British losses were 1,744 killed, wounded or missing. O'Connor, having reached El Agheila, was for pushing on into Tripolitania in the hope of completely driving the Italians from Libya, despite being at the end of considerably extended and, therefore, attenuated supply lines. Wavell prevented him from doing so.

The campaign was a masterpiece of all-arms co-operation based on established principles and was possible because of the quality of the highly trained forces at O'Connor's command. In this regard it harked back in many ways to the later battles on the Western Front in 1918. It was the high water mark of British military operations in the Western Desert for over eighteen months but, for many, it was the *radix malorum* of all subsequent failings in those operations. This was through the inappropriate application of its lessons, through the slavish adherence of first 7th Armoured and then other armoured formations to an erroneous tactical doctrine, and because it gave the misleading impression that all Italian formations could be easily overcome in battle.

This critique presupposes that circumstances would have allowed a different approach. They did not. Just as the British Expeditionary Force (BEF) in the Great War had struggled to inculcate 'the lessons of the fighting' in its forces whilst engaged in almost continuous conflict on the Western Front, with few opportunities for meaningful tactical training schemes incorporating, for example, tanks and artillery, so circumstances dictated possibilities for the British Eighth Army (as Western Desert Force became known on expansion to a two-corps organization in September 1941). There was simply no time to review the lessons of the offensive at the level of detail required before events intervened. The strategic situation in the Mediterranean and Africa required Wavell to dispatch a large part of O'Connor's command to Greece. The units that replaced them were newly formed and inexperienced (especially in desert warfare). There was little continuity of learning and few opportunities for training. There were also fundamental problems with the structure and organization of British formations which were not addressed and which were to present particular problems.

British armoured divisions were too heavy on armour and too light on infantry and lacked sufficient artillery (with no self-propelled guns). In tactical terms, this encouraged them to focus on tank-versus-tank operations in which there was no co-operation with the other arms – something which O'Connor believed *was* a result of the influence of Liddell Hart's theories on commanders of armoured units.[7] As a consequence, *ad hoc* formations of all arms *except* tanks were formed. These 'Jock Columns' – named after their inventor Lieutenant-Colonel J.C. 'Jock' Campbell VC of 4th Royal Horse Artillery (RHA) – were typically made up of a battery of 25-pounder field guns, a motorized 'motor' infantry company, an armoured car troop, a troop of 2-pounder anti-tank guns and a section of 40mm Bofors anti-aircraft guns, plus ancillary arms such as medical personnel and signallers. Until July 1942, these seemingly aggressive formations were actually responsible for dissipating the artillery strength of the British in the desert and impeded effective co-operation between the infantry and armour.[8] This tactical schism was exploited repeatedly by the new, and extremely skilful, tactician who arrived soon after the defeat at Beda Fomm to lead their opponent's forces.

The leader of Nazi Germany, Adolf Hitler, was not prepared to see his ally defeated in North Africa and was swift to act. In doing so, he abandoned the 'parallel warfare' approach that had seen Germany and Italy allied but not co-ordinating military action. In view of the critical situation for his Italian allies, a *Sperrverband* (blocking force) of two German troops was sent to Libya to their aid under Operation *Sonnenblume*. The newly promoted, forty-nine-year-old Generalleutnant Erwin Johannes Eugen Rommel was to take command of this Deutsches Afrika Korps (DAK). Rommel was an experienced commander of armoured forces, who had distinguished himself leading 7. Panzer-Division during the invasion of Belgium and France in the previous year. Leutnant Heinz Werner Schmidt of the Deutsche Motorisierte Kompanie recorded his impressions of the Afrika Korps commander soon after arriving from Eritrea to join Rommel's staff:

> The General stands before me. His figure is compact and short. I gain a measure of confidence as I note that, although I am only of middle height, the General is shorter. He gives me a brief, powerful shake of the hand. Blue-grey eyes look steadily into mine. I notice that he has unusual humour-wrinkles slanting downward from above the corners of his eyes to the outer edges of his cheekbones. His mouth and chin are well-formed and strong, and reinforce my first impression of an energetic, vital personality.[9]

From the first, Rommel demonstrated qualities that characterized his entire command of the German and Italian forces in North Africa: a shrewd cunning which, in connection with tactics, earned him the nickname (from his own troops) of *der Wüstenfuchs*, the Desert Fox,[10] and a flagrant disregard for the orders and opinions of the Italians. He was, notionally, under the command of Generale di Corpo Armata Italo Gariboldi, who had succeeded Graziani after the latter's resignation. However, neither Gariboldi nor Generale d'Armata Ettore Bastico, who in turn succeeded Gariboldi in July 1941, could control Rommel. From the first arrival of German troops, Rommel's decisions were the critical ones for the deployment and use of both German and Italian units.

A misleading impression resulted in that it was seemingly solely the arrival of the Germans that saved the Axis war effort in North Africa. But Rommel also benefited from Italian reinforcements, including 132ª Divisione Corazzata 'Ariete' – the first complete armoured division to arrive – under Generale di Divisione Ettore Baldassarre and a motorized division, 102ª Divisione Motorizzata

'Trento'. These were formations better suited to desert conditions by virtue of possessing motorized transport, although Italian tanks were both under-gunned and not as well armoured as the German Panzer III and IV.

It was Italian formations that were initially sent forward to Sirte on 14 February, at Rommel's insistence, to oppose any further British advance. On the same day Aufklärungs-Abteilung 3 (mot), the first German Army unit, landed at Tripoli. The next day, the first tanks of Panzer-Regiment 5 were landed. By 10 March the regiment, consisting of twenty-five Panzerkampfwagen (PzKpfw) I forty-five PzKpfw II sixty-one PzKpfw III, seventeen PzKpfw IV and seven *Panzerbefehlswagen* (armoured command vehicles), had disembarked. Rommel covered this build-up of armour by two acts of deception. The first was intended to fool British aerial reconnaissance, as Oberleutnant Hans-Otto Behrendt, an *Ordonnanzoffizier*, or staff officer, in the blocking force, explained:

> In the port of Tripoli in February 1941, Rommel told my friend, Leutnant Hundt
> – an engineer: 'Hundt, here you can build me 150 tanks'. The man looked stupefied
> and Rommel told him 'Don't you have timber here in the harbour and canvas of
> sails to make 150 covers for Volkswagens? So you can give me 150 tanks.' And
> those tanks misled the British in the first campaign.[11]

A parade of German armoured strength through Tripoli offered the second opportunity. Behrendt's fellow *Ordonnanzoffizier*, Heinz Werner Schmidt, provided a vivid description:

> Singly and at regular intervals the Panzers clattered and rattled by. They made
> a devil of a noise on the macadamized streets. Not far past the saluting base the
> column turned into a side street with mighty squeaks and creaks. I began to
> wonder at the extraordinary number of Panzers passing, and to regret that I had
> not counted them from the beginning. After a quarter of an hour I noticed a fault
> in one of the chains of a heavy Mark IV Panzer which somehow looked familiar
> to me although I had not previously seen its driver. Only then did the penny drop,
> as the Tommies say, and I could not help grinning. Still more Panzers passed,
> squeaking and creaking round that bend.[12]

Thus, a relatively small force of tanks was made to appear much larger simply by following a circuitous route. These *ruses de guerre* bought Rommel useful time. On 21 February his force was officially named the Deutsches Afrika Korps, when Generalmajor Johannes Streich's 5. leichte-Division arrived. Rommel was helped by the British reorganization of units, which included the withdrawal of 7th Armoured Division to the Nile Delta to refit. With the British forces taking a defensive posture, initiative passed to the Axis commander. Rather than staying on the defensive, he decided to attack and, on 31 March 1941, a series of battles began which were to ebb and flow eastwards and westwards across the Western Desert for the next fourteen months.

Rommel's initial advance had been intended as an armoured reconnaissance in keeping with his orders for defence, but soon became a fully fledged offensive. Fifteen convoys had delivered 25,000 German troops, 8,500 vehicles and 26,000 tons of supplies to Tripoli by the end of March.[13] This included the first elements of 15. Panzer-Division. With this strength, his forces no longer had to be shielded by the Italians. On 19 February, the Luftwaffe (in the form of Messerschmitt Bf-110s of Zerstörergeschwader 26 (ZG-26)) claimed its first victories in the Desert Air War whilst Fliegerführer Afrika, Generalmajor Stefan Fröhlich, now had two *Gruppen* (squadrons) of Junkers 87 'Stuka' dive-bombers, a *Jagdgeschwader* (fighter wing) of Messerschmitt Bf-109s and an *Aufklärungsgeschwader* (reconnaissance wing) with which to support land operations.

Under attack, the British forces were forced back out of Cyrenaica in a matter of days and several senior commanders including O'Connor, Lieutenant-General Sir Philip Neame VC (O'Connor's successor), Major-General Michael Gambier-Parry (2nd Armoured Division) and Brigadier John Coombe, who had played an important role in the successful British operations in late 1940 to early 1941, were all captured. As the retreat continued Wavell decided that the port of Tobruk must be defended. Lieutenant-General Sir Leslie Morshead's 9th Australian Division and a brigade from 7th Australian Division with four regiments of British artillery and some Indian troops occupied fortified positions around the port, which was soon invested. The remaining British formations withdrew eastwards to the Egyptian border. Tobruk remained besieged from April to November with the defenders supplied and reinforced by sea thanks to the Royal Navy and Royal Australian Navy.

With Tobruk surrounded by the main German–Italian force, a proportion of Rommel's forces pressed eastwards, capturing Fort Capuzzo and Bardia before advancing into Egypt. By the end of April, Sollum had been taken and the tactically important Halfaya Pass was reached. Here the advance was stopped and Rommel garrisoned the captured positions. Significantly, repeated attempts to take Tobruk failed.

The importance of logistics in the Desert War was again emphasized by this failure. Rommel's most advanced units were at the end of a vastly overextended supply chain stretching back to Tripoli. Without possession of Tobruk as an advanced supply base, it was doubtful whether the Axis forces could remain in these dispositions for an extended period. The wider strategic situation was also influential as the Luftwaffe Fliegerkorps X, which had been attacking British land and naval forces and the besieged island of Malta, was moved to Greece in May to support the Axis forces there and against Crete. This allowed Malta to be resupplied and sustained as a threat against the German–Italian North African force's supply routes.

With Churchill demanding action, Wavell launched two attempts to relieve Tobruk. Neither Operation *Brevity* in May, nor a larger-scale offensive Operation *Battleaxe* in June, was successful. *Battleaxe* was a triumph for the German 88mm Flak anti-aircraft guns, numbers of which were deployed in an anti-tank capacity.[14] These knocked out even the most heavily armoured British tanks, the Infantry 'Matildas', at ranges of 1,500 yards, although the 88mm was not recognized as the weapon responsible until some time afterwards.

Rommel's first offensive operations included several features that were significant throughout the North African campaign. The influence of the problems arising from supplying both British and Axis forces cannot be understated. Theoretically, the much shorter supply routes from Italy to the theatre of operations should have been to the German and Italians' advantage. Supplies of equipment and troops from Britain had to be sent round the South African Cape and into Egypt 'via the back door'. These extended supply routes were still vulnerable to German U-boats, aircraft and surface raiders – especially in the North Atlantic. Nonetheless, the efforts of the Royal Navy and the Royal Air Force and the continued presence of an untaken Malta as an advanced base for attacks by aircraft and submarines on the Italian shipping chiefly responsible for transporting all necessary supplies to the Axis forces meant that an important threat remained unconquered, with significant consequences later.

However, the chief problem for Rommel and his Italian allies was the limited capacity of the Libyan ports that restricted Axis supplies. In ideal circumstances, Tripoli could deal with, at most, only five large cargo ships or four troop transports at any one time, and about 45,000 tonnes of supplies per month could pass through. Benghasi could manage only three cargo ships or two troop transports, and deal with 24,000 tonnes per month. It was also often subject to bombing. When Tobruk was captured and used by the Panzerarmee, its capacity was found to be about the same number of vessels as Benghasi but only 18,000 tonnes of supplies per month. Because of these restrictions, generally the requirements of the Axis forces operating in North Africa greatly exceeded the capacity of the ports to supply them.

There were more problems when transporting supplies from the ports. From Tripoli to Benghasi alone was about 600 miles and there was only one proper road along the coast which could be used for this. By comparison, it was only 600 miles from the Polish border to Moscow and there were many roads and railways along this route.[15] Almost all supplies for the Axis fighting formations had to be transported by large numbers of lorries – an enormous logistical operation which used up perhaps as much as a third of all the vital and scarce supplies of fuel landed. The lorries were also constantly at risk from air attack on this road.

Further east, British transport and supplies were transported with the same risks in similar circumstances. However, it was the Axis forces, rather than the British and Commonwealth troops, who were forced to lead a hand-to-mouth existence for much of the time. Allied troops could also be supplied from India – although the soldiers might rail at the quality of some 'essentials' (particularly cigarettes) they received from this source. The Germans and Italians seldom had sufficient supplies for their needs and often struggled to have even the most basic requirements on occasion. At best, they had to do without many non-essential items. At worst, even supplies of fuel or ammunition dropped to critical levels.

This dearth of essentials meant that Axis troops soon turned to other sources of supplies – especially those of their opponents. Uniforms, vehicles, equipment, weaponry, rations and fuel were all captured and used – although in some cases the quality of their own issue was markedly better. The supply question was a source of acrimonious dispute between the Axis allies. Many German commanders and their men blamed the Italians for the inadequacy of supplies, although, in fact, the Oberkommando der Wehrmacht (OKW) – the German High Command – had set the priorities after June 1941, with the war against the Russians foremost. The Italian war economy was not geared to supply its own forces on land, sea and in the air with adequate resources and, in struggling to do so, had nothing to spare for the Germans. The failure to address these logistical problems was an indication of Rommel's weakness in a crucial area of generalship at the level of command he now held.

A further feature of the fighting was Rommel's aggressive personal style of leadership, more suited to the command of an armoured division than a corps or army. Hans-Otto Behrendt described him as follows:

> He was a commander with instinct, as he told me once. An instinct to know where the enemy was weak – but he found that out personally. He was a good leader because he did not ask more of his troops than he was ready to give himself.
>
> The Afrika Korps soldiers sensed instinctively that he knew his business as a leader; he was never indecisive and, above all, he was often right up there with them, at the front facing the enemy. There he often issued orders that asked a lot of his troops and more, but thanks to their efficiency and devotion they resulted in victories in the 'good times' and were faithfully executed without grumbling during the retreat.[16]

This energetic and high-risk approach inevitably took its toll on his health but whether in a Fieseler Storch aircraft on personal reconnaissance or in a captured AEC Dorchester command vehicle known as a *Mammut*, Rommel maintained close contact with his front-line troops. Frequently, he was well forward with only his *Begleitkommando,* or escort group, for protection. This body later became the basis from which his *Gefechtsstaffel* (his tactical operations command and signals unit) or *Kampfstaffel* (combat echelon) was formed.

It should be emphasized, however, that this 'personal example' command style was not uniquely Rommel's. The nature of the Desert War and the employment of mobile formations often necessitated this approach. British formation commanders – particularly those of armoured divisions but also corps commanders – adopted similar approaches, either by choice or because of necessity. Often, like Rommel, it was because of their background at lower levels of command. Thus, for example, Lieutenant-General William 'Strafer' Gott, who had commanded 7th Armoured's support group and the division itself, had a similar command style whilst Lieutenant-General Sir Charles Willoughby Moke Norrie commanded XXX Corps in late 1941 from a mobile tactical headquarters consisting of four vehicles carrying a couple of staff officers, a wireless tuned to his own corps message net and a second tuned to intercept messages from Rommel's Panzer units.[17] Whilst these men may not have been in direct combat situations, neither is it suggested that Rommel himself *fought* when with his leading units. The difference between the British commanders and Rommel was the unreliability of the British communications. It was all too often the case that at critical junctures in the key battles, British formation commanders in forward positions could not communicate or be contacted. In the battles of manoeuvre, Rommel had more than proved himself, but he had been greatly assisted by the work of his signals units.

The single most important influence on all the campaigns was the desert itself. 'All against the desert' was a truism even before it was used in a memorable post-war film.[18] In combination with the supply situation, the environment had an enormous impact on the conduct of military operations and on the participants in them, as Havildar Nila Kanten of the 5th Indian Brigade, 4th Indian Division, vividly recalled:

> Oh, it was a miserable thing! I wondered why the hell are we fighting here!? Godforsaken place, no water, nothing. No place to hide. Of course, the desert is not completely flat, there are many folds. Two convoys can pass each other without being noticed at a distance of 100 yards. There are so many folds, you see. The only thing is that movement cannot be concealed because of the dust clouds. That's the only handicap.[19]

The desert was not pure sand; it was gravel and rocky outcrops, soft sand and steep ravines. Conditions and 'going' varied between the coastal strip and the desert proper beyond the line of two steep escarpments which was a limestone plateau. This was largely table flat with some depressions and low-lying ridges. The further south one went, the more rugged and variable the terrain became. During daylight hours the heat of the sun on the exposed desert was relentlessly oppressing. At night, temperatures plummeted and it would be bitterly cold – especially in winter. Sudden heavy rainfall was not unknown and could produce floods and boggy ground preventing tanks and vehicles from moving. At all other times, the dust mentioned by Nila Kanten was a major problem, clogging men's throats and the engines and tracks of tanks and reducing visibility to only a few yards.

The desert and its conditions were also a state of mind, depending upon how the individual responded to it. For Major Alf Flatow of the 45th Royal Tank Regiment (Leeds Rifles):

To see the desert sprinkled with tanks, soldiers, tents and lorries was to see a hot Hades of flies, and sand and discomfort. But I sometimes used to get into the Jeep and drive off alone and then it was different. For a long time we had camping places on what once had been a huge primeval forest. Petrified trunks of trees were lying about half covered in the sand and in one or two odd places trunks were still upright to a height of six or seven feet. To the imaginative it could not fail to thrill or stir in a peculiar manner, but I doubt if half a per cent of the Middle Eastern Force who reached the desert went so far as to look at the desert in this way. It was just 'a hole and the sooner we leave it the better' which of course was surely the only materialistic way to look at it.[20]

Water, or rather its absence, was also a hugely important influence on how men lived in this hostile environment. Each man was issued with between four and six pints of water a day but a proportion went to the cookhouse for the preparation of communal food. With significant numbers of troops from the Indian sub-continent, water rationing presented particular problems, as Nila Kanten remembered:

We used to get a gallon of water a day. Out of that gallon sixty-five per cent or seventy per cent went to the cookhouse, for food, tea and everything. The rest of the contribution went for our own drinking and washing. When we joined the army we completely forgot the religion. No purification. Nothing of the sort. We never bothered. The situation made us forget. Nobody was telling us. Even the Sikhs with all their beards and everything, they were the most affected. They had to wash.[21]

The water was especially disliked for what it did to tea – a beverage considered such an essential to the British and Commonwealth men's morale that in 1942 the British government endeavoured to purchase the entire Indian and Ceylonese tea crop. Bombardier Cyril Mount of the 11th Field Regiment, Royal Artillery (RA), told how:

It was salty so the tea always curdled. When you put evaporated milk in the tea it curdled. Whether the salt was put in to replace the salt we were losing through sweat or whether it was coming from wells that had been contaminated by the sea or from salt in the ground, I don't know.[22]

Maintaining personal hygiene was also difficult because of the shortage of water. Cyril Mount continued:

> The water cart would come up and you could fill up. A lot of us still had our canvas buckets from the horse days which you used to carry on your saddle and so you could fill up your canvas bucket, and you could fill up your water bottle. And you might be able to fill a petrol can and if that was the case, if the water was plentiful, you were alright. You were able to wash, never bath. You may have a sponge-down to get rid of the soreness between your crutch. You'd get sweat rashes and prickly heat and so on. But there were no baths. You were expected to shave.[23]

Near the coast, men might be lucky to bathe in the sea, but elsewhere the heat and lack of water posed the risk of illness and disease being spread by inadequate sanitary facilities and attempts were always being made to address this. Cyril Mount recounted:

> Normally people would go off with a spade leaving a good fifty yards from anybody else's position and dig a hole and afterwards fill it in. Like a cat. Eventually some hygienic officer decided we would have a battery command post latrine and we dug this very deep hole and we put ammunition boxes on the soft sand and we put planks across it and a tin of some sort with a hole in to sit on and people used to go and sit on this throne. Until one day it collapsed and we were back to the old system. It fell in. I don't think anyone fell in with it! But it did fall in. That was the end of the attempt to civilize us. [24]

Decent latrines were in fact an essential for every unit camp: Trooper Ian King of the 3rd Hussars, described the arrangements:

> The first task on setting up a camp was to dig a latrine, a narrow hole about nine feet long by six feet deep and three feet wide. Over this was placed a box-like structure with holes cut into it. As there was no need for privacy in the desert, the latrine was open to view. Urinals, commonly known as 'desert roses', were made from cut-down petrol tins, pierced at the base, filled with stones and slightly canted when set in the ground. These were set some distance from the tents and were hygienic enough because the fierce sun soon dried them. Finding them at night was not without risk of becoming lost in the featureless

desert and only the most fastidious used them after dark. It was safer to walk within earshot of one's friends and kick sand over the wet patch.[25]

The desert night was so dark that there was a real risk of a man getting lost when walking even a very short distance in camp – a risk described in a letter home by Lieutenant Charles Potts of the 1st Buffs (Royal East Kent Regiment), 8th Armoured Brigade:

> We find one of the biggest snags in the desert is to find our way about on a dark night, when there is no moon. One can lose one's way going to the latrine only 100 yards away or so, and after walking round in circles for hours one gives up hope of finding the way back, scoops a trench in the sand and sleeps in it, then one wakes up in the morning and finds the camp half a mile away. It's a great life. Here's another cyclone going by and a hellofabig one – wow! And another dust storm – again the camp is wrapped in a cloud of white dust.[26]

These dramatic desert sandstorms, or *gibli*, were, like the desert night sky, an incredible thing to behold.

With the wreckage and detritus of men and battle lying all around the desert, soldiers of all nationalities were plagued by enormous quantities of flies, a problem bitterly recalled by Kannoneer Martin Ranft of Artillerie-Regiment 220, 164. leichte Afrika-Division:

> They were really beastly. They weren't flies like the ordinary house flies. They were horrid. So much bigger and so much more aggressive. We had those nets over our heads but even with those nets they'd cling against the net, trying to get in your eyes – everywhere where they sensed there was moisture. The eyes and the mouth. All day long you'd walk about like that – trying to flick them away with your hand. And they don't really go away. They go a little bit and they come straight back again. They were horrible.[27]

Sergeant Fred Hunn of the 12th Lancers remembered how his squadron of armoured cars spent some time encamped in an especially fly-blown area:

> The squadron was in a wadi thickly populated by millions of flies which settled in hundreds on the face, hands, everywhere. If one made a mug of tea, within seconds the whole of the brew would become a black mass of heaving insects.

Never had so many pests been encountered in all the days spent on the desert. The only relief came when one was covered completely by a mosquito net. Thirty six hours in this place was torture.[28]

Despite best endeavours, the health of the men suffered and especially during the periods between battles. Cyril Mount recalled:

Everybody had desert sores. If you nicked yourself on anything – and there were a hell of a lot of sharp edges ... wherever you nicked yourself, you immediately got what seemed like every fly in Egypt trying to get onto that sore, on that bit of dried blood and no matter what you did you couldn't get rid of them. They'd probe. Their little tongue would be probing right inside that wound and eventually they would become septic. People would be going round with their faces bright violet. I don't know what it was but the MO would paint stuff on their faces and hands. But that didn't keep the flies away. That just disinfected. It was permanganate of potash or something. But it was a very bright violet stuff and it to some extent stopped the infection from spreading. But you still had the flies coming on it.[29]

What helped many men cope with these hellish delights was their youth and general fitness, as Canon Gervase Markham of the 124th Field Regiment (RA) recorded:

I got this dysentery after a bit. I got boils on my face so had to have bandages all over my face and so looked an awful sight for some time. In fact I had to be sent back and be treated at one time. This was very ignominious because to be classed as 'undesertworthy' was a very humiliating thing. But we were all very young and probably very healthy. I was in my twenties and in fact I can remember speaking to a Sergeant who was forty! 'Forty!! A man like you! You ought to be at home!' Forty was an ANCIENT age and it was very unusual to find anyone as old as that – most of them were just lads in their early twenties.[30]

As in any war, despite all the awfulness some men were exhilarated by the experiences they had and relished the desert's challenges. The majority however gritted it out, seeing it as something to be endured with only the hope of leave in Cairo, Alexandria or Tripoli and the desire to see the war ended to sustain them. Meanwhile they did what they could to make themselves as comfortable as possible and took what pleasures life offered, as Heinz Werner Schmidt recounted:

> Although it was against orders, we listened every night to the news and to music broadcast from Cairo. The British had a fairly objective propaganda station there. We learned from Eighth Army prisoners that they too listened to the 'enemy,' particularly to hear *Lili Marlene* played from Belgrade or Athens. The sentimental tune reminded us on both sides that there were other things than aerial bombs and desert warfare.[31]

As a result of the failure of Operation *Battleaxe*, Churchill replaced Wavell as Middle East commander with General Sir Claude Auchinleck. The change was effected on 21 June. It was Auchinleck's fifty-fifth birthday. On the following day, the German attack on the Soviet Union began. Both events had a major influence on the course of the Desert War.

It was in this context that operations in North Africa for the next twelve months took place. Instead of becoming the main focus of the Axis war effort, North Africa now became of secondary importance. On 26 June Italy accepted the change in priorities when Mussolini sent the first units of a *corpo di spedizione Italiano* to Russia. This expeditionary corps subsequently grew into an army of 230,000 men, 22,300 vehicles, 1,100 guns, fifty tanks and eighty-three aircraft – a larger organization than Italy deployed in North Africa. These forces could have had a major impact in North Africa but were sent to Russia in an attempt to maintain the illusion that Italy was a significant power.

On the British side, the new Middle East Commander-in-Chief Auchinleck had been warned by the almost equally new Chief of the Imperial General Staff, General Sir Alan Brooke, that Churchill would expect quick results from an early offensive. However, Auchinleck was a plain-speaking soldier, unable or unwilling to do anything other than offer statements of fact to anyone, including the Prime Minister – no matter how far diplomatic answers might help his cause. He bluntly maintained that launching an offensive with the inadequate means at his disposal was not justifiable. Despite Churchill's relentless pressure he responded with stark facts to explain his forces' unreadiness. Intelligence intercepts via the Ultra network suggested the weaknesses of the Axis forces but Auchinleck judged his troops inadequate in numbers and training. Reinforcements were sent to bolster his forces but Auchinleck still maintained, rightly, the inferiority of the tanks and guns with which they were equipped. On each occasion Auchinleck got his way. However, in September, he appointed Lieutenant-General Sir Alan Cunningham to command what now became Eighth Army. Cunningham arrived fresh from success in East Africa where he had retaken British Somaliland, captured Addis Ababa and forced the surrender of the Duca d'Aosta's forces. The build-up of this army continued with the inclusion of forces from many nationalities including Australian, New Zealand, South African, Indian, Polish and French units. Against them now was the Panzergruppe Afrika (as it became known from August 1941) consisting of three experienced German divisions (15. and 21. Panzer-Division and Division z.b.V. Afrika (Division zur besonderen Verwendung,* which soon became 90. leichte-Infanterie-Division)) and some Italian formations, especially Divisioni 'Ariete' and 'Trento', which might by now be termed veteran. Another motorized formation, 101ª Divisione Motorizzata 'Trieste', had joined in August.

Not until 18 November did Eighth Army open Operation *Crusader*, by advancing against the southern flank of the Axis forces' positions. A deception plan was also used to persuade Panzergruppe intelligence that the main attack would not take place until early December and would be a much more ambitious outflanking manoeuvre than the one planned. This succeeded to the extent that Rommel was not in North Africa when the attack began. Eighth Army's plan relied once more on air co-operation from what was now the Desert Air Force to give them two clear days without serious air opposition. However, bad weather before the offensive resulted in the cancellation of all the air raids planned to interdict the Axis airfields and destroy their aircraft on the ground.

Cunningham's plan depended on the destruction of the Afrika Korps and the Italian armour but this came apart when, after a number of inconclusive engagements, 7th Armoured Division was defeated at Sidi Rezegh. The Axis units fought well, including the Italian Divisioni 'Ariete' and 'Bologna' – a 'semi-motorized' formation. Rommel then made a dash for the Egyptian border with the remnants of his Afrika Korps armour and Divisioni 'Ariete' and 'Trieste' – both placed under his command by Comando Supremo after the success at Sidi Rezegh. He hoped to contact and destroy the main body of Eighth Army. However, he missed his target and Tobruk was relieved on 27 November. Rommel was forced to withdraw his armoured units to fight at Tobruk. His forces were so weakened by the fighting in *Crusader*, that he later

---

* 'for special purposes'.

withdrew to defensive positions at Gazala, west of Tobruk, and then all the way back to El Agheila.

Meanwhile, Auchinleck, realizing that Cunningham had lost belief in the possibility of winning the battle, sacked the army commander and replaced him with Major-General Neil Ritchie from his Middle East Command staff. Ritchie, who had no experience above divisional command, was originally intended as a temporary appointment until a suitable alternative could be found, but ended up leading Eighth Army for more than six months.

Auchinleck himself saw the tactical lessons of *Crusader* clearly. Eighth Army was well short of the necessary standards in combined arms tactics to have any hope of defeating its enemies in the short term. As Auchinleck pointed out:

> We have got to face the fact that, unless we can achieve superiority on the battlefield by better co-operation between the arms, and more original leadership ... we may have to forego any idea of mounting a strategical offensive, because our armoured forces are incapable of meeting the enemy in the open, even when superior to him in numbers.[32]

What Auchinleck leading Middle East Command needed was an Eighth Army commander with 'grip' who would appreciate the problem and work to resolve it. Neil Ritchie was never intended to be that man, but Auchinleck was yet to see how far he fell short.

The wider strategic situation now exercised its influence on the North African campaign as the Japanese attacks in the Far East saw reinforcements meant for North Africa dispatched to Burma, Malaya and India. The stranglehold on Axis supplies gradually developed by the Royal Navy and RAF was broken by the loss of Force 'K' on mines on 18 December, a highly successful and daring attack by Italian mini-submarines ('human torpedoes') on Royal Navy battleships in Alexandria harbour and the deployment of Generalfeldmarschall Albert Kesselring's Fliegerkorps II to Sicily with the explicit purpose of neutralizing Malta and giving support to the Italian–German land forces in the region. Malta was soon being pounded by regular and frequent air attacks. As plans were laid for Operation *Herkules* – the invasion of Malta – Rommel pushed the British back once more and began planning operations with the capture of Tobruk and a subsequent advance to the Egyptian border as the goals. When Malta was taken, supplies would be easier to dispatch to Panzerarmee Afrika (as it became known in January 1942) and an invasion of Egypt could be prepared.

———————

Rommel gathered resources and reorganized ready for his attack. In February 1942 he formed a combat detachment, or *Kampfstaffel*, under his personal command which could be thrown into the fighting at vital points and times to overcome opposition. This formation was well equipped and Rommel himself began to use the SdKfz 250 half-tracks 'Greif', 'Igel' and 'Adler' which were highly mobile and equipped with powerful radio equipment allowing him a greater measure of control over his forces. He was reinforced by more Panzers, especially the Panzer IIIs which were now the workhorses of his two Panzer divisions. Another Italian armoured formation, 133ᵃ Divisione Corazzata 'Littorio', arrived as well as forty Semoventi da 75/18s, Italian self-propelled guns with a low profile, which proved excellent as support artillery and anti-tank guns. The Italian M13/40 tanks, though increasingly obsolescent, were still welcome as, used against the right targets – including the not so well-armoured British 'Cruiser' tanks (such as the Crusader I and II now in use) and 'soft-skinned' i.e. unarmoured vehicles and infantry – they could still perform a useful role, freeing up the heavier Panzers for other work. Italian reinforcements also included 105mm guns and 90mm anti-aircraft guns, which could perform as well as the German '88' in an anti-tank role.

Rommel's force of 90,000 men, 561 tanks and 542 aircraft was opposed by 100,000 men, 849 tanks (including the first supplies of the American M3 'Grant' tanks that had a 75mm gun, mounted in a side sponson, capable of outmatching the Panzer III's 50mm gun) and 604 aircraft. A few 6-pounder anti-tank guns were also available. These were eventually intended to replace the by-now-inadequate 2-pounder gun with which most infantry units and Royal Artillery anti-tank regiments were equipped and which was the gun on all British-built tanks at this time.

Important changes in the Desert Air Strategy also took place. The Commander-in-Chief of the RAF forces in the Middle East, Air Marshal Sir Arthur Tedder, and Air Vice-Marshal Arthur Coningham, commander of the Desert Air Force, now introduced a new strategy focusing during battle on ground support rather than destroying the Luftwaffe and Regia Aeronautica. Fighter-bombers were developed for this task. The contrast was noted by Squadron Leader Billy Drake of 112 Squadron, a pilot with experience in the Battle of Britain:

It was a very interesting period for us who had just come out from England where we'd been a part of the 'interceptor' Fighter Command concept and to come out to the desert where most of the flying was involved in air support of a sort. So, twenty per cent of your time was involved in air-to-air, the rest – eighty per cent – on strafing and releasing bombs in a rather haphazard, but effective way.[33]

The P-40 Curtiss Kittyhawks of 112 Squadron bore distinctive markings leading them to be called the 'Shark Squadron'. Now, as Drake described, an aircraft outclassed in high-altitude air fighting gained a new lease of life in a more appropriate role:

It was obvious when I first arrived that the powers-that-be had decided to use the fighter aeroplane in a form of ground-support aircraft in support of the Eighth Army. To do that we were equipped with bomb racks and carried 500lb bombs with what was called a 'stick' – which was a protuberance in the nose of these bombs so that they would detonate at about a foot above ground to be used as anti-personnel weapons and against soft vehicles. They were also very effective against tanks if you got a bomb close enough. So my life when I took over 112 Squadron was basically in the ground attack mode in support of the Eighth Army.[34]

There was, however, as Drake made clear, a considerable gap between the knowledge of the task and an understanding of the manner in which to accomplish it.

Quite frankly we hadn't a clue what we had to do to carry out this role except it was a *fait accompli* I had a bomb underneath this thing and that it had to be delivered against the Afrika Korps. So, it was a new experience to me and caused me a degree of apprehension particularly as, for the first time, I was up against light ack-ack – which is probably the most frightening aspect of ground attack fighting. Without any warning, the closer you got to the enemy, the more and more light flak. You couldn't see it until you heard a bang. Or they were using tracer. All you saw was tracer coming at you. It was a new experience and it took a few months for me to get used to the idea that this was probably my future in the air force.[35]

Meanwhile, Coningham moved himself and his staff close to Ritchie's headquarters to improve co-operation.

Churchill had, once again, been pressing Auchinleck to make an attack before Rommel whilst, at the same time, General Sir Alan Brooke was telling the Commander-in-Chief, Middle East of the probable loss of units to cope with the Japanese threat. Once again, Churchill believed Auchinleck had substantial superiority in the air, in armour and in other forces over his enemy and reminded Auchinleck of Malta's precarious position, all of which necessitated Auchinleck acting as soon as possible to seize airfields in Cyrenaica for aircraft to operate in the island's defence. Auchinleck's factual evidence backing a conclusion that an attack before 1 June was too laden with risk was unpalatable to the Prime Minister and the British High Command in the shape of the Chiefs of Staff. Although based on solid evidence, it did his standing as a commander a great deal of harm.[36]

In the Gazala position in May 1942, Ritchie was preparing an attack by Eighth Army when he received intelligence via Ultra that Rommel intended to launch an offensive towards the end of the month. This valuable information did not, however, say what Rommel's plan was, although it was known that the main effort would be made in the south. Eighth Army found itself having to prepare for defence *against* an attack in dispositions ready to *launch* an attack. Auchinleck had been tempted to take over command of Eighth Army from Ritchie after *Crusader*. Witnessing Ritchie's preparations, which he realized were inadequate, he had become more and more deeply involved in Eighth Army affairs which were, after all, only one (albeit important) part of Middle East Command. Auchinleck knew what had to be done but did not wish to cramp Ritchie's style by telling him how to do it. Instead, with respect for the chain of command, he offered suggestions and advice. This approach was extremely unsatisfactory but circumstances had not yet merited Auchinleck making any change.[37] Ritchie also lacked the confidence of his corps commanders, Gott and Norrie. Both were notionally senior to him and definitely more experienced. Then, on 26 May, the threat against Eighth Army became a reality as the Panzerarmee pre-empted Eighth Army plans and attacked.

Rommel initially feinted with an assault in the north which used various means of deception to suggest that this was the main thrust. Small numbers of Afrika Korps and 'Ariete' tanks accompanied the predominantly Italian infantry. Lorries carrying aircraft engines were used to stir up dust to suggest movement of large numbers of vehicles. However, this was all recognized for what it was and when the Panzerarmee advanced in force southwards towards Bir Hacheim late that evening Eighth Army HQ could have done more to interfere with its intentions, but did not.

The fighting soon demonstrated the weakness of the 'Jock Columns' as the Afrika Korps, now commanded by General der Panzertruppen Walther Nehring, brushed aside these formations. The chief obstacle to initial Panzerarmee success was the presence of a defensive 'box' – a position surrounded by wire and minefields – at Bir Hacheim, occupied by Général Pierre Koenig's 1ère Brigade Française Libre which continued to resist repeated Axis attacks from 27 May until the night of 10–11 June when the brigade was withdrawn largely intact.

Rommel hoped first to destroy Eighth Army's armour and appeared to be succeeding as brigade after brigade was committed piecemeal to the fighting. Yet it was the Panzerarmee which was soon in difficulties as its units were widely dispersed and running low on supplies. The British had suffered heavy losses in Grant tanks and 6-pounder anti-tank guns, but both had inflicted many casualties on the Axis tanks and jolted the Panzer units' morale. Seemingly trapped by minefields in an area that became known as the 'Cauldron', the Afrika Korps shielded itself with an anti-tank gun screen whilst clearing gaps in the minefields. It then destroyed 150th Brigade from 50th Division which, supported by thirty tanks from 1st Army Tank Brigade, had attempted to bar its way. However, during this fighting, Rommel's deputy Panzerarmee commander, General der Panzertruppe Ludwig Crüwell, was shot down and captured whilst flying in a Storch light aircraft over 150th Brigade's positions. Generalfeldmarschall Albert Kesselring happened to be at Crüwell's former headquarters when news of this loss arrived. Oberstleutnant Friedrich Wilhelm von Mellenthin, a staff officer in the Panzerarmee Afrika, recounted:

> He wanted to know how the battle was going – and I asked him to take command of the group until Rommel could make other arrangements. Kesselring was amused, and remarked that as a Generalfeldmarschall he could hardly take orders from Generaloberst Rommel. But I pointed out that it would not suit us to have an Italian general in command of Crüwell Gruppe at such a critical juncture, and Kesselring agreed to take command for a few days.[38]

This ensured continued German control of this formation which was chiefly Italian in composition.

Meanwhile, Ritchie delayed in making a concerted attack on the Cauldron and lost the initiative. When this attack was finally launched on 5 June as

Operation *Aberdeen*, it was comprehensively defeated. Rommel secured his supply lines and set about overcoming the resistance at Bir Hacheim. Rommel's 'personal' command style was once again in evidence, as Leutnant Klaus Michaelse of 90. leichte-Infanterie-Division described:

> Near Bir Hacheim, during a sandstorm (a *gibli*), a larger and larger vehicle came out of the dust. It was an eight-wheeled car. Rommel. 'What troop?' '90th Light'. 'Who is commanding?' 'Behind.' 'Well, I'm rolling ahead in that direction. He has to follow. We meet at point so and so.' The commanding officer, General Kleeman, had to follow. So, half an hour later we met both generals, C-in-C and General Kleeman, with about twenty-five English lorries who had to bring ammunition and so on to Bir Hacheim.[39]

With resistance at Bir Hacheim ended, Rommel's aggressive thrusts now produced disaster followed by disaster for Eighth Army. In a major clash of tank forces in an area termed 'Knightsbridge', British command, communication and control mechanisms broke down and Ritchie's armoured reserve was largely destroyed. The shattered remnants of the armoured brigades involved had to retire, leaving behind many damaged tanks that they might otherwise have recovered and repaired.

On 14 June, Auchinleck authorized Ritchie to withdraw from the Gazala line. The chaotic nature of the army's situation now was such that 151st Brigade, which had become isolated and separated from 69th Brigade, the other surviving 50th Division formation, had to escape encirclement by a move *westwards* into the Axis positions before swinging south and then east. The escape was fraught with danger and packed with incident. Corporal Tom Russ of the 6th Durham Light Infantry (DLI) told the story:

> We were going to go out of the 'box' turn left, go along the line and down south and come back from the back – that's what I was told. I had to make sure that everyone had got plenty of petrol, plenty of water and everything was roadworthy – which was quite a job to do to make sure everybody had jerry cans and they were all topped up, and their tanks were full and everything was functioning alright. That particular night, there was bloody shit flying all over. We just drove through the 'box', turned left and away we went. There were one or two little 'knock-ups' and what have you. First the autovac went dicky, so we were out with a four gallon drum de-siphoning the autovac. Then I heard a hell of a knocking noise – 'Oh, my

god, what's…?' Either the big end had worn or something. There was a chappie called Bill Nimmo. I said, 'Bill, there's a drum of oil in the back of there, get on this mudguard and when she knocks tip oil into the hole'. We'd got well and truly behind the column and I said, 'Right, this is our final fling, we'll fill her up and let go'. I put my foot down and caught up the last truck and we just dumped everything. We grabbed our rifles and water bottles and all jumped into the back of the truck. A Scottish chap called Dan Callow was driving. He stopped to pick us up and away we went.[40]

Despite losing most of their vehicles, ninety per cent of 151st Brigade personnel managed to escape back to Mersa Matruh.

Under pressure, the British continued to retreat and Tobruk was isolated on 17 June. The port city had previously withstood a nine-month siege before being relieved in December 1941, but this time the Royal Navy was too stretched to be sure of supplying a garrison which could, nevertheless, hold out for two months with its existing supplies. Auchinleck however had already decided Tobruk should not be held at all costs this time and informed Ritchie. Nevertheless, the loss of almost 35,000 men, including the entire 2nd South African Division, when Tobruk fell after little more than a day's fighting, was a catalogue of disastrous elements that might have been avoided if each had been addressed. Churchill had insisted that Tobruk be held, but its defences had been allowed to decline since the first siege. Had it been abandoned, the South Africans might have been withdrawn in good order. Their commander, Major-General Hendrik Klopper, did not attempt a serious breakout. Ritchie and Auchinleck disagreed about the former's decision to break contact between the defenders and the rest of Eighth Army, which he had ordered to regroup back at the Egyptian border.

Tobruk's fall was a shocking blow to British and Commonwealth morale. It was the latest in a succession of disasters which included the sinking of the *Prince of Wales* and *Repulse*, the loss of Malaya and Burma, the fall of Singapore, the threat of a Japanese invasion of Australia and the heavy losses in shipping in the Battle of the Atlantic, as well as the losses amongst Mediterranean naval forces previously mentioned. Ironically, it prompted American action in offers of troops (which Churchill declined) and equipment and weapons, which he accepted gratefully. None of this help would arrive in time for Eighth Army's immediate crisis. With Tobruk lost, Ultra intelligence was interpreted at Eighth Army Headquarters as indicating that Rommel would now stand and gather his forces before reorganizing for an attack on Egypt. But they had reckoned without their chief protagonist's appetite for further glory and were soon to be disabused of this complacent analysis.

It had originally been agreed that after Tobruk was captured, the Panzerarmee would stand on the defensive on the Egyptian frontier, and that all available aircraft and shipping would be used to attack and conquer Malta. To that end, on 21 June Kesselring flew once more to Africa, and met Rommel in his *Mammut* command vehicle. According to Friedrich Wilhelm von Mellenthin:

> Rommel insisted that he must follow up his victory without waiting for an attack on Malta, but Kesselring pointed out that an advance into Egypt could not succeed without full support from the Luftwaffe. If this were given, the Luftwaffe would not be available for operations against Malta, and should the island recover, Rommel's communications would be in serious jeopardy. Kesselring maintained that the only sound course was to stick to the original plan, and postpone an invasion of Egypt until Malta had fallen.[41]

Rommel argued that although the Panzerarmee had suffered in the Gazala battles, Eighth Army was in a far worse state and there was a unique opportunity to drive forwards to the Suez Canal. Even a short delay would allow the British commander time to regroup with reinforcements and dig in. Rommel had already issued an order of the day urging:

> Now for the complete destruction of the enemy. We will not rest until we have shattered the last remnants of the British Eighth Army. During the days to come, I shall call on you for one more great effort to bring us to this final goal.[42]

But that evening he also sent a personal liaison officer to put his views before Hitler. The following day he signalled to Rome that 'the state and morale of the troops, the present supply position owing to captured dumps, and the present weakness of the enemy, permit our pursuing him into the depths of the Egyptian area.'[43] This contrasted strongly with the views of Maresciallo d'Italia Conte Ugo Cavallero, Badoglio's successor at Comando Supremo, who announced that Comando Supremo intended to defend the Egyptian frontier whilst withdrawing aircraft and shipping for an attack on Malta.[44] Rommel gained Hitler's support, in spite of these strong objections. The decision was made to postpone *Herkules* until September, and throw everything behind Rommel's invasion of Egypt. Hitler had never been keen on the prospect of invading Malta, probably fearing heavy losses like those suffered in capturing Crete, but Kesselring also blamed Rommel for misleading Hitler and OKW. Kesselring recorded:

> At that period Rommel exercised an almost hypnotic influence over Hitler, who was all but incapable of appreciating the situation objectively. This curious fact no doubt accounted for the ... order I received when Hitler, impressed by Tobruk, and probably at the instigation of Rommel's mouthpiece, Dr. Berndt, told me not to meddle with Rommel's operational plan and to back him to the hilt.[45]

The Panzerarmee began to move east on 22 June and Rommel's Rubicon-crossing moment came the following day as he travelled into Egypt. In his own words, the whole enterprise was a 'try-on'. He was counting on bluff and the superb morale of his men. He had also received notification that in reward for his victory at Gazala, he had been promoted to Generalfeldmarschall. The lure of Cairo, the Nile and the Pyramids and greater fame proved too great. Rommel had courted celebrity whilst a desert commander. Now he succumbed to the need to feed it with new victories.

Rommel's eagerness to continue the advance was owed in no small measure to intelligence received via the *Gute Quelle* ('Good Source'). The 'Good Source' was unaware of his value to the Italians and Germans who eagerly read his every word for the information it might contain on their enemy's strengths and weaknesses. This was because the *Gute Quelle* was Colonel Bonner Fellers, Military Attaché in the United States' Embassy in Cairo. Fellers, had been sending back detailed encrypted reports on the combat performance, tactics, strength, location and morale of Eighth Army units to Washington since 1941. However, the diplomatic cipher he used had been compromised by the theft of the cipher keys by Italian agents from the US Embassy in the Vatican in September 1941. The quality of military information received by the Italian and German high commands for the North African theatre was at least as good as similar intelligence that the British received via Ultra.

Fellers had provided a detailed summary of British tank strength and losses during the Gazala battle and Rommel had received a decrypted version of this report by 20 June. It undoubtedly convinced Rommel that his 'try-on' with the small number of surviving Afrika Korps tanks was definitely worthwhile against a force with virtually no serviceable tanks at all. Fellers also provided information that the 9th Australian Division was still in Palestine and Syria, which was true and of crucial importance, and that only one brigade of 50th Division was still in existence, which was inaccurate. Taken together, these factors must have suggested a very rosy picture to Rommel.

This proved to be one of the last of Fellers' reports to be intercepted and disseminated by the Axis. Allied intelligence (ironically using Ultra decrypts) had already pinpointed the US Embassy in Cairo as the source of high-grade intelligence, resulting in a change in the American cipher code. Fellers returned to the United States in July before serving in the Far East under General Douglas MacArthur. His detailed reports from Cairo were praised for the valuable information they gave the Americans on the conduct of the war by both Britain and Germany.

On 25 June 1942, Auchinleck finally intervened in an attempt to give Eighth Army the strong leadership it needed. He advised General Sir Alan Brooke of his intention to take over command of Eighth Army, with Major-General Eric Dorman-Smith, the most capable and intellectually gifted officer on his Middle East Command Headquarters staff as his 'unofficial' Chief of General Staff. 'Chink' Dorman-Smith (his nickname came from his prominent front teeth) was a remarkable man with an excellent record of service in the Great War (three times wounded and winner of a Military Cross in 1915) and an interesting inter-war career which included spending his army leaves with Ernest Hemingway in Switzerland, Paris and Pamplona, where he mixed with Gertrude Stein, Ford Maddox Ford, Ezra Pound, James Joyce and F. Scott Fitzgerald. He was godfather to Hemingway's first son. At Staff College he was unconventional and anti-tradition and as he rose in the army he made many enemies and was seen as arrogant. He was a close friend of Basil Liddell Hart, the influential military theorist – a friendship that did not help his standing with many fellow army officers. He had been Director of Military Training, India prior to 1939 and he and Auchinleck worked closely together and got on well. On the outbreak of war, he was commandant of the Haifa Staff College in Palestine before Wavell involved him in some of the planning for Operation *Compass*. At a time of great crisis, Auchinleck looked to use the best he had. Dorman-Smith represented the best and most senior staff officer available with the skills necessary for the role Auchinleck envisaged. The two men understood each other and had a successful working relationship. It remained to be seen whether they could communicate effectively enough to win over a difficult and resistant group of combat-weary and demoralized commanders.

The task was immense. Time was extremely short. There was no pause in operations to allow a comfortable transition between Ritchie and the 'Auk'. Anything that could be done to save the situation required instant and definite action. The crisis was such that Auchinleck had abandoned his senior strategic role to deal with what was the most important and definite threat. In choosing to do so, he had already demonstrated the singleness of purpose that Ritchie had lacked, and thereby greatly reduced the chances of success for Rommel's attack, which gambled on exploiting the command uncertainties he had witnessed at Gazala.

By the time he was photographed at El Daba on 28 June, Auchinleck had enacted most of the critical decisions concerning how he would defeat the Panzerarmee. He no longer needed reports from subordinates to assess the state of Eighth Army's morale and fitness for battle. He was able to witness it first hand. Part of his command style now was to share the same conditions as those he commanded, their rations and their discomfort. It was an admirable attempt to break away from any accusation of 'chateau generalship'. It probably made little difference to most men's opinions of the situation in the short term. It needed time before word of mouth made such a thing widely known in the army but Auchinleck believed in its value. It was one of many small things that earned him the soubriquet of the 'Soldier's General'. What was needed most now was an end to defeat and retreat. A demonstration of purpose and resolution and, above all, a victory.

CHAPTER TWO

AN OASIS OF CALM

Claude Auchinleck and Eric Dorman-Smith had made many of their plans for stopping the advance of Rommel and the Panzerarmee on the floor of an otherwise empty Boston bomber that transported them on 25 June from Cairo to Eighth Army Headquarters at Maaten Bagush, between Mersa Matruh and Fuka on the coast. The chief and most pressing need was to abandon Matruh, where Eighth Army ran the risk of being destroyed by the imminent onslaught of Rommel's forces. Instead units were to withdraw approximately 150 miles back to El Alamein. The latter occupied a position offering natural obstacles in support of the defender; these advantages being absent at Matruh. The deep and almost impassable Qattara Depression to the south and the sea to the north were only forty miles apart here, creating a narrower front that might more easily be defended. Captain Tom Witherby of the 46th Royal Tank Regiment, 23rd Armoured Brigade, explained:

> The 'Alamein Line' was little more than a line on a map. Much work had been done in 1941 and a little later. There were three posts. The most important of these surrounded Alamein Railway Station and had been likened to a small Tobruk. There were concrete works in a semicircle surrounding the station and extending about five miles inland, so that the defences dominated a distance of about seven or eight miles from the coast, about halfway to Ruweisat Ridge. The central post in the 'Alamein Line' was at Bab el Qattara* about twenty miles south from the coast

---

* The Axis forces referred to this position as the Qaret el Abd.

where there were some completed concrete works, but no wires or mines. About the same distance to the south west was the third post at Naqb abu Dweis at a point where a track ran along the side of the Qattara Depression. These three posts were too far apart to be mutually supporting and it was intended that strong armoured forces would manoeuvre round them.[1]

Preparations were immediately put in hand for Lieutenant-General Sir Willoughby Norrie's XXX Corps to improve the defences of the Alamein Box and 1st South African Division set to completing the considerable work already done on a defensive system originally laid out by Lieutenant-General Sir James Marshall-Cornwell, whose experience with Field Marshal Sir Douglas Haig's staff in the Great War had given him plenty of knowledge of the configuration of strongly fortified positions.

After he assumed command of Eighth Army, Auchinleck authorized important fundamental changes which attempted to address two years of tactical error and shaped how Eighth Army would fight from this point forward. Many of these ideas came from Dorman-Smith's incisive analysis. A vitally important change was the centralization of artillery control at the highest possible level of command. Concentrated *control* of artillery (as opposed to concentration by location) would ensure concentrated effect, as would the decision not to spread the available forces along a forty-mile front. Concentration of effort as an army and not isolated corps was another absolute necessity, Auchinleck and Dorman-Smith agreed. A reorganization of armoured formations separating Grants from Crusaders would allow the latter to operate in a more mobile role, with the Grants operating within the range of the British field artillery. Armoured car units were to be grouped together in a light armoured reconnaissance brigade. Finally, Auchinleck was persuaded that a stagnating defensive battle might offer opportunities to launch focused attacks on the Italian infantry in the Panzerarmee, which Rommel would be forced to use in the front line.[2] None of this sound analysis of Eighth Army's operational flaws matches the opinion of one XIII Corps junior staff officer of the time that Dorman-Smith was 'a trenchant critic but not so good when it came to proposing a course of action' whose 'principal motive seemed to be to suggest some startlingly novel solution, regardless of whether or not it had a hope of working.'[3] Neither did it suggest, as Lieutenant-Colonel Charles Richardson, a fellow Eighth Army staff officer, did, that Dorman-Smith was a 'dangerous supernumerary'.[4] These appear as the responses of men who, as experienced but weary and demoralized desert staff officers, had to endure the sudden imposition of an outsider, whose 'knees were not brown'[5] in their opinion, making sharply critical observations on all they had been doing 'wrong' in their war against Rommel.

Disengaging units from their existing positions around Matruh was not going to be easy but it was absolutely essential. Both Auchinleck and Dorman-Smith could see the obvious gap in the dispositions of the Army's two corps through which the Axis forces could advance and encircle Lieutenant-General William Holmes' X Corps, which included 2nd New Zealand Division and was recently arrived from Syria, in its inadequate defensive positions near Matruh. The New Zealanders' commander, Lieutenant-General Sir Bernard Freyberg, had been unhappy at the prospect of his men being the defenders of Matruh itself, which had all the makings of another Tobruk, and used political pressure (an option always available to the Commonwealth generals who were not answerable to the British government) to secure a redeployment at Minqar Qaim, due south of Mersa.[6]

Eighth Army was still using 'Jock Columns' or 'battle groups' which had proved too weak in too many actions. Two such formations, 'Gleecol' and 'Leathercol', notionally defended the gap between the two corps. When 90. leichte-Afrika-Division and 21. Panzer-Division advanced and swept these two formations aside, the feared separation of XIII Corps from X Corps became a reality. Co-ordinated action by the two corps was rendered impossible as poor wireless communications once more let the British down. Holmes and Gott fought separate battles despite Auchinleck's prior urgings that 'the corps commanders must be in the closest possible touch so as to ensure that if one corps or part of it has to give ground the other is immediately able to take advantage of the situation by rapidly and boldly attacking the enemy in the flank'.[6]

Auchinleck had intended to keep Eighth Army fully mobile in a fighting withdrawal to the Alamein defences. However, it was his opponent who dictated events, driving Eighth Army's scattered units before him. The New Zealanders were forced to fight their way out of an encirclement at Minqar Qaim; Freyberg was wounded in the process. Gott, who had visited the New Zealanders under a heavy bombardment, witnessed the destruction of the division's transport soon afterwards and assumed the New Zealanders had been wiped out. Meanwhile, Kampfgruppen Kost and Kaiser cut the road east of Matruh, effectively completing the encirclement of X Corps. On the night of 28 June, X Corps' units attempted to break out. This was accomplished with desperate hand-to-hand fighting in which the staff of Gruppe Menton was especially involved for the Panzerarmee.

In the breakout, Captain Geoffrey Armstrong, an officer in the 11th Royal Horse Artillery, had been ordered by his column commander to clear a way for the infantry with his guns and the regiment's carriers:

I gave the signal and went forward at carrier pace, compass set at 180° in one hand, revolver in the other and shouting blue murder at the top of my voice. At once we seemed to be among them. Tracer flew in all directions from a score of flashes of light, AP [Armour Piercing] rushed past our ears or kicked up the sand, the Brens from the carriers on either side clattered and flashed. Boche rose from the ground and scattered from our path. We ran them down – and over. I took pot-shots at Huns; my driver was ducked to dashboard level; I glanced at my compass and over the open truck back to my guns. Bullets seemed to pour through quads or bounce at angles from the wheels. One was fired; it blazed and men jumped on to the next one; the mass came on. The carriers creaked steadily forward firing burst after burst and magazine after magazine. I was never so excited in my life.[7]

There was a tremendous rush of adrenalin and a feeling of exhilaration which found its release when the fight and flight were over. Armstrong continued:

We ran our two miles and pulled up in the first clear space while others came in. Our order of march was gone. We recced round our area, found a Boche column in leaguer on our flank, raked it with fire and withdrew to our bridgehead. Slowly, our nerves relaxed; we began to laugh. We were alive again.[8]

Another artilleryman, Bombadier Jim Brooks of the 64th Medium Regiment (RA) wrote home describing the chaos his unit experienced in escaping the pursuing Axis forces:

During this withdrawal or should I say stampede, we lived like lords. All NAAFI or Service Corps food dumps were left and we simply went and helped ourselves. Consequently every lorry was loaded up with beer, tinned fruit, fags and sweets. The Gerrys must have done well out of us. I won't tell you how many men, trucks and guns we lost. I doubt whether the censor would pass it, it was a big loss anyway.[9]

Lieutenant-General Holmes later estimated that about sixty per cent of his command was saved in the Matruh breakout. By midday on 29 June, the small port had been captured and 10th Indian and 50th Divisions were both in a disorganized mess as they fell back to the vicinity of Alexandria. Considerable quantities of vital supplies had been lost when Tobruk fell. Now the vast supply dump at Belhamed, with 20,000 tons of stores carefully gathered well forward in preparation for Ritchie's offensive, had to be destroyed. The destruction of supply dumps was not wholesale, but, where it occurred, it did nothing to lift the impression for men already in retreat that they were in a situation of chaos. According to Lance Corporal Douglas Waller of the 1st Rifle Brigade:

> One dump we went past, we had time for a breather and we stopped. I said to one of our chaps: 'Nip over. See if you can get anything out of there.' The red caps stopped him and said 'You can't come in here, we're going to blow it up.' So he said 'Well, can't I take something?' but they wouldn't let us. They just blew the lot up... They were blowing up the dumps of food, petrol, on the way back. As you went down, all the way in the rear there were people saying, 'Move, move move,' and keeping everybody moving. It was a complete rout almost – that's not described in the annals of the British Army – but it was. We were just flapping back until we got to Alamein.[10]

In fact, although the army was now streaming back in retreat, as Auchinleck witnessed from his roadside position, there was sufficient order established in a very short period of time that, soon after the retreat ended, Eighth Army's supply infrastructure was fully restored and functioning – an achievement for which the army commander and his staff should be given much credit.

The retreating forces might have been made to suffer more if the Luftwaffe had had the ability to launch air attacks on the traffic on the coastal highway. However, Kesselring's aircraft were not yet able to use advanced airfields or landing grounds sufficiently far forward to operate in strength against such prime targets. This was not because of problems with aircraft but rather because of difficulties in supplying and maintaining those aircraft, which was hampered by lack of transport for ground crews and for the necessary fuel and ammunition. Instead, the Panzerarmee approached the Alamein 'line' – still no line at all but rather a defensive 'box' combining minefields, barbed wire and concrete strongpoints around the Alamein station and other defended localities to the south and east – with little air support.

On the other hand, the Desert Air Force was dedicating itself to hundreds of sorties per day. However, instead of responding to requests received from

Eighth Army, co-operation between the two had broken down to the extent that Air Vice-Marshal Arthur Coningham, the Desert Air Force's commander, was setting the targets for his aircraft and had his fighters and bombers doing a shuttle service focused solely on ground attack. Coningham took a considerable risk in telling his pilots to ignore enemy fighters and ordered them not to fly above 6,000 feet. He admitted that it was a lot to ask that they think only of the ground and submit themselves to unmolested attack from above but it was necessary.[11]

Much criticism was made at the time, and subsequently, of Auchinleck's re-siting of Eighth Army's Advanced Headquarters at the eastern end of the Alam Halfa Ridge in the middle of the desert. This was a considerable distance from the Desert Air Force's headquarters at Burg-el-Arab and a half-hour's drive from the nearest airfield. Auchinleck clearly did not fully appreciate the importance of air power in the ground battle. Air Marshal Sir Arthur Tedder, the head of the Middle East air command, even went so far as to say: 'This complete failure on the part of the Army even now to understand some of the most elementary principles of modern warfare defeats me'.[12] However, two points deserve mention. Firstly, Coningham's possession of a captured Fieseler Storch light aircraft enabled him to visit Auchinleck *and* retain touch with his squadrons in this period. Secondly, Auchinleck's command style meant that he needed to be in touch, *and visibly so*, with the formations he commanded. The location of his Advanced Headquarters did this. Co-location of army and air headquarters was a regrettable casualty of this rationale.

As Commander-in-Chief, Middle East Command, Auchinleck had a wider responsibility than the fighting against the Panzerarmee. Now, this strategic vision ensured that the approach to defence at Alamein was not a last-ditch all-or-nothing one. Dorman-Smith was given the task of drawing up an 'appreciation' (the bread and butter of a staff officer in initial planning) regarding the defence of Egypt. This document's most important section described Auchinleck's intention with which Tedder was in full agreement: 'to keep Eighth Army in being as a mobile field force and resist by every possible means any further attempts by the enemy to advance eastwards'.[13] This was because he recognized, like the Chief of the Imperial General Staff, General Alan Brooke, that 'the oil in the Persian Gulf was more important to the war than Egypt'.[14]

Orders were issued on the basis of this 'appreciation', firstly by Eighth Army HQ and then by Lieutenant-General Tom Corbett, Auchinleck's Chief of General Staff (CGS) at General Headquarters, Middle East. On 30 June General Holmes and his X Corps staff were sent back to organize the defences of the Nile Delta in co-operation with Lieutenant-General Robert Stone, Commander of British Troops in Egypt. Problems arose, however, from the misinterpretation of these orders and especially the instructions from Corbett by several Eighth Army commanders. The New Zealand Brigadier, Howard Kippenberger of 5th New Zealand Infantry Brigade, encountered 'Strafer' Gott – a prime example:

> General Gott was in his Armoured Command Vehicle (ACV), the first I had seen. He came out at once and walked a few yards clear of it. 'Inglis has gone to Cairo', he said, and handed me a letter. It was a short note from General Corbett... I remember very clearly the opening sentence: 'The Chief has decided to save Eighth Army.' The note then went on to say that the South Africans would retire through Alexandria and the rest of us down the desert road through Cairo. I asked what was meant by the first sentence. 'It means what it says – he means to save the Field Army,' the General said. [15]

Gott interpreted the order as an indication that a general retirement and evacuation of Egypt was being contemplated. The justification for his view is unclear, and may have had more to do with his state of mind after the recent events involving the New Zealand Division, as indicated by his response to Kippenberger's vehement demonstration of 'fight':

> I protested that we were perfectly fit to fight and that it was criminal to give up Egypt to 25,000 German troops and a hundred tanks (disregarding the Italians) – the latest Intelligence estimate – and to lose as helpless prisoners perhaps 200,000 Base troops. Strafer replied sadly that NZ Division was battle-worthy but very few other people were and he feared the worst.[16]

Gott, by reputation supposedly unflappable, was certainly not the only senior commander to be viewing events in an extremely pessimistic light at this time. Major-General Dan Pienaar, the commander of 2nd South African Division, was especially voluble and bleak in his opinions, according to Lieutenant-General Sir Willoughby Norrie, the General Officer Commanding XXX Corps:

Pienaar was openly saying that he thought it was wrong to stand at El Alamein, and that the best place was to go behind the Suez Canal. Even allowing for Pienaar's well-known exaggeration of speech, these expressions were a source of considerable embarrassment, both to the Commander-in-Chief and myself.[17]

Kippenberger's confusion actually arose from the question of whether Corbett's memo was at variance with the very clear instructions he had already received on 29 June. Kippenberger recorded:

We were told that Eighth Army would stand and fight on the Alamein line, which ran from the sea to where the Taqa plateau overlooked the impassable Qattara Depression… There was no fear of being outflanked. We heard that 1 South African Division under Dan Pienaar was holding the Alamein Box in the north and that an Indian brigade was in the Deir el Shein Box with 50 Division Group in a near position. Then came 2 NZ Division and south of us on the Taqa plateau was another Indian brigade. The armour was in support and the leading Australian brigade from Syria had arrived at Amiriya. In addition there were a number of 'Jock' columns, at this time called 'Monthly' columns, between us and the plateau. We made contact with 'June', 'July', and 'August'. They were each composed of a battery of twenty-five-pounders and a company of motorized infantry and, acting independently as they usually did, had little fighting and no stopping value whatever. Nor could we ever find out where they were, which would have been annoying if they had been serious fighting troops. The whole position looked weak but it was reasonable to suppose that the enemy was getting weary and he was certainly at the end of a terrific line of supply.[18]

This was a clear reflection of information communicated from Auchinleck to his Eighth Army command. There should have been no doubt about the decision to stand and fight.

However, although the opinions and doubts of some senior commanders had a corrosive influence on some men's morale in the forward areas, they were not the cause of another crisis in morale that was arising. This became known as the 'Cairo Flap' and was almost as much a product of the determined steps Auchinleck was taking to resolve the military crisis as it was a consequence of Rommel's success.

It was ironic, but the 'Cairo Flap' probably began in Alexandria. The Royal Navy took the cautious step of evacuating the Mediterranean Fleet from the port on 28 June. This news and the subsequent lootings convinced large numbers of people that Rommel's arrival in the city was imminent. This was compounded by the large numbers of troops passing eastwards and westwards through Alexandria in particular. Whilst many ancillary units such as workshops, supply companies, administrative, engineering and other troops not expected to bear arms in the front line were being evacuated, a number of reinforcement units were being sent forward for the defence. This created a sense of terrific confusion with troops everywhere and crowds milling at railway stations, in the already-crowded streets and on the main roads. There were many amongst the Egyptian population who had hoped to see the end of a British presence and nationalist groups did what they could to encourage the disorder and sense of panic. The most notable signs of panic were the actions of some government offices and military headquarters. On Wednesday 1 July, Brigadier George Davy returning from Eighth Army Headquarters to Middle East General Headquarters (GHQ) in Cairo witnessed an unusual sight:

> As I approached GHQ, I saw clouds of smouldering paper fragments in the air and fluttering down like black snow. It was carried on a light breeze in a broad belt and deposited over the streets of several square miles of Cairo. I sent for Douglas Packard and asked what it was all about. He said that the embassy had started burning their secret documents and that the CGS, at the morning conference, had ordered that all secret documents in GHQ were to be burned at once.[19]

The orders seem to have originated with Sir Richard Casey, the Minister of State, and the British Ambassador, Sir Miles Lampson, but military personnel at GHQ were involved too. With sardonic humour, the day became known as 'Ash Wednesday'. This was all a source of great amusement at the front, where, despite flagging morale, most men responded with a grim determination to defeat Rommel now that a stand was being made.

In many standard military histories, the whole situation is usually portrayed as a jolly farce based on false rumours and British incompetence. It was, for large numbers of people, rather more a real threat to life and limb. For lurking behind the Axis forces in this supposed 'War without Hate' between the Panzerarmee and Eighth Army was very real hatred. Even as plans were made for the advance on Cairo, an SS *Einsatzkommando* was created to murder tens of thousands of Jews who lived in Egypt.[20]

On the last days of June, significant reinforcements arrived to boost the resources at Auchinleck's disposal. The first were from 18th Indian Brigade, who, having been rushed over to North Africa from Mosul and attached to 10th Indian Division, had only two days to prepare an additional 'box' at Deir el Shein. This was because XXX Corps' commander, Norrie, was worried about the width of the gaps between the existing boxes. Deir el Shein was halfway between Alamein and Bab el Qattara.

The brigade was made up of 2/3rd Gurkhas, 4/11th Sikhs and 2/5th Essex Regiment. It had no desert experience and only one battalion had seen combat. Their hasty transfer from Iraq meant they were disorganized, having lost their brigade commander and their organic artillery regiment. This had been made good by odds and sods of field and anti-tank guns by XXX Corps' artillery commander, Brigadier Mead Dennis, but the field guns were from several regiments and their fire could not be co-ordinated. Meanwhile, the infantry had discovered what a difficult position they had been selected to defend, as Private Arthur Page of 2/5th Essex reported:

> After being allocated to our positions, we dug ourselves in as best we could, but not far underneath the sand were shelves of rock. We were given very little time to prepare so it was extremely hard work. Everything was hurried. We even had our kitbags with us.[21]

Only the fact that this was a small depression with raised lips offered any real protection.

By comparison, the move of 9th Australian Division from Syria was well managed – except for efforts to maintain secrecy by hiding the national identity of the men. Warrant Officer Eric Watts of 2/12th Field Regiment remembered:

> The captain in charge of the troop ordered a parade and told everybody that there was a move and it was going to happen in the next twenty-four hours. They had to take all the signs indicating that they were the Australian 9th Division off the trucks, guns and anything that indicated that we were Australian had to be done away with – all the signs. We weren't allowed to wear our slouch hats on the move

and we moved within twenty-four hours of being told this. But only one little point had been forgotten. Australians were the only troops who wore tan boots. All the other British troops wore black boots. But we wore tan boots. Well, it didn't take anyone long to wake up to this and they knew and they used to sing out 'Aussie, Aussie' and this sort of stuff as we were travelling through their villages and everything. So that was our top secret move – it was a bit botched really.[22]

The Australians would not arrive until 4 or 5 July, which meant they could not take part in the critical opening phase of the defensive battle. Dorman-Smith had specified that, if necessary, they would be used with 1st South African Division in defence around Alexandria. Wherever they were to be deployed the response was typified by the resolute Corporal Ray Middleton of 2/28th Battalion:

Well, somebody's got to stop the bastard. We can prove we've done it before, and we can do it again. The way we saw it, we're in desperate straits. If they've got to call on the Australians, alright, we'll show them. It's clean muck and stop that. Then we can go home.[23]

On 30 June Auchinleck issued an exhortation to his men prior to what he knew would be a crucial fight. Whilst its effects on Eighth Army morale have been doubted, this message was uncannily accurate concerning his opponent in stating 'the enemy is stretching to his limits and thinks we are a broken army. His tactics against the New Zealanders were poor in the extreme. He hopes to take Egypt by bluff. Show him where he gets off.'[24] The fighting in the last ten days of June had taken a heavy toll on the Panzerarmee and, in particular, the Afrika Korps. Rommel had fifty-five German tanks in total, with perhaps 500 infantry for each of the two divisions. 90. leichte-Afrika-Division possessed fewer than 1,100 infantry. The Germans had 330 guns of all types, including thirty-nine captured British 25-pounders and twenty-nine 88mm guns. The Italians, with only thirty, actually possessed fewer serviceable tanks, 5,500 infantry and 200 guns.[25]

Rommel attempted to marginalize these shortcomings with a display of confidence and ambitious plans. The latter, outlined to his commanders on 30 June, was based on splitting the two corps facing him and getting behind the British defences, at which point experience suggested the British would collapse. The Italian XXI Corpo d'Armata would 'pin' the defenders of the

Alamein Box. Divisione 'Littorio', which had been mauled by the hastily retreating 1st Armoured Division and had lost heavily in tanks, was to be bolstered by two units of 88mm guns before tackling 1st Armoured (believed to be in front of the Bab el Qattara Box) again. The 10th Indian Brigade in a box at Deir el Abyad was to be bypassed as the Afrika Korps with Divisioni 'Ariete' and 'Trieste' thrust through the centre of the British positions before turning to attack the New Zealanders in the Bab el Qattara Box. This was all to be followed by a triumphal drive on Alexandria.

These plans were full of intelligence errors, false optimism and high expectations. The identification and positioning of several units was wrong – partly in misplacing 1st Armoured Division but especially in relation to 18th Indian Brigade. The armoured units were expected to capture the necessary fuel to reach Alexandria and the mere presence of *der Wüstenfuchs* amongst them was presumed enough to scatter the Eighth Army, like chickens, and put them to flight. Rommel and his forces were still confident that they had smashed the Eighth Army and expected to be able to break through what resistance remained, despite tiredness amongst all ranks.

The first exchanges at Alamein began on 30 June 1942 when 90. leichte-Afrika-Division came into sight on the coast road near Tel el Eisa and exchanged fire with South African Artillery stationed outside the Alamein Box. This and 1st Armoured's clash with 'Littorio' aside, there was something of a hush as the armies closed with each other. Eighth Army was warned that the anticipated attack would begin on 1 July. Auchinleck, meanwhile, finalized his plans. He expected XXX Corps units in and around the Alamein and Deir el Shein positions to hold the Axis advance, allowing XIII Corps in the shape of 1st Armoured (actually to the south-east of the Alamein Box) and New Zealand Divisions to strike from the south against Rommel's right flank. There was no suggestion of withdrawal in his mind. Early on the morning of 1 July, he wrote a brief note of these ideas. His first stated purpose was crucial: 'I intend to defeat the enemy and destroy him'.[26]

During the night, the Afrika Korps advance had been confused and disorganized so that, at dawn, they were still not ready to attack. This was the time for the attack against the Alamein Box by Divisione 'Trento' to begin and 90. leichte-Afrika-Division's advance was supposed to start. The latter was soon halted by fire from the Alamein Box, which prevented further forward movement all morning until a sandstorm allowed a withdrawal. Only at 0645hrs did General der Panzertruppe Walther Nehring's men advance and that was after enduring a heavy bombing raid. At about 1000hrs their approach was seen from Deir el Shein and soon afterwards the position was shelled by artillery. After about an hour a bren gun carrier approached the 2/5th Essex under a white flag. The occupants were two supposedly British soldiers with no badges of rank sent by the Germans to encourage surrender to prevent further losses. The words used to dismiss this suggestion have clearly been sanitized in every account with only 'Stick it up and be damned' offering a clue to the real terminology employed.[27]

This unexpected opposition gave Nehring a dilemma as he could not leave Deir el Shein untaken as the Afrika Korps pursued its primary objective. He chose to eliminate the Indian brigade. During the whole day 18th Indian Brigade was under attack and stubborn resistance delayed and prevented the Axis breakthrough and frustrated their whole plan. At 1130hrs Schützen-Regiment 104 deployed under long-range covering fire from the few Panzer IVs they had and moved to the attack but were repeatedly beaten back by the Essex and Gurkhas, eventually finding a gap close to the former's B Echelon. Lieutenant-Colonel Steve May of 2/5th Essex recalled:

At this time every available man, cooks, mess staff, clerks, MT [Motor Transport] personnel and QM [Quarter Master] and his staff were firing steadily and there is no doubt they took steady toll of infantry who tried to force a gap. Towards 1300 hours the ammunition situation was getting desperate and finally the enemy got a lodgement, blew the wire and forced a gap, and exploited it with tanks. However, he had not had it all his own way. The 25-pounders had some excellent targets, some at point-blank range.[28]

The brigade had nine Matilda 'infantry' tanks in support. These offered determined resistance too but armed only with 2-pounder guns, they were no match for the Panzers. The Sikhs, who had now been subjected to heavy attack, were driven from their positions and forced to surrender and, by 1900hrs, it was all over. The circumstances of Private Arthur Page's surrender must have seemed strangely familiar to many who were taken prisoner in the two wars against Germany:

By evening all of our battalion were captured. One of our officers told us to come out of the trenches with our hands up. We were, as the saying went, 'in the bag', slang for Prisoner of War. 'For you, the war is over,' a German said to us.[29]

The destruction of 18th Indian Brigade was complete, but in accomplishing it, the Afrika Korps had suffered significant losses in armour and elsewhere things unravelled rapidly too. Friedrich Wilhelm von Mellenthin described the situation:

> We lost eighteen tanks out of fifty-five, and the fighting edge of the Afrika Korps was finally blunted. 90. leichte advanced during the afternoon, and attempted to bypass the El Alamein Box; it ran into a crescent of fire from the 1st, 2nd, and 3rd South African Brigades and their supporting artillery, and was thrown into confusion not far removed from panic. Rommel himself went to 90. leichte to try and urge the division forward but the volume of fire was so heavy that even he was pinned down.[30]

Von Mellenthin recognized the significance of this hold-up: 'Our prospects of victory were hopelessly prejudiced on 1 July. Our one chance was to outmanoeuvre the enemy, but we had actually been drawn into a battle of attrition'.[31] For Rommel, 90. leichte-Afrika-Division's crisis must surely have brought home to him the extent to which his plans for the day had failed when he decided to put everything into supporting this effort by using his *Gefechtsstaffel* in conjunction with Kampfgruppe Kiehl. Rommel recorded:

> Furious artillery fire again struck into our ranks. British shells came streaming in from three directions, north, east and south; anti-aircraft tracer streaked through our force. Under this tremendous weight of fire, our attack came to a standstill. Hastily we scattered our vehicles and took cover, as shell after shell crashed into the area we were holding. For two hours Bayerlein and I had to lie out in the open. Suddenly to add to our troubles, a powerful British bomber force came flying up towards us. Fortunately, it was turned back before it reached us by some German fighters who had been escorting a dive-bomber raid.[32]

It was indeed fortunate that the Luftwaffe fighters saved Rommel since his units were still complaining of the air arm's absence over the battlefield.[33] Slowly, this was being rectified but the Desert Air Force still maintained the ascendancy for the moment.

Rommel's descriptions of the power of the artillery bombardment give some clue to the cause of 90. leichte-Afrika-Division's crisis in morale. Apart from the South African Field Regiments in the Alamein Box, the heavier guns of 7th Medium Regiment, under Lieutenant-Colonel 'Toc' Elton were also present.

Elton had already embarked on re-educating his gunners to tried-and-tested techniques which fitted closely with Auchinleck and Dorman-Smith's aim for improving the artillery's effectiveness, as one of his officers, Lieutenant Charles Westlake, noted:

> His idea was to have a concentration of all artillery that could reach certain targets so that you brought a massive firepower to bear coming from various directions and by this means you were pretty well sure of destroying the target.[34]

This simple, but effective, technique now became a possibility in a defended locale like the Alamein Box and an early version was employed on 1 July.

The attack on 1 July had not produced the victory Rommel needed but buoyed by aerial reconnaissance reports of the British Eastern Mediterranean Fleet's departure from Alexandria, he determined on a further effort. Auchinleck, who throughout the day had been plagued by communication problems and particularly the frustrating experience of being unable to contact one of his corps commanders (Gott again), was relieved when the latter appeared at his headquarters. This enabled him to deliver plans for a more compact defence of his positions, abandoning the boxes at Bab el Qattara and Naqb abu Dweis. He hoped to meet Rommel's expected second effort with a counter-attack by XIII Corps. However, Gott's forces were separated and fragmenting still further with the creation and deployment of 'mobile artillery battle-groups' – which Auchinleck had intended for use in 'fluid defence' to preserve his limited numbers of tanks for use at critical moments. These formations appeared to be 'Jock Columns' in all but name and to have the same weaknesses i.e. they could not, in Auchinleck's opinion of their predecessor, 'press home an attack against anything but very weak opposition'.[35]

Despite enjoying a peaceful night and the opportunity to recover, 90. leichte-Afrika-Division was soon under heavy fire again when trying to go forward. Rommel therefore decided to reinforce it with an Afrika Korps attack striking east and then north around Alam el Onsol. Now both formations were subjected to more air attacks by formations of fifteen, eighteen or even twenty-one bombers with fighter protection. 90. leichte-Afrika-Division was now thoroughly demoralized. Meanwhile the Afrika Korps struck resistance first from 1st South African Brigade and then from a column from 10th Indian

Division, called 'Robcol' after its commander, Brigadier Robert Waller.[36] There followed a heated argument between Pienaar on behalf of 1st South African Brigade and Norrie, his superior, over the South African commander's insistence on the brigade being withdrawn after both its brigadier and brigade-major were wounded. Norrie reluctantly acceded.

'Robcol' consisted of two companies of 1/4th Essex, three platoons of Northumberland Fusiliers, two batteries from 11th (HAC) Regiment, Royal Horse Artillery and 11th Field Regiment, Royal Artillery. According to Cyril Mount:

> Some intelligence must have come through that we were going to take the brunt of the attack and this column was very hastily formed by Waller with the 1/4th Essex as the main fighting unit. There were no other fighting units at that moment there, just the 11th and the Essex. We still had OPs [observation posts] on Ruweisat Ridge and we were firing on observed targets from Ruweisat Ridge. We weren't defending the ridge, we were on the left of the ridge. The orders were that we were to hold that line where the main prod was coming from the Germans.[37]

Fierce action began after the sudden retirement of the artillery OPs from Ruweisat Ridge, as Mount related:

> German tanks had occupied the western end of the ridge and the OPs came hurtling back, tearing back, zig-zagging across the gravelly flat stuff and being shot at by tanks. From then on there were no OPs. It was direct firing over open sights. The whole regiment was in. 83rd and 85th were forward and they took the full brunt of it. My battery was maybe 400 yards out to the left and rear. I was in the waggon lines. I was helping to load ammunition into the 3-tonners. The 3-tonners were taking ammunition up to the guns and dumping it and food was taken up. We could see what was going on – about 200 or 300 yards ahead of us. We were getting a lot of 'overs' from these tanks – they were firing at the guns. There were casualties coming back. It was just total pandemonium and chaos. We were expecting all the time to be overrun. There was damn all we could do about it. The guns were tackling the tanks.[38]

It was not a wholly uncommon experience for Field and Horse Artillery regiments of Eighth Army equipped with 25-pounders to find themselves isolated and overrun by Axis armour during the Desert War. A typical incident was the destruction of 107 (South Nottinghamshire Hussars Yeomanry) Regiment, Royal Horse Artillery during the Gazala battle on 6 June 1942.[39] However, on this occasion, guns of the same type, operating in the open desert against the same enemy, halted their opponent's advance. Mount continued:

> The gun positions weren't overrun but a whole troop, E Troop, was lost and it was re-formed from stragglers that came from other regiments. It was lost to tank fire and small arms fire. The tanks were quite close but a hell of a lot were knocked out. They eventually withdrew. Had they broken through, they would have gone on straight through.[40]

There were three crucial differences on this occasion. Firstly, the attacking forces were a great deal weaker than at Gazala and did not have the advantage of surprise – although 11th Field Regiment still suffered almost one-third casualties. Secondly, the defenders enjoyed considerably more air support than on the previous occasion. Thirdly, Auchinleck's 'mobile artillery battle groups' as indicated by their name had the 25-pounder batteries at their heart and, with more batteries attached, could concentrate more firepower than the 'Jock Columns'. This made them more appropriate for the fluid defensive battle now being fought by Eighth Army around the Ruweisat Ridge. There was a difference between the two *ad hoc* formations after all.

Nevertheless, 'Robcol' would have been overrun if it had not been for the arrival of 22nd and 4th Armoured Brigades who clashed with tanks from 21. Panzer-Division and 15. Panzer-Division respectively. There was an element of 'smoke and mirrors' illusion behind the armoured brigades' deployment and particularly the use of the 6-pounder anti-tank guns the brigade had had since Gazala. Now, as Private Laurie Phillips of 1st Rifle Brigade, 22nd Armoured Brigade, recalled, they were to be employed in an unusual way:

> Because of the shortage of tanks they decided to use us as 'armour'; with the guns up 'on portee'. We reversed into action alongside the tanks. Because there was a lot of soft sand in the area where we were operating, south of Ruweisat, we had Honey tanks standing by to tow us out if we got stuck and Crusaders to bring us up ammunition and petrol. We put in an attack in the afternoon and met the 21st Panzer Division head on as it advanced to attack us; we fired over 100 rounds with our gun (we had to pull back for more after we had used the 70 we carried) and it got pretty hot.[41]

THE FIRST BATTLE OF EL ALAMEIN

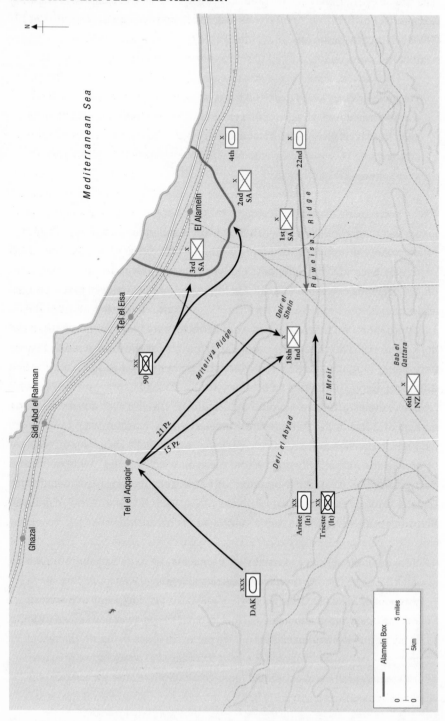

The advantages of the 6-pounder anti-tank gun over its predecessor were ably demonstrated on Ruweisat Ridge. Lance Corporal Douglas Waller, also of 1st Rifle Brigade, described the benefits:

> With a 6-pounder you definitely had a chance as long as you could hit them [i.e. tanks] in the side or the back. Not too much if you hit them on the front. A 2-pounder would knock out an Italian M13 but it wouldn't touch a Mark III or Mark IV. You could knock them out with a 6-pdr, but a 2-pdr was hopeless. If you get them side-on or even partially side-on. You're not likely to get one at the back unless it swung round. You aimed at side-on, because the front had reinforced plate in front of it. If you couldn't get a side-on, you aimed for the turret, below the gun because there was a chance that if you hit it, it would dip down and it was not so thick there or at least it would cause flakes of metal to fly off inside the tank and at least put the gunner out of action.[42]

By the end of the day, the two Panzer units possessed a total of only 26 tanks between them.[43] A good percentage of the casualties were due to the 6-pounders. This demonstration of the gun's capabilities certainly boosted morale – as did the arrival of the 6-pounder generally, for which men were prepared to forgive a great deal. As one sergeant in another anti-tank regiment pointed out: 'The 6-pounders were there – that was the important thing. The fact that they weren't polished and finished and you could cut your hands on the raw welding didn't really matter. We'd got them'.[44]

On 3 July, a resumption of the Afrika Korps attack was ordered by Rommel with Divisione 'Ariete' and 'Littorio' on its southern flank. Meanwhile 27ª Divisione Autotrasportabile 'Brescia' was to hold El Mreir. This time the British armoured brigades were awaiting the attack and were ready. After an hour and a half of fighting, the Axis forces were driven off with the Panzer units again complaining of lack of air and artillery support.

Twenty M14/41 tanks of XII Battaglione Carri of 'Littorio' also advanced on British positions on Ruweisat Ridge, but ran into opposition. Tenente Armando Luciano was in one of them:

> We're lined up facing east, with the sun blinding us and making our tank armour shine. In the distance in front of us, I can make out the silhouettes of the enemy

tanks backed up against a large mound of earth. This is it – the moment of our first combat has come. Maggiore dell'Uva gives the final orders, the battalion advances to get in range, then the exchange of fire starts and tank platoons start moving. At the same time we are bombarded with enemy artillery fire, which gets more and more frequent and well-aimed.[45]

The Italian tanks had always struggled to compete with Eighth Army's armour. Now Luciano's men had another shock, confirming the information provided by those who have already been in combat:

In the distance in front of me I make out an enemy tank flying a pennant from its radio antenna; it must be a command tank... 'Halt!' I cry to Ramazzotti, 'Aim 600, fire!' Following the trail of the tracer, I see the shell hit the enemy armour, but I wait in vain for the usual black smoke of burning fuel to pour from the tank, or to see the crew throw themselves out of the vehicle. Our armour-piercing shell must have misfired – it is probably an American Grant tank, a beast with too thick a skin. I try again with another armour-piercing shell, but almost simultaneously I feel a blow on our right flank and hear the screams of the radio operator who seems to be going mad and whom Vizentini, the gunner, is trying to calm down. The tank has taken a hit, fortunately not a direct hit, but on its right side, on the track, which is now hanging uselessly while the exchange of fire is getting more intense and other tanks are being destroyed.[46]

Now, the few remaining tanks of 'Ariete' were attacked by 4th Armoured Brigade, whilst 'Trieste', the right flank guard to 'Ariete', was pinned down by incessant air attacks. They offered a superb target for the New Zealand artillery which pounded the Italians. A 'silent' attack by infantry from 19th Battalion of 4th New Zealand Brigade overran the positions held by the *Bersaglieri* of 'Ariete' and captured 350 men and forty-four assorted guns, including twelve 105mm, eleven 88mm, sixteen 75mm, five captured 25-pounder guns, some 20mm infantry guns and mortars and 100 assorted motor vehicles, for the loss of two killed and twenty wounded.[47]

––––––––––––

It was these losses that finally convinced Rommel of the need to call off his attacks for the time being. Low on both fuel and ammunition and over 1,400 miles from Tripoli, its main supply port, the Panzerarmee needed time to regroup, and to collect reinforcements and supplies. Although Stukas had now reappeared in the skies over the Eighth Army, any pause would offer a chance to get more Luftwaffe support forward. However, given the original premise on which Rommel had, firstly, gone into Egypt and, secondly, attacked the Alamein positions – neither of which he was obliged to do – it was questionable whether any further opportunity would be offered. In all probability, the situation before Gazala occurred to him. Then the British had raced to gather their forces and mass supplies and ammunition ready for an attack, only to be pre-empted by Rommel. It would, however, take a long time to recover the Panzerarmee's strength. Rommel indulged in some bitter remarks regarding the performance of his Italian ally, complaining that the losses in 'Ariete' had occurred without the division offering any real resistance. He subsequently admitted, however, that he had demanded too much from the Italians, whose equipment in all areas except artillery was no match for that of his German units.

In the meantime, Auchinleck had correctly detected the change in his opponent's stance and issued orders for preparation to pursue, presuming that Rommel would need to withdraw because of his very vulnerable supply route. If no retirement occurred, it would be Auchinleck who would have the initiative. On 4 July, Auchinleck could truly claim to have defeated his enemy's designs on Egypt, Cairo and Suez. However the victory was not a decisive one; Rommel had only been forced onto the defensive. This was like the 1916 naval battle of Jutland, where Jellicoe had, by the very act of *not losing*, frustrated German plans for the destruction of the Royal Navy's main fleet, which was an essential prerequisite for invading Britain. The German *Hochseeflotte* (High Seas Fleet) could make repeated attempts to destroy the Grand Fleet; Jellicoe need only lose once to jeopardize Britain's chances of victory. Auchinleck, however, wanted a definite victory and now set to making plans to secure it.

CHAPTER THREE

DIMINISHING RETURNS

On the morning of 4 July 1942 the Panzerarmee Afrika was in great danger. Its main attacking force, the Afrika Korps, had only thirty-six tanks in running order and no more than a few hundred exhausted infantry. The non-motorized units of its Italian allies were still in fair shape but not yet in the front line whilst Divisione 'Littorio' and, more particularly, Divisione 'Ariete', had suffered heavy casualties. The latter reportedly had only five M14 tanks and two field guns left after the New Zealand assault on the previous day. Fortunately for Rommel, given the need for defensive action, his artillery (both Italian and German) was otherwise still strong and a number of captured British guns were being used. German guns were very low on ammunition but 1,500 captured 25-pounder rounds were found in Deir el Shein, and the Italians had some reserve stocks. There was no doubt amongst some on his staff that the Axis forces could not have resisted a determined attack by Eighth Army and there was relief that the Panzerarmee survived the day 'with no real damage except to our nerves.'[1] This was despite a crisis for 15. Panzer-Division caused by a shortage of ammunition and confusion over the supposed surrender of 600 men of Schützen-Regiment 115.[2] On 5 July there was still little belief amongst Eighth Army that Auchinleck would have the temerity to attempt serious counter-attacks against the man whose reputation was such that every rumour now referred to 'Rommel' as opposed to 'the enemy' or 'the Germans and Italians', as in 'Rommel will be in Cairo in a week'. There was no clear point for the fighting troop at which they were able to see that they had actually defeated the intentions of their 'invincible' opponent. There were no two 'halves' of the First Battle of El Alamein. There are some who argued later that there was not even a battle that was 'First Alamein'.[3]

Eighth Army was bolstered on this day by the arrival and deployment of 9th Australian Division, but only after a dispute between Lieutenant-General Sir Leslie Morshead, the divisional commander, and Auchinleck. The Australian commander refused to detach brigades from his command to form the 'mobile artillery battle-groups' Auchinleck favoured for infantry formations. Morshead invoked the rights of a 'Commonwealth commander' in refusing to co-operate with a policy which he disliked, only accepting a temporary detachment of 24th Australian Infantry Brigade to positions on Ruweisat Ridge after tough negotiations. This was the only one of his brigades trained in mobile operations, which was how Auchinleck hoped it would be used.[4] Lance Corporal Phil Loffman, 2/28th Battalion, remembered the preparations:

> We were full of confidence. Actually, as the South Africans were retreating, they were saying 'Oh, Aussie, you're gonna get cleaned up, you're gonna get cleaned up'. They were disheartened and demoralized and they were a bad influence on the diggers. I didn't want them talking to our blokes because they were just gloom and doom. We were full of fight at that stage of the game.[5]

The Australians were unaware of the South Africans' involvement in the fighting of the previous days. Their opinions on the South African forces as a whole were now coloured by their unchangeable view that it was the South Africans who had lost Tobruk after they themselves had held it for so long in the siege. There was, on the other hand, admiration for their British counterparts and a feeling of mutual respect, as Private Peter Salmon, also of 2/28th Battalion, recalled:

> We always complained, we Australians, about our conditions but the British troops really their rations and things were a lot worse than ours. The morale amongst the British troops was extremely high. There was a tremendous lot of admiration for them. They were very good soldiers, wonderful soldiers, a lot of those British battalions. A lot of Australians, of course, called the British soldiers 'Poms', but it's in many cases an affectionate term. I think we generally had an admiration for each other really. There was never any bad feeling between ourselves and the British soldiers. Far from it.[6]

On 6 July Rommel continued to regroup his forces, laying mines to strengthen his front. The still-fragile 90. leichte-Afrika-Division received reinforcements and the number of tanks in the Afrika Korps rose to forty-four thanks to reinforcements and recoveries. This permitted the formation of a small mobile reserve. The great opportunity for destroying the Panzerarmee had passed, but Auchinleck rightly retained belief in the possibility of defeating his opponent given the steady and strong stream of reinforcements now arriving in the Middle East and coming forward to the front line. He, therefore, planned and gave orders accordingly.

Auchinleck cannot have been aware of the extent to which he was now the focus of the Prime Minister's criticism and concern. Auchinleck's correct refusal to attack before June 1942 had rankled with Churchill who had watched the events of June and early July from afar and with an increasingly jaundiced eye. It had been all that General Sir Alan Brooke could do to prevent the Prime Minister going out to Egypt at the end of June. Churchill, blocked in his designs, now used Cabinet meetings as a forum for ill-informed remarks on events in the Middle East [ME]. Typical was the meeting on 8 July, as General Brooke recorded:

> PM ran down ME army in shocking way and criticized Auchinleck for not showing a more offensive spirit. I had an uphill task defending him and pointing out the difficulties of his present position. Also the fact that any rash move on his part at present would very quickly lose us Egypt. However PM was in one of his unpleasant moods going back over old ground and asking where the 750,000 men in ME were, what they were doing, and why they were not fighting. After being thoroughly unpleasant during the Cabinet meeting, with that astounding charm of his he came up to me afterwards and said to me 'I am sorry Brookie if I had to be unpleasant about Auchinleck and the Middle East!'[7]

This apology was of no value to Auchinleck and the men of Eighth Army who continued to fight and die in defence of Egypt. Churchill's inability to differentiate between the enormous breadth of Auchinleck's responsibilities as Commander-in-Chief, Middle East and those connected with the necessary temporary assumption of Eighth Army command produced relentless and counter-productive criticism. It is doubtful whether even a great victory on Auchinleck's part could now have saved his position. As a professional soldier, however, he stayed firmly focused on the immediate challenge of defeating Rommel.

———————————

Since the Gazala battle opened, the Desert Air Force had been engaged at an incredible level in operations in support of the ground forces. In June, there had been heavy losses in aircraft with 113 British against eighty German and eighteen Italian. In July the effort was still being maintained and on 3 July, 770 sorties were flown – the greatest effort to date. When the lull in operations occurred, Air Vice-Marshal Arthur Coningham ordered most of his fighters onto fighter-bombing operations, especially attacks against the Panzerarmee supply route along the coastal road and, from 6 July onwards, the German airfields.

Squadron Leader Billy Drake had by now developed an effective modus operandi for airfield attacks:

> Airfields were very nasty. You only did one attack and never, never a repeat attack because that's where everybody got killed, if they were going to get killed. 'Surprise, surprise' was the essence. Ground attacks were always very carefully looked at before attack. You usually had photographs of where the aeroplanes were and the answer was you did one strafing attack, destroyed whatever you could on the ground and then went home and got the hell out of it. Never, never, never a second attack.[8]

The airfield attacks supported those of the bomber formations which were now being undertaken both night and day. The regular formations of bombers were usually accompanied by three squadrons of Kittyhawks with roving extra-high top cover from Spitfires. These were for protection against the 'Snappers' – the high-flying Messerschmitt Bf-109s and Macchi C202s who continually dived and pecked at the formations.[9] Meanwhile, the Luftwaffe was now finding plenty of opportunities amongst the stationary Eighth Army units for its Junkers 87 Stuka dive-bombers, which now reappeared (reportedly boosting the Panzerarmee's morale). However, as Cyril Mount noted, they operated under a law of diminishing returns:

> The Stukas were scary because we'd never come across anything like that before. [We were] very, very scared at first, then you realized you'd be very unlucky if you copped it, because they were a terrorizing thing, more than damaging. They only

had two bombs and they had a siren. They'd come when the sun was coming down at only a couple of degrees up and they would come out of the sun. The sirens were quite scary AAAAAAARRRRRRRRRRR!!!! and they seemed to be coming straight for you. At the beginning, you thought you'd had it but, later on when you got used to them, you realized they just weren't coming straight for you and the bombs they dropped very often did no damage at all to anybody. They just buried themselves in the sand and blew up great clouds of sand. You'd have to be very unlucky to get a direct hit from a Stuka.[10]

This growing contempt developed to the extent that, in mid-July, one fellow artilleryman, Bombardier Louis Challoner of 2nd Royal Horse Artillery, was reporting that he and his mates 'were inclined to look on them with some derision'.[11]

The dive-bombers also presented problems for the Luftwaffe. Oberleutnant Friedrich Körner of Jagdgeschwader 27, an 'ace' with thirty-six 'kills', noted their need 'for a fighter escort – being very slow and having poor defensive armament' and that a particular problem was 'they were scattered over a wide area after the dive and were very hard to protect'.[12] Körner was himself shot down by a Hurricane IIc flown by Lieutenant Lawrence Waugh of 1 South African Air Force Squadron and taken prisoner on 4 July whilst trying to attack a formation of allied bombers as German air operations grew in intensity. The Germans now dispatched large formations of Stukas and Junkers-88 conventional bombers with strong fighter escorts to pound their opponent. As a consequence, the count of aircraft shot down on both sides mounted steadily.

On 8 July Auchinleck relieved Lieutenant-General Sir Willoughby Norrie of command of XXX Corps and replaced him with William Ramsden, commander of 50th Division. Ramsden was immediately instructed to prepare an operation to capture two low ridges at Tel el Eisa ('the Hill of Jesus') and Tel el Makh Khad at the extreme *northern* end of his opponent's front. This was at a time when Rommel's attention had been drawn to the more open southern flank once more. Auchinleck was still thinking well ahead of his opponent. He had decided as early as 3 July that he would abandon the Bab el Qattara Box, but then considered using it as the basis for a thrust northwards towards El Mreir. Having decided against this, and with this box now offering little value defensively or for the attack, he ordered Gott to abandon it and withdraw the New Zealand defenders eastwards on 8 July. This pre-empted any effort by Rommel against the southern part of the Alamein line where the Panzerarmee commander dispatched 21. Panzer-Division, Divisione 'Littorio' and elements of 90. leichte-Afrika-Division to make 'a full-dress attack' on the well-built concrete strongpoints and gun emplacements. These forces consequently arrived too late and encountered only slight resistance from the retiring rearguard. Neither Rommel nor Generalmajor Georg von Bismarck, commander of 21. Panzer-Division, were able to understand why the position had been given up.

Auchinleck's northern attack would make a strike against the coastal highway a possibility and would be focused principally on the Italian infantry, now brought into the line. In this way, Auchinleck was not only out-thinking Rommel, he was also unwittingly anticipating his successor's plans by several months.

The attack was preceded by a raid on 7 July in which 2/43rd Battalion killed at least fifteen Germans, took nine prisoners and destroyed four anti-tank guns and one field gun. This led to sharp criticism by Rommel of his subordinates and severe strictures concerning officers sleeping in front-line positions at night because of the raid threat. Perhaps the Australians' reputation in two world wars for aggressive raiding was responsible for this rather edgy response.

The capture of Tel el Eisa was to be 9th Australian Division's responsibility, whilst 1st South African Division was to take Tel el Makh Khad. Thirty-two Valentine tanks of 44th Royal Tank Regiment (RTR) (with one squadron of 8th RTR attached) were to assist the Australians; the South Africans received only eight A12 Matilda II tanks. The 2/48th under its redoubtable commander, Lieutenant-Colonel Heathcote Hammer (known variously as 'Tack' or 'Sledge' and whose motto was 'hard as nails'),[13] would lead the Australian attack with 2/24th following and operating along the coast. A veteran tank officer, Captain Stuart Hamilton of the 8th RTR, witnessed the Australian methods of preparation at first – and was suitably impressed:

> We had just had our usual 'O' Group Orders for the forthcoming attack, done in the traditional format and style of: 1. Information; 2. Intention; 3. Method; 4. Plan; 5. Administration; 6. Questions etc. I then noticed a crowd of Aussie infantry gathering around an empty 44-gallon oil-drum to get their orders, so I wandered up to hear how this was to be done. They were an incredibly scruffy crowd with no one appearing to be dressed the same: some stripped to the waist with dirty, ragged shorts and scuffed boots: others in dirty slacks and equally dirty singlets: some wearing slouch hats, others with tin hats or bare-headed:

talking, smoking and laughing amongst themselves as they grouped around this oil-drum and waited for an RSM to stand on the top of it. He looked magnificent and would have done credit to a Guards battalion. He was a good 6' tall with a fine physique to match: deeply bronzed and bare-chested: wearing immaculately clean and well-pressed shorts, puttees and highly polished boots and a clean slouch hat with polished chin strap. He stood with his hands on his hips, looking down at them and bellowed, 'Friends, Romans and Countrymen' – this is going to be good I thought – 'lend me yer fuckin' ears you heap! You lucky bastards are going to have the chance once more of putting the shits up the fuckin' Jerries! Aren't you the lucky ones...?!'[14]

When the operation began, the tanks found the 'going' near the coast difficult even during the approach march. The hard crust of the salt pans broke up and several tanks and support vehicles bogged down, effectively limiting their participation. The attack went ahead, however, preceded by the sort of concentrated artillery fire that Auchinleck and Dorman-Smith had hoped for in their reforms to centralize artillery control. The availability of 7th Medium Regiment's heavier 4.5-inch guns provided depth to the barrage beyond the capabilities of the 25-pounders from three field regiments and from batteries of three more. The war diarist of the Afrika Korps witnessing the barrage from twenty miles away was sufficiently impressed to note that 'particularly heavy artillery fire can be heard from the north. Veterans of the Great War say it is even stronger than the *Trommelfeuer* [drum fire] of the Western Front'.[15]

The recipients of this concentrated 'hate' were troops of the inexperienced 60a Divisione di Fanteria 'Sabratha'. Just how ill-prepared for its task this Italian division was is indicated by the fact that the attacking infantry had already penetrated the Italian front-line positions and captured 400 men garrisoning Point 26 without a single casualty before the barrage started. Now it had begun, the infantry followed it and 2/48th seized Tel el Eisa station despite heavy fire from German and Italian field guns. Meanwhile 2/24th had taken its first objective, Trig 33, in spite of delays caused by crossing the salt marsh. However, without supporting tanks and machine guns, the battalion commander ordered them to dig in on these positions. Elsewhere, the South African attack on Tel el Makh Khad saw the position taken.

The attack prompted a crisis for the Axis forces. There was a gap near the coast where the 'Sabratha' had broken – a fact recognized by Oberstleutnant Friedrich Wilhelm von Mellenthin, now Panzerarmee Afrika's acting Chef der

Operationsabteilung. His prompt action prevented any possible further exploitation of the Australian success:

> Panzerarmee headquarters was on the coast, only a few miles behind the front, and early that morning I was startled to see hundreds of Italians rushing past the headquarters in the final stages of panic and rout. Rommel had spent the night in the Qaret el Abd Box, far to the south, and it was for me to decide what to do. When a headquarters is threatened the first instinct is to move and safeguard its irreplaceable equipment and documents. It was clear to me, however, that Sabratha was finished – their artillery was already 'in the bag' – and something must be done immediately to close the road to the west. I called on the staff and personnel of headquarters to form a rough battle line, which I strengthened with our anti-aircraft guns and some infantry reinforcements which happened to arrive.[16]

The infantry reinforcements were from Infanterie-Regiment 382, which was one of the advance units of what was to be 164. leichte-Afrika-Division and had just flown in from Crete. Mellenthin continued:

> Without these reinforcements the northern flank of the Panzerarmee could have been broken through. At noon Rommel came up from the south with his Kampfstaffel and a hastily organized battle group from 15. Panzer-Division. He attempted to cut off the Australian salient at Tel el Eisa by an attack from the south, but the artillery fire from Alamein Fortress was too strong.[17]

Throughout the day the infantry endured artillery fire, five visits by Stukas (with as many as thirty to forty planes in each attack) and tank assaults against which 2/3rd Anti-Tank Regiment's 2-pounders achieved exceptional and surprising success. In the early evening a penetration of the positions near the railway station was repelled by a determined counter-attack in which Corporal Tom 'Diver' Derrick of 2/48th Battalion took part:

> We were to move forward in one long extended line, cross the railway line without a sound and on a shot from the OC [Officer Commanding] we were to open up with everything and continue to advance firing as we went and calling out 'Come on Australianoes!'... From the din of the light machine-guns, tommy guns, rifles and grenades, also the blood-curdling cries of advancing men, the enemy must have thought there were thousands and I think the Australianoes business helped a lot.[18]

Attempts by the Germans to drive the attackers from their positions eventually ended in failure and the Australians set to constructing better defences for their gains. The attack had been a classic of Great War 'bite and hold' tactics in which the seizing of limited gains provoked a succession of counter-attacks which were decisively destroyed by a combination of the infantry defenders' own firepower and strong artillery support. It succeeded in relieving the immediate pressure on the Alamein Box and reducing Axis observation over the defences.

Like all salients, the captured ground *might* offer a position of potential from which further attacks could capitalize on the initial success but, equally, it placed the defenders in relatively crowded positions on which their opponent could pour concentrated artillery fire. In Auchinleck's view the necessity outweighed the probable consequences. *Post facto* suggestions of a connection between this attack and Basil Liddell Hart's 'Strategy of the Indirect Approach' are spurious.[19] The threat to his northern flank was something Rommel had previously failed to appreciate. The attack drew his attention back from grandiose schemes for a further effort towards Cairo to the very real need for effective defence. His deployment of an Italian infantry division to hold the line showed he had seriously underestimated the growing power of his opponent. In this sense, the attack was a shattering, though not decisive, blow.[20]

It had a shattering effect in another way too. This was the destruction of Nachrichten Fernaufklärungs Kompanie 621. This 'radio intercept company' under its ambitious commander, Hauptmann Alfred Seebohm, had provided Rommel with an immediate and extremely valuable insight into Eighth Army's plans, intentions, manoeuvres and actions since April 1941 by the simple expedient of listening to British wireless traffic. Under the pressure of events on the battlefield, these messages were usually sent 'in clear' i.e. without being encoded using a cipher, but with some codewords for places, units and so on. It was a flawed system, as even its users recognized, including Major Anthony Wingfield of the 10th Hussars:

> There was a system of code words and disguised language which had been adopted by the Eighth Army, and which now had to be learnt for use when wireless communication was in operation. I cannot help feeling that the Germans and Italians soon understood that 'Sun-ray' meant one's senior commander, etc. Those units who had recently served in India often adopted some Urdu words; but as there were Indian troops in the Desert it seemed obvious that the enemy would have Indian interpreters in their ranks.[21]

Seebohm's unit therefore consisted of skilled linguists with powerful wireless receivers. However, the men he commanded were also able to stand up to combat if necessary, as they had proved on several previous occasions. Supposedly out of the way at the northernmost end of the Axis line, this specialist unit fed back to Rommel details of Eighth Army deployments and intentions. It was extremely effective and had been working well both at Gazala and at Alamein, as one of its members, Leutnant Berno Wischmann, attested:

> Since the beginning of June, I had been assigned to Rommel as liaison officer with two operators. Any important message intercepted by the company reached me a few minutes later and thereby Rommel. I kept the wireless situation map for him. Not infrequently, the intercepted enemy signals had been deciphered and were in Rommel's hands whilst the [less well positioned] enemy signallers were still querying them. Rommel thus often had signals in his hands before the enemy commanders to whom they had been addressed. It was to achieve such brilliant results that Seebohm had taken the risk of putting our company in such an exposed position by the sea, just a few hundred yards behind a sector defended by Italian troops.[22]

When 2/24th Battalion attacked on 10 July, NFAK 621 was directly in their path. Seebohm was badly wounded and died in captivity soon afterwards and most of his unit were killed or captured after an hour's fight against the Australians and some Valentine tanks. Rommel's response to this news indicated how significant the loss was. According to Berno Wischmann:

> When Rommel asked me at about 09.00 on 10th July, for the latest intercepts, I had to tell him that we had still not established radio contact with the company yet. 'Where is the company positioned?' he asked. I showed him on the map. 'Then it is *futsch* – lost!' he said, absolutely furious.[23]

This was the second intelligence loss Rommel had suffered in less than two weeks. Firstly the 'Good Source' – *Gute Quelle* – had been blocked and now NFAK 621. The former could not be replaced. The latter was reconstituted in September but was never as effective again, although British wireless discipline continued to be lax.

The fighting around Tel el Eisa continued the next morning when at 0630hrs 2/24th Battalion with 44th RTR took the easternmost of the two 'Point 24' features and, once more, held it against repeated counter-attacks whilst another of Auchinleck's 'mobile artillery battle-groups' termed 'Daycol', operating in the manner he and Dorman-Smith had envisaged, but reinforced by 'infantry' tanks, managed to capture a battalion of Italian infantry before encountering resistance and withdrawing. On 13 July an attack by 21. Panzer-Division intended to break into the Alamein Box and 'supported by every gun and every aircraft'[24] the Panzerarmee could muster, failed badly under heavy artillery fire from the Box. Information from Ultra had warned Eighth Army of Rommel's intentions. Although Point 24 was lost on 14 July, the losses to the German forces were too heavy to sustain and the attack was broken off.

A major factor in the effective defence of the Alamein Box throughout the first half of July had been the successful use of centralized control of artillery to defeat specific threats. The value of the medium guns in this regard was recognized by Eighth Army and the power of 7th Medium Regiment was increased still further with the arrival of the South Nottinghamshire Hussars Yeomanry which had been overrun during Gazala and was now reconstituted as 107 Battery and the first to be equipped with the 5.5-inch medium gun. Lieutenant Charles Laborde, from 107 Battery, recalled:

> We set to to learn how to operate these guns which of course were quite different. They were split-trail and the barrel had to be lowered so that the 100-pound shell could be put into it and rammed home and the charges and so on. Then it would be raised up again and then laid in the normal manner. When the men had learned sufficiently how to operate the guns, we then had to take all these guns out into the desert and calibrate them. It was then we discovered what wonderful guns they were because they proved to be quite extraordinarily accurate. We found that their 'hundred per cent' and their 'fifty per cent' zones were so small that we could really hardly believe it. On Charge One where the range wasn't very great – only about 4,000 or 5,000 yards, the shells almost fell in the same hole. It was quite an extraordinarily accurate gun.[25]

The 'five-fives' not only brought greater accuracy, they also provided the gunners with more hitting power, as Charles Westlake found:

> The reaction we had was that it packed a fairly healthy wallop. You did feel that if you dropped one of those shells near the enemy you were certainly going to do him some damage. In fact we knocked out quite a few tanks with these.

Not by hitting the tank but by dropping the shell in proximity – you stunned the crew inside. A hundred pounds of explosive – well, it's obviously four times the power of the 25-pounder. They were a very effective weapon.[26]

Towed by diesel-engined four-wheel drive AEC Matadors which later, after much fruitless manual toil, were found to be the best means to haul and push these enormous guns into their battery position, the battery came into the line on 15 July under the watchful eye of an important, and greatly admired, observer. Sergeant David Tickle, also of 107 Battery, recounted:

When we moved up into the line at Alamein, we pulled up on the roadside in the evening. The idea was to go and take up our positions in the dark and a staff car came down and lo and behold, who got out the staff car but Auchinleck. He stopped and he hadn't seen anything of the five-five. He probably heard they were around, but he hadn't seen them. He stopped and he came right down the line and I think he had a word with most of the people lined up then. I thought that was extremely good. I know he wanted to look at the five-fives but he took time out to come and talk to us. He was a good lad.[27]

These guns were the means to deliver Auchinleck's vision of artillery power for his army.

———————

During the Great War, a challenge for the high command of all armies had been to maintain 'operational tempo' through co-ordinated attacks in quick succession that ensured that different sectors of the enemy's line were attacked and their opponent kept off balance. Auchinleck's operations in the second half of July, beginning with the launch of Operation *Bacon* – an attempt to capture the Ruweisat Ridge in the centre of the Axis front – were seemingly intended for precisely this end: a succession of blows against the Panzerarmee coming on the heels of the fighting at Tel el Eisa to maintain the initiative and break his opponent's resistance. All these operations were fatally compromised in conception and execution.

———————

Operation *Bacon* began on the night of 14 July when 5th Indian Brigade (part of XXX Corps, but under XIII Corps orders) and 4th and 5th New Zealand Brigades attacked. The New Zealand division was temporarily under the command of

Brigadier Lindsay Inglis, who appeared exceptionally keen to prove his own mettle as a divisional commander in Freyberg's absence. Two brigades of 1st Armoured Division were ordered to be ready to fight off Axis counter-attacks and, if possible, exploit any success the infantry units achieved. The attack was to be made at night with the New Zealanders advancing nearly six miles to seize their objective and the Indian brigade on their right flank. The objectives were known to be held by 27ª Divisione Autotrasportabile 'Brescia' and 17ª Divisione Autotrasportabile 'Pavia'. Once again Italian non-armoured formations were being targeted.

Problems in the planning, preparation and delivery of this operation did a great deal of harm in Eighth Army, reflecting badly on Auchinleck and Gott. It was later criticized as being 'hastily conceived, loosely coordinated, and abound[ing] in examples of poor staff work on matters which might be supposed to be within the knowledge and experience of those responsible.'[28] It featured many flaws – the first being the repeated cancellations (three all told) which seriously prejudiced men like Brigadier Howard Kippenberger, commanding 5th New Zealand Infantry Brigade, against both the High Command and the British armour commanders. Kippenberger explained the background to the attack as he saw it:

> Ruweisat Ridge, a long, bare, narrow ridge of an average height of 180 feet, ran east and west into the centre of the army position and gave enough command to make it of great tactical importance. Apparently [XIII] Corps thought we might seize it by something in the nature of a *coup de main*... The plan was a daring one and looked well on paper, or rather on the map, for there were no written orders. It was asking a great deal of the infantry. Two brigades were to move in trucks two and a half miles under fire to an assembly position, easily marked on the map but not so easily located on the ground. Then they were to form up and make a night attack without artillery support on an objective five miles distant. There was no time for co-ordination with the armour, through which we were advancing at right angles to the way it was looking and thinking.[29]

Kippenberger's doubts grew with the cancellation of the attack on 12 July and after discussion of the plans:

> We had a conference about the projected attack and heard with some scepticism that when we had taken the ridge our tanks would go through and exploit. I do not think anyone then realized how much training and care and forethought are

required to get good co-operation between infantry and tanks. We merely cursed one another when it was not achieved. Nor was the problem of command dealt with: the tank brigadiers naturally and emphatically intended to keep their regiments under their own command and to act merely 'in support'. In the absence of any clear direction from Army they had to be left with their way. We knew there were minefields to be passed but I do not remember any particular plan for clearing and marking gaps: at least there is no mention of the matter in 5 Brigade Orders. Fortunately the Italians had left some gaps on their own initiative and had also gone to the trouble of marking them.[30]

Many of Kippenberger's criticisms have the benefit of hindsight but other errors are obvious – especially the failure of Gott and XIII Corps to understand and *convey* the purpose of the operations. Their orders only stated: 'XIII Corps will secure Point 64.'[31] This objective (elsewhere termed Point 63) was not mentioned as a bridgehead from which the armour would then operate. Kippenberger had other frustrations too:

There was no time to do any proper reconnaissance – or any at all for that matter – to circulate orders, to let the men know what they had to do. I spoke to several company officers during the advance and found that they had not the faintest idea of the intention. There was no time to make proper arrangements for bringing up antitank guns or clearing and marking any minefields we might encounter or ensuring artillery support in the morning. In fact these matters were not very clearly thought about by anybody in those days. The whole operation was typical of Eighth Army's methods and ideas while it was dominated by what I heard one very senior officer describe as 'the vested interests of the British cavalry'.[32]

British armour was to become Kippenberger's particular *bête noir*, so his critique needs to be treated with caution. It was, however, based on the events of Operation *Bacon* where, clearly, infantry and armoured co-operation went seriously awry. What was also clear was that the prior reconnaissance for the advance was not performed and that XIII Corps' approach was at the root of many of Kippenberger's complaints:

We heard that 4 Indian Division, advancing on a converging bearing, would be on our right, but there was no more liaison with the Indians than with the tanks. The affair was a Corps attack delivered by one armoured and two infantry divisions, but there was no Corps conference for lower than divisional commanders and none of us had much idea what the other divisions were to do.[33]

It is interesting however to note that in his description of the final New Zealand divisional conference on 14 July, he unwittingly brings criticism on his own acting commander, Inglis, in noting the absence of any representative of the armour or of the Indian brigade there – something which the New Zealanders themselves could have ensured.[34] Finally, he concluded:

> Odd things always go wrong in the preparations for a battle and the only course is to be patient, correct them as far as possible, and remember them for future reference. More than usual went wrong in the preparations for this unlucky battle.[35]

The New Zealand advance began at 2300hrs on 15 July. The advance first met opposition soon after midnight. Private Richard Hewitt of 22nd Battalion, 5th New Zealand Brigade, remembered:

> It was all quiet and orderly, we just trudged along over the sand. I can't say I was very excited or even very scared. One felt that one had been at that sort of thing all one's life. As we moved in closer the Jerries and Ites started up the odd bursts of machine-gun fire as if they were a bit uneasy about things. Then the fire became more prolonged and after a few flares had been put up they started giving us all they had. Big mortars came whistling over to land with nasty bumps and shattering explosions beside us in the dark, while at times the night was lit up with flares and tracers from different types of shells and bullets, also a burning truck or two.[36]

Both New Zealand brigades had problems from the start with wireless communications and frequently lost touch with their battalions. The battalions themselves could not maintain inter-company contact when they got involved in the fighting. The heavy and temperamental No. 18 infantry pack set was not robust enough and the sets did not stay adjusted to the correct 'net' and interference made renetting on the move impossible. The wireless vehicle for 4th New Zealand Brigade was hit early in the fighting. Communications also broke down in Kippenberger's brigade and, in the darkness, units got dispersed and fragmented.

Nevertheless, the advance went into the heart of Divisione 'Brescia' and 'Pavia' and, indeed, through to the rear areas of the Panzerarmee. There was panic amongst the Italian troops. In fact, however, the night advance meant many German and Italian positions were not tackled. Therefore, on their final objective, the infantry's problems came to a head. Second Lieutenant Roy Johnston, also of 22nd Battalion, recounted:

> Dawn found us on a slight feature looking down to a shallow basin. In daylight we moved into the basin. We were halted. We were told to dig in. No one could inform us as to our front, or direction of anticipated counter-attack. We were told to dig in anywhere. The men were being very philosophical about it all but there was confusion. Soldiers trained to do what they were told 'dug in anywhere'.[37]

The brigade's anti-tank guns had got lost in the advance so 22nd Battalion had no protection except four guns under Captain Mick Ollivier. Operating beyond the range of their field guns, the New Zealanders needed armoured support but the orders to Major-General Herbert Lumsden's 1st Armoured Division did not make clear this need and no provision had been made for close support by Valentines or Matildas from 1st Army Tank Brigade. Consequently, the Grants and Crusaders of 2nd and 22nd Armoured Brigades waited well to the south of Ruweisat Ridge. Richard Hewitt described the scene:

> Those with shovels and picks started digging while the 'diggers' who had nothing to dig with built up rough little shelters of stone. I had a few rocks in front of me and even one or two on each side which was better than nothing. Suddenly there was an ear-splitting crack and a fiery projectile flashed past a few feet above ground and got a direct hit on a truck in front of us which promptly went up in flames.[38]

Eight tanks from Panzer-Regiment 8 which had not been dealt with during the night advance had arrived to attack the vulnerable 22nd Battalion from the rear. They made shrewd use of natural cover, light and a dust haze. Ollivier's four anti-tank guns opened up, but were soon overwhelmed. Most infantry had been expecting British armour to appear and mistook the Panzers for this armoured support. Too late, they realized their mistake, as Hewitt recalled:

> One platoon on our right that was near a bit of a ridge got up and made a run for it, they had of course to run a hell of a gauntlet of machine-gun bullets, and it was

pretty grim to see these men running with dust being kicked up all round them as they fell or dived to the ground and then up and on again.[39]

This was Sergeant Keith Elliott and 11 Platoon, who successfully escaped the debacle. As they began running, men shouted: 'What the hell are you running for – they are our tanks.' Elliott's adventures had only just begun. Although wounded, he subsequently led a growing party of men from three New Zealand battalions against various parties of Italians, capturing five posts and returning with over 200 prisoners. He was later awarded the Victoria Cross.

Most of his battalion was captured that morning, however. Hewitt's narrative continued:

> The tanks having knocked out our guns came rumbling and clanking towards us with nothing to stop them. We could do nothing but keep hoping some of our own tanks would turn up to the rescue. A big Mark IV was only about 70 yards off me by this time and I was … wondering what the hell to do next. Some of our chaps were right under the damned monster, and I can still see clearly the silly little bits of white paper they waved for a white flag. Then all seemed to rise up out of the desert with their hands up.[40]

Fourteen officers and 261 other ranks were 'in the bag', including four wounded who were considerately treated. Apart from these prisoners, the entire Ruweisat action had cost 22nd Battalion one killed and eighteen wounded (two of whom died later). The men went into captivity feeling bitterly let down by the British armour.

When 22nd Battalion was overwhelmed, Kippenberger had trekked to find the British armour to ask for help for his men on the ridge. Eventually he reached Brigadier Harold Briggs' 2nd Armoured Brigade:

> In every turret someone was standing gazing through glasses at the smoke rising from Ruweisat Ridge four miles and more away. I found and spoke to a regimental commander, who referred me to his Brigadier. The Brigadier received me coolly. I did my best not to appear agitated, said that I was Commander of 5 New Zealand Infantry Brigade, that we were on Ruweisat Ridge and were being attacked in the rear by tanks when I left an hour before. Would he move up and help? He said he would send a reconnaissance tank. I said there was no time. Would he move his whole brigade?[41]

Lumsden's arrival did nothing to placate the increasingly frustrated Kippenberger:

> I gave him exactly the same information. Without answering he walked round
> to the back of his car, unfastened a shovel and with it killed a scorpion with
> several blows. Then he climbed up beside the Brigadier, who was sitting on
> the turret of his tank... The General asked where we were and the Brigadier
> pointed out the place on the map. 'But I told you to be there at first light,' General
> Lumsden then said, placing his finger on Point 63. I jumped down and did not
> hear the rest of the conversation but in a few minutes the General got down and
> in a soothing manner which I resented said that the Brigade would move as soon
> as possible.[42]

In fact, this was only confirmation that the tanks could now go forward in the
manner envisaged in XIII Corps' plans but never adequately explained to the
New Zealanders. This incident assumed greater importance when at 1700hrs
General der Panzertruppen Walther Nehring launched his first counter-attack.
When Eighth Army's attack was recognized by Panzerarmee as more than a raid,
Panzer-Aufklärungs-Abteilung 3 and part of 21. Panzer-Division were sent
against the ridge from the north and Panzer-Aufklärungs-Abteilung 33 and
the Baade Gruppe[43] from the south. These units took time to gather and organize
but now they counter-attacked through the late afternoon haze and the dust
and smoke of the battlefield. The New Zealanders had frequently used their
2-pounder anti-tank guns mounted on the lorries that transported them.
But these 'portees', as they were termed, were dangerously exposed on the
bare ridge and were targeted by the German tanks and armoured cars. The
headquarters of 4th New Zealand Brigade was overrun and Brigadier James
Burrows was captured, but subsequently managed to escape. The tanks of
2nd Armoured, operating in hull down positions, then stopped any further
German advance and the Panzers soon broke off the action as night descended.

As something more than an interested observer, the opinions of Major-
General Francis 'Gertie' Tuker of 4th Indian Division on the failure of the attack
are valuable and explain the fundamental flaw in the plan:

> The divisional objectives were on a vast front of something like 7,000 yards; the
> depth of attack was on the same scale; the attackers were six weak battalions.
> All that amounted to was that this division had been given a task which should
> have been beyond its powers. Unless the ground it covered at night could be well

scoured by our tanks at crack of dawn and unless other tanks could be up with the forward infantry to hold while the antitank guns were being sited at first light, then many enemy posts and other defences were bound to be missed, only to come to life at dawn and dislocate the divisional plan to hold its gains.[44]

Attacks by single divisions or two or three brigades with over-ambitious objectives, and without full consideration given to the problems of supporting the infantry beyond the range of the field artillery, are recognisable issues afflicting British operations on the Western Front in the summer of 1916. It remained to be seen if Auchinleck would repeat these mistakes in his subsequent operations.

The antipathy between infantry and tanks in Eighth Army was now very real. It could be put right out of the line only through revised doctrine, training and effective liaison. These options were unavailable to Auchinleck's forces. Limited by lack of trained reserves, they remained in the front line for extended periods. It seemed that only when the reinforcements arriving in the shape of 44th, 51st and 8th Armoured Divisions were in good shape could this situation be rectified. However, under pressure of events, this situation was soon to change.

Both Ultra and the British 'Y' (wireless intercept) Service provided timely warning of an Axis counter-attack against 5th Indian Brigade on 16 July. Both Panzer divisions were used and the attack was preceded by heavy Stuka attacks – the Luftwaffe was now fully geared up for operations and its fighters were also operating more aggressively again. Although the attack was made in 'classical' Afrika Korps fashion with the setting sun behind the Panzers, it was defeated by an effective combination of Grant tanks and anti-tank guns with the former a 'lure' to draw the German tanks onto the latter guns. The destruction of the attack was brutally efficient, as Francis 'Gertie' Tuker described:

Major Waller of 149th Anti-Tank Regiment and Lieutenant-Colonel Hutton of the 5th Royal Tank Regiment were the two stalwarts on the spot who hastily planned and then fought this important action, the tanks retiring and drawing the panzers on to Waller's well-concealed 6-pounders. It is to the credit of 149th that, after only a few days' training on the new gun, it could demonstrate in battle that, co-ordinated with other arms, our 6-pounder was the master of the German armour. Our infantry casualties were negligible and 149th lost only three killed and three wounded. The news spread quickly through the Eighth Army and up went the men's spirits from doggedness to elation.[45]

This important, but often-ignored victory resulted in losses of twenty-four tanks, six armoured cars, one self-propelled gun, eighteen anti-tank guns and six 88mm guns.[46] It demonstrated that Eighth Army could now mount defensive actions making effective use of its new weaponry.

The following day, however, the Australians made their latest attempt to expand the Tel el Eisa salient. Initially successful, with the capture of 736 prisoners from 102ª Divisione Motorizzata 'Trento', 101ª Divisione Motorizzata 'Trieste' and 7º Reggimento Bersaglieri, the Australians were later counter-attacked and suffered approximately 300 casualties. Both Auchinleck and Morshead, despite several disagreements in this period, both saw the value in maintaining pressure on Rommel's northernmost positions.

Auchinleck's next major attack – Operation *Splendour* – was to be against the centre of the Axis defences where he hoped finally and conclusively to break the Italian infantry and induce a collapse in the Panzerarmee. It began on the night of 21–22 July and was a true tragedy in many ways. The whole attack had the virtue at least of combining the efforts of XIII and XXX Corps. At Tel el Eisa 9th Australian Division with 50th RTR tanks in support would make another effort to expand the salient and threaten the Axis northern flank. The main attack forces included 161st Indian Motor Brigade (recently arrived from Iraq), 6th New Zealand Brigade (brought up to the line from the Delta after the loss of 4th New Zealand Brigade) and the remaining two Territorial RTR battalions of 23rd Armoured Brigade equipped with Valentines, whose experiences since their very recent arrival in the desert had not been happy ones, as Captain Tom Witherby of 46th RTR attested:

We had found our vehicles by 10th July and were horrified by their state. We considered that they were OUR tanks and they had not only been sent off from our Camps in England in tip top condition but they were also stowed with personal kit. Nearly all the kit was looted and the tanks were in a terrible state after being 'overhauled' in workshops. Brigadier Misa, the Commander of 23rd Armoured Brigade, went to Cairo and saw General McCreery, our former divisional commander, who was at GHQ as Armoured Fighting Vehicles Staff Officer Class

One. McCreery came down and forbade all further work and allowed us to have our tanks to ourselves. We were also given tanks from 24th Armoured Brigade stock to use for 'cannibalization'. By 17th July we were more or less ready.[47]

Nor did the brigade's briefings inspire confidence, as Witherby described:

Two Warrant Officers arrived as tank instructors. One of them walked out to the tank park and went up to a Valentine. He stood looking at it as if admiring it and then pointed at the turret and asked 'What is that funny little thing sticking out of the turret'? Someone said it was the two pounder gun. He said 'They'll murder you if you go up there with that. You might as well go into action with a pea shooter'.[48]

Brigadier Misa did not consider his brigade ready for battle and protested at its being sent straight into action, but he was overruled.

The first tragedy occurred when it was discovered that Panzer-Regiment 8 had grouped to make a counter-attack against positions taken during the first Ruweisat battle on 15 July. This was the same ground over which 6th New Zealand Brigade was making its night attack on the El Mreir depression. Howard Kippenberger told the story:

We could see and hear that the attack was progressing slowly but little else. Our fire programme ended but I ordered part to be repeated as it was clear that the infantry were not yet on their objective. After the repeat, we carried on at a slower rate, for some ammunition had to be kept for the morning. We were concerned to see explosions and fires in the path of the advance.[49]

Soon after daylight, the reports of the wounded indicated that there had been another disaster. The three battalions and headquarters of 6th New Zealand Brigade had reached the depression, but had lost their anti-tank guns and transport. Two liaison officers – one being the son of a very famous father – had been assigned to the New Zealanders from 22nd Armoured Brigade in an endeavour to avoid the previous week's debacle, but these too had problems. Major Dawyck Haig, one of the assignees from 22 Armoured's HQ Staff, recalled:

I had a tank which should have had good communications with 22nd [Armoured] Brigade but those communications were not much use because our wireless was jammed – stopped by the Germans. They wouldn't allow it. Anyway, the attack went through quite well. Everything would have been alright had the armour, the 22nd Brigade, been ready to liberate us and defend us at first light. Not a sight of our armour![50]

Signals communication had supposedly advanced rapidly since the days when his father had been a Field Marshal and Commander-in-Chief of the British Expeditionary Force in France, but this was not Dawyck Haig's experience.

The expected tanks from 2nd Armoured Brigade had made no appearance and German tanks had attacked the brigade at first light and forced them to surrender. Brigadier George Clifton was captured and taken to Rommel. The New Zealanders did not even have the compensation of substantial captures of prisoners and equipment; plenty of prisoners were taken but hardly any retained. As Kippenberger wrote, 'Worst of all, we had again relied in vain on the support of our tanks and bitterness was extreme.'[51]

The experience of the armoured division's liaison officers, as voiced by Dawyck Haig, was equally bitter:

There we were in a sort of bowl and I'm in my tank. We're being shot at by German armour and guns at quite close range really and they had 88s – a lot of 88s. We were absolutely mincemeat. There was no way that we could have survived. Sooner, rather than later, my tank got brewed up. You suddenly realize you've been hit. It was a Crusader tank with a 2-pounder gun and it didn't have much armour. It was really an uncomfortable position to be in. You realized full well that you had been hit, which was really what one was hoping to happen quicker and we wouldn't be either obliterated or lose our legs or whatever. I got into the nearest slit trench with some New Zealanders. One New Zealander was very grateful to have me guarding his bottom by lying on top of him![52]

Haig was captured and spent much of the rest of the war as a prisoner in Colditz. He recognized that, being in a tank, he and his crew could have escaped but felt this would have been dishonourable:

It's quite a shock, but on the other hand it's also a big relief. You've had this night battle – which in itself is a bit frightening and then you realize you're not in a very happy position and you couldn't really move. You didn't want to leg it – we could've legged it straight off, but it would not be looked on very well by the New Zealanders, if of the only tanks they had, one of them – which was us – legged it off into the

Delta. So, one more or less said 'Well, there's nothing else to do but just to wait and be a prisoner'. We had no firepower – I mean a 2-pounder against 88s![53]

Although 161st Indian Motor Brigade managed to achieve some success, capturing 190 prisoners in their attack, they could not take the troublesome Point 63. Neither had the minefield gapping operations which were essential to the plan's success been accomplished satisfactorily. This work was essential for the advance of 23rd Armoured Brigade to succeed. Strenuous efforts were being made to call off the attack because of the problems encountered during the night by the New Zealanders and Indians. Nevertheless, the attack still went in at 0800hrs on 22 July with 40th and 46th RTR side by side. The long-range fuel tanks which the Valentines had carried to enable them to reach the front line with enough fuel were dropped off and lay on the desert in three lines to mark the position occupied by the Valentines and Matildas. Tom Witherby recounted:

In broad daylight, we moved up a track to the top of Ruweisat Ridge and formed up ready to start. The scene was unreal. The tanks were freshly painted, pennons flew from radio aerials, jeeps and scout cars moved up and down, but there was no massive bombing, no saturation bombardment, no accompanying Infantry. Our Armoured Cars, which would have been a useful screen, had been sent elsewhere. To attack a German-Italian force in broad daylight and without surprise was like trying to break a block of concrete with a woodman's axe.[54]

More than one hundred Valentines armed with 2-pounder guns and Matildas with three-inch mortars rolled westwards along Ruweisat Ridge, with Bren carriers, 2-pounder anti-tank guns and artillery following. Ironically, here was a mass of 'infantry' tanks being used without infantry. The New Zealanders would have welcomed the presence of squadrons from these regiments in their two disastrous attacks.

Very soon the tanks came under tremendous anti-tank fire in which at least four types of gun were used: the 88mm Flak, 50mm Pak 38, Russian 76mm anti-tank gun and captured British 2-pounders. Trooper Geoff Bays of 46th RTR recalled:

I was LOB – Left Out Of Battle – as reinforcements. You trailed up in one of the ammunition wagons or the fuel wagon, waiting for your call. They went straight up and virtually straight into action with appalling staff work – very amateurish – and of course they got cut to ribbons on their first action. Starting off in the morning, I think they had forty-four per cent dead by midday.[55]

Many tanks were stopped on the minefield and destroyed when trying to find a way through non-existent gaps. At 1100hrs the remnants were attacked by 21. Panzer-Division and were ordered to withdraw. The disastrous 'Charge of the Light Brigade' attack cost the brigade 203 casualties, with about forty tanks destroyed and forty-seven badly damaged. Attempts further south to get 2nd Armoured Brigade into action to support the New Zealanders and 23rd Armoured eventually saw a narrow lane being cleared through the minefields and at 1700hrs 9th Lancers and 6th RTR attempted to go through the gap, only to suffer heavy tank casualties. After forty minutes, the attack was called off by Major-General Alec Gatehouse, the acting divisional commander, who was well up with the attack. Lieutenant Gerald Jackson of 6th RTR, 1st Armoured Brigade, remembered:

> Major-General Gatehouse came up to visit us, just then we were heavily shelled and one fell about five yards away from me as I was going to Frank's tank. It blew me head over heels but the only damage was a cut finger and cut knee. Gatehouse was more unfortunate and got a nasty wound in the arm and another chap next to him was killed.[56]

The experience of the delays in this mine-clearing were to colour the opinions of armoured commanders like Gatehouse and Fisher, 2nd Armoured Brigade's commander, in future operations.

The attack by 9th Australian Division with 50th RTR was also a failure. The inexperience of the new tank unit was evident, certainly to Company Sergeant Major Alan Potter of 2/28th Battalion:

> It was the 50th Tank Battalion [sic]. British tanks who'd never been in action before coming to the desert. They had poor training, and I believe they were on their way to Burma. Once they got under fire, they really didn't know where they were at and the Germans by this time had the 88 millimetres, which were superb guns.[57]

To transport the infantry a dangerous expedient was adopted. Lance Corporal Phil Loffman, with 2/28th Battalion, was one of those involved:

> We had to sit on the Valentine tanks and go into the attack – which is quite
> a precarious position to be in when you go into an armoured attack, sitting on
> a front row of the armour. Officially there was going to be a full company to go
> on the armour, but in the finish I don't know what happened but it was only
> 10 Platoon. That was only 30 Diggers.[58]

These were the battalion pioneers who, despite their own war experiences,
could not fail to admire the tank men's courage from their new vantage point:

> Anyway we perched ourselves on the front of these guns and before we went in
> I said to the chap 'they're little guns you've got' and he said 'Yeh, 2-pounders'. I
> said 'You know what you're up against?' He said 'We know'. So these fellows were
> bloody heroes. They were going to take this armour straight on and meet these
> 88s and the bigger tanks head on. We knew what would happen – and it did![59]

Slow-moving tanks could still outdistance burdened infantry advancing on the
ridge. Consequently, the tanks soon left their 'partners' behind and, without
adequate infantry support to overcome the anti-tank gunners, began to take
many casualties. The men riding the tanks soon also suffered losses to their
numbers, as Loffman discovered:

> Our platoon commander ... lost his life. He was on a tank fifteen metres from me
> and I thought they were throwing a red flag off the tank and he got a direct hit
> with an anti-tank shell and was just blown to pieces. The platoon sergeant, he had
> both legs taken off and wanted to commit suicide with a grenade. He died of loss
> of blood. Two or three of them went up on the minefield. We got heavy losses on
> that day. The chap who got blown up, he'd only just finished his officer training
> course in Cairo. Came out in his new uniform with his pips on and his batman,
> sat on the tank and lasted about ... 20 minutes.[60]

The failure in co-operation saw twenty-three tanks knocked out. Some advance
had been made but the attackers were forced to withdraw and their objective,
Ruin Ridge, remained untaken.

———————————

Auchinleck's final effort – Operation *Manhood* – was prepared with more time
than most of the previous operations. It saw XXX Corps reinforced by 4th Light

Armoured Brigade and 69th Brigade and aimed to break through between Miteirya and Deir el Dhib. It was a return to a single corps attack and enjoyed as little success and as much failure as many of the previous attacks. The attack relied on minefield gapping – an operational task for which Eighth Army was still inadequately equipped and trained. Nevertheless, on the night of 26–27 July a wide gap in the Axis minefield south of Miteirya was made by the South Africans assigned to this task. Meanwhile 2/28th Battalion, Australian Infantry Force (AIF), though delayed, took its objective on the eastern end of Miteirya Ridge. Private Patrick Toovey, from 2/28th, was present:

> It was all supposed to be 'hush hush' but we set off at midnight and from my memory we started having casualties before ten minutes or quarter of an hour was gone. The firing started almost as soon as we got going. We had a lot of casualties on the way in.[61]

Despite heavy fire the Aussies made good, though delayed, progress. Phil Loffman recalled:

> The artillery barrage was magnificent. It built up confidence. It gave us all the sting in the world and I actually felt sorry for the Germans. I said 'If those blokes see that how're they going to get through to Cairo with guns like that in front of them?' The firefight wasn't that bad – we got onto the ridge. We accepted casualties on the start line so you're going to get a few going in too, but we got onto the ridge and the battalion was pretty well intact.[62]

The barrage on Ruin Ridge was supposed to ensure the Australians had less opposition. Whilst waiting for it to lift, a company commander from 2/28th Battalion, Captain Vernon Northwood, noticed a disturbing development:

> I saw a gun coming up on the ridge just as we were going forward over on my left, a gun was being pulled into position. And I thought 'That can't be one of ours'. And, in any case, it wouldn't be on the back side of the ridge, it'd be forward here somewhere where there was danger. I watched as we were waiting – because we had to wait to go onto the ridge... Then two truck loads of men came up and they turned this gun round. It was an 88mm. An anti-tank gun. They were vicious. They were the worst gun that we ever encountered.[63]

Northwood's response was immediate – he knew it had to be. He ordered his company to turn to their flank and made ready to make a bayonet charge:

> There's no chance to take up a firing position. We could see men coming forward where this gun was obviously taking up firing positions to protect the gun, so we had to act more quickly than they were acting. So I got I'd say two platoons on a fairly good line, and the other one – 8 platoon – hadn't much further to come round and I thought 'I can't wait for them to come round'. So, I thought 'Better go in now with the bayonet'.[64]

Northwood's rationale relied on the bayonet charge's threat to morale more than its reality:

> You know that if they're in a position to run, they will. They won't face you. Moonlight night. Moon glinting on bayonets and they know you're charging with the bayonet and it would be a very powerful man – a person dug in in a gun position would stay there and fight but a man who's a rifleman won't – they'll get up and run. Or they'll stay with their hands up.[65]

His choice made, it was time for action:

> I said 'Right. Into them!' It's really hard to lead a bayonet charge from fellers lying on the ground. For a moment I'm the only one up. I really thought, 'One Man Bayonet Charge'. You get that horrible feeling 'I'm the only one. Oh, where are they?!' I was shouting like a madman. And you shout all sorts of things. Obscenities. 'Get the bastards,' you say. Because you've got to get yourself into a state of frenzy because you can't attack a man with a bayonet or group of them. All of a sudden I heard this noise behind me and I got the fright of my life! My hair started to stand up on the back of my neck. It's the most frightening thing. To be in a bayonet attack and everyone else is shouting. Mind, it's an awful noise you can make when you're in fear – that you're on the top of the ground and you think someone's going to shoot you.[66]

His personal charge was soon brought to a halt:

> Anyway, I'd only gone about 15 or 20 paces, I suppose. And first of all I got a bullet through my steel helmet. I threw my head back and then in this position I felt

a cut through the top of my arm, and then WHAM! It was a compound fracture of the arm. It was four shots. A bullet went through just above my forehead and out the top. It cut my scalp – I had a big scar on my scalp for quite some time. The other one – a little bit of metal lodged in the back of my neck. I very nearly lost the arm. It was just like a kick from a horse. I have been kicked by a horse and it was ooh! The one on my helmet threw my head back and I felt stinging pain with the other two but this one, because it hit the bone, just threw me round. I was out of control – just went round and round. My rifle and bayonet flew out of my hands and I was just like a crazy thing. I just pitched to the ground... Somebody shouted out: 'The Skipper's been hit' and I called back 'I'm all right!' because it's fatal if someone stops so I said 'I'm all right'. So they went on.[67]

Northwood, though badly wounded, lingered with the front-line troops long enough to ensure the ridge was taken before making his way back to the rear on foot.

I thought: 'I am worried now why the vehicles are not getting through'. I waited there for a while. No ambulance came up and I said 'I'm going back to find out why the vehicles aren't coming through.' Our supply vehicles. Ammunition and all the company vehicles. Bringing forward ammunition, extra weapons, anti-tank guns. One anti-tank portee came through – I saw that and I thought, 'No, we've got more than that.' We had anti-tank guns coming in to help us if we had trouble in the morning.[68]

One vehicle was hit and set alight and before long, the whole ridge was lit up with burning vehicles as the fires drew more fire from the 88mm guns. Alan Potter described the position:

With first light came the first German attack. They came in on armoured vehicles, which swung round and disgorged the contents – the German infantry – who advanced on us. And because at this time we had enough ammunition, we were able to repel two, perhaps three attacks. And we were pretty confident of holding our position. But the shortage of ammunition was becoming something of a problem.[69]

Short of ammunition and expecting armoured support, the situation seemed desperate but the arrival of tanks seemed to suggest relief. One officer raced out in a car to guide the tanks in, only to be blown up by what turned out to be German armour. From their sangars and shallow scrapes in the poor ground of the ridge, the men were rounded up. Corporal Ray Middleton was one of them:

> The tanks that came through, unfortunately, had black crosses on. So, we were rounded up by a batch of 20 or 30 tanks. They cut us off. Our anti-tank guns were wiped out.
>
> I said 'Stick your head out, Jack, and tell me if it's clear.' He stood up and Jack never swore much and he said 'Christ! Corp!' 'What is it, Jack?' And so I climbed out and stood up. We'd had to remove our equipment and rifles to get into this little sangar and there was a German half-track a few yards from me, in front of me, and a German standing up on it with a machine-gun aimed at me and a 2-pounder gun aimed at me. And all he said was 'Come on out, Aussie'. And I didn't have a darned thing except a rifle down there. So I came on out. One or two of the men bending down to pick up equipment got shot at so I'm glad I didn't bend down. We just left everything behind. The food we had. Even our change of socks – I'd taken to filling my clutches with spare socks and chocolate and things of use and I had to leave it all behind.[70]

The 2/28th, without support from 50th RTR, which had been unable to get through, were rounded up as POWs. But disasters occurred elsewhere in the attack too.

The plan had called for 69th Brigade to pass through the 'South African' gap and clear any further minefield gaps beyond to allow 2nd Armoured Brigade's advance. But there was confusion over the work completed and once more the armoured advance was delayed. Such delays in operations at night when only a limited period of covering darkness was available would always prejudice operations of this type. The consequences were great on this occasion as both 6th Durham Light Infantry and 5th East Yorkshire Battalions were cut off and overrun by a counter-attack.

Auchinleck's last attempt at a major operation in July 1942 had ended in ignominious failure. Whilst operations in the first half of the month had shown his and Dorman-Smith's sure command of the situation and Auchinleck's intelligent analytical mind backed by good intelligence information received via Ultra and the Y Service, operations in the second half of the month (with one or two notable exceptions) had been rushed, increasingly desperate in their intentions and badly executed by his subordinates – especially his corps commanders. Most noticeable was the poor co-operation between tanks and infantry on which all the operations of late July depended. Only in defence had Eighth Army demonstrated its abilities and effectiveness to advantage – circumstances unlikely to win over Churchill. The victor of the 'Defence of Egypt' stood, perhaps unknowingly, on the edge of the abyss with his political masters considering whether they should force him to jump. However, it remained to be seen how his military superior, the Chief of the Imperial General Staff, would react with better understanding of the realities of military command.

CHAPTER FOUR

THE LITTLE MAN WITH WHITE KNOBBLY KNEES

The right opportunity for the Chief of the Imperial General Staff (CIGS) arrived on the evening of 15 July in the garden of 10 Downing Street. It was a lovely evening and Alan Brooke found the Prime Minister, Winston Churchill, in a pleasant mood. Choosing his moment carefully, Brooke asked Churchill for permission to visit the Middle East as soon as possible to ascertain for himself how matters stood with Eighth Army.

> I knew that the odds would be heavily against getting his sanction; that he would say he could not spare me, whilst in the back of his mind the real reason would be that he would hate me to go off on my own without him. Meanwhile the situation in the Middle East was not improving; the Auk was suggesting giving the Eighth Army to Corbett. It was essential that I should go out to see for myself what was really wrong, and for that job I did not want Winston treading on my heels![1]

Surprisingly, Churchill acceded to the request but Brooke was still wary that 'there was always the danger of Winston changing his mind or deciding to come with me'.

It was natural that Brooke should wish to visit Britain's main theatre of land operations in mid-1942. Victory there had been a cornerstone of his strategy since he had become CIGS and with agreement over Anglo-American strategy being forged in July that included commitment to joint military landings in French

North Africa, Brooke was more keenly aware than ever of the need not just to hold, but to defeat, the Axis forces attacking in Egypt:[2]

> From the moment I took over the job of CIGS I was convinced that the sequence of events should be: a) liberate North Africa; b) open up Mediterranean and score a million tons of shipping; c) threaten Southern Europe by eliminating Italy; d) then, and only then, if Russia is still holding, liberate France and invade Germany.[3]

His anxiety about North Africa may have been increased the following day when he had dinner with Neil Ritchie, who had returned to Britain after his dismissal from command of Eighth Army. Perhaps as a consequence, Brooke wrote a long letter to Auchinleck on 17 July offering sympathy, support, advice and information. The sympathy and practical support came first:

> You have constantly been in my thoughts since Rommel started his attacks, and I have so well realized the difficult and anxious times that you have been through. I only wish that it was possible to do more to help you from this distance. It is such a joy to see you gradually regaining the mastery over the enemy. I do hope that this heavier equipment in the shape of 6-pounder tanks, and the latest American tanks, will arrive soon enough to provide the additional striking power you require.[4]

This was followed by advice concerning Churchill's character:

> It is his confidence that is the important factor. You know how temperamental he is apt to be at times, so I hope you do not attach too much importance if occasionally his telegrams are not quite as friendly as they might be. I can assure you that I do all that is within my power to guard you against unnecessary repercussions from outside, and to let you carry on with the least possible interference.[5]

Both Brooke and Auchinleck knew that the latter's responsibilities as Commander-in-Chief (C-in-C), Middle East extended far beyond the 'western front' of Egypt and Libya and much of the letter concerned the provision of adequate numbers of divisions to cover any collapse by the Russians in the Caucasus. Brooke ended with a hint regarding his plan to visit Auchinleck at the earliest opportunity.

His letter, which reached the C-in-C on 23 July, elicited an extensive reply on 25 July which demonstrated Auchinleck's unfortunate tendency to report honestly on the state of affairs in his command. Such correspondence was not private – Auchinleck undoubtedly knew it would be referred to by Brooke when asked by Churchill about the Middle East situation. Instead of comprising platitudinous statements designed to mollify the Prime Minister, however, the letter was full of hopes and disappointments rather than confident statements of how victory would be achieved, and quickly, as Churchill wished:

> I was disappointed when our big effort of July 21–22 came to nothing, as I had great hopes of it. I still do not know the full story of the battle in the centre, but it does seem as if the 23rd Armoured Brigade, though gallant enough, lost control and missed direction. The infantry, too, seem to have made some avoidable mistakes. Perhaps I asked too much of them, but one can only plan on the information available. Well, there it is; we undoubtedly gave the enemy a rude shock, judging from the many intercepted messages from various enemy units, but we failed to get our object, which was to break through.[6]

He continued in the same vein. He was 'not too hopeful' about the possibility of getting around his opponents' southern flank. He was grateful for the support of Brooke and Churchill, doing his utmost to repay their faith in him and remove the threat to Egypt but 'I do not want to hold out hopes of an early decision'. Perhaps most damaging to himself were the details he provided concerning his contingency plans for the defence of Egypt which began 'We may yet have to face a withdrawal from our present forward positions, but I hope this will not be necessary'.[7]

The factual content of this letter was not at issue; the problem was the manner in which Auchinleck explained his extensive preparations and understated how Eighth Army under his command had defeated the Axis forces during First Alamein. It was probably receipt of this letter late on 28 July or early the next morning, together with news of the failure of Operation *Manhood*, that prompted frustration on Brooke's part, expressed in his diary:

> PM in very depressed mood as result of Auk's second attack being repulsed. Pouring out questions as to why Auk could not have done this or that and never giving him the least credit for doing the right thing. He is quite heart-breaking to work for. It is very trying having to fight battles to defend the Auk, when I am myself doubtful at times why on earth he does not act differently.[8]

Churchill, meanwhile, had had enough. It was time for him to step in to galvanize Middle East Command.[9] An invitation to visit Russia from Stalin sent via the British Ambassador in Moscow provided the opportunity. Brooke had feared the possibility, but was still caught by surprise:

> 29 July. At 6.30 pm PM sent for me to 10 Downing Street where I spent an hour with him in the garden discussing the points he wishes me to look to whilst in the Middle East, Persia, Iraq, India etc. He is evidently very intent on following along close behind me if possible and wishes me to report what journey is like.
>
> 30 July. A short COS* at which Portal broke the news that Winston had decided to follow me at once to the Middle East! I was sent for by him at 12 noon and told that after I left him yesterday he decided at dinner that he would fly out on Friday! He called War Cabinet meeting immediately after dinner and obtained their approval. Since then wire from Ambassador in Moscow had been received suggesting visit from Winston to Stalin was advisable! He was therefore contemplating going on to Russia and wanted me to go with him!! All my plans upset.[10]

It was decided, therefore, that Brooke would travel out via Gibraltar and Malta, where he was anxious to visit the Governor, General the Viscount Gort, whilst Churchill would follow the day after, but arrive on the same day. Churchill's frequent expressions of impatience with Auchinleck had finally culminated in action.

Focusing solely on the negative tone of Auchinleck's letter to Brooke of 25 July ignores a great deal of other information it contained concerning developments in Eighth Army and Middle East Command at this time. Firstly, concerning Panzerarmee tactics, he wrote:

> The enemy has now got his German infantry, irrespective of what formation or unit they belong to, sandwiched in between the remnants of his Italian divisions along the whole front, so that we can no longer fall on Italians and put them in the bag as easily as we did at first. I feel that owing to the great length of front he is holding the enemy can not have much depth to his position, except in the centre, where he holds his German armour in reserve.[11]

---

* Chiefs of Staff Committee.

This policy became known as 'corseting' – a term devised at this time by a brilliant young Captain 'Bill' Williams of the staff of the Director of Military Intelligence, Brigadier Freddie de Guingand.[12] Recognition of its existence was to prove important for later operations.

Auchinleck was also at pains to mention the important changes in Eighth Army's artillery tactics organized by his Brigadier-General Royal Artillery (BGRA), Brigadier Noel Martin:

> The troops have recovered themselves wonderfully, I think, and have acquired a new tactical technique, based really on the proper use of artillery and the retention of mobility, remarkably quickly. They have still a great deal to learn of course, but the gunners have been very good indeed, and the Boche does not like our shell-fire at all, now that it is centrally controlled and directed.[13]

Auchinleck's correspondence with Brooke also contained several references to his subordinate commanders. He singled out Lieutenant-General Tom Corbett, his Chief of General Staff (CGS) in Cairo, for particular praise for the support he continued to give, without which Auchinleck would not have been able to function in his dual role. He suggested Lieutenant-General William 'Strafer' Gott as a possible future army commander – perhaps replacing General Sir Maitland 'Jumbo' Wilson, Ninth Army's commander.

He also indicated one important change that he had decided was necessary. This was the replacement of Brigadier John 'Jock' Whiteley as Brigadier General Staff (BGS) of Eighth Army with de Guingand. Whiteley, in Auchinleck's view, was not cut out for staff work in a field formation but would be worth promoting to a senior staff job at a General Headquarters. These changes give the lie to the suggestion that Auchinleck was a poor judge of men, as both had very successful wartime careers.[14]

Auchinleck's letter did not detail other changes he was planning. On 29 July, he met Major-General Richard McCreery, his adviser as C-in-C on armour, and Major-General John Harding, the Director of Military Training, to discuss a reorganization of British armour. His intention was 'To find the correct organization for the fighting troops to enable them to defeat the enemy under the peculiar conditions of mechanised war in the desert'. In an official dispatch, he noted that:

> At the conclusion of the Eighth Army's offensive in Cyrenaica it was plain to me that our existing divisional and brigade organisation did not allow of that very close

co-operation on the battlefield between the armoured corps, the artillery and the infantry which was to my mind essential to success. The Germans had reached a very high standard of co-operation between the three arms and I felt that we must try at least to equal and, if possible, surpass them. There was no doubt, too, that as a result of the recent fighting an impression had been created in the minds of some junior leaders and soldiers, other than those of the Royal Armoured Corps, that our armour had not altogether pulled its weight in the battle. It was very necessary to eradicate any such feeling, and I felt that the best way to do this was to associate the three arms more closely at all times and in all places.[15]

To discourage the idea of the Royal Armoured Corps as 'an army within an army' and to have more armoured divisions, Auchinleck had already reorganized the armoured divisions, giving to each an armoured brigade group and a motorized infantry brigade group instead of two armoured brigades and a support group. This reorganization was still in progress and was in advance of similar organizational changes in forces in Britain. Now he wanted to go further, abolishing distinctions between infantry and armoured divisions and creating a more mobile formation with greater striking power in place of the infantry division.

These radical proposals were met with horror by 'traditionalists' like McCreery and Major-General Douglas Wimberley, the recently-arrived commander of 51st Division, although at least one experienced desert general, Tuker of 4th Indian Division, saw them as a 'logical and sensible'.[16] Harding had a view but was 'really primarily interested in the tactical training of the individuals, the units and the formations':

> My view at the time was that what was needed was to retain the armoured division formations as such and also to maintain the distinction between armoured divisions and infantry divisions. Dick McCreery held the same view. I think the Auk and Dorman-Smith were rather inclined to think that he should be able to have a number of homogeneous divisions equipped with both armour and infantry. I'm not sure that I was right from subsequent experience – particularly in Italy.[17]

However, there already existed 'a definite antipathy between McCreery and Auchinleck'[18] which resulted in McCreery refusing to implement the changes and Auchinleck effectively sacking him, telling him that if 'he would not obey orders he could consider himself relieved of his appointment'.[19]

Wimberley had 'had his card marked' by Lieutenant-General Sir Leslie Morshead regarding the manner in which divisions might be organized:

> He gave me a lot of sound advice, and it was clear talking to him that the Australians at that time did not have a very high regard for the British Armour, which they thought had let them down. He told me that the Staff were mad on breaking Divisions up into 'Jock Columns' and that if I allowed them to break my Division up, when it arrived, I would never be able to collect it together again, and that he had very firmly resisted any attempt to 'muck about' his Australians.[20]

It was almost two weeks later, however, before Wimberley's resolve was directly challenged:

> Soon after the Division arrived, I was told that it was probable that one of my Brigades would be taken away from me to go to some armoured division or other, and in return I was to be given some armour. It was rapidly becoming clear to me that I would have to take a firm stand to prevent what Morshead had already warned me about, 'the mucking about' of my Division, which had trained as a single fighting formation for two years and more.[21]

These reforming changes, which would have meant making changes to new divisions arriving in Egypt as well as existing formations, were probably unworkable and certainly so without the willing co-operation of senior commanders. They were never implemented. However, they were part of a wider programme of changes and rethinking in Eighth Army at the end of July 1942 and indicated that despite a prolonged period of hard fighting, neither Auchinleck nor Eighth Army was suffering from the 'inexplicable inertia' ascribed to them.[22] Auchinleck's mind was firmly on achieving success in future operations. Of great importance to him in that process was the work of his 'field' Chief of Staff, Major-General Eric Dorman-Smith. Auchinleck's appointment of de Guingand had been intended to free up Dorman-Smith for work on these organizational reforms, but events were to intervene.

Much of Auchinleck's information regarding the state of Eighth Army and its opponents provided to Brooke in his letter of 27 July was from an 'appreciation' produced by Dorman-Smith. This was the most controversial document of the

Desert War, chiefly because for supporters of Auchinleck (and, by implication, of Dorman-Smith), this was a superb model of analytical thinking and clear expression that correctly predicted many of the subsequent events around El Alamein as well as defining how Auchinleck would defeat any further offensive by Rommel by fighting a 'modern defensive battle'.[23] For the critics of Auchinleck (usually the supporters of Montgomery), it was a depressing and sorry document – proof positive of Dorman-Smith's 'unsound'[24] ideas that had caused 'a state of complete muddle and disorganization'[25] in Eighth Army. This was because of their influence on Auchinleck, who had 'sent for "Chink" Dorman-Smith as a kind of personal evil genius.'[26] Dorman-Smith was a prime example for some of Auchinleck's being a poor 'chooser'.[27] Comparisons between him and John Frederick Charles Fuller, the gifted but flawed Tank Corps staff officer and military theorist, do not help his cause.

Dorman-Smith's 'Appreciation' began by stating the obvious. It recognized that the Axis positions were now too strong to assault with the available resources and suggested that Eighth Army would not be strong enough to attack again until mid-September at the earliest and, even then, the British and Commonwealth forces might not have a sufficient superiority to justify a direct attack. However, Dorman-Smith went further in his analysis. He anticipated an attack by the Axis forces before the end of August and predicted that the attempt would be made on the southern flank of the Alamein position where it would be met by his plans to fight a 'modern defensive battle'. However, the document also gave considerable attention to the defensive preparations in the Nile Delta and around Alexandria and Cairo. Although these details provided important context to the rest of his analysis and were intended to indicate that planning did not stop with front-line preparations, they had an unfortunate influence, according to some historians, for their suggestion of confused thinking and pessimistic outlook.

It is too easy to see Dorman-Smith's 'Appreciation' with the benefit of hindsight and unhelpful to consider it solely as a paper exercise. What was important about it was its *influence* at the time. In this regard, it worked in both negative and positive ways and its detail is better considered in connection with these influences.

In a positive way, it influenced Auchinleck in deciding Eighth Army's short-term goals, which he expounded at a meeting with his corps commanders, Gott and Lieutenant-General William Ramsden, on 30 July – a meeting at which Corbett was also present – and further developed in an 'appreciation' of his own on 1 August. Thus, Auchinleck accepted Dorman-Smith's advice that Eighth Army adopt the tactical defensive until strong enough to attack. In the meantime, raids would be mounted to harass the Panzerarmee's rear.[28] He also accepted Dorman-Smith's assessment of the importance of the air superiority the Desert Air Force had fought to achieve during July in harassing Axis supply routes.

It was also a positive influence on Gott's thinking and planning for the defence of XIII Corps against a possible Axis attack in the south of the Alamein position: in particular, the employment of a mobile harassing wing of light tanks, armoured cars and Crusader i.e. faster, more lightly armoured tanks. Gott's ideas about the Alam Halfa Ridge as the likely first objective of an Axis attack were his own (although he made reference to Rommel's shortages in infantry mentioned by Dorman-Smith as a possible influencing factor). However, he accepted Dorman-Smith's assessment that the attack could come at a critical time for Eighth Army – the second half of August – when the Panzerarmee might have between 150 and 200 tanks and before new divisions sent to Egypt were ready for action.[29] From this point forward, the staff of XIII Corps developed and honed plans for defence of the Alam Halfa Ridge and began to implement extensive defensive preparations.

It was undoubtedly the case that the negatives outweighed the positives and were more obvious in their influence. They may have been partly the result of the cumulative effect of the 'appreciation' and Auchinleck's 28 June assessment of the situation (also drafted by Dorman-Smith). In June, the C-in-C had outlined to Brooke how he would fight if driven from the Alamein position.[30] This had also been passed to Corbett and, through him, to Gott and Ramsden. Its meaning had been the subject of considerable misinterpretation throughout all levels of the army and the defensive preparations it outlined had perturbed some at even the most senior levels.

Now Dorman-Smith's 'Appreciation' suggested a possible retreat once more. Indirectly, therefore, it was responsible for a crisis in morale. Men could see for themselves the continued preparations many miles behind the front line aimed at putting the Delta and other localities in a state of effective defence. The effect on morale was obviously detrimental. It was compounded still further by the extensive forward defensive preparations organized by Dorman-Smith and Brigadier Frederick Kisch, Eighth Army's Commander Royal Engineers. These involved men digging trenches and laying out barbed wire and minefields seemingly in the middle of the open desert without an obvious reason (at least to those doing the work).

After some months of hard fighting, Eighth Army needed clarity regarding its position and plans. Both Dorman-Smith and Auchinleck possessed a clear vision of how they would fight defensively, but they failed to communicate this to the wider army. The ambiguity remained unresolved.

In plans for a future attack, however, Auchinleck was clearer. On 2 August a further 'Appreciation' outlined Eighth Army's approach to offensive operations planned for mid-September. Based on ideas from Ramsden, the suggestion was for 'a deliberate attack on the extreme NORTH of the enemy's position' with deception measures to suggest an attack in the south. The army was to 'train and rehearse intensively for the main operation' and motorized and armoured forces were to be organized to exploit any successful breakthrough.[31] This plan would not be implemented whilst Auchinleck was C-in-C, but army staff continued to work with it as a general aspiration for a future when the Allied forces would return to the offensive.

———————

Brooke's stopover in Malta was a salutary reminder of the misery of civilian life in the front line of total war. Continued attempts at an air and sea blockade of the island were gradually starving the inhabitants. Repeated air strikes were destroying their homes and killing or wounding many. The constant threat of a Crete-like invasion was sapping morale. Brooke witnessed it all and described how 'the destruction is inconceivable and reminds one of Ypres, Arras, Lens at their worst during the last war.' Brooke continued:

> The conditions prevailing in Malta were distinctly depressing, to put it mildly! Shortage of rations, shortage of petrol, a hungry population that rubbed their tummies looking at Gort as he went by, destruction and ruin of docks, loss of convoys just as they approached the island, and the continual possibility of an attack on the island without much hope of help or reinforcements.[32]

Brooke's visit was a brief one. He hoped to have convinced Gort, at least, of the possibility that if Allied plans came to fruition Malta, rather than being a backwater, might be an outpost of an advance that would ultimately win the war in the Mediterranean.[33] Meanwhile, it was vital for the British forces in the desert for Malta and the forces based there to survive.

———————

Both Brooke and Churchill arrived in Cairo on 3 August. Astonishingly, given the supposed premise for the visit, major changes in the Middle East High Command had been decided on, and the detail agreed between Churchill and Brooke, within 24 hours. The first decision was that Corbett was not the man to command Eighth Army. Brooke's verdict, with its unwitting puns, was severe:

> Went over to GHQ after breakfast and had long talk with Corbett the CGS. The more I saw of him the less I thought of him — he is a very small man. One interview with him was enough to size him up. He was a very, very small man unfit for his job of CGS and totally unsuited for command of the 8th Army, an appointment which the Auk had suggested. Consequently Corbett's selection reflected very unfavourably on the Auk's ability to select men and confirmed my fears in that respect.[34]

For the moment, Brooke did not disabuse Corbett of his belief that he was to succeed Auchinleck as Army Commander.

Churchill, having discussed matters with the South African Prime Minister, Jan Smuts, then met with Brooke and Auchinleck. Afterwards, Churchill was clearly unhappy that no attack was planned before 15 September. Later, in a discussion with a weary Brooke that lasted until 0130hrs, they agreed that a new Eighth Army commander was needed; Churchill first suggested Gott, who Brooke felt was 'very tired', and then Brooke himself. Flattered, Brooke discussed the offer with Smuts, before very reluctantly declining. It was an agonizing choice. Brooke, seemingly, had in mind the man he wanted:

> I did not feel that Gott in his present state was the man to instil a new spirit of self confidence in the 8th Army. It would require someone like Montgomery, bounding with self-confidence and capable of instilling this confidence in those under his command. At any rate I wanted to see Gott for myself to find out how tired he was before putting him down definitely as unfit for the 8th Army.[35]

The following afternoon Brooke discussed his ideas for command changes with Auchinleck. It says a great deal about Auchinleck's character that he accepted Brooke's suggestions for change, which were:

> a) new commander for 8th Army Montgomery; b) new CGS to be selected vice Corbett; c) 'Jumbo' Wilson too old and to be replaced by Gott; d) Quinan unsuitable for 10th Army, to be replaced by Anderson. These changes should

lead to improvements but I must still pass them through the PM and there will be the difficulty.[36]

Brooke, aware of a personal enmity between the two men, had not expected that Auchinleck would accept Montgomery and doubted, in any case, that the combination would work. Brooke's *idée fixe* was now to see his protégé, Montgomery, command Eighth Army. He was prepared to move Auchinleck to another command, if necessary, to achieve this.

Churchill, meanwhile, was obsessed with launching attacks before Eighth Army, regardless of its commander, could be ready. However, he had also taken reconnaissance in typical fashion, as Brigadier Davy discovered when summoned that morning to the British Embassy:

Winston came in, followed by a waiter with a beaker of neat whiskey. He made me sit beside him at his desk, and let his cigar go out. It did this many times in the next two hours, as he only took one puff each time he re-lit it. He just quietly grilled me. He wanted a lot of detailed information and in his characteristic fashion he asked questions which cut at right-angles across one's normal method of assessing military strength. At school I had been fairly quick at mental arithmetic and it stood me in good stead at the interview. How many tanks have we? How many cannon have we? How many bayonets have we?[37]

Churchill demanded details of the state of training of divisions not in the Eighth Army and their dates of readiness; the reserves of mines and ammunition, and a vast number of administrative details.

He horrified me by taking notes of what I said on a bit of embassy writing paper, as I was answering 'off the cuff' and with probably not more than 80 percent accuracy. Having pumped me on statistics and the tactical and strategical situation in the desert, he threw a tactful fly over me on personalities. I gave it merely a sniff, as I did not wish to be disloyal to the Auk and I felt that Casey* would already have said enough about Corbett and Chink. When someone came to announce luncheon, the PM said to me, 'Thank you and you might let me have confirmation of these figures by five o'clock'. And he handed me his notes, much to my relief, and took his neglected cigar with him.[38]

---

* Rt Hon Sir Richard Casey, Minister of State responsible for Egypt.

After another exhausting late-night discussion, he and Churchill still disagreed about Montgomery's appointment. An early morning start and a visit to Eighth Army's spartan headquarters the next day decided matters for Churchill. Auchinleck had always seemed sensitive to the idea of personal comfort whilst his men endured privations and hardship. This was not Churchill's style at all, even as a battalion commander in the Great War. In Cairo, he had enjoyed 'princely' hospitality and an air-conditioned bedroom and study. In the desert, he was given breakfast in a 'wire-netted cube, full of flies' and high-ranking people.[39] He did not enjoy the heat. Conditions drew no comment from Brooke who, in typical soldierly style, got a good feel for the terrain and its differences from his expectations.

A briefing for Churchill by Auchinleck and Dorman-Smith using maps proved an unmitigated disaster. According to Dorman-Smith:

[Churchill] quickly began to demand that Eighth Army should attack afresh. He thrust stubby fingers against the talc; 'Here', he said, 'or here'. We were alone with him, for the CIGS had gone forward up the line. It was a little like being caged with a gorilla. Eventually Auchinleck said quietly, and finally, 'No, Sir, we cannot attack again yet'. The Prime Minister swung round to [me]: 'Do you say that too; why don't you use the 44th Division?' 'Because Sir, that division isn't ready and anyhow a one-division attack would not get us anywhere.' Churchill rose, grunted, stumped down from the caravan and stood alone in the sand, back turned to us. The chill was now icy.[40]

Nevertheless, Churchill got his opportunity to meet Gott and afterwards was happy that this was the man to command Eighth Army. He returned to Cairo eager to put matters in chain with Brooke to enact his decisions. However, his next move was unexpected – in more ways than one!

6 August
Whilst I was dressing and practically naked, the PM suddenly burst into my room. Very elated and informed me that his thoughts were taking shape and that he would soon commit himself to paper! I rather shuddered and wondered what he was up to![41]

Churchill had never liked the Auchinleck/Montgomery combination. Now his plan was to give Brooke Montgomery as Eighth Army commander – with Brooke as C-in-C of a 'Near East Command'. Auchinleck would be given a new Persia–Iraq Command (confusingly termed 'Middle East Command') instead. Gott did not feature in this at all, although presumably Churchill still had an army in mind for him. Thwarted by Brooke's polite declining of a second appointment in 48 hours, Churchill tried a new tack that evening, sending for Brooke to hear the decisions he had reached, guided by discussions with Smuts. Churchill had drafted a telegram to the War Cabinet recommending a splitting of Middle East Command in two with Auchinleck to be C-in-C of the new command. General the Honourable Sir Harold Alexander was to take over the 'Near East Command,' with Gott commanding Eighth Army. There were other purges including removal of the commander of XXX Corps, Ramsden, the diminutive Corbett and Dorman-Smith.

Brooke concurred and the telegram was dispatched. Churchill was unaware, however, that it had been Brooke who had persuaded Smuts of the virtues of Alexander as the new C-in-C. The CIGS was learning how to exercise a degree of control over the Prime Minister. He could not have predicted how fate would now intervene. Having been told of his new appointment, on the afternoon of 7 August Gott flew back to Cairo in a Bristol Bombay transport of 216 Squadron flown by 19-year old Sergeant Hugh 'Jimmy' James. His intention was to take a few days' leave. However, the aircraft, crew and its passengers had the misfortune to encounter Messerschmitt Bf-109s from Jagdgeschwader 27 led by Leutnant Emil Clade. The transport plane was forced down and then attacked on the ground by Feldwebel Bernd Schneider. Although Sergeant James and three others survived, Gott and fifteen of the passengers died when the plane caught fire.

When he heard the news, Brooke was horrified at losing one of the 'linkpins' of the planned changes. However, on later reflection, 'it seemed almost like the hand of God suddenly appearing to set matters right where we had gone wrong'.[42] Once more Brooke benefited from Smuts' support in convincing Churchill to select Montgomery, and a telegram was duly dispatched summoning him to Cairo. The War Cabinet's chief objection in all this seemed to be the nomenclature – Middle East Command remained and the new one was called Persia–Iraq Command.[43]

The following day, 8 August, Lieutenant-Colonel Ian Jacob was sent to Eighth Army Headquarters with a letter from Churchill advising Auchinleck of the decision to replace him as C-in-C and offering him the Persia–Iraq Command. Auchinleck took time to consider this offer, but ultimately rejected it. This decision has subsequently been criticized as an emotional response – a fit of pique at losing both the Eighth Army and Middle East Command. In fact, as Jacob's account of their meeting makes clear, Auchinleck had clear reasons for not accepting the appointment, which he never veered from:

> I felt as if I were just going to murder an unsuspecting friend… I handed the C-in-C the letter I had brought. He opened it and read it through two or three times in silence. He did not move a muscle, and remained outwardly calm, and in complete control of himself. He then asked me whether it was intended that Persia should be under India… He felt that sooner or later they would inevitably come under India… He was convinced that he could not accept what was offered. He had been C-in-C, India and C-in-C, Middle East, and now he was asked to take a position which was virtually that of one of his own Army commanders. The fact that he was being moved would indicate to the Army that he had lost the confidence of the Government, and had failed in his task… He had always determined, when his time came, to set his face against accepting any sop. I felt bound to say that I had never imagined that he would take up any other attitude, and that I had told the CIGS this straight… I could not have admired more the way General Auchinleck received me, and his attitude throughout. A great man and a great fighter.[44]

Brooke, on the other hand, thought he was 'behaving like an offended film star'.[45]

It was a harsh judgement on a man who had performed more than adequately in both roles in which the crisis occasioned by Rommel's offensive had required him to serve. He had not failed as an army commander. Indeed, he had decisively beaten Rommel during the fighting around Alamein in early July. There had been no suggestion of failure as C-in-C, although there was concern about possible future direction – especially the possibility of Corbett being given Eighth Army.

By working in a dual role, Auchinleck had encouraged Churchill to concatenate the positions of Eighth Army commander and C-in-C, whereas his real concern was for an energetic fighting army commander to defeat Rommel – what else mattered but beating him? Here was where the change was needed – as Auchinleck also admitted. However, it was Brooke who perceived, probably correctly on the balance of evidence, that it was time for a change. With his vision of a British war-winning strategy mapped out, Brooke pursued a combination of new commanders who he believed could realize his vision in North Africa. Ultimately, this path led to General the Hon. Sir Harold Alexander and Lieutenant-General Bernard Montgomery.

Harold Rupert Leofric George Alexander arrived in Egypt with an impressive record of service in both the Great War and the Second World War. Commissioned in the Irish Guards, he had ended the first war as an acting brigadier-general, having been twice wounded and awarded a Military Cross and a DSO. In 1940 he had been a divisional commander at Dunkirk and responsible for the withdrawal of all British forces that could be saved. He had performed this role skilfully and effectively. With a reputation, therefore, as a good man for a crisis, he had been sent in February 1942 to Burma where he had organized the evacuation of Rangoon and the withdrawal into India. As the new C-in-C, Middle East, he was satisfied to learn that Montgomery, with whom he had been both friend and military colleague for many years, was to command Eighth Army.

Bernard Law Montgomery had been an officer in the Royal Warwickshire Regiment on the outbreak of the First World War. Wounded in 1914, he subsequently served as a brigade, corps and divisional staff officer. His official biographer has wrongly credited him with writing one of the most important of the British Expeditionary Force's multiplicity of training documents, produced as the army strove to 'learn the lessons of the fighting' and master the greatest military conflict in which British forces have ever been involved.[46] It was actually in the inter-war years that Montgomery developed a reputation as a trainer. This period included time as an instructor at the Staff College, where he worked alongside Alan Brooke, and work for the War Office in revising the Infantry Training manual. On the outbreak of the Second World War he was a divisional commander whose confident and capable performance in France in 1940 was noted and remembered by his corps commander, Brooke. As a corps commander himself in Britain, he fell out with his superior, Auchinleck, and the resulting feud was never resolved. It was, therefore, undoubtedly pleasing for him that he was replacing his rival.

Montgomery benefited greatly from Alexander's support and confidence. Had he been required to deal with many of the matters Auchinleck had in his dual role, Montgomery's abrasive personality would probably have seen him fail. Instead, he could concentrate on Eighth Army, and especially in using the opportunity now offered by the exhaustion of both sides for training (which was always necessary even in well-organized and established formations) to continue the reorganization that was already under way. Meanwhile, Alexander adopted a policy of non-interference, although he ensured he was kept informed of Montgomery's plans and the latter duly ensured that he sought appropriate approval for his intentions. The time was right for change, if a change was needed. The *perception* was that it *was* needed – that was what counted in the end.

The 'Cairo Purge' continued with the departures of Corbett and Dorman-Smith and the promotion of McCreery to be Alexander's CGS. With this shake-up in the High Command came Churchill's attempt to provide focus to the new leadership pairing. George Davy recorded:

> The Prime Minister was still in Cairo and almost my first job was to translate his instruction to Alex into an instruction from Alex to Monty. Like his notes of my statistics, the original was written on a sheet of embassy writing paper and was in two short paragraphs. The first served as Alex's instruction to Monty without the alteration of a word: 'Your prime and main duty will be to take or destroy at the earliest opportunity the German-Italian Army commanded by the Field-Marshal Rommel, together with all its supplies and establishments in Egypt and Libya.' The second paragraph referred to 'such other duties as pertain to your (i.e. Alex's) command', subject to the paramount importance of para 1. This part did not have to be put into the instruction to Monty.[47]

Alexander was not to take over from Auchinleck until 15 August, so it was from the latter that Montgomery received his instructions on his arrival on 12 August. The meeting was not officially minuted so what passed between the two men is unknown, but Auchinleck's professionalism would have ensured he briefed Montgomery on the latest Eighth Army plans including those for possible resumption of an offensive. In addition, Montgomery had access to all the recent appreciations, reports on operations and correspondence relating to the conduct of operations in the desert. These he had thoroughly digested.

After seeing Auchinleck, Montgomery met Alexander and John Harding (now Deputy Chief of General Staff). He asked Harding to produce plans for a strong armoured formation akin to the Afrika Korps to act as a spearhead for future operations. This formation he termed a '*corps de chasse*'; it was intended to comprise two armoured divisions and one of mobile infantry. That evening Harding outlined how this would be formed from 1st and 10th Armoured Divisions with 2nd New Zealand Division – the latter with 9th Armoured Brigade as an integral component. This last element mirrored Auchinleck's scheme which McCreery had disputed.

The following day, at Eighth Army Headquarters, Montgomery outlined his view on the current situation and his plans to his staff. He had already made a strong impression on Guingand by his observations on Eighth Army's need for a clear lead and a firm grip from the top for the creation of a winning team. Now he explained how this would be achieved. His first concern was with the atmosphere in which staff, commanders and troops would live, work and fight. In his view, doubt and loss of confidence were prevalent, with some looking back to select the next place to withdraw. There were 'desperate defence measures' under way to prepare positions in Cairo and the Delta. All this was to cease.

Critical to the new 'atmosphere' were his next observations:

The defence of Egypt lies here at Alamein and on the Ruweisat Ridge. What is the use of digging trenches in the Delta? It is quite useless; if we lose this position we lose Egypt; all the fighting troops now in the Delta must come here at once, and will. *Here* we will stand and fight; there will be no further withdrawal. I have ordered that all plans and instructions dealing with further withdrawal are to be burnt, and at once. We will stand and fight *here*. If we can't stay here alive, then let us stay here dead.[48]

This was classic motivational speaking by a skilled orator. Strategically, this approach was ridiculous. Measures for the defence of Cairo and the Delta remained in place. Churchill even intervened to influence the contingency plans at the end of the month by placing General Maitland Wilson, who took the Persia–Iraq Command refused by Auchinleck, in charge of Cairo's defence.[49] If Rommel did attack, and break through, Montgomery's words would have meant nothing. Eighth Army would have fallen back on the Delta and, if necessary, beyond. Montgomery would have been required to preserve Eighth Army 'in being' in that process. But, as an exemplar of inspirational rhetoric, his speech did touch a chord with its audience, who could see the value in the simple message and relayed it to the men they commanded without issues about comprehension. The speech's principal contribution, therefore, was in terms of its influence on morale – many men mentioned it when writing letters home, for example.[50] It certainly removed any concern about confused thinking.

Montgomery also explained that fresh divisions and weapons were arriving from Britain along with reinforcements for the existing units. Between 300 and 400 Sherman tanks were being unloaded at Suez. (On this, he was mistaken; one of Corbett's last duties as CGS had been to tell Churchill these tanks would be about three weeks late). He was confident in the case of an attack by 'Wommel' (Montgomery had a slight speech impediment) and his plans for an attack would 'hit Rommel and his Army for six right out of Africa' but he was determined not to attack until he was ready. He would not tolerate 'belly aching' or excuse-making, expecting his orders to be swiftly obeyed.

It is difficult to know what to make of Montgomery's next remarks. Certainly, they must have bemused some amongst the Eighth Army staff:

> I have little more to say just at present. And some of you may think it is quite enough and may wonder if I am mad. I assure you I am quite sane. I understand there are people who often think I am slightly mad; so often that I now regard it rather a compliment. All I have to say to that is that if I am slightly mad, there are a large number of people I could name who are raving lunatics.[51]

A strange mix of eccentricity and paranoia, with a degree of challenge and irreverence – all of which may have passed for humour with Montgomery. Fortunately, he soon returned to more familiar themes, including an important desire for all soldiers to understand what they were required to do. It was perceptive of Montgomery to see that from this a 'surge of confidence throughout the Army' would result.

A move of Eighth Army Headquarters was also outlined. Montgomery had no time for Auchinleck's desire to share the conditions of his men and endure the hardships and privations they endured. He would not be sleeping in a 'fleabag' under the stars. Instead, his headquarters would be:

> a decent place where we can live in reasonable comfort and where the Army Staff can all be together and side by side with the HQ of the Desert Air Force. This is a frightful place here, depressing, unhealthy and a rendezvous for every fly in Africa; we shall do no good work here. Let us get over there by the sea where it is fresh and healthy. If officers are to do good work they must have decent messes, and be comfortable.[52]

This is especially ironic given that Montgomery was a critic of the 'chateau generalship' of the Great War. In fact, the new headquarters at Burg-el-Arab were further behind the front line than Haig's GHQ at Montreuil but, like Haig, whose position was actually more closely analogous to Alexander's, Montgomery made use of modern transport to maintain a Tactical Headquarters closer to his subordinate commanders. For Haig's train, Montgomery substituted staff cars and later tanks. The move to re-establish physical proximity with the Desert Air Force Headquarters was sensible and demonstrated a desire to improve inter-service relations.

———————

Montgomery now embarked on daily tours of his command, attempting to see as many units as he could. This was a first opportunity for many of them to see him – although some knew him from their time in Britain before coming to the desert. John Harding recalled:

> He went round and saw everybody. They saw him. He told them what was what and what they had to do and why. This is the way to get morale going the right way. He was brilliant at carrying people with him by explaining to them what was going to happen: what was planned and then, of course, by carrying it out.[53]

For those who did not know him, his extraordinary abrasive self-confidence was a shock – as was his appearance, which was very different to the patriarchal Auchinleck. Brigadier Philip ('Pip') Roberts of 22nd Armoured Brigade remembered:

> Within two days of his arrival General Montgomery had toured the whole front and visited all the units in it. I well remember my first meeting with him; he and the new Corps Commander, General Horrocks, were to meet me at a certain point on the Alam Halfa Ridge at 0845 hours. At 0830 being afflicted with gyppy-tummy I felt there was just time to disappear over the nearest ridge with a spade, and plodding my way back a few minutes later complete with spade I saw a large cortege arriving at the appointed spot and some 5 minutes ahead of schedule. There was General Horrocks, XIII Corps Commander, whom I saluted, there were Bobbie Erskine, Brigadier General Staff, XIII Corps, and Freddie de Guingand, Chief of Staff, Eighth Army and several other characters including a little man with white knobbly knees, an Australian hat and no badges of rank who I took to be a newly arrived war correspondent. Monty, whom I had not previously met, was obviously going to arrive later. I was just about to ask Freddie de Guingand from which direction the Army Commander might be expected when the gentleman in the Australian hat said to me 'Do you know who I am?'– 'Yes, Sir,' was the prompt reply. It was quite clear that whoever he was it was better to know! And, of course, it was Monty.[54]

On 14 August, whilst visiting 24th Australian Infantry Brigade Montgomery had accepted an Australian slouch hat as alternative headgear to his traditional general's hat. The gesture was popular with the Australians. It suggested a degree of non-conformity on their new Army Commander's part. But, even so, some in the ranks were less impressed, including Warrant Officer Eric Watts of 2/12th Field Regiment, Royal Australian Artillery:

> We were told about him. He did come round to the gun positions. We used to think he looked terrible. He was a slight, thin-faced man and the Australians were big, stronger-looking – I'm not saying that he wasn't, he was obviously pretty fit. But he wore one of these turned-up hats and he looked terrible in it because nobody can wear a turned-up hat like an Australian. But he knew he had the Australian forces under him and he wanted to look like them and I suppose it meant something to him. He wanted to indicate to us that he could wear an Australian hat. But, anyway, it was a morale-builder and the fact was that he was round the gun positions. A very short visit too it was. He was just in and out, talked to the officers and then off again because he had a fair area to cover. He was just more or less there to say 'Look I'm the new boy on the block. I'm the bloke that's going to be responsible for what happens now and I want you to know what the situation is.'[55]

From any 'Tommy' or Digger', there was always a likelihood of resistance to any initiative from those in authority. Montgomery's attempts to ensure every man knew his role in the fight against Rommel provided one opportunity. Cyril Mount recorded:

> The first thing we got were a whole pile of pamphlets – leaflets – being dished out. We knew that Montgomery had taken over from Auchinleck. We were very sceptical because I think most people were fond of Auchinleck. We were very sceptical of this guy who'd come out and he was going to break eggs with a big stick, sort of thing. But he kept sending these pamphlets which were sort of semi-religious: 'With God's help. We will hit him for six out of North Africa' and that type of stuff which people very ostentatiously used as bog paper. I don't know whether that had any effect on morale or not but that was coupled with the new regime of physical training and leaping about in the sand and becoming fit.[56]

As a divisional and corps commander, Montgomery had insisted on a rigorous training regime for all men for which many who served under him cordially detested him. Now he brought his zealous views on personal fitness to the desert. Captain Carol Mather, a liaison officer in Eighth Army General Headquarters, observed:

> He was a bit sceptical of the Desert Army because, as he said, the men looked very fit and bronzed and all the rest of it but none of them had walked a mile since they came into the desert. Everyone was riding in vehicles, so they really weren't quite so fit as they looked. I think this was quite true.[57]

The reaction from Eighth Army old hands was much as it had been in Britain. Cyril Mount recalled:

> There were orders for PT, which was absolutely ridiculous. We had to do PT in the sand, jumping up and down with our arms waving. It irritated a lot of people. We were incredibly unfit, I think, at the time. We weren't exercising, we were lying around reading. But I think we started to feel OK in the end.[58]

There were many who were enthusiastic about Montgomery despite appearances, for example Lieutenant-Colonel John Anderson Smith of 57th Anti-Tank Regiment:

> We had only been in the desert a few days when I was summoned with the other COs to meet the Prime Minister Winston Churchill. He shook hands with all of us but said practically nothing at that time. Amongst others there was a little man in a bush hat who looked slightly familiar and who I took to be a CO of one of the Australian units. Only as I was going did I realise it was Monty. He had taken over 8th Army only a day or two before. In the first week that he had command the whole atmosphere notably changed and took on a much more confident tone.[59]

Others admired what they took to be indications of a strong personality. Trooper Ian King of 3rd Hussars 'was struck by the intensity of his eyes as he out-stared each man when he passed.'[60]

Crucially, Montgomery won over many senior commanders and their staff. Those he didn't adapted strategies they'd used under Auchinleck to deal with the new man, as Carol Mather remembered:

> Lumsden was a very dapper, beautifully dressed, beautifully turned-out man – quite a difficult character and he didn't care for Monty... Those who were under

his command greatly admired him. But he wanted to go his own way and he resisted Monty's orders as to what he was to do and what he wasn't to do.[61]

The majority of Eighth Army was indifferent to the change in commander. What affected them was any change to their personal comfort or their job as they understood it. It was fortunate for Alexander and Montgomery that other factors worked in their favour at this point.

The new commanders took over at a time when the British, for the first time, held many of the advantages in the Desert War. Rommel's forces were exhausted and diminished in size and equipment by the attempt to take Egypt. It would be some time before the Panzerarmee could resume the offensive. Meanwhile, reinforcements and replacements were arriving in great numbers. New divisions (8th Armoured, 44th and 51st) were training in the Delta and the desert. The growing strength of Eighth Army was obvious to even the casual observer, including Lance-Corporal Laurie Phillips of the 1st Rifle Brigade:

> Back here in the Alamein position, we found the desert much more crowded than we had been used to; with a comparatively narrow front, and Alex only sixty miles away, most of the desert seemed to be occupied by the vehicles of some sort, whereas in the wide open spaces of Libya one could go for miles without seeing another unit. (It is one of the features of the army that it seems to take 100 men at the rear to keep one soldier at the front.) Moving up from the rear, one passed through a mass of camps – supply depots, ordnance workshops, pioneer units, tank delivery squadrons, sub-area HQs and heaven knows what. Then at varying distances depending on how far forward the front was, there would be Army HQ, Corps HQ, Corps and Divisional supply columns and transport units, then Main Div HQ, the 'B' Echelons, and Main Brigade HQ. Then the country started to look relatively uninhabited as one reached the business end – the battalions, batteries and tank regiments, usually fairly widely scattered and with vehicles well dispersed as unobtrusively as possible.) At Alamein we could not disperse as much as we would have liked, but the RAF were keeping the Luftwaffe away, and when they did appear they had such a wide range of targets that one was unlucky to cop it, although we did, once or twice.[62]

Der Stern von Afrika – Hans-Joachim Marseille recording his 100th 'victory'. (Courtest of Jerry Scutts)

A newly-arrived Sherman tank attracts close attention, 15 September 1942. (Imperial War Museum, E 16861)

Lieutenant-General William 'Strafer' Gott, XIII Corps commander. (Imperial War Museum, E 2623)

A 6-pdr anti-tank gun in action, 29 October 1942. (Imperial War Museum, E 18802)

A Crusader II tank of 22nd Armoured Brigade returning from action, 28 July 1942. (Imperial War Museum, E 14950)

Crew of a Humber Mk II armoured car of 4th Armoured Brigade keep a sharp look out whilst on patrol, 10 August 1942. (Imperial War Museum, E 15509)

A solitary soldier: General Sir Claude Auchinleck watches retreating transport on the North African coast, El Daba, 28 June 1942. (Imperial War Museum, E 13882)

M3 Grant tank and its Royal Scots Greys crew, 19 September 1942. (Australian War Memorial)

Der Wüstenfuchs: Generalfeldmarschall Erwin
Rommel. (Imperial War Museum, HU 5623)

General Major Georg von Bismarck, commander
21 Panzer Division, in front of one of his division's
Panzer IIIs. Von Bismarck was killed during the
fighting on the first day of the battle of Alam
Halfa on 1 September 1942. (Bundesarchiv
1011-784-0231-35)

A Panzer III Ausf. H – the workhorse of the Panzer Divisions. (Imperial War Museum, MH 5852)

Panzer III negotiating a sand dune. (HITM)

German infantry occupy a heavy machine-gun position, probably in the Alamein defences, 1942. (HITM)

After Tobruk's fall, Italian Bersaglieri guard two British prisoners in a captured Bedford MWD 15cwt lorry, June 1942. (ACS)

Italian M13/40 tanks of Divisione Ariete. (Private Collection)

A German Luftwaffe Flak battery moving forwards during the First Battle of El Alamein, July 1942. SdKfz 7 half-track pulling an 88mm gun. (Imperial War Museum, MH 5869)

A German 88mm gun in action. (Imperial War Museum, MH 5853)

Brigadier Freddie de Guingand, Chief of Staff to Lieutenant-General Bernard Montgomery. (Courtesy of Tim Moreman)

General Sir Claude Auchinleck, British Commander in Chief, Middle East Command. (Imperial War Museum, E 13794)

Lieutenant-General Sir Willoughby Norrie. (Imperial War Museum, E 13290)

Lieutenant-General William Ramsden, XXX Corps commander. Dismissed by Montgomery: 'You're not exactly on the crest of a wave, Ramsden.' (Imperial War Museum, E 13566)

Despite the crowding of the army's positions and the need for dispersal, ground units acknowledged that the Desert Air Force was doing a good job in providing protection against the Stukas and ground-attack Messerschmitt Bf-109s. The crews of the 40mm Bofors anti-aircraft guns worked hard with little credit despite shortcomings in their equipment. The combination of aircraft and anti-aircraft guns proved effective in diminishing the threat from the air, whilst the ineffectiveness of the attacks encouraged men to treat them as 'normal' thereby diminishing their effect on morale still further. Private Ernie Kerans of the 9th DLI, 151st Brigade, described the routine:

> His air force could be expected to put in hourly visits during the daylight, strafing and bombing. Casualties were remarkably light, the desert sand killed most of the blast. We got used to these low-flying strafing fighter-pilots. As soon as we could estimate we were no longer in the direct line of fire, out would come the rifles and Brens and we would have a 'Bird Shoot'. It must have been worse for the pilots than for us with our nice deep 'funk holes'. When the enemy planes came over the New Zealand artillery threw everything including their mess tins at them. What a display. Once I saw them knock out eight out of ten ME109s in less than three lively minutes. During the latter days of our stay in the Southern Box we saw less of the German and more of the RAF. The lads used to sit on the sides of their trenches and in comparative safety watch for hours one dogfight after another. The area was a graveyard of planes.[63]

New equipment was also available in greater quantities than ever before. Eagerly anticipated were the Sherman tanks. Churchill was to some extent responsible for raising expectations when on 8 August he had visited various yeomanry regiments, as Lance-Corporal Mick Collins of the Wiltshire Yeomanry, 9th Armoured Brigade, recalled:

> It gave us all a feeling of being less cut off and it was heart-warming when we saw the old boy, sat up on the back of his open Staff car, give the well-known 'V' sign and puffing away merrily at his interminable cigar. In his speech to the Regiment he said that we had not been given a proper chance so far and that we were to be issued with the new Sherman Tanks that were even then on the high seas. You can imagine the feeling that went through the camp after those promises.[64]

Troops were instructed to refer to the new tanks by the code name 'Swallow' – something, it was observed, Churchill singularly failed to do. The code name's origins were fairly obvious but, in fact, the swallows did not arrive until summer was almost over and, for the moment, it was the promise they offered rather than anything of substance that boosted morale.

Montgomery also actively encouraged one aid to unit cohesion that had been discouraged under Auchinleck, as Douglas Wimberley recounted:

> One of the delights to me of now being under Monty, was that he really understood the value of morale and esprit-de-corps. I had been very worried, when I had arrived in Egypt, to be told that no Divisional signs were allowed to be worn. I was quite determined that we in the Highland Division would wear our signs, and indeed had brought many thousand shoulder patch signs with me for this very purpose, to be donned as soon as it was beyond doubt to the enemy that the 51st were in the Middle East – and with our pipes, kilts and accents, this fact could obviously be kept secret for a very short time in a country like Egypt. I went at an early date to Monty to tell him I intended now to put up our Division sign again on all the troops, and on all the vehicles. He heartily agreed, and it was not long before the custom extended to every formation in the 8th Army.[65]

Unfortunately, this caused friction with other units. According to Captain David Elliott of 107 Battery, 7th Medium Regiment:

> These extra divisions had come over to support us – one of which was the Highland Division. Arrived from England and didn't have a tremendous reception from the old stagers much because they started plastering the area with 'HD' – which was their divisional sign. Before that there had been the jerboa – 7th Armoured Division's sign – but nothing to the extent that the 51st Highland Division did. Everywhere was 'HD'.[66]

Other factors also worked to maintain and improve morale in Eighth Army now. The food and the sanitary arrangements remained largely unchanged. But with a more static front line, occasional comforts came more often. Cyril Mount remembered:

> Occasionally you got a mobile NAAFI, but things were severely rationed. You could have one tin of peaches OR one tin of pineapples. One bar of chocolate

or whatever. And you also got decent cigarettes. We were still getting these Victory V cigarettes with weevils in from India. But you got a ration which was 50 cigarettes – they were Wills Navy Cut – but they were sealed. On the lid there was a little point which you slid along and then you pressed it, and you turned it, and it opened this foil on the lid. And the smell of real tobacco was so beautiful! You tried to make these 50 last, because the other things were so awful.[67]

Other suppliers of variety to the monotonous diet were available occasionally but the goods they offered were popular and soon ran out. Private George F. Bartle of the 6th Cheshires, 44th Division, recalled:

> Visited a YMCA truck which stopped in an infantry unit's lines but not in time to buy fruit and drinks. Food still mostly bully and biscuit but some dried fruit in the evening and 'baaksheesh' bread at mid-day.[68]

Parcels arrived from home – both personal ones and those sent by well-wishers themselves living under rationing. Ernie Kerans was touched by the genuine, but impractical kindness of an old family friend:

> My mother died when I was young and she felt she was a bit like my adopted family because I used to go there a lot and she used to send us letters. Well, when I was abroad, you didn't get any parcels or anything like that but she used to put five Woodbines in an envelope – you can imagine what they were like when they came about three weeks after. When you opened up, they all poured out. Well, I didn't like to say anything because she was so good to send them. But she used to put them in an envelope and brown paper tape all the way round and a letter used to come like a little parcel with five woodbines in.[69]

This, once more, was not a result of Montgomery's appearance. Even in the midst of the July battles, efforts to maintain morale were regularly being made, as Louis Challoner recorded:

> A radio van came up to RHQ on July 11th and took recordings of messages from several of us to be broadcast in Blighty on the 17th. I was fortunate enough to be chosen and got a good message over which was well received. We all felt brighter and with increasing mail and prospects of a rest of a few days we were quite ourselves again. Some desert sores were awkward.[70]

One other factor played an important part in ensuring that morale remained high during August and September. Neither Auchinleck or Montgomery can claim credit for it, it was not unique to Eighth Army nor was it unique to the desert campaign, but 'environmental factors' certainly assisted its development. The character of the Desert War was such that it encouraged small mutually supportive groups to thrive – gun and tank crews, infantry sections, groups of sappers. The manner in which such groups sustained morale is perhaps best explained by the comments of Lieutenant Charles Potts, 1st Buffs, 8th Armoured Brigade:

> We live in tiny communities attached to our various vehicles. I have my batman, my driver and my wireless signaller with me. They quarrel and argue constantly. I sleep on the ground on one side of the vehicle and they sleep on the other. Vehicles are nearly always at least 100 yards apart for fear of bombing. Hundreds of vehicles moving around the desert like unsociable ants, rarely getting close to one another. Surprising really how we keep cheerful – grumbling always, but still fairly cheerful.[71]

These communities tackled practical problems together and gave many a sense of 'family' – including the arguments! They shared the bad and good things and fought, lived and died together. Most men in such groups hoped at the very least not to let their mates down. These bonds carried them through much adversity.

CHAPTER FIVE

SUMMER MADNESS

On 10 August, as generals Sir Alan Brooke and Sir Harold Alexander breakfasted on the terrace of their hotel in Cairo with Churchill, events of great significance for the war in North Africa and the Mediterranean were taking place at sea. A convoy of fourteen merchant ships, escorted by two battleships, three aircraft carriers, seven cruisers, and twenty-four destroyers with various ancillary vessels, and screened by submarines, had passed through the Straits of Gibraltar during the night and was now sailing in the Mediterranean. Operation *Pedestal* – the largest undertaking of the war to supply the beleaguered island of Malta – had entered its most critical phase.

During the next six days, harassed by German and Italian air attacks, motor torpedo boats and submarines, and threatened by mines and a force of cruisers from the Regia Marina, the convoy battled through to its destination. Of the original fourteen merchantmen, only five managed to complete the voyage. Nevertheless, 47,000 tons of supplies were landed, ensuring that the island's inhabitants could hold out until December 1942, albeit on very meagre rations. Crucially, one of the surviving vessels was the *Ohio*, which limped into Grand Harbour, Valletta, with two destroyers lashed alongside for support on the morning of 15 August. Although badly damaged, this tanker was carrying 12,000 tons of oil which ensured that aircraft and submarines from the island could once again undertake offensive operations against Axis shipping in the Central and Eastern Mediterranean. Meanwhile, in connected operations, the aircraft carrier *Furious* flew off a total of sixty-six Spitfires, which considerably enhanced the island's air defences.

The Royal Navy paid a heavy price for *Pedestal*. The aircraft carrier *Eagle*, the cruisers *Manchester* and *Cairo* and the destroyer *Foresight* were all lost. Many of the other vessels were damaged in various degrees. Thirteen Fleet Air Arm and five RAF aircraft were shot down. Even so, the Germans and Italians had failed to prevent a major strategic success for their opponents. Furthermore, two Italian cruisers, unable to intervene against the convoy, had been badly holed by a British submarine, *P42*. Two Italian submarines were also sunk, and a third damaged.[1] More, and larger, Italian naval vessels had not been able to put to sea to attack the convoy because of the chronic shortages of fuel that inhibited all Italy's endeavours in the war.

Pedestal showed Malta's continued importance to the Allied war effort as a base from which aircraft and submarines could attack supply routes of the Axis forces in North Africa. Between June and September, aircraft from the island and Egypt flew nearly a thousand sorties in search of enemy shipping, sinking fifteen ships over 500 tons, with consequent losses of 60,588 tons of vital supplies. Similarly, submarines accounted for fifteen ships and 56,642 tons. During July (when shortages of aviation spirit had limited air operations out of Malta chiefly to those aimed at defending the island, and when the 1st and 10th Submarine Flotillas had temporarily moved bases from there) only five ships were sunk by submarines or aircraft, with a loss of little more than 11,000 tons of supplies. In August, when fuel brought by the *Ohio* enabled 10th Submarine Flotilla to return to Malta and resume patrols in the Central Mediterranean, the figures were ten and 52,056 – and this despite the fact that *Pedestal* did not reach the island until the middle of the month.[2] Similarly, only six per cent of all Axis supplies to North Africa were lost in July, but twenty-five per cent of general military cargo and, significantly, forty-one per cent of fuel in August, with twenty per cent of all cargo (including fuel) in September. Malta had, therefore, despite its travails, an important part to play in the Allied cause.

Malta's chief influence on the North African campaign, however, was its maintenance as a *threat* to Axis supplies. Having captured Tobruk, Rommel expected the port to serve as an advanced base for the landing of supplies for the Panzerarmee. In July, however, Comando Supremo chose to use Benghazi and Tripoli instead – chiefly because Tobruk lay within range of aircraft based in

Malta and the Desert Air Force in Egypt. These alternative ports were 800 and 1,300 miles respectively behind the front. Transporting vital supplies these distances was logistically unsustainable. At the beginning of August, Rommel forced a temporary switch back to Tobruk, which resulted immediately in a dramatic rise in shipping losses. The Italians reverted once again to the safer ports.[3] Whilst Malta remained unconquered, Comando Supremo's concerns about shipping losses would continue to impact on the flow of albeit-inadequate supplies to the Panzerarmee, compounding the fundamental supply problems they were facing.

Despite the efforts of British aircraft, submarines and surface vessels, the losses to Axis shipping came in peaks and troughs. On average, almost eighty-six per cent of all supplies dispatched, arrived – including eighty per cent of oil and eighty-eight per cent of munitions.[4] However, the quantities of supplies being dispatched to the Axis forces fighting in North Africa were insufficient *before* they left port. The Axis powers were already stretched beyond their resources. Furthermore, sufficient quantities could be neither loaded nor unloaded quickly enough because of problems with port facilities in Italy and North Africa. Once a cargo was unloaded, the Panzerarmee's transport infrastructure was inadequate.

Both the Regia Marina and the Regia Aeronautica did what they could to ensure that Italian ships with supplies arrived in North Africa, but the ships sent were frequently not full. The same problems with the Axis, and especially the Italian, war economy that prevented the Regia Marina putting to sea with its largest capital ships against the *Pedestal* convoy, also ensured that Rommel would never receive adequate supplies for his forces. According to the Afrika Korps Chief of Staff, Oberst Fritz Bayerlein, 'To build a stock pile for the decisive battle of the future was impossible' because they were receiving only one-fifth of their normal requirements.[5]

It was ironic that the senior German commanders in North Africa not only blamed their allies for the inability to supply their forces but, taking their lead from Rommel, also cited this as a reason for their subsequent flawed decisions. Friedrich Wilhelm von Mellenthin wrote that:

> Benghazi and even Tobruk were very far from the front and the long haul between the supply ports and Alamein imposed an unbearable strain on our road transport. All these factors, combined with the incompetence or ill-will of the Italian transport and shipping authorities, made it obvious that we could not stay indefinitely at Alamein. The general staff of the Panzerarmee studied the whole

problem carefully and prepared detailed appreciations. A possible solution was to withdraw all non-mobile formations to Libya and to leave only armoured and motorized divisions in the forward area.[6]

But this was not really an option, as Mellenthin made clear:

> Hitler would never have accepted a solution which involved giving up ground, and so the only alternative was to try and go forward to the Nile, while we still had the strength to make the attempt.[7]

Agreement for withdrawal from Egypt might have been almost impossible to secure, but it would undoubtedly have reduced the Axis supply problems. The practicalities were not even examined closely. The other alternative – establishment of strong defensive positions against which Eighth Army might be encouraged to smash itself – was not fully endorsed either. The means to do this were available, as minefields were already being laid to protect key positions, but not to a definite plan. Concentration on this, combined with time spent addressing his supply situation (a senior staff officer with a better understanding of logistics and more tact than Rommel would have been able to achieve this), would have represented a better option in the circumstances than the one chosen. Nevertheless, to keep the initiative, but with inadequate supplies and forces that he acknowledged were weak in terms of equipment and numbers, Rommel recklessly gambled on all he knew – attack.

On 15 August, in a bullish memorandum that described well-fed troops with adequate supplies of ammunition and growing tank strength, Rommel advanced the case for going on the offensive before Eighth Army's supplies of equipment and reinforcements swung the advantage to his opponent.[8] Clearly, the real state of his forces was considerably better, by the Panzerarmee's own reports, than Rommel was subsequently prepared to admit. Good quality infantry reinforcements, including 164. leichte-Afrika-Division, Fallschirmjäger-Brigade Ramcke and the Italian Divisione Paracadutisti 'Folgore', had arrived during July and August. The 'Folgore' were particularly good, although the harsh desert conditions still surprised them, as Tenente Emilio Pulini recalled:

> We arrived in northern Africa in very good condition. We had had very tough training in southern Italy before. For a couple of months we had been training in difficult ground and in a very hot climate too. When arrived we were very fit.

Unfortunately in the desert the conditions were not the same as we had in Italy. The climate was very hot at that time because we arrived in the middle of July. We were taken immediately to the battle front and that too was a rather sudden change. There were a few things which we did not like very much and these things were flies, mainly, and very hot sun which was above us all day long. Being on the front line we had no means of being in the shade.[9]

They soon adapted, however, and their quality drew admiration from their opponents, who referred to them as 'the cream of the Italian Army'.[10]

The Italians had also embarked Divisione 'Pistoia' in order to guard the extended lines of communication through Cyrenaica. Much to Rommel's disgust, this division (unlike the other units) was well-equipped with vehicles, and Italian units generally were re-equipping with new motor transport, whilst the German units struggled on with worn equipment. Rommel's vague criticism of perceived Italian prioritization of cargoes towards their own forces seems to amount to little more than jealousy on his part. Previously, he had always seemed to understand Kitchener's adage regarding the need to 'make war as we must and not as we should like'.[11]

As Rommel made his proposal for a further attack, the Panzerarmee was reporting that it had seventy-five per cent of its nominal strength in personnel, fifty per cent of its tanks, eighty-five per cent of its artillery, sixty per cent of its Pak anti-tank guns and seventy per cent of its heavy Flak artillery (chiefly 88mm guns).[12] Its strength continued to rise. In tanks, for example, the Afrika Korps reported at the end of August having 203 tanks.[13] With about 250 M13/41 Italian tanks as well, the tank forces of the opposing forces (in numerical terms at least), seemed roughly comparable. In an intelligence summary of 22 August, Major Ernst Zolling of the Panzerarmee staff estimated British tank numbers as between 350 and 400.[14] In fact, they were closer to 700.[15] Based on his estimate, Zolling argued 'It can therefore be assumed that the enemy will remain on the defensive in his Alamein position for the time being'.[16]

With this flawed intelligence and promises from Oberbefehlshaber Süd (Luftwaffe Commander-in-Chief South), Generalfeldmarschall Albert Kesselring, and Maresciallo d'Italia Conte Ugo Cavallero, and despite his own increasing ill health, Rommel decided to proceed. Mellenthin recorded:

In the end he accepted Kesselring's assurance that he could fly in 90,000 gallons of gasoline a day, and we relied on a large tanker due in Tobruk at the end of

August. Kesselring did in fact fulfil his promise but most of the gasoline was consumed on the long journey to the front... We were compelled to launch our attack on the night of 30/31 August to take advantage of the full moon. Any further delay would have meant a postponement of three weeks, which in the circumstances was out of the question.[17]

As the planned start date approached, Rommel heard what he *wanted* to hear. In his own words:

Cavallero informed me that tankers had been despatched to get to us in time for the offensive. If these were sunk, other ships, which were being assembled, would sail at once under appropriate escort. Kesselring promised the Panzer Army that in an emergency his transport squadrons would fly across 500 tons of petrol a day. Cavallero said he would use submarines and warships for the carriage of the most urgent material.[18]

Fritz Bayerlein heard much the same:

Marshals Kesselring and Cavallero guaranteed him that he would receive 6,000 tons of gasoline, of which 1,000 would come by air. Rommel stated, 'The battle is dependent upon the prompt delivery of this gasoline.' Cavallero answered, 'You can begin the battle now, Herr Feldmarschall, the gasoline is already under way'.[19]

Kesselring, on the other hand, was more equivocal:

The precarious plight of our communication system made it impossible to give a positive assurance that all supply requirements would be met. I promised to do all I could and to use my influence with the Comando Supremo to keep the stream flowing.[20]

Despite his doubts and the unreliable promises given, the lure of the possible prize proved too much of a temptation for Rommel to ignore.

Rommel had issued his orders for the attack on 22 August. It was scheduled to begin on the night of 30 August. His plans were as outlined by his operations chief, Friedrich Wilhelm von Mellenthin:

Since we could not pierce the Eighth Army front, we had to seek a way round the flank, and Rommel adopted a plan broadly similar to that of Gazala. The Italian infantry, stiffened by the 164th Infantry Division and other German units, were to hold the front from the sea to a point ten miles south of Ruweisat Ridge; the striking force, consisting of 90. leichte-Afrika-Division (on the inner arc of the circle), the Italian armoured corps, and the Afrika Korps, was to swing round the British left flank and advance on the Alam Halfa Ridge. This was a key position, well in rear of Eighth Army, and its capture would decide the fate of the battle. In case of success, 21. Panzer-Division was to advance on Alexandria, and 15. Panzer-Division and 90. leichte-Afrika-Division towards Cairo.[21]

The plan was simple and bold. It was also expected. Almost immediately upon taking command of Eighth Army, Montgomery had warning via Ultra of the likelihood of a new Axis offensive. The exact date was unknown but night operations in the desert without the benefits of moonlight were fraught with additional risks, suggesting it would coincide with a time when the moon was full. Ultra subsequently confirmed this. What was definitely known by the more traditional means of aerial reconnaissance was the approximate strength and location of the planned Axis thrust. This confirmed Eighth Army's expectation in August that any attempt by Rommel would be made in the south, as a consequence of which XIII Corps (first under Gott, and then Horrocks) had been working to fortify the Alam Halfa Ridge. In the desert campaign both sides were aware of the problems in maintaining supplies to any force making a deep thrust through the desert away from the coastal plain and escarpment. Ultimately, any such advance would have to turn northwards to regain the coastal road, either to cut off its opponent's retreat or to establish sustainable lines of communication. The Alam Halfa Ridge running east–west, therefore, offered protection to the southern flank of the Alamein position and observation over the open and difficult desert to the south. Its advantages to the defenders were clear, as John Harding recorded:

The position was that the front at Alamein was held by the infantry. In the north it was the Australians and the New Zealanders and so on. It was held by infantry divisions with the armour in support and with most of the armour on the left flank. There was a feature that runs back from Alamein almost at right angles to it which overlooks the line of advance that the German armour would have to take in order to break through into the Delta.[22]

Harding ascribed responsibility for the plan to meet the attack to Montgomery and three other men newly appointed to positions in Eighth Army – Brigadier Freddie de Guingand, Lieutenant-General Brian Horrocks (Gott's replacement as XIII Corps commander) and Brigadier Roberts of 22nd Armoured Brigade. In fact, the plan was already being developed, first by Dorman-Smith and then by Gott. In Harding's view:

> What really matters is the execution of a plan. Monty and de Guingand with 'Jorrocks' and 'Pip' Roberts organized a defence on that high ground which overlooked the open area where Rommel would have troops. They put the armour in position and Rommel had to attack and defeat that before he could safely continue his advance on the Delta. And that was the battle of Alam Halfa. It was rarely that you had your right hand holding the front ... with your left hand held back in mid-air, overlooking the line in which the German advance would have to take place.[23]

The existence of a plan on which schemes were already being developed gave Montgomery the framework he needed not only to continue the Alam Halfa preparations, but also to ditch those elements he disliked – such as any plan for a withdrawal to, and subsequent defence of, the Nile Delta. This allowed him to promulgate his 'no retreat' policy that was an immediate boost to the morale of most ordinary soldiers. Crucially, the refrain was taken up by his corps and divisional commanders in outlining the plan to their officers. Lieutenant-General Sir Bernard Freyberg of 2nd New Zealand Division made things plain in his address to the New Zealand Divisional Headquarters Conference on 16 August:

> I want you to make the Army Commander's views clear to everybody. This looking over your shoulder and cranking up to get back to the position in the rear is to cease. Here we are going to stay and here we are going to fight. There is no question of going to any back position from here. We are to make this position as complete as we can.[24]

There was, consequently, a great deal of sensitivity regarding the shape and terminology of the defensive positions. The 44th (Home Counties) Division had only recently arrived in Egypt but had been rushed up to the Ridge on Montgomery's orders, despite being inadequately trained. One of its officers, Lieutenant-Colonel John Anderson Smith of the 57th Anti-Tank Regiment (RA) recalled:

Each Brigade was in what we were forbidden to call a 'box'– a defensive position entirely surrounded by wire and minefields – and usually there was wire and sometimes minefields between Brigade positions. Divisional HQ and my HQ were not in a box but were between 131 and 133 Brigades.[25]

This ban on certain terminology for defensive positions, which originated from Montgomery, had echoes of the controversies over the defensive arrangements of the British Army in March 1918 against the German Spring Offensive. Then 'defence in depth' was based around wired-in redoubts or strongpoints intended to delay the attackers' advance and use up their ammunition and resources. The tactics were poorly understood and very unpopular, summed up in the observation of one anonymous non-commissioned officer (NCO): 'It don't suit us. The British Army fights in line and won't do any good in these bird cages'.[26] 'Boxes', like 'bird cages', suggested restrictions on freedom of movement and inevitable capture. Instead, 'Every post was to have All-Round Defence, with its own stores, and supplied within itself.'[27]

The Alam Halfa position extended beyond the ridge itself, presenting problems for siting the 2-pounder guns and headquarters of Anderson Smith's unit:

Owing to the extreme flatness of the area although one could get fairly good fields of fire for the guns it was extremely hard to conceal them. My HQ was a small area of desert, we had about five vehicles up scattered about. The second afternoon we were there we were dive bombed by four or five Stukas. At the time we were digging a bit of a hole to use as an office. It had a bank about a foot high against which I flung myself. One signaller was slightly wounded in the back. He had crawled under a lorry and a splinter had hit the chassis and 'splashed' him. He was back two days later. It had a very good effect ever after in that I never had much bother getting RHQ to dig in.[28]

Horrocks, new to the desert, made his preparations around a static defensive combination of tanks and anti-tank guns – especially the new 6-pounder guns of 1st Rifle Brigade and the Grant tanks of 22nd Armoured Brigade. Manoeuvre was not contemplated, except by 7th Motor Brigade and the armoured cars and Stuart tanks of 4th Armoured Brigade, both from 7th Armoured Division. Valentine tanks from 23rd Armoured Brigade had trained as a mobile corps reserve to support the infantry – especially 2nd New Zealand and 44th Divisions. Tom Witherby remembered getting to know the area with 46th RTR:

We had to know how to get to five places by day or night at top Valentine speed. In particular, I remember going to 'Scotland' and seeing the Grant tanks of the Royal Scots Greys. They were not in 'dug-in' positions but were on a steep hill at the back of the Alam Halfa Ridge. Nearby we examined the dug-in emplacement of a six-pounder anti-tank gun, with a very solid breastwork of sandbags, carefully camouflaged. This gun was half-way down a little 'wadi' or chine and was largely hidden from the ground in front and could only be attacked by tanks as they climbed up the wadi itself.[29]

Considerable care was taken in siting the precious 6-pounders for their fire to achieve optimum effect. Douglas Waller recalled:

There were two of us in front and the other two were slightly on our flanks and further behind us. They put us out there and said 'Mark out something 300 yards away'. Well, we put an empty petrol tin there and they said 'That's your maximum range. Don't open fire above 300 yards'. Our tanks were not as heavily armoured and didn't have as big guns as they [the Germans] did. Really they were outranged. That was the trouble. So where they were in a hull-down position, they didn't want to be at extreme range because they weren't going to inflict any damage. They didn't want us to open fire until they were in the range of the tanks.[30]

The plan was simple and clear, the preparations to execute it obvious to all. Captain Tom Witherby spoke for many ordinary Eighth Army soldiers when expressing the view that 'the days of complicated, obscure plans, of constant pointless movements and of the splitting up of formations were gone for ever.'[31]

The credit for the clear plans for battle at Alam Halfa should be assigned to Auchinleck, Dorman-Smith and Gott for the work they had already accomplished before Montgomery took over. However, when Churchill returned from his meeting with Stalin in mid-August, Montgomery told him of the measures being prepared against the expected attack – all of which were based on existing plans. This was a masterly exposition of the situation, according to Churchill, which left him delighted at the speed with which the new Army Commander had grasped the situation.[32] This ascribed the credit to Montgomery, who without demurring, accepted it and perpetuated the lie ever after.

Each night from 25 August onwards – the start of the full moon period – the men of Eighth Army had been in a state of nervous expectation. On 29 August, Rifleman Reg Crimp of the 2nd Rifle Brigade wrote in his diary:

At night each of us in the Signals section has a couple of hours listening-duty, sitting in the dark PU, with the set humming and the night-light glowing, hearing also the planes droning across overhead. Everyone now is on the 'qui vive'; there's a general sweat on. The moon is full and Jerry has been 'more or less definitely' expected to launch an attack during the last three nights, but so far nothing's happened.[33]

The next night, the wait was over.

After sunset on 30 August the armoured divisions of the Afrika Korps and the Italian Divisioni 'Ariete' and 'Littorio' began their advance, screened by light reconnaissance units on the right and with 90. leichte-Afrika-Division on the left. Mellenthin recorded:

To turn the Eighth Army front it was necessary to pierce a thick minebelt, which the British had laid almost as far as the Qattara Depression. Right from the start the offensive got into difficulties, for the minefields were far more elaborate than we imagined, and the British covering forces inflicted heavy losses on the mine-lifting parties. This threw our whole timetable out of gear.[34]

Sergeant Fred Hunn commanded a Humber Mark II armoured car of B Squadron, 12th Lancers. The armoured cars operated in front of the rest of Eighth Army and occasionally behind enemy lines in a 'light cavalry' role. Now, at the southern end of the Alamein line minefields, they were to provide advanced warning of the Panzerarmee attack and track the advance.

It was on the night of 30 August. I remember the night. So clear. It was beautiful. A full moon, and of course the sand and everything. It looked so good and still, everyone was very quiet and looking and listening to see if they could see or hear any sight or sound. I think round about midnight, No.3 Troop reported some movement in his area as if he could hear the German engineers clearing a gap through the minefield. A thousand yards or perhaps a bit more. In the moonlight, you could probably see a fair way but the sound was travelling more. This sound came and then slowly through the minefields came the tanks. We all sort of kept in line with them, observing, pulling back – it'd be pointless to stay where we were because we would have been cut off. We kept in touch and started reporting back.[35]

The Lancers withdrew through gaps in the minefields, which were then shelled by the Axis artillery. This, in effect, broadcast the attack's start to the rest of the Eighth Army. Brigadier Philip 'Pip' Roberts recounted:

> Shortly after midnight I was awakened by gunfire in the distance and it was quite clearly more than some little affair. I look outside and the sky is lit up by flashes, so I get up and stroll over to my ACV (Armoured Command Vehicle) to find that the staff have not, as yet, had any reports; I go out into the cool night air again. To the northwest the shelling seems to be dying down a bit, but in the southwest the noise continues. German Verey lights lob forward and an occasional tracer tears across the sky. I am called into the ACV and find that information has come through. It seems that there is a very determined attack against 7th Motor Brigade towards the south of the minefields and we are ordered to our defensive position.[36]

Despite the efforts of Panzer-Pioniere-Bataillon 33 and 200 who set to with mine detectors to clear routes for the Panzers under cover of heavy artillery fire, the Afrika Korps was still passing through the minebelt at 0500hrs. The concentrated mass of tanks and vehicles was bombed repeatedly by Wellingtons from the Desert Air Force and attacked by 7th Motor Brigade. The targets were illuminated by parachute magnesium flares dropped by the 'pathfinder' Fairey Albacores of 821 Squadron, Fleet Air Arm. Reg Crimp wrote in his diary:

> Tonight, the relay of aircraft overhead is more concentrated than ever. They can be seen passing in two-way procession against the grey velvet sky, and the flares, some of which seem suspended even nearer than usual, give the desert a strident face, like a painted mask. Once, suddenly, a plane is heard diving, fairly near – a sinking, menacing, loudening roar. Instantly everyone's awake, hearts in mouths. The roar reaches its nadir, and there's a brief, surprisingly distant, explosion. And more surprising still, no fast, strong, exultant up-climb, but instead, a mile away, a brilliant blossoming of white fire, inset with vivid sperms of incandescence, ascending into a spire of smoke – and silence.[37]

The prolonged fighting at the minefield gap was important for two reasons. Firstly, it considerably delayed the Panzerarmee advance. By 0800hrs, when Rommel and his staff had a clearer picture of the situation, his forces should have been twenty-five to thirty miles beyond their starting point. Instead, they had

THE BATTLE OF ALAM HALFA

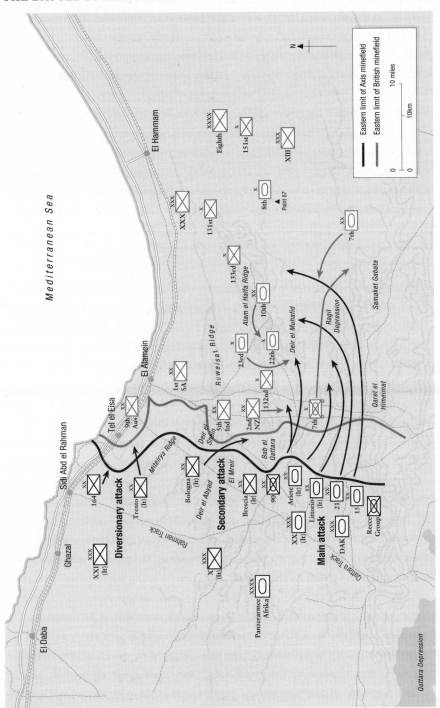

accomplished between eight and ten miles. The Italian armour was still largely hung up in the minefields. Equally important were the losses amongst senior commanders in this fighting. Generalmajor Georg von Bismarck, the experienced and energetic commander of 21. Panzer-Division, was killed whilst near the front of the advance. The Afrika Korps commander, Generalleutnant Walther Nehring, was severely wounded and several of his staff killed in an air attack. Generalmajor Ulrich Kleeman, 90. leichte-Afrika-Division's commander, was also severely wounded. Oberst Fritz Bayerlein assumed temporary command of the Afrika Korps until Generalmajor Gustav von Vaerst of 15. Panzer-Division arrived to take over. There was inevitably a period of adjustment whilst replacement commanders were organized and moved to their units; Oberst Carl-Hans Lungerhausen, originally destined for 164. leichte-Afrika-Division, took over from Bismarck temporarily and Oberst Eduard Crasemann became acting commander of 15. Panzer-Division. Mellenthin recorded:

> Rommel was half-minded to call off the attack but decided to continue when the Afrika Korps, under Bayerlein's resolute leadership, got through the minefields and made a substantial advance to the east. A heavy sandstorm blew up during the day, and although this added to the difficulties of the march it did give considerable protection from the British bombers.[38]

Probably influenced by fuel shortages rather than a captured 'going' map which supposedly showed terrain suitable for tanks but which was, in fact, a piece of deception produced by Middle East General Headquarters intelligence staff, Rommel adjusted his force's 'wheel' to approach the more westerly half of the Alam Halfa Ridge, instead of the eastern.[39] The attack would now fall exactly where Gott and, subsequently, Horrocks, had hoped it would.

The enforced command changes, together with refuelling, wireless communication problems and a sandstorm, further delayed the German forces. However, there were also problems for the units shadowing and harassing the advance. Fred Hunn remembered:

> We got a call where 2 and 3 Troops were running out of petrol. Of course, we couldn't send a lorry up that area because it was under fire. I got a jeep and I put in the back a load of jerry cans. I took enough petrol to give them about nine gallons each – two jerry cans each I suppose – and drove up behind each armoured car and said 'Here you are. Petrol' and threw it up on the back for them

and drove back as quick as I could. That would see them through for the day, certainly the speed they were going back.[40]

Manoeuvres and the difficult terrain were using up a lot of fuel on both sides.

The problems for 7th Motor Brigade were in disengaging from contact with the advancing Afrika Korps – something which Major-General Callum Renton, commanding 7th Armoured Division, agreed to but which infuriated Horrocks, who had expected the brigade to stand and fight for longer. Having accomplished this, however, the chief concern was to provoke the Germans into attempting an attack on 22nd Armoured Brigade. 'Pip' Roberts described the situation from the viewpoint of the latter:

> Now I can see the enemy myself through my glasses. They are coming straight up the line of the telegraph posts which lead in front of our position. On they come, a most impressive array. And now they are swinging east and look like passing us about 1,200 yards from our forward positions. I had given strict instructions that we would not open fire until the enemy tanks were at under 1,000 yards range. Here was something of a dilemma... General Gatehouse is with General Horrocks on Alam Halfa itself and a bit further east than we are; it seems that he can see this mass of enemy tanks about to pass our position ... at that moment he speaks to me ... 'I don't want you to think that we are in a blue funk here or anything like that, but if these fellows continue on as they are doing you will have to come out and hit them in the flank'.[41]

But, then, the advance halted, before turning to advance on Roberts' brigade:

> It is fascinating to watch them, as one might watch a snake curl up ready to strike. But there is something unusual too; some of the leading tanks are Mark IVs, and Mark IVs have, in the past, always had short-barrelled 75mm guns used for close-support work and firing HE only, consequently they are not usually in front. But these Mark IVs have a very long gun on them; in fact it looks the devil of a gun. This must be the long-barrelled stepped-up 75mm the Intelligence people have been talking about.[42]

This was the first encounter with the PzKpfw Mark IV 'Special' whose new weaponry brought about a change in German tank tactics and which soon established a fearsome reputation.

And now they all turn left and face us and begin to advance slowly. The greatest concentration seems to be opposite the CLY [4th County of London Yeomanry] and the A/T [anti-tank] guns of the Rifle Brigade. (Eighty-seven German tanks were counted at this time opposite this part of the front.) I warn all units over the air not to fire until the enemy are within 1,000 yards; it can't be long now and then in a few seconds the tanks of the CLY open fire and the battle is on.[43]

The Mark III tanks came forward to engage the Grants of 4th CLY, offering tempting targets for the 6-pounders. Douglas Waller viewed the scene:

We were dug in these positions at Alam Halfa and we saw an armoured car come whizzing back. 'Tanks are coming!' We sat there and waited. We could see them then. About 70 of them. The first tank started moving forward and the first commander's tank came up and, very obligingly, almost stopped on top of this petrol tin that we'd put out. I said to Bill: 'That one's ours'. Nothing had been fired then so we fired and he was a goner because he was side-on. Once we fired of course other tanks started firing at us. One came up and two of the crew bailed out of this one to get on the back of this other tank. We fired at it. On the front it just bounced off so we fired at the turret and the track but it still kept going and it started backing away and the machine guns opened up on us which went through the front shield and deflected off the curved shield behind. Also went through and knocked the sights out of our gun. But nobody was hit. If it hadn't been for the shield we'd have all been goners.[44]

Doctor Alfons Selmayr in his *Arztpanzer* – one of a few PzKpfw II light tanks still in use by the Panzer units – was with Panzer-Regiment 5:

We were received by raging tank, anti-tank gun and anti-aircraft gun fire. By the time we looked around, several of our tanks had already been finished. I received a call for help from the 8th Company and was in the process of moving around the 7th Company when my left track was shot off. Since everyone was pulling back and only the adjutant and the battalion commander were ahead of me, I had to dismount and abandon the tank. My tunic over my shoulder, the two medical bags in my hands, I walked back, covered by a withdrawing tank.[45]

To the watching Brigadier Roberts, the success of the anti-tank gunners was balanced by his tank losses:

It seems only a few minutes before nearly all the tanks of the Grant squadron of the County of London Yeomanry were on fire. The new German 75mm is taking a heavy toll. The enemy tanks have halted and they have had their own casualties, but the situation is serious; there is a complete hole in our defence. I hurriedly warn the Greys that they must move at all speed from their defensive positions and plug the gap. Meanwhile the enemy tanks are edging forward again and they have got close to the Rifle Brigade's anti-tank guns, who have held their fire marvellously to a few hundred yards. When they open up they inflict heavy casualties on the enemy, but through sheer weight of numbers some guns are overrun. The SOS artillery fire is called for; it comes down almost at once right on top of the enemy tanks. This, together with the casualties they have received, checks them. But where are the Greys? 'Come on the Greys!' I shout over the wireless 'Get out your whips!' But there is no sign of them at the moment coming over the ridge and there is at least another half hour's daylight left.[46]

Much damage was due to the new German tank – the Mark IV Special, whose long-barrelled 75mm gun, even at relatively long range, was able to penetrate the frontal armour of the Grants. In the midst of the action was Laurie Phillips:

Luckily the one nearest to us (about 10 yards) although hit, with two of the crew killed, did not brew up, or we would have had a very warm time. We did not fire a shot from our gun, as nothing came within our arc of fire, and we were defiladed from the front by a bit of a bump in the ground. I would have been less scared if I had been busy firing back than just lying there with the earth erupting all around. But the company was said to have knocked out nineteen tanks in all, including five credited to an old friend of mine from Farnham days, Lance Corporal Norman Griffiths.[47]

The Mark IVs could stand off and shell their opponents with little concern about being hit. Meanwhile the attacking PzKpfw IIIs rallied to come again against the anti-tank gunners, only to suffer more losses, as Sergeant Stephen Kennedy of 1st/6th RTR, observed:

I don't think the Germans were expecting that they would be dug in so near to them. They really created havoc. They brought on some more Mark III tanks around and, with our help, firing from further back and mainly the infantry with their anti-tank guns, they destroyed them. There was a great area of destroyed

German equipment – which was a great boost to our morale and the Germans started to withdraw. Instead of coming round the south of us, they went back and formed a straight line back against the reinforcements that they'd got.[48]

The use of SOS artillery fire and the timely appearance of tanks of the Royal Scots Greys clinched matters. Laurie Phillips remembered:

The German tanks were gradually edging closer, from a direction in which we could not fire at them, and I was anxiously calculating how long it would be before the sun went down, and how near the tanks would be by then, when there was a rumble, and over the ridge behind us roared the Grant squadrons of the Royal Scots Greys. It was a marvellous sight to see 30 Grants come roaring down and open fire simultaneously – one of them stopped only a few yards behind us, and the blast deafened us; when we made our presence known, the tank commander said 'Good God, I didn't know anyone was still alive down there'.[49]

The attackers now withdrew but were granted no respite as the bombers of the Desert Air Force once again appeared in strength. Alfons Selmayr recalled:

They constantly flew past us in air-show formation and dropped their loads wherever there were even just a few vehicles close together. Directly in front of me, the tank of a company commander was hit right on the turret. The commander and the loader were badly wounded; both of them died later. The gunner and the radio operator had critical wounds. Other than a few field dressings, I no longer had any dressing material... The dressing I had in the bags had already been used in the morning and last night for smaller injuries and wounds. I set the wounds with shovels and camouflage material and sent the people to the rear.[50]

The bombing continued through the night and into the next day. The Allied air effort (now including United States Army Air Force B-25 Mitchell day bombers) and the strength of the defences his forces encountered were two of three critical factors Rommel identified in forcing him to withdraw his forces. Third in importance was the fuel shortages the Afrika Korps now had – primarily as a result of the quantities used in traversing the minefields and difficult terrain.

On 1 September, only Crasemann's 15. Panzer-Division was able to make any attempt at attacking again, but these attempts were unavailing and the attacking tanks were again mauled by the Royal Artillery and what Rommel described as 'Part Rally' formations of bombers – a reference to the perfect formations of fly-pasts at Nazi 'celebrations'.[51] According to Bayerlein:

> All day the ceaseless attacks of the British bomber formations continued on the battlefield. Enemy artillery fired immense quantities of ammunition into our positions. Movement on the battlefield was impossible. Again and again our outnumbered fighter aircraft threw themselves against the British bomber formations. But seldom did they succeed in getting close to the British bombers, since they were always engaged in aerial battles with extraordinarily strong fighter formations of the RAF which were assigned to protect the seemingly endless flight of the bomber squadrons.[52]

Yet this was the day on which the fighter ace Oberleutnant Hans-Joachim Marseille of Jagdgeschwader 27 – 'Der Stern von Afrika'* – enjoyed the most successful day of his career in claiming seven victories, four of which could definitely be identified – a feat for which, on landing that evening, he was personally congratulated by Kesselring. All of his victims were fighters. On 1 September, not one Allied bomber was shot down by fighters; such losses as there were (three day bombers) resulted from anti-aircraft fire.[53] The large numbers of aircraft engaged in unglamorous bomber escort duties were proving effective in pursuit of Air Vice-Marshal Arthur Coningham's concept of tactical air power in which securing air superiority was the necessary precursor to interdicting enemy supplies and reinforcements, as well as the means of permitting direct air co-operation with ground forces in the land battle. The following day, Marseille claimed five more victories against fighters, bringing his 'score' to 126. Yet, crucially, the effects of these losses on both the ground operations and the efforts of the Desert Air Force were practically nil.

On the ground, the problems of fuel supply to the North African theatre of operations continued, but it was the distances required to transport fuel deep into the southern flank of the Axis forces that were now taking their toll. The Panzerarmee command also mistakenly expected to get a large proportion of the fuel landed from the vessel *Giorgio*, which landed at Tobruk with 2,474 tons on 28 August, but all but 120 tons was intended for the Luftwaffe.[54] Malta-based aircraft damaged the *Abruzzi* carrying 611 tons on 1 September and sank the

---

* The Star of Africa.

Picci Fassio with 1,100 tons of fuel on the following day but these losses came too late to influence Rommel, who had already decided to withdraw – disappointing news for at least one young officer, Oberleutnant Heinz Werner Schmidt of Sonderverband 288:

> On the third day of the battle our own *Sonderverband* still lay inactive in the reserve area. Reports from forward became steadily more non-committal. We began to feel that the 'final shot' at Alexandria had misfired. I had been thinking regretfully that in the Nile Delta I should miss the three white tropical uniforms I had left in the hotel in Asmara when I flew out of Eritrea; now my regrets began to fade. I developed serious doubts as to whether I should ever, as a soldier, set eyes on the Pyramids.[55]

Thus far, Montgomery's control of the battle had been beyond reproach. Adopting an existing plan he had tailored it to his needs and conducted the battle on terms that used the strengths of Eighth Army as they appeared to its new commander in the short time he had been in Egypt. He had committed the necessary reserves in support of his corps and divisional commanders when circumstances required and had, otherwise, allowed Horrocks to fight the battle as he wanted. He had regularly visited his subordinate commanders with his Tactical Headquarters whilst leaving de Guingand as Chief of Staff to run matters at GHQ in Burg-el-Arab. However, Rommel's withdrawal and its connection with fuel supply problems, about which Montgomery was well-informed, represented a significant missed opportunity. Montgomery was slow to reorganize his forces to seize the initiative and, though he was informed via Ultra on 2 September that the Panzerarmee was temporarily going on the defensive owing to lack of fuel, it was only that evening that he ordered specific action and then it was with the caveat that it was important not to rush into the attack.[56] Overly cautious, Montgomery achieved nothing on 3 September and it was, once again, the Desert Air Force which did the most damage.

It was only that night that Operation *Beresford*, involving 5th and 6th New Zealand Brigades flanking 132nd Infantry Brigade of 44th Division, was launched. It would be 132nd Infantry Brigade's first desert attack. The purpose of the attack was ill-defined being seemingly a set of probes to test the Panzerarmee reaction.[57] Very little, if anything, was prepared for what would happen in the event of the attack's success or failure. One squadron each of Valentine tanks from 46th and 50th RTR were to support 132nd and 5th New Zealand Brigades respectively.

In the event, 'a great many things went wrong'. Brigadier Cecil Robertson of 132nd Brigade failed to follow the advice of the more experienced Brigadier Howard Kippenberger in his preparations and was subsequently severely wounded when his brigade was late reaching its starting positions – by which time the Germans and Italians were alert to what was happening. The 'greenness' of the 4th and 5th Royal West Kent battalions and 2nd Buffs showed in practically all they did. It was an especially chastening experience for Lieutenant Harry Crispin Smith of 4th Royal West Kent Regiment:

We were really not terribly trained for desert warfare and we were thrown into this night attack without any artillery support – the idea being to have a silent attack – and yet silence was sacrificed because we took lorry loads of mines with us. There were these lorries grinding about, and I think the enemy had plenty of warning. Luckily we were the reserve company just behind the three attacking companies. On our particular front a three-ton lorry load of mines was hit and went up with a cataclysmic roar. We had some tanks on the flank that were blazing away but a lot of their fire was misdirected. With A Company we had to cover the withdrawal of the attacking companies after they'd made their attack and had been repulsed and were streaming back. We had the Bren guns out giving covering fire as best we could in the moonlight and then this German Spandau opened up and the bullets came whistling in amongst us. Several men were killed – but of course you never know at the time who's been killed and who wasn't. A burst hit the ground just in front of my face and then another just behind my feet. I thought, 'Well, the third one's not going to be so good'. The bullets just skimmed over me excepting two which succeeded in perforating my backside. I remember thinking it was quite like being caned by my housemaster when I was a boy at school.[58]

Eventually the battalion pulled back at first light and took up a position about a mile back.

We weren't in very good shape by then. The rifle companies had very heavy casualties and of course we had to leave the dead and the wounded. So we withdrew and we licked our wounds back in the rear area of the Alamein line.

The battalion had taken quite a lot of casualties and it took quite a while to get organized again. The same applied to 5th Battalion and 2nd Buffs. None of them had had a very successful night.[59]

In spite of the success of 28th (Māori) Battalion and the gallantry of the Valentine crews of Major Alan Hughes' B Squadron, 50th RTR, who knocked out a detachment of German 88mm guns from Flak-Regiment 135 and were last seen charging another – an example of 'mixing it' much admired by the New Zealand infantry – Brigadier Kippenberger was forced to order a retirement. The plan had unravelled and his counterpart, Brigadier George Clifton of 6th New Zealand Brigade, had been captured. Witnessing an incipient counter-attack by Italian M13/40s and *Bersaglieri* from 22nd Battalion's headquarters, Kippenberger prepared to contact his brigade-major, Monty Fairbrother, to organize concentrated fire from his division's supporting artillery. Kippenberger recorded how the battalion commander, Lieutenant-Colonel John Russell:

pointed out, some 3,000 yards away, four or five tanks and perhaps a hundred infantry, with more coming into view every moment. 'This looks like it, Sir,' John said. I grunted agreement and said I would go back and get the guns on; there was time enough yet. More and more infantry and more tanks appeared. Several of the tanks were firing at long-range, and from them and the 88's the Twenty-second was getting quite a preparation. The sight fascinated me and I still dallied. Another minute and John said: 'You'd better go now, Sir, this is where I do my stuff.' I rang Monty and told him to call for fire from every gun we had on to the map squares that I estimated the counter-attack would be passing through in ten minutes. Then I scrambled into my jeep and bolted off, not so much out of timidity as out of the virtuous realization that my right place was at my own headquarters.[60]

Five minutes later, at his own headquarters, Kippenberger found Fairbrother giving final telephone instructions to the artillery:

He finished, said 'Make it snappy', and we waited in silence. The gunners responded splendidly... In this case it was eleven minutes before the first shell howled overhead. Very good for those days. A few seconds later every gun was firing, while we gloated. It was a magnificent, overpowering concentration. After five minutes it stopped. I called for a repeat, searching back. Down it came like the hammer of Thor. We rang the Twenty-second and asked how things were. 'That's fixed 'em,' said the Adjutant. 'They're fixed.' So they were.[61]

It was a landmark moment. 'For the first time in our experience, the immediate counter-attack had been crushingly defeated,' Kippenberger noted.[62] The reforms of Brigadier Noel Martin, Eighth Army's Brigadier-General Royal Artillery (BGRA), in centralization of artillery control were now bearing fruit (although, shortly afterwards, Martin lost his job as Montgomery culled commanders and replaced them with those he favoured).

Later, with his battalion now in reserve, Harry Crispin Smith took the opportunity to hop a ride to Alexandria to visit a hospital to have his wound properly dressed:

I went riding the truck down the desert, which didn't do my backside any good as you can imagine. It was very bumpy. They kept me in for a night. That made the wound official. It went down in the hospital records as 'Gunshot Wound: Buttocks'. Gunshot Wound Buttocks! GSW Buttocks. So my wife got the telegram in due course. I never realized this was going to happen and in actual fact I'd only been superficially wounded.[63]

Beresford was a failure with hazy aims and uncertain armoured support. It demonstrated that there were many things that Montgomery's arrival had not fixed, and suggested that the new Army Commander's cautious approach to operations might itself be the source of future difficulties. After the battle there was a heated exchange between Major-Generals Gatehouse and Lumsden over why the former had not pursued and 'annihilated' Rommel during the withdrawal. According to Gatehouse:

I informed him that previous to the battle I had had a long briefing by Monty, and that this had been one of the main points insisted upon – viz not to be drawn on a wild goose chase on to the muzzles of waiting 88mm guns – as Rommel had so often managed to make his enemy do in the past. [Lumsden] would not believe me and when I repeated I had had definite orders on this point, and that I heartily agreed with them, he quivered with rage and left my HQ in a hurry.[64]

Montgomery's cull of commanders, in which Brigadier Martin was a casualty, began soon after Alam Halfa. Lieutenant-General William Ramsden, an Auchinleck appointment, was allegedly dismissed with the memorable 'You're not exactly on the crest of a wave, Ramsden'. He was replaced by Sir Oliver Leese. Brigadier Sidney Kirkman came out from England to be the new BGRA of Eighth Army. Major-General Callum Renton went because of his falling-out with Horrocks during Alam Halfa, and was replaced by John Harding – already a 'Monty favourite'. Montgomery could not sack the three Dominion commanders, nor could he dismiss 'Gertie' Tuker of 4th Indian Division. Neither did he promote them; Morshead and Freyberg were both angry at being passed over for corps commands. Ability sometimes lost out to the known quantity – but many of those appointed proved very successful.

Whilst a great deal of work began on preparing an Allied offensive, there was a further brigade-sized operation undertaken by 44th Division at the end of September. The attack by 131st Brigade, which consisted of three territorial battalions (1/5th, 1/6th and 1/7th) of the Queen's Royal (West Surrey) Regiment, was intended to retake the Deir-el-Munassib (Munassib Depression), which the Panzerarmee had held since Alam Halfa, and, to keep Axis attention focused on the southern part of the front. Preparations for the attack were better than for 132nd Brigade's participation in *Beresford*. Nine field artillery regiments were to support the attack, which was scheduled for 29 September. Private Jack York of 1/5th Battalion recalled:

> The enemy had still retained their hold on part of this area after the September push, and the result was quite a large bulge in our front line. Our task was to straighten this out – and rumour had it that the enemy here consisted of Italian pioneer units and second-rate troops, in which case we were told, the attack would be a piece of cake.[65]

This was clearly the terminology of reassurance, reeled out at the briefings. Private Fred Daniels, also of 1/5th Battalion, heard the same message:

> The Company Commander called a meeting of officers and NCOs during the afternoon and we learned that the job that night was likely to be no trouble at all – a 'bit of cake' – as the Army says. We were to take an Italian position and hold

it for forty-eight hours until relieved – just a matter of straightening up the line. Tank and air support was promised, and an Artillery barrage would effect a preliminary 'softening up.'[66]

There were also hints that little opposition was expected owing to the surprise nature of the attack. Corporal Ernest Norris, from 1/5th, remembered his thoughts at the time:

> I hoped that he was right. Sitting there under the hot sun, letting the sand pass through my fingers and cursing the flies, the war had suddenly become a very close and personal thing. The speaker spoke in the customary 'old school tie' manner with reference to the honour of the Regiment. And, indeed, why not? It was solely a Queen's affair and was to be named '*Braganza*'. I wonder if the ghost of King Charles II's wife … was also there, nodding her approval… For most of us, this was the first time we had taken part in an attack and we heard the news with a mixture of fear and excitement. Of course we joked about it and said things like 'We'll show the bastards' but in each man's mind was the hope that he would show out well once the chips were down.[67]

Dressed in Celanese shirts, shorts, woollen cardigan and battle order equipment, the men were taken in trucks to a gap in the protective minefields, arriving at midnight. Carriers, anti-tank guns and mortars arrived at the same time. One vehicle accidentally exploded a mine at the side of the track, making a terrible sound. The rifle companies now advanced, quietly moving into the Depression. Jack York painted an evocative picture of the scene:

> Each man was carrying extra rations and ammunition, and we were all wearing desert boots made of soft suede leather, with a thick crepe sole – very useful for night attacks as they made little sound. The floor of the Depression was quite flat, with soft sand in places. We had to walk about four or five miles. The night was chilly. On and on we plodded, with a muttered curse now and then, as someone tripped over camel thorn or stumbled into soft sand. The Depression seemed to assume quite a ghostly atmosphere, as the pale moonlight filtered through, and we could see the grotesque shapes and outlines of the hard high sides of the Wadi – about half a mile away on either side – where the moon was making weird patterns of light and shadow on twisted column and crested ridge. The whole of the desert outside seemed so unusually quiet it was almost sinister to our tensed

nerves. Not a sound of a gun or burst of fire in any direction. Almost as if we had entered a prehistoric world, and were disturbing the virgin sand for the first time. Just a gentle chill wind in our faces and the faint unmistakeable smell of the desert. Hardly anybody spoke, but many of us gave an apprehensive glance now and then at the sides of the Depression, dreading to hear the burst of fire from some inquisitive enemy patrol.[68]

Arriving near the area to be attacked, they then rested until 0510hrs when the advance began. At 0525hrs supporting artillery opened fire and 1/5th moved forward in a vast saucer rimmed with fire. Ernest Norris described the start:

Our artillery opened fire with the shells screaming over our heads and the noise rising to a crescendo. That made me feel better and when we were ordered to fix bayonets and spread out in line, I felt proud that I was there. Sounds corny perhaps, but it's true nevertheless.[69]

The 1/6th Queens were on the right flank of the Depression, the 1/7th on the left. Norris continued:

We started forward in line at a steady plod with our eyes fixed on the exploding shells, shoulders hunched, but determined. I well remember the sudden feeling of nakedness when our guns stopped firing and the grim silence as I stalked forward in fear. It was dark and eerie and felt bloody dangerous. Then they let us have it. They were using tracer and it came over like a broken curve of light seemingly slowly at first then suddenly rushing in followed by a sharp crack. Men were being hit and shouting as they went down and our line must have broken. I found myself crouching in a dip with Sergeant Wakefield and a great deal of noise. He said that we had better get on forward and he edged himself to the lip of the hollow. But I must admit that we were both a bit reluctant to move.[70]

The attack had run into serious trouble, failing to reach the main objective amidst noise and confusion. Norris went on:

It was still dark but that desert dawn was very close at hand. Clearly through all that noise I heard Captain Clark calling out 'Carry on Mr Cole-Biroth, I've been hit'. From behind us came one of the signal section with his set strapped to his back and he asked us where he could find Captain Clark. We told him that he was wounded and Cole-Biroth was in command. He complained that he couldn't get BHQ [Battalion Headquaters] only atmospherics, and that either we were too far forward or his set was fucking useless. He needed orders.[71]

Then, with characteristic suddenness, daylight came:

We found ourselves lying just outside the barbed-wire perimeter of the Italian position, in full view of the defenders and their compatriots in machine-gun nests in the rocks above us, who proved their vigilance by sending single shots every time we moved hand or feet. But the company commander now decided he ought to contact Battalion HQ. When we tried to get through we found that the set had been damaged and was useless. No message had been received and none sent from our company throughout the engagement.[72]

The coming of morning helped orientation but also showed the desperate nature of the situation. It also brought heavier and better-directed fire:

It was daylight now and I could see in front of me the rising ridge with lots of hard ground and masses of rocks and stones leading to the sky line. I could also see some of my company crouched behind cover where there was a fair-sized dip – or drop – just below the summit. We were being mortared and that, coupled with the machine-gun and rifle fire, was very frightening. I heard our Bren-gunner screaming: 'Me arm's gone! Me arm's gone!'. This was George Church. His arm was slung round his back and was lying on top of his small pack. He had been machine-gunned in the shoulder, four or five bullets smashing it completely and slinging his arm to where it was now like a kicked-open door with broken hinges. He was not bleeding much so maybe all that sand that filled his wounds was blocking the flow. We could only try to dress them with a couple of field dressings and leave his arm where it was. He was taking it very well and making little of it. I think it was a great relief to him to know that the arm was still there. He had really thought that he had lost it. Not that it looked much good to him now. I remember George asking me to light a cigarette. We were copping it again and fear made me speak sharply. Within seconds I was apologizing and George was smoking but that didn't excuse me to myself.[73]

With only one unwounded sergeant and a mortally wounded officer left in A Company, the company's few survivors were fatalistic:

We sprawled there in that hot bowl not expecting to survive. Then came a lull and what seemed a relative quiet. We heard them coming. They were not keeping their voices down. On the contrary, they seemed to be talking excessively loud. Possibly to frighten us. Suddenly they were standing above us shouting, and ordering us by signs to take off our equipment and come out.[74]

The 1/5th had reached its objective only to find itself surrounded by men from Fallschirmjäger-Brigade Ramcke and Divisione Paracadutisti 'Folgore'. The prisoners were hustled through a minefield and barbed-wire defences. Then Italian soldiers took all their equipment. Fred Daniels picked up the tale:

To our surprise an English-speaking Italian who came up shortly afterwards told us who we were and knew all about our units. During our short march to a waiting lorry, the soldiers conducting us noticed our shirt pockets and were soon searching for and confiscating fountain pens, wallets, watches and rings. We learned later that there were known cases of our chaps having fingers cut off when they refused to part with wedding and other rings of sentimental value.[75]

The paratroopers had allowed the two leading companies to get well inside their defensive system before opening fire, and then their heavy machine-gun fire had made withdrawal impossible; all had been taken prisoner, killed or wounded. Jack York, with Battalion Headquarters, was a fortunate survivor:

As a result of this action, the first to be fought by the battalion in this campaign, we lost about eight or nine officers, and nearly 300 NCOs and men. The sudden loss of so many of our comrades put the rest of us into a state of depression and low spirits, and it was a very hard task for the battalion to pull itself together.[76]

Elsewhere, both 1/7th and 1/6th battalions took all their objectives. According to Colonel Dennis Gibbs of 1/6th Battalion:

That perhaps, albeit unpleasant enough, was the easiest part of the operation. Reorganisation on the objectives in what seemed to be a very open, naked and coverless sandy arena was quite another matter. We were in that situation, pretty visible to the enemy, and under mortar and shell fire for a couple of days or so, and were then relieved. All in all the battalion did extremely well but we had several sad losses including two splendid Officers – Arthur Trench and

Jim Priestly. The former was badly wounded in assisting with his company to repel a counter-attack at night. I went forward to see him and his company. As he lay wounded he said to me, 'We really knocked them back, didn't we, Colonel?' I can remember this and his quiet, brave and almost smiling face so well.[77]

Soon after the battle, Gibbs was told of Major Trench's death:

I think this was one of the biggest shocks one sustained up to that period of the war. I had seen soldiers die and soldiers wounded; I had been at Dunkirk. I had amongst many, both military and civilian refugees, been the target of German dive-bombing, but, somehow, nothing had affected me so personally up till then as those one or two deaths in September 1942 at Deir-el-Munassib, perhaps, partly, because it was my 'command,' and deaths within it were part of me.[78]

The action of 131st Brigade at Deir-el-Munassib, coming as it did, in the build-up to Montgomery's major offensive, has not received much attention. It almost certainly influenced Montgomery's thinking regarding his attack plans and definitely reassured the Panzerarmee commanders that they still had the measure of their opponents. Like *Beresford*, it demonstrated the fighting abilities of well-led Italian troops and especially Divisione Paracadutisti 'Folgore'.

On 30 September, as Operation *Braganza* was being decisively beaten, the 'Star of Africa' fell. Flying a relatively new Messerschmitt Bf-109G, the 'ace' Hauptmann Hans-Joachim Marseille was forced to bail out when the cockpit filled with smoke from a fire in a fractured oil pipe. In doing so, he was struck by the aircraft's tail rendering him incapable of opening his parachute. At the time of his death he had 158 confirmed claims for aircraft he had shot down.[79] Yet his death, like his most successful days at the beginning of the month, did not have a significant influence on the desert campaign. The Desert Air War was already being won by Coningham's strategy, a developing superiority in numbers (if not types) of aircraft and important tactical differences between the opposing ai forces. The last of these depended on the Desert Air Force fighter pilots conducting unglamorous tasks such as escorting bombers with courage and determination. Attacks on airfields and supplies would yield, in the long run, better results than aerial combat with their opposite numbers.

Fundamentally, there was a flaw in the Luftwaffe's approach to the Desert Air War – a fact acknowledged by a fellow 'ace' from Marseille's *Gruppe* in Jagdgeschwader 27, Oberleutnant Werner Schroer:

> I think one of the great vices of the German fighters was the growth of 'free-lance hunting'. Free-lance sorties (*Freie Jagd*) against enemy fighters were the most popular missions. Perhaps we could have shot down more bombers, but it is possible that we were not too interested – they had tail gunners. I have sometimes wished I could get a Ju52 or Ju87 in front of my guns, but I never had such luck![80]

Schroer himself may have shot down as many as six fighters in a single day during September 1942 and had 114 'confirmed claims'. However, between 30 May and 4 November 1942, he was credited with having shot down just two bombers. Similarly, another 'ace' (with 59 'victories') from the same *Jagdgeschwader*, Leutnant Hans-Arnold 'Fiffi' Stahlschmidt, who was killed on a *Freie Jagd* on 7 September, never claimed a single bomber. The *Freie Jagd* may have been popular with Luftwaffe pilots, but it was losing them the Desert Air War.

CHAPTER SIX

SOMETHING OLD, SOMETHING NEW

With the Panzerarmee's defeat at Alam Halfa, matters returned to a familiar state of affairs so far as the higher direction of British military operations. The Prime Minister, Sir Winston Churchill, demanded an immediate return to the offensive by Montgomery who, in turn, sought time to absorb reinforcements and train men in the use of new equipment. Churchill wanted a British victory over Rommel before the Anglo-American landings in Algeria and Morocco planned for early November 1942. Circular arguments over the need to capture airfields in Cyrenaica by mid-November to protect convoys engaged in the continued supply of Malta and, thereby, maintain it as a threat to his enemies' supply routes, could not be ignored by Montgomery. But any attempt to overcome the Axis defences, and especially the already-extensive and growing minefields, required moonlight. The September full moon period would be too soon to complete preparations, so the fourth week of October was chosen. Crucially, Montgomery enjoyed the full support of Alexander, his immediate superior, over this matter.

By its very nature, the relatively narrow frontage with secure flanks occupied and defended by Eighth Army in July and September now served to limit options for its offensive operations. One accusation laid at their door by their adversaries was that Second World War British Army generals understood only positional warfare and not more fluid operations.[1] This, then, was an opportunity for the same generals to attack in familiar and favourable circumstances. It would be necessary to breach the strong defensive positions of the Axis forces in one or more places and then to expand rapidly through the gap made. Montgomery settled early on making two simultaneous attacks: the main one in the north and a lesser one in the south.

On 14 September, he issued his 'General Plan' for the battle – to be known as Operation *Lightfoot*.[2] The following day he discussed it with corps and divisional commanders. The plan in outline was for four infantry divisions of Lieutenant-General Sir Oliver Leese's XXX Corps (9th Australian, 51st (Highland), 2nd New Zealand and 1st South African), with massive artillery support and tanks of 23rd Armoured Brigade in close co-operation, to break the Panzerarmee defences in the northern attack, establishing bridgeheads for armoured operations. Immediately, the armour of Lieutenant-General Herbert Lumsden's X Corps would go through passages cleared in the minefields and take up position on the Axis supply routes, provoking the intervention and, hopefully, consequent destruction of the German and Italian tanks. In the south, the tasks of Lieutenant-General Brian Horrocks' XIII Corps, including 7th Armoured Division, were explained by Montgomery to his protégé, Harding:

> 7th Armoured Division was on the south flank – the left flank. The task that I [Harding] was given would be to launch an attack against the enemy's position on my front working up from the south from Himeimat which was a particularly awkward feature northwards, primarily to hold the German armour down there and prevent them from being able to be moved north to take part in holding the main offensive. I was told personally by Monty: 'Your job is to keep 21 Panzer down here by offensive action but, at the same time, to keep your division in being so that it can take part in a further offensive, in pursuit or whatever, later on.' So it was 'Heads you win, tails I lose'.[3]

Amongst Eighth Army's most senior commanders many had served on the Western Front in the Great War.[4] This had grounded them in the necessary principles for dealing with an enemy well-established in prepared positions of strength incorporating sophisticated defensive techniques. The German *Teufelsgarten* ('Devil's Garden') minefields and wire defences were not the 1918 Hindenburg Line, but those who had been part of Haig's British Expeditionary Force (BEF) – including Montgomery – knew, as a consequence of their experience, what was necessary. As liaison officer Carol Mather recognized:

Monty's idea, we thought, initially, was going back to the First World War. It was really. He was the first person to make proper use of artillery. He concentrated the artillery. The divisional artillery or the corps artillery. Previous to that the artillery had been used in 'penny packets' and 'jock columns' and small battle groups and this kind of thing.[5]

Positional warfare offered an ideal opportunity for the concentration of artillery resources under divisional, corps or even army command. Montgomery had a very capable senior artilleryman in Brigadier Sidney Kirkman (who had replaced the unfairly sacked Noel Martin), but he now took a close personal interest in the development of the artillery plan for his battle. This task was assigned by Kirkman to Brigadier Bryan 'Frizz' Fowler, Commander Royal Artillery (CRA) of 1st Armoured Division, and a hand-picked group of artillerymen, including Major Brian Wyldbore-Smith (otherwise known as 'Madcow-Jones'). The 'first class' Fowler was 'very experienced – [he] knew the desert backwards and he'd been a gunner all his life'.[6] Nevertheless, Montgomery continually shaped the process as the plan was developed. Brian Wyldbore-Smith recounted:

He gave us what his plans were and we then made a plan to support each of those attacks which we submitted to him and he then amended as he saw fit: 'No, I want more guns on here and less guns on here and more artillery fire and a longer and a deeper artillery barrage here'. Every single regiment – of which there were probably 30 regiments – each had in writing what its role was in the fire plan [with] variations in case there was a difference in how the battle went. It was vast – must have been about 30, 40 or 50 pages, I should think.[7]

Working around a single table the artillery planners continually refined arrangements:

You worked as a team. You'd say 'Let's deal with Attack A', which was the attack on the coast, and then you'd produce a plan for that. Then you'd see what you'd got left available for Attack B, which was the one inland. Then you'd say 'we've got a bit too much in the north than in the south' and you'd try and adjust it. Then you'd have to save something for eventualities. You'd go on like that till you'd got a plan. You'd produce a first draft, give that to the CRA and he'd alter it or approve it and that would go to Monty's headquarters.[8]

Appropriately, given that more than twenty years had elapsed, the technical and mathematical aspects of gunnery had become more sophisticated since the Great War. Yet their importance to the weapon's successful use would have been well understood by artillerymen of the earlier conflict. Advances always aimed, essentially, at improvements in accuracy and effectiveness. For Montgomery, 'the concentration of artillery and mortars [was] a battle-winning factor of the first importance'.[9] Hence his desire for centralized command of his army's artillery: concentration of resources, but also concentration of impact. Thus the artillery plan ultimately had a sophistication that included synchronization from the BBC time signal and calculations to ensure that shells from guns of all calibres fell on their targets at precisely the same time, but was still based on important principles such as gun calibration, and meteorological checks.[10]

A creeping artillery barrage had been employed for Operation *Braganza* in late September and was championed for the coming attack by Lieutenant-General Sir Bernard Freyberg and his CRA, Brigadier C.E. 'Steve' Weir. Weir remains a highly regarded artillery tactician but it is remarkable that this is based, at least in part, not on innovation but on a return to principles of artillery use tried and tested in the Great War and, specifically, his reintroduction of the creeping barrage at Alamein. Whilst ultimately chiefly employed in this attack as a directional aid to the infantry, its use depended on 25-pounders calibrated for the greatest level of accuracy to minimize risk of casualties amongst the attacking infantry.

The artillery depended on accurate maps. Most of these were made by 512 Field Survey Company and 46 South African Survey Company. A drawing section of 514 Field Survey Company was attached, principally for locating and plotting enemy battery positions on specially prepared 1/25,000 scale maps. The maps would be used by the counter-battery organization for concentrating artillery fire onto Axis gun positions and defences. Meanwhile, this counter-battery work of locating enemy gun batteries for them to be 'silently registered' and targeted at Zero, began in earnest. This was helped by a flaw in their opponents' methods, as highlighted by Captain Vero Bosazza of 19th South African Field Park Company:

In September, the Artillery must have drawn attention to the fact that the Axis artillery and particularly the 88mms either did not have alternate positions, or did not use them. The 88mms positions with desultory fire were easily identified. Sometime before this, a British Survey Company officer came up and helped us with 'secret' and unmarked (except for a steel pin), trig. stations far forward. At the same time, tubular scaffolding towers were erected, one being near the ruins on the Springbok Road, another further south and a low one, on the Alamein Ridge. Their headquarters were an underground plotting office in the 9th Australian lines.[11]

The flash-spotters were from 4th (Durham) Survey Regiment (RA). One of these was Captain Jack Scollen:

Flash-spotting began, with theodolites set up on steel towers erected by the Royal Engineers to give as much forward visibility as possible over the flattish desert. Headquarters plotted the bearings to enemy gun-flashes which were reported by the OPs and passed on the resulting locations to the Counter-Battery Officer. But, apart from occasional shelling, there was a strangely quiet atmosphere as preparations proceeded for the next battle. Here and there in our area there were dummy guns, carefully camouflaged as though they were the real thing, but there was a policy of artillery silence to deny the enemy, as far as possible, information about our actual artillery positions.[12]

Captain Vero Bosazza regularly visited the survey unit as its work progressed:

Most of their work was done at night but they maintained a 24-hour watch and gradually built up what no Army Commander wants his enemy to do: an accurate plot of the order of battle of almost his complete artillery.[13]

This vital work depended to a great extent on the scaffolding towers which, to Bosazza's amazement, remained untouched throughout September and October:

The remarkable thing about these towers is that they were distinctly visible, with a sandbagged position for the observer at the top. To make the towers stable, they were very well guyed with steel cables and I doubt whether they could have been knocked down by arty fire. I doubt whether the Axis Commanders ever really appreciated what was being done from these towers, for I think much more determined efforts by Stukas or direct fire from '88s' would have been attempted. After all, the top of these towers presented to an '88' no more difficult a target than say a stationary tank.[14]

Artillery was vital to Montgomery's plan and all these preparations were intended to ensure that when the attack opened, the Royal Artillery would immediately establish fire superiority.

As his corps and divisional commanders set to work to develop detailed plans, Montgomery devolved much of the planning to four key men. His close interest in the artillery planning should not diminish the important role of Sidney Kirkman, whom he had brought out with him from Britain. Kirkman had overall responsibilities beyond the artillery plan and the medium- and field- artillery, and these included co-ordination between artillery formations across Eighth Army. The other men were his chief of staff, Brigadier Freddie de Guingand; the Chief Engineer, Brigadier Frederick Kisch; and Brigadier Sir Brian Robertson, the head of administration.[15]

Guingand was responsible for co-ordination of operational planning across all of Eighth Army, whilst Kisch and his sappers applied themselves to the many practicalities of the forthcoming assault and especially the problem of getting through the minefield defences. Robertson's work was critical for the forthcoming battle. The tenacious, dour and ruthless 'business manager'[16] was responsible for the army's logistical arrangements – including the supply of petrol, oil and lubricants (POL), the provision of motor transport, the establishment of prisoner of war cages, the creation of forward dumps and the stockpiling of supplies. Great stocks of ammunition were accumulated and hidden in the sand at pre-determined, but as yet unoccupied, gun positions. Robertson demonstrated an ability to address a problem's scale with a proportionate solution. An example was his requisitioning of all captured German 'jerrycans' – the 'excellent stout returnables with a hinged, air-sealing, levered stopper'[17] used for transporting petrol. They were given to X Corps so that its tank operations would not be impeded by fuel shortages caused by using British petrol 'flimsies' which had a tendency to leak.[18]

Montgomery himself preferred to be out and about. He spent a great deal of time visiting troops who were training, and talking with corps, divisional and battalion commanders and, often, with their officers and men. Towards the end of September, he acquired a 'Personal Protection Force' consisting of a troop of Grant tanks, a troop of anti-tank guns, and an infantry company. This force was intended to defend Eighth Army GHQ in the event of a German commando raid, like one the British had attempted on Rommel's headquarters in November 1941.

Montgomery's own Grant became his frequent mode of transport in the forward areas. Sergeant Stephen Kennedy of 1st/6th RTR recalled:

> Each day, the General would visit Corps Headquarters from GHQ. He didn't want his generals to come back to him. He would go forward to them. We would go off earlier on and wait for him just at Tel el Eisa, which was in the Australian area. We would wait by the side of the road. He would come along after a while in his staff car and then get into the tank and go into the desert to meet up with corps HQ – to meet up with the other generals – which was within range of the enemy.[19]

It was Kennedy and his crew who were responsible for Montgomery's famous two-badged beret, which he subsequently frequently wore (in defiance of army regulations). According to Kennedy:

> We heard the General was wearing an Australian hat and it was blowing off. They say Corporal Fraser, the driver, said 'You can have my beret'. If this happened, so well it be, but they asked his ADC [aide-de-camp], Captain Poston, 11th Hussars, would the General wear a beret? He said 'I'll ask him' and our Lieutenant got permission from the ADC that he would wear a beret. They also asked him would he wear the badge of the regiment and he said he would. They were able to order a brand new beret with the badge in and Corporal Fraser, who was the one he thanked for driving him, stepped forward and said 'General, will you wear our beret?' He'd already been tuned in and knew the form and he said 'Of course I will'. He wore the beret that day and the next day he appeared in that beret and he had his general's badge beside it. He's probably the only general in the army who had two badges.[20]

If Montgomery's Australian hat could be dismissed as flamboyantly idiosyncratic, his new headgear was a statement challenging anyone who still questioned his authority; an army commander did things his way.

Alexander, as Commander-in-Chief, maintained close contact with Montgomery through the simple expedient of setting up a small advanced base close to Eighth Army Headquarters. He visited Montgomery often during this period, offering his assistance in overcoming difficulties but, otherwise, not intervening in any way. With Air Vice-Marshal Coningham's Desert Air Force Headquarters also at Burg-el-Arab, the land and air commands were co-located, even when the commanders themselves were frequently not.

In Montgomery's plan it was essential that X Corps got beyond the Axis minefields by first light. In preparation for the battle, both armoured divisions of the corps (1st and 10th) had been taken out of the line, reorganized, and given opportunities to train. For the training, special areas had been marked out to represent the minefields and defences, though giving no indication of where the actual place would be 'on the night'. Sergeant Fred Hunn, 12th Lancers, recalled:

> We had to train at going through the minefields in darkness as though we were attacking. It was all preparation and training so we could move at night as though it was more or less second nature. They had the minefield all taped and they'd simulate the minefield being cleared and there'd be tape with little lights, little red lights that could show – not from the enemy side but facing you – and you could then motor through them. This was done with all the tanks, the whole division would then go forward. We [the armoured cars] would then follow through ready for when the tanks would break out and, once the breakout had been accomplished, we would take up our role of going forward shooting up any transport, or whatever and following the enemy up.[21]

The process of creating armoured divisions as 'divisions of all arms', which had begun before Alam Halfa, was still going on. Amidst a host of other changes, 7th Motor Brigade's move to 1st Armoured Division created some resentment at being transferred from 'the Desert Rats', as Rifleman Reg Crimp observed:

> Training is strenuous, and there are many portents of approaching action. All the other camps in the area are now filled with infantry, tank and artillery units. A large draft arrived yesterday from Geneifa to bring this Battalion up to full strength. Evidently a purge has been going on lately at the base, combing out surplus personnel, and many faces I haven't seen for months are now re-appearing. The anti-tank company has been re-equipped with the latest, and much more formidable, 6-pounder guns, in place of their piddling 2-pounders. Quite a lot of new trucks have been drawn to replace our desert-weary veterans, and new signs are being painted on all vehicles as a result of our now belonging

to another division; the old red jerboa on the white circular field, famous badge of the Desert Rats, having had to give way to a white rhinoceros on a black oval field – the 'pregnant pig', as some of our fellows, regretful of the change, scornfully describe it.[22]

Reorganization and training in the armoured divisions had been intended to be complimentary. They were nothing of the kind. The transfer of 7th Motor Brigade was to help create an armoured formation akin to the German model. However, the integration of the motorized infantry and armour could not happen overnight. It took time.

At the same time, Auchinleck's scheme for concentrating tanks by their types in the various formations was still being implemented. This entailed many transfers as the squadrons received new or reconditioned tanks. Every commander did his best to acquire the newly arrived Shermans in place of the Grants or Crusaders. However, even some of the units allocated Shermans were not happy, as Lance-Corporal Mick Collins of the Wiltshire Yeomanry, found:

> We got our tanks but they were not the brand new Shermans that Winston Churchill had said we were to have. The tanks were certainly not in their first flush of youth as they had been taken over from American armoured units and consequently had considerable mileage on their clocks. So much for promises, but at least they were of the latest type even if they were well-worn.[23]

Even less happy was Captain Stuart Hamilton of 8th RTR:

> Imagine our great disappointment when we were informed that we were not going to get the new Sherman tank but that we were to be re-equipped, once again, with blasted Valentines with their pathetic little 2-pdr pop-gun, and that we would be joining the 23rd Armoured Brigade. It was reckoned that the forthcoming battle was going to be a very tough one indeed and that they should have the backing of a battle-experienced Valentine Tank Regiment.[24]

Against this background, training in X Corps was necessarily basic and disjointed and the *corps de chasse* remained far from being in the shape Montgomery wanted. Some close to Montgomery felt that the root of many problems was the attitude of the corps commander. Carol Mather commented:

> I think he [Lumsden] felt this was a misuse of his armour. He wasn't really convinced that the plan was the right use of armour. That's why I think he was reluctant. He didn't agree with the strategy.[25]

However, as Mather admitted, Lumsden and his divisional commanders all had genuine and complex concerns about the planned operations.

> He was being 'sticky', but one must remember that the armoured troops had suffered terribly in the desert up to that moment. The number of tanks and lives lost was very high. We were continually suffering from the fact that we were outgunned by the Germans and when they started using the 88 millimetre anti-aircraft guns in a ground role, of course, they by far outgunned us. The armour commanders were very sensitive as to how the armour was to be used. They didn't want to be exposed to being sitting ducks in the front line.[26]

There was general apprehension amongst the armoured unit commanders about the possibility of getting their tanks and, very importantly, the vehicles needed to keep them supplied, through the minefields in one night. Training exercises confirmed their fears. Experience of the July battles also led them to doubt the infantry's ability to clear a path through the minefields in sufficiently quick time for their armour to pass through. More pertinently, however, they did not attempt to test this in their exercises – which focused on the problems of manoeuvring at night and retaining order. Exercises began with the *assumption* that XXX Corps had done its job.

Neither Lumsden nor Leese worked to bridge this gap in the training. Leese had only recently assumed command of XXX Corps from Ramsden after the Alam Halfa battle, and on arrival in Egypt, 'had been horrified at the controversy between infantry and armour', noting 'neither had confidence in the other'.[27] Nevertheless, he did not address this schism. Yet amongst his divisions the suspicion that the armoured leaders were likely to act too cautiously was so strong that Morshead, Pienaar and Freyberg, the three 'Commonwealth commanders', approached Leese to express their concerns. With no first-hand experience of the Desert War, and an unwillingness to believe that the armour would not follow Montgomery's orders to the letter, Leese took the matter no further. His over-simplistic analysis was that the armoured divisions were too worried about mines and the 88mm anti-tank guns.[28] Much criticism has been levelled over this matter at Lumsden, but at least some should also be directed at Leese and also at Montgomery and Guingand for not insisting on closer corps co-operation. This was, after all, one of Eighth Army Headquarters' chief roles.

The exception to this lack of trust in infantry–armour relations was in 2nd New Zealand Division where 9th Armoured Brigade, commanded by John Currie, became an organic component of Freyberg's division. Trooper Len Flanakin of the Warwickshire Yeomanry remembered:

> We settled down with the 2 NZ Division very well and found them to be a jovial lot. They were tough as soldiers but a damn sight tougher on the rugby field. They accepted us for who we were... General Montgomery paid us a visit while we were at 'Happy Valley' and I shall always remember him referring to us as 'wonderful material'.[29]

Flanakin's remark about rugby indicates the work being done in a crucial aspect of infantry–armour co-operation. Freyberg went further still in pursuit of effective collaboration, as Howard Kippenberger recalled:

> The General gave a dinner party in Alexandria to the senior officers of the Division and of 9 Armoured Brigade, and it can be said that thereby a lot of reserve and shyness was broken down. The regiments put the New Zealand fern-leaf, our distinctive emblem, on their tanks and vehicles. We were pleased that they were clearly proud to wear it. We sent our men to examine and admire their Shermans, and our bands to play at their ceremonial parades and church services. We called on one another at every opportunity and got to know as many individuals and personalities as possible.[30]

In the Great War, the benefits of 'social activities' which followed the 'formal' training exercises to successful co-operation between infantry and tank crews had been recognized, since they fostered a stronger empathy between the two arms which, in turn, encouraged teamwork.[31] But, above all, the two arms 'trained together, did TEWTs, and prepared and carried out exercises together.'[32] The six weeks of training granted to the New Zealanders and 9th Armoured were used to good purpose and contrasted with 23rd Armoured Brigade's disastrous introduction to battle back in July.

Both Leese and Lumsden were present at an exercise conducted by the New Zealanders and their attached armour which ran from 24–27 September and from which Freyberg concluded that 'considerably more collective training would have to be undertaken before the tanks and infantry could work as one.'[33] But, whilst Freyberg trained his division to address the problem, the lessons were not applied elsewhere.

Amongst XXX Corps infantry, the training opportunities were harder to come by. Both 1st South African and 9th Australian Divisions were in the front line. Consequently, brigades were withdrawn from these positions and trained in turn. In 51st Division, Major-General Douglas Wimberley was guided by the principles he had learned from his Great War mentor:

> It was very necessary that every man should go into his first action knowing exactly what he had to do. I had had that lesson well drummed into me by the teaching of 'Uncle' Harper, our General, in 1917 at Ypres and Cambrai, and there was no time to be lost in practising![34]

A small proportion of Wimberley's command was also in the front line. But here they were receiving valuable instruction in the techniques of desert warfare from the Australians:

> Our officers in the line were attached to Australian officers, our sergeants to their sergeants, if the Australians sent out patrols they were composed of a mixture of Aussies and Jocks under instruction. We were very fortunate in our instructors. They were veteran troops and they could not have been kinder to us.[35]

Wimberley laid out an exact replica of the defences his men would face in the coming attack. Then each brigade practised its battalions in their role in the initial attack. Wimberley strove for realism in the training:

> I used our Divisional artillery to fire the exact barrage they would have to fire in the battle, at the same rate and with the same pauses for leap-frogging. Meanwhile Divisional Signals carried out the same outline plan, reporting the capture of objectives: and the Sappers did their clearing of mines through dummy minefields, of what we believed were the same breadth as the ones we had actually to gap in the battle.[36]

Attempts to create realistic conditions in the largest of his division's exercises (this time involving both 153rd and 154th Brigades covered by the divisional artillery), tested the infantry's mettle but, unfortunately, led to the death of the second-in-command of 1st Black Watch, Major Arthur Wilmot, mortally wounded by an artillery 'short'. Private Frank Devaney of the 1st Black Watch remembered:

> We did mock attacks with live artillery. They tried to do something they'd never done before. They tried with a 50-yard lift. To walk behind it – this curtain of fire – to ensure that we were on the objective before Jerry could get his head up and man his machine-guns, etc. [Then] the whole thing was revised. The reason why it was altered was because the second in command at HQ was killed by a shell – Sir Arthur Wilmer [sic]. They said it would have to be done with a hundred yards' lift. Even a hundred yards' lift was terrific. Can you imagine these 800 guns firing a hundred yards just in front of you when you're walking forward as close as you probably can? The idea was that we could walk so close as when a 25-pounder strikes, all the blast goes forward so you can be as tight as you like up behind that curtain of fire. It's not affecting you but everything is affecting everybody in front of it, but you're getting the concussion, you're getting the noise. You're getting it coming down over the top of you. The projectiles are coming lower and they swish.[37]

Opportunities to train were welcome, but the training focused narrowly on the tasks required to get through the Panzerarmee defences. As in the planning, no thinking was directed towards the detail of the hoped-for exploitation.

On 6 October, Montgomery modified the battle plan.[38] The revised plan aimed at the methodical destruction of the Panzerarmee through 'crumbling' operations aimed at the Axis infantry after XXX Corps had made bridgeheads in the defences. In Montgomery's colourful expression, the attackers having 'eaten the guts out of the enemy', the Germans and Italians would be unable to hold their positions. If the Afrika Korps attempted to interfere by launching counter-attacks, this would play into the hands of the numerically superior Eighth Army. With the line-holding infantry destroyed, the Afrika Korps could not avoid destruction anyway. Montgomery's tone was now altogether more cautious and warned that 'we should keep well within ourselves, and should not attempt ambitious operations beyond the capabilities of our somewhat untrained troops'.[39] This change in approach was influenced by intelligence analysis of the likely Panzerarmee response to a surprise attack. Montgomery's stated reason was the inadequate level of Eighth Army's training.

Many of the plan's most ambitious elements were unchanged. At a corps conference the following day, the continued expectation that the armour of X Corps would, and must, break through the minefields in one night was again debated. Lumsden, despite his own strong opinions on the approach, dutifully reflected the Army Commander's views during the discussions but allowed consideration of an alternative approach by which the armoured operations started a night after XXX Corps had seized the bridgeheads. Guingand, who was present, afterwards told Montgomery of the armoured commanders' continued unhappiness with the plan. Montgomery moved to quash the continued rumblings of discontent, forcefully telling Lumsden that his orders allowed no latitude in interpretation.

Montgomery continued to suggest that the state of training had been his principal reason for changes in the plan, going even further to indicate where the inadequacies might be, when it was appropriate for his audience. According to Kippenberger:

> The Army Commander called together all officers of the rank of brigadier and above. With a big map he explained his plan for the battle and his view of the way it would be fought, in four phases: 'the break in, the dog-fight, the breakthrough, and the exploitation'. All the infantry brigadiers were a little maliciously pleased when he said that he had altered his plan after seeing that the armour was not trained.[40]

Kippenberger's account suggests an even closer correlation between Montgomery's *four* phases of the planned battle and the four necessary stages of war which, according to Field Marshal Sir Douglas Haig, 'have marked all the conclusive battles of history'.[41] These were: the manoeuvre for position, the first clash of battle, the wearing-out fight and the decisive blow.[42] The influence of their Staff College training on the military theories of both men was clear.

Montgomery also visited 1st South African Division's headquarters to allay Major-General Dan Pienaar's concerns regarding the likely casualties to his division in the attack. Their meeting, as recounted by Carol Mather, provided an example of the value of Montgomery's ebullient and confident public persona:

> The South Africans had very few men on the ground. Getting reinforcements was quite difficult. Pienaar was casualty conscious. The South Africans it has to be said had had a pretty good beating on several occasions. They'd lost a lot of men.

Pienaar started saying to me that he didn't believe in this plan of Monty's. I didn't think that was a very good 'ord group' for a battle and then he started drawing figures in the sand showing how he would have done it. The next moment Monty arrived and they disappeared into this dugout. Monty came out saying 'Splendid chap, splendid chap. He wants to kill as many Germans as possible!'[43]

In a coalition force like Eighth Army, it was vital that good relations were maintained with the commanders and troops of all the nations. Both Montgomery and Leese excelled at this work in the weeks before the battle.

In July 1942, Eighth Army's operations had foundered repeatedly on the ability of the engineers to deal with mines. Yet, only two months later, in planning for the Alamein battle, there was tacit acceptance that the problems posed by mines could be overcome. Chiefly, efforts were directed towards providing the means for this task to be accomplished as swiftly as possible, and educating men about the relative risks of the various types of mines. Progress was due to a variety of factors, but the influence of Brigadier Frederick Kisch was especially important.

In August, Kisch had co-ordinated analysis of Eighth Army's experiences of mine-clearing operations and, from this and training exercises and experiments, distilled the key lessons. He now selected the man he thought capable of tackling the task of minefield clearance which, he recognized, would form an essential part of the work of Royal Engineers in all future offensive operations. Major Peter Moore of 3rd (Cheshire) Field Squadron, Royal Engineers, had just left hospital when he was told Kisch had a job for him.

He got me into his caravan and told me that I was to open the Eighth Army School of Minefield Clearance. He said that the nature of the Desert War had changed. There was no longer an open flank. There were continuous deep minefields right across our front and that we were to be prepared to force our way through it against heavy opposition. There must be a drill for clearing mines just as there was a drill for the loading and firing of field guns. The old methods of detailing a sub-unit, giving them a mine detector or two and telling them to get on with it were all right for clearing minefields not under fire or those met during a night approach march, for extricating vehicles from our own minefields or for getting through very shallow minefields. The lack of a uniform method had led to divisional engineers being asked to perform impossible tasks or being asked to make gaps which were quite inadequate for the tactical operations in view.[44]

Moore's brief was to define a standard method for minefield clearance that could be taught at an Eighth Army School of Mine Clearance, which he was to establish at Burg-el-Arab. This School's work was soon seen as sufficiently important for it to merit a visit from Montgomery, as Moore recounted:

> We had a good commander who wouldn't ask us to do more than was reasonable and generally an air of confidence grew up. Not least was the fact that the army commander himself came to this quite small unit that had just been formed. This created a very favourable impression on all ranks. All I can say was that he was like a tonic.[45]

Two technological innovations had been devised in time for use at Alamein and the School worked with both. The first, and most important, was a reliable portable mine detector, of which the most noted example was invented by a Polish officer, Józef Stanisław Kosacki. This was capable of detecting mines with some degree of accuracy and 500 Mine Detectors No 2 (Polish) and other types were rushed to the Western Desert in time for the attack. Their use dramatically increased the rate of clearance in heavily mined areas. Based on experimental use, and the evidence of the employment of detectors in earlier operations, Moore concluded that:

> the detector – except on very rocky ground or in newly laid fields was the quickest means of clearing mines and the only reliable one; the choice of ground for a gap was extremely important; that tapes were required to keep the clearance parties going straight; that the operation of the detector itself was an important skill which must also be taught as a drill.[46]

The drill eventually adopted was a mix of choreography and gradual enhancement from small beginnings.

The first task was for a 'confirming reconnaissance party', usually of five men and an officer, to find and mark the near edge of an enemy minefield. The men could walk through the minefields with little likelihood of setting off the anti-tank mines but the reconnaissance party 'had to find and neutralize any tripwire-operated [anti-personnel] S-Mines as these with their hundreds of steel balls were murder to detector operators who had to stand up and swing their detectors' coils in front of them'. Having gone through, the far edge was also marked. In each case a shielded blue light facing the British lines was used. Moore described the procedure:

> Initial gaps were to be eight yards wide and these were to be widened to sixteen yards as soon as possible. Three detector men were each to sweep an eight-foot lane and were to be echeloned back at ten-yard intervals. This echeloning back was most important. It ensured that a mistake by one detector man would not write off all three. They could advance using detectors at a rate of three yards a minute or three times as fast as it took to locate mines by prodding. Each detector man had an assistant – No 2 – who paid out a tape to the left of the detector man's swing and pegged it down, put a half-inch nail through the safety pin hole of any S-mine with horns and marked all mines with a conical hat – light enough to be safe, but robust enough not to be blown away. We soon found that laying out the tapes was best left to a separate party. Altogether we required an NCO to supervise, a man – No 3 – to pull mines while everybody else lay down, a party to mark the edge of the gap with signs and coloured lights, a medical orderly and four stretcher bearers, a reserves party to replace casualties of one NCO and six sappers. Then there was an 'O i/c gap'* plus four sappers and a control party. We also needed a party carrying gap-marking stores. These were quite heavy but could be carried on the back of a Dingo Scout Car.[47]

Only the mention of a medical orderly and stretcher bearers hinted at the incredibly dangerous and stressful nature of the work. The detector men, carrying portable battery packs and wearing headphones, had to walk upright and concentrate their eyes and ears for the tell-tale indications of mines: all this under fire from shot and shell that they could not hear. These men started their task thirty yards behind the tape-layers, with the disarming and lifting parties fifty yards behind the detectors. This last group had to take particular care because of booby traps.

The ultimate aim was a 'lane' forty yards wide. Gap-marking parties placed signs on each edge of the cleared lane. Small electric torches on posts were used at night. For Alamein, each track and minefield lane would be named. These tracks were, starting from the North: Sun, Moon, Star, Bottle,

---

*   Officer in charge of gap

Boat and Hat. They were marked with signs corresponding to these names by empty petrol cans with a patterned hole cut into them and illuminated from the inside.

Eight training teams went through the Minefield Clearance School and taught seven eight-day courses each between 26 August and 20 October. By mid-October, the courses incorporated a competitive element to hone the sappers' skills. Lieutenant Robert Pearson of 276 Army Field Company recorded:

> This p.m. we have a competition – four teams of eight clearing an eight-yard gap 200 yards long of mines; missing a mine means disqualification. The Highland Div swept the board and won the sixteen bottles of beer. All very bucked because best time was fourteen minutes and worst only sixteen.[48]

The basic drill remained unchanged but refinements and improvements were made by individual divisions, as Moore described:

> Perhaps the biggest and the best of these was the establishment of a minefield clearance task force by 1st Armoured Division with an infantry battalion headquarters, a close infantry escort of at least a company, provost, line and wireless communications as well as sappers to clear the mines. This recognized the truth of the saying I heard as a young officer, 'Sappers can either work or fight; they cannot do both simultaneously'.[49]

Another advance tested by the Mine Clearance School was the 'Scorpion'. Major-General Francis 'Gertie' Tuker of 4th Indian Division noted:

> In early October we went to a demonstration of mine clearing by 'Scorpions' near Burg-el-Arab. The Scorpion was the old infantry tank stripped of its superfluities and fitted with a roller and chains to flail the ground ahead of it in order to explode the mines. These had been under design and construction for some months but it was heartening to see that we British were at last thinking in terms of machines to do the job of men.[50]

However, the Scorpions were not available in large numbers and were usually held in reserve for emergencies.

It should be stressed that not every unit required to clear mines had detectors. For those that did not, the procedure was to probe with a bayonet – a much slower method. Any approach was laden with risk from booby traps, as Frank Devaney experienced:

> If they hit anything metallic they cleared round about it and cleared underneath it because you could often get what they called an anti-personnel tripwire attached – a small barbed-like thing screwed into the base of the mine which had a small wire attached. A trigger effected a spring inside which when you lifted the mine out, this wire was locked and set off this other anti-personnel detonator which, of course, blew the whole lot up and took the RE with it.[51]

The work of all the specialists involved drew admiration, summed up by infantryman Jack York:

> These courageous men made possible the breakthrough at Alamein. In doing so they suffered wounds, hardships and disappointments – but saw their task through to the end. Perhaps they were the real heroes at Alamein.[52]

———

Further training exercises by 1st and 10th Armoured Divisions were still being carried out in mid-October, striving for a preparedness to match Montgomery's expectations for the battle. In 1st Armoured Division exercises on 12 October, after several daylight rehearsals, the whole process of passing the division including tanks, armoured cars, 25-pounders, self-propelled guns, anti-tank and anti-aircraft guns, ambulances, HQ armoured control vehicles, and infantry was tried at night and took 'about three hours'.[53] Any delay in starting, or during the advance, would be critical.

The supply of battle-ready tanks to armoured regiments was not completed until early October. Generally, opinions on the new tanks were positive, and a welcome boost to morale. Len Flanakin noted:

> More tanks arrived and gradually the Regiment became fully equipped. One Squadron had British Crusaders while B and C Squadrons had American Grant and Sherman tanks. HQ Squadron had a mixture of tanks, recce vehicles and Dingo scout cars. C Squadron, my Squadron, was equipped with Shermans, the newest of the American tanks whose main armament was a 75mm gun along with Browning machine guns of different calibre. The Sherman was a

magnificent machine. It had a stabilized turret with full 360 degree traverse while the telescopic equipment, if tested and adjusted properly, made the gun deadly accurate. Its power supply came from a nine cylinder aero engine running on high octane fuel giving a top speed of approximately 30mph.[54]

With the new tanks came new tactical possibilities – in particular those offered by the 75mm gun which could fire both armour-piercing (AP) and high explosive (HE) ammunition. Sergeant Douglas Covill of the 10th Hussars soon learned the benefits:

> This was the first time that we had a gun that was equivalent to the Germans'. We were then taught how to fire the gun properly. We had a man called Henri Le Grand who was a Belgian artillery officer – a major – attached to the squadron, and he said we don't need to fire direct; we can fire indirect. That is to say that we could lay behind a ridge and fire as long as the commander could see where the shots were going. We could then go up 200 or down 300 and we were able to do that on the sights. The gunner could do it.[55]

This was a revelation and of great importance for the coming battle. Crews adopted their new tanks, naming them and adding other personal markings, like those produced by Trooper Arthur Reddish of the Sherwood Rangers Yeomanry:

> Before the Sherman faced its baptism of fire, our commander prevailed on me to paint the 'Eye of Horus' on its side. I used a toothbrush and a mixture of sump oil and boot polish. The sign was said to be lucky. But years later, I learned the Ancient Egyptians put the 'Eye' on coffins to allow the soul of the departed to peer through![56]

About 100 Crusader Mark IIIs equipped with 6-pounder guns in place of the 2-pounders on earlier marks were also available. This provided the less heavily armoured tanks with more firepower. However, the tank proved mechanically temperamental, perpetuating the poor reputation of British tanks amongst the units equipped with them. The first few Churchill Mark III 'Infantry' tanks – intended eventually to replace the Valentine – had also arrived in August 1942. In the same month it had been decided to create a separate organization for the vital work of tank and vehicle maintenance, repair and recovery; the creation of the Royal Electrical and Mechanical Engineers on 1 October was timely and the nature of the change was not disruptive to preparations.

Other new armoured fighting vehicles (AFVs) also appeared but these were for service with the Royal Artillery. The '105mm Self Propelled Gun, Priest' with its pulpit-like machine-gun position was the most important. The ninety available presented a logistical problem because their 105mm gun required ammunition not in use elsewhere in Eighth Army. Approximately eighty British-made 'Ordnance QF 25-pdr on Carrier Valentine 25-pdr Mk 1', universally known as the 'Bishop', were also available. The 'Bishop' was disliked because of its high-profile silhouette, but both weapons, significantly, offered mobile firepower to support armoured operations.

By October 1942, the Royal Artillery was better equipped for its many roles on the battlefield than at any point since 1940. There were 849 6-pounder anti-tank guns, and 554 2-pounders, in service. The Anti-Tank Regiments, with sixty-four 6-pounders in armoured formations and forty-eight in infantry formations, offered a strong, primarily defensive, capability. The fact that each motorized infantry battalion also had sixteen of the new guns increased the all-arms armoured division's options in the attack.[57]

What was more important for the attack against prepared positions was the availability of the BL 5.5-inch Medium Gun to supplement the 4.5-inch gun already in service. Although present only in small numbers, both Medium guns (like the 6-pounder anti-tank gun), freed the 25-pounders from tasks for which they were ill-suited. They excelled in counter-battery work beyond the range of the 25-pounders. Aware that the Eighth Army's few Medium Regiments could not deal with all the hostile batteries, twenty-five such Italian and German formations were prioritized as targets.[58] The 25-pounders would focus on firing the creeping barrage and concentrations on strongpoints, etc.

Under Kirkman, Eighth Army's artillery had also worked to develop its Defensive Fire (DF) techniques still further with the onomatopoeic 'stonk' – a reinvention of the Great War 'Zone Call'. Howard Kippenberger recorded:

The practice had developed of having defensive fire tasks prepared, code-named, and issued to gunners, infantry, and armour, before any operations. With that system the infantry could get a 'stonk' wherever it was wanted within three or four minutes of asking for 'Napier' or 'Nelson' or whatever the appropriate code word might be. The quickest I remember was two and a half minutes.[59]

As the battle's start drew near, the close co-operation of the Desert Air Force grew in importance. A superficially impressive 736 aircraft, of which 420 were fighters, had few aircraft capable of matching the Messerschmitt Bf-109Fs and Gs with which the Luftwaffe in Egypt was equipped. This sometimes required fighter squadron leaders to make the best use of available equipment by combining tactical changes with half-truths, as did Lieutenant-Colonel (Squadron Leader) Cyril Gardner of 40 Squadron, South African Air Force:

> During the first ten days of September we worked at re-equipping and revitalising the Squadron. I arranged to be supplied with new Hurricane IIs, not the clapped-out Tomahawks and Kittyhawks that had been provisionally allocated. We set about training the pilots in the tactics to use when 'bounced' by enemy fighters. I also introduced as a firm policy a 'Pairs, line abreast' system of doing tactical reconnaissance, as opposed to the rather pointless 'Line astern'. We also suggested to our trainees that the German fighter pilots were just as nervous at the thought of combat with the Hurricanes and their machine-guns, and were unlikely to press home an attack if our pair kept a good look-out, and looked alert and aggressive. As the 109s invariably flew higher, and were undoubtedly faster, in level flight, and in the dive, this advice was received with a certain amount of scepticism. But the tactical training and demonstrations were, quite clearly, a morale-booster.[60]

In the hands of experienced pilots like Billy Drake, however, even the Curtiss P-40 Kittyhawk could give a good account of itself against the best Axis aircraft. The aircraft was used in a variety of roles including 'air superiority' fighter (fundamental to Air Vice-Marshal Coningham's doctrine of tactical air power), bomber escort and fighter bomber. Drake's principal reputation was as a fighter 'ace'. Many of his victims were Junkers 87 'Stukas' crews:

> In each case they would be against formations of about 20 Stukas with a number of '109s' guarding them. They were, particularly for the leader, fairly easy targets. One just got behind them, fired, and then waited for them to either explode or catch fire or something and then gently ease away from that attack – as against the few occasions in France and the Battle of Britain where life was so hectic that one just shot at something and then moved away because someone was shooting at you. You did your best to do [the rear gunner] in at the same time as the aeroplane itself. I wouldn't have been a Stuka rear gunner for all the tea in China.[61]

In the lead-up to the offensive Drake's squadron of Kittyhawks operated in all three roles.

> Quite a few of our trips were in that role of fighter escort. It was a brand new role so we weren't quite certain how to do it. So my first thoughts were not to do what the Germans did in the Battle of Britain – formate closely with the bomber forces – but to be in the area. That was our method of protecting the light bombers agreed by their commanders as well. As a floating air cover.[62]

This flexibility on the part of the 'fighters' was matched by the efficiency of the medium bombers in their regular formations which attacked airfields and landing grounds by day and night to keep the Luftwaffe and Regio Aeronautica under pressure. Nightly medium and heavy bomber raids by aircraft from the Desert Air Force and United States Army Air Force against Tobruk and Benghazi were also undertaken. Air operations followed Coningham's model for tactical air power. Hurricanes of Nos 6 and 7 Squadrons, South African Air Force, were also now equipped with 40mm 'cannon' to act as 'tankbusters'. However, the need for surprise meant that a more aggressive approach had to be tempered until land operations commenced.

A remarkable amount of work in planning and delivering Montgomery's attack was expended on the deception plan – Operation *Bertram* (actually consisting of many sub-plans). Its intention was to convince the Panzerarmee that the main effort would come in the southern sector of the line, as it often had done in previous attacks, as well as disguising preparations by X Corps for the northern attack. This work was co-ordinated by Lieutenant-Colonel Charles Richardson, GSO1 (Plans) at Eighth Army. Thus, supply dumps were camouflaged or buried, and dummy supply centres were mocked up in the southern sector. Guns and tanks were concealed in assembly and battle positions using 'sunshields' or 'cannibals' which made them appear as 'soft-skinned' i.e. unarmoured vehicles. According to Brigadier George Davy:

> The real armoured divisions were withdrawn from their forward positions behind the right of the line and dummies were skilfully erected approximately in the same area, where the armour was to be concentrated for the eventual offensive. The actual armour was placed for training some 80 miles behind the

front. It was hoped that the Germans would get used to the sight of both lots of armour so that when, a few days before the offensive, the tanks and the dummies began to change places, no difference would be noticed and no suspicions be aroused of the impending attack.[63]

Large unit concentrations were ostentatiously formed behind XIII Corps in the south by the real move of tanks and vehicles from 10th Armoured Division. More dummy vehicles were constructed from canvas and steel when these units moved again to their real assembly positions.

Deception had been a crucial part of successful operations such as the Battle of Amiens in August 1918 and, consequently, Montgomery was well aware of its potential value. Wireless deception, also a feature of Amiens, was used to suggest that 8th Armoured Division – already disbanded and its units dispersed to other formations – was fully functioning and preparing an attack. Meanwhile, in an important but often forgotten parallel strand, Lieutenant-Colonel Dudley Clarke was responsible for the deliberate passing of false information concerning Allied intentions to the Italians and Germans by controlled and captured agents.[64]

The extent to which this massive undertaking genuinely deceived the Panzerarmee's senior commanders is difficult to assess. Evidence suggests that some measures did succeed. Certainly Heinz Werner Schmidt remembers that:

> He deceived us by starting to lay a new pipe line, complete with pumping stations, away in the south. Its completion was deliberately prolonged, and it began to look as though some time must pass before the Eighth Army could mount what seemed to be obviously an offensive planned in the southern sector of the El Alamein line. Air reconnaissance could not reveal that the pipe line was a dummy constructed out of old petrol tins.[65]

However, in the weeks prior to the battle, there was no significant redeployment of Panzerarmee units in response to these efforts. The German–Italian forces were already committed to a defensive plan prepared in outline by Rommel before he departed on sick leave to Germany on 22 September. His replacement, General der Kavallerie Georg Stumme, and his senior German subordinate commander, General der Panzertruppen Wilhelm von Thoma, both understood and adhered to this plan.

The defensive preparations were not completed until 20 October. Under them, the Panzerarmee weakened and deepened its advanced defensive positions – concentrating on deployment around company strongpoints – and deployed Italian and German infantry together in front of extensive minefield 'boxes' which were designed to confine an attacking force until counter-attacked by Axis armour. In the north, a further line of defence was formed by large numbers of anti-tank guns near the Rahman Track.

The British characterized the mixed deployment as 'corsetting'. It was, in fact, unnecessary in the case of Divisione Paracadutisti 'Folgore' and the *Bersaglieri* units, whilst the armoured formations were grouped together as mobile reserves to increase their power in the counterattack: 15. Panzer-Division and Divisione 'Littorio' in the north, 21. Panzer-Division and Divisione 'Ariete' in the south. Its disadvantage was in its effects on the Italian formations' command and control structures since, on many occasions, they received no direct orders or information and were obliged to conform to sudden movements by their German 'partners'.

Stumme, like Rommel, had hoped to hit the British hard before they could launch an offensive but, in the absence of any such opportunity arising before Eighth Army attacked, he (like Rommel) placed much faith in the *Teufelsgarten* and hoped the attack's defeat might, in turn, lead to a successful advance on Alexandria.[66]

Gradually, details of the plan were made known through the ranks of Eighth Army: brigadiers, corps and divisional Royal Engineers commanders – 29 September; colonels and majors – 10 October; captains and subalterns – 17 October; NCOs and 'other ranks' – 21–22 October. Montgomery gave a final address to his regimental commanders at the Amariya Cinema on 19 October. He repeated it the next day. Its effect on those present was unforgettable, according to Lieutenant-Colonel Cecil Lucas Phillips of 102nd (Northumberland Hussars) Anti-Tank Regiment:

> To many it was a day of revelation. It was the day Montgomery finally and firmly impressed upon the Army not only his professional personality but also the inevitability of victory. In a rapt silence the gatherings of officers – sunburnt, experienced, not easily impressionable, most of them already proved leaders, many of them bearing upon their persons or their clothing the scars and emblems of hard service – listened to that incisive, rather metallic, completely matter-of-fact voice telling them in professional form exactly what was going to happen. It was no mere pep-talk, no homily on heroics.[67]

By spelling out how 'crumbling operations', the 'dog-fight' and constant pressure would in a battle lasting twelve days achieve ultimate victory, he overcame scepticism and generated a feeling of utter conviction of victory. He also forged the bond with many that day that survived every kind of adversity and hardship the war offered and which remained unbroken till the end of their lives.

With definite confirmation of imminent combat, men reacted in a variety of ways: eager anticipation, trepidation, anxiety, fear. There was more than disappointment amongst many chosen to be 'LOB', as Stuart Hamilton recalled:

> We had a new CO of whom we weren't quite sure because he didn't seem to be a fighting soldier, rather more an administrative type bloke. He called me into his tent one day, 21st October, and said, 'Ham I have got some news for you which you won't like but it's an order so you will just have to listen and take it.' He then went on to say that the forthcoming battle was going to be a very tough one indeed as a result of which heavy casualties were expected and as I was the senior Captain in the Regiment and probably one of the most experienced tank commanders, being one of the old originals left, that I was going to be 'LOB' (Left Out of Battle). I was absolutely furious but he said it was no good being furious about it as this was being done to all Regiments. I could see the sense and reasoning for this but I was very upset and extremely downcast when I said goodbye to the Squadron and my fellow officers.[68]

The Chief of the Imperial General Staff, General Sir Alan Brooke, knew the details and probable date on 14 October, but did not tell Churchill:

> As I had no confidence in Winston's ability to keep anything secret I decided not to tell him about this plan. I knew, however, that I should have difficulties as Winston was continually fretting to advance the date and asking me why we were not being informed of the proposed date of attack. I had to judge between the relative importance of maintaining complete secrecy and on the other hand of stopping Winston from wiring to Alex and Monty and upsetting their plans with his impatience.[69]

Relenting a week later, Brooke was horrified to learn that Churchill 'after giving me a solemn undertaking that he would not tell anybody what I had told him about details of [the] impending M[iddle] E[ast] attack had calmly gone and told Eisenhower and Bedell Smith!!'

I had had great doubts as to whether Winston would keep his secret, and my doubts were not misplaced! The newspaper reporter in him was coming to the fore. News was not something to sit on, it must be cashed in on at once, even if that cash only meant importance. He had no reason whatever to tell Eisenhower, this attack did not concern him in the least at that moment, and what is more important, Ike's HQ was conspicuously leaky as regards information and secrets at that time.[70]

Back in Egypt, Brigadier Davy visited XIII and XXX Corps to check on preparations:

Both the corps commanders, Horrocks and Leese, explained their plans to me. Both were confident, as were all the subordinate commanders I met. I played polo as usual the day before the battle, for the sake of security. Dick [McCreery] and Alex had conferred together on the various aspects of my polo, as soon as they took over, and decided that from the point of view of security and morale it was a good thing that I should continue. I gathered from Freddie that Monty did not approve.[71]

On the evening of 23 October, Major-General Wimberley watched his men quietly move into position in the moonlight and hoped his command would maintain its illustrious reputation:

Platoon by Platoon they filed past, heavily laden with pick anti shovel, sandbags and grenades – the officer at the head, his piper by his side. There was nothing more that I could do now to prepare for the battle, it was only possible to pray for their success, and that the Highland Division would live up to its name and the names of those very famous regiments of which it was composed.[72]

Sergeant James Harris of 4th 'Sharpshooters' County of London Yeomanry wrote that 'Today will go down in history as the start of a great battle, we all feel confident as to the outcome of it.'[73] Colonel 'Flash' Kellett of the Sherwood Rangers Yeomanry, perhaps subconsciously echoing Montgomery's August intent to 'hit Rommel and his army for six, right out of Africa', told his navigating officer, 'Put on your white flannels. You're batting first for England'.[74] For Captain Robert Angel, a Great War veteran and now 7th Rifle Brigade's quartermaster, 'It all seemed a pretty desperate venture and I was very conscious that I had probably seen the last of some of my friends.'[75]

In London, Brooke saw the impending battle's tremendous significance. With it and the imminent *Torch* Landings in North Africa, his strategic plans, outlined on taking office the previous year, were once more possibilities. On the evening of 23 October, he received word that the attack 'had started'.

> We are bound to have some desperately anxious moments as to what success is to be achieved. There are great possibilities and great dangers! It may be the turning point of the war, leading to further success combined with the North African attack, or it may mean nothing. If it fails I don't quite know how I shall bear it, I have pinned such hopes on these two offensives.

In his own words, therefore, 'The stage was now set, after much trouble, for a possible change in the tide of the war.'[76]

CHAPTER SEVEN

AN END HAS A START

It was a full moon, a gloriously calm, warm night. All the men were at their guns, ammunition was being polished. Fradd, the GPO (Gun Position Officer), was standing at the command post, watch in hand. Inside, the telephonist was listening to instructions from battery command post. Down the wire came 'five minutes to go'. The lamp on the post from which the guns take their angle went black, the wick having been turned up too high. A man ran across with an electric torch. He had thirty seconds to go! Five seconds to go! FIRE! And as Fradd shouted down his megaphone, the whole regiment let go together and all along the horizon flash after flash appeared and the air began to crack and rumble as the near and distant guns fired on their tasks. The Battle for Africa had begun.[1]

At 2140hrs on 23 October 1942, this, as penned by Canon Gervase Markham, was how the opening of the battle appeared from a battery position of one field regiment: an almost-tangible sense of tension and drama and the inevitable last-minute hitch before the guns roared into life.

For many witnessing it, the bombardment was stunning, but although 408 field guns and forty-eight medium guns were concentrated in the northern sector under the control of the XXX Corps Commander Royal Artillery (CRA), Brigadier Mead Dennis, the majority of available guns were actually spread along the entire forty-mile front.[2] Consequently, in places the noise was barely noticeable, a fact that made a great impression on Major-General Francis 'Gertie' Tuker:

There was no roar of cannon, at least none that we heard as the sound came through the muffling sands below Ruweisat – none even from our own divisional guns hard by. Wide to the north and south played the swift flickering lightning flashes, dead white, as if giants danced a Khuttack war dance whirling their swords about their heads under the moon. And the sound, too, it fluttered all around us and above us. Many a time have I been in a bombardment, our own and the enemy's, and never have I listened to so seemingly gentle a noise of guns. When I say fluttered, I mean fluttered like a thousand moths – no other. It was hard to believe that 500 field- and medium- guns close by were pounding the enemy's batteries with shell.[3]

However, where the guns were concentrated, it was undoubtedly impressive. At the artillery observation posts (OP), officers and men enjoyed a 'grandstand' view of the sights and sounds as the gunners stepped through their fire programme. Bombadier Cyril Mount recounted:

You can't describe it. It was like millions of wild swans going overhead, mixed with the sort of noise you sometimes get when a tram car goes round the bend – or a tube train – a squeeching. That'd be one probably turning over and you'd think 'God, is it going to hit us?!' It seemed to be about six inches above our heads all night long – this barrage. At times it was as light as daylight there were so many flares going up. We just got very, very pissed that night on Canadian Club whisky and yet not so pissed that we were incapable. It was adrenaline mixed with the alcohol somehow. It was an incredible night.[4]

To see such devastating destructive power in use against his fellow man was assuredly a challenge to Canon Markham's faith but, despite this, he rationalized the end as justifying the means:

They were just the enemy. You didn't see them, you didn't know them. You knew that they were trying to win the war for a cause which you regarded as an evil cause – Nazism – and so you were glad to be fighting a battle that would help to win the war. There was no opportunity or occasion for sympathizing with the individual soldier who was on the opposite side. Even as a chaplain, that was only a very secondary thought.[5]

As in the Great War, when men witnessed or endured such massed artillery fire, the weapon in its effect was seemingly a bludgeon, disguising the sophisticated science required to wield it successfully.

Montgomery claimed to have slept through the bombardment,[6] but wrote elsewhere that it was 'a wonderful sight, similar to a Great War 1914/18 attack'.[7] Lance Corporal Douglas Waller of 1st Rifle Brigade called it 'a little bit of World War One stuff'.[8] On the front of XXX Corps, a complex 'hurricane' bombardment benefited from the thorough preparatory counter-battery (CB) work of units like 4th (Durham) Survey Regiment in locating the Axis guns. Now the flash-spotting, sound-ranging, aerial reconnaissance, secret trig points and the surprisingly unscathed observation towers reaped their dividends. With medium guns attacking the more distant targets and the 25-pounders concentrating fire on forward batteries, Eighth Army quickly established fire superiority.[9] The German and Italian gunners were totally unprepared when the bombardment opened, as Kannoneer Martin Ranft recalled:

> I was talking to a comrade of mine and I was facing the front line which was roughly about 5 miles away from our guns. Suddenly I saw the whole front line – the sky went red with the gunfire. I said 'Look at that!' We thought then 'That is going to be the end'. But we survived. When the shells came over it was just horrible. You know, you had the shells howling over you and then exploding all round you. It wasn't a very nice thing.[10]

The headquarters of 15. Panzer-Division immediately reported problems from the destruction of telephone communications by artillery fire. General Georg Stumme was also completely surprised. His efforts to grasp the details of the situation were ineffectual and the Panzerarmee fought the first few hours of the battle 'blind'.[11]

―――――――――――――

At 2155hrs, the bombardment stopped. The gunners made the necessary adjustments to begin the barrage and fire concentrations on targets in the vicinity of the front line; the infantry lying flat while the change took place. Then, as the firing recommenced, the infantry and the Royal Engineer mine-clearing parties started forward again. Rifleman Reg Crimp looked on:

> Groups of Jock infantry, in shorts and shirts and tin-hats, with bayonets fixed, begin filtering forward through the gap. Poor devils – I don't envy them their

SECOND ALAMEIN: OPERATION *LIGHTFOOT*

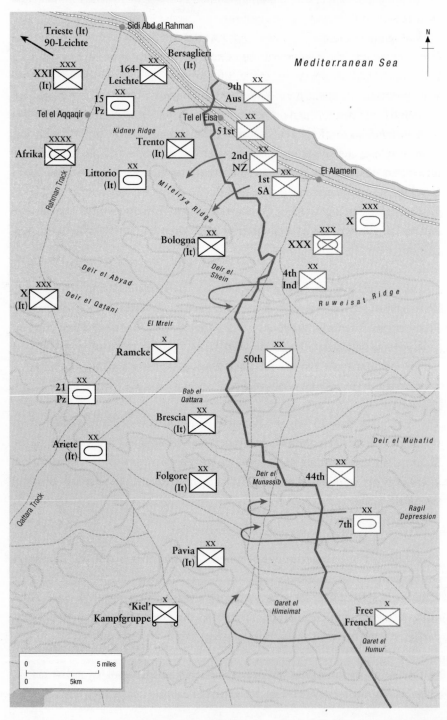

night's work. Not much reaction from the enemy seems forthcoming, though – only an occasional soughing plunge and the hoarse crash of a shell landing somewhere forward.[12]

The waiting tank crews watched without envy from behind their protective armour. Trooper Len Flanakin of the 9th Armoured Brigade remembered:

> Across the minefields we could see the shadowy figures of the Sappers engrossed in a job I would not have had for the world. Infantry men bent low moving in to attack. The barrage ceased for a moment. Then the gunners having adjusted their sights began in unison again. These men must have got into their stride as this encore seemed heavier than ever.[13]

Air superiority was crucial to British success at Alamein. The Desert Air Force was to assist by attacking 'deep' targets, permitting the artillery to focus on the close battle.[14] From 2200hrs, when the artillery commenced attacking the forward defensive positions, twenty Fleet Air Arm Albacore 'pathfinders' and sixty Wellingtons worked through the night in a counter-battery role on the front of XXX Corps. Major Alan Newson, Royal Marines, was commanding 821 Squadron, Fleet Air Arm:

> We were doing the usual job of illuminating concentrations behind the enemy lines. Of course we had to fly over the battlefield of Alamein itself. It was a wonderful sight. I can remember the barrage stretching for miles in either direction, tracer going in all directions and in the distance were explosions and fires and the flares dropped by the Wellingtons and ourselves. The chief opposition was enemy night fighters and light ack-ack. The other thing that used to worry us quite a lot was our own Wellingtons and their bombs because they used to bomb from 10,000 feet and we used to bomb from 5,000. That was one of the risks we had to take because we had to keep the illumination going the whole time they were bombing.[15]

The Wellington 1C crews from 148 Squadron had been given a line of longitude which they mustn't bomb east of. Anything visible west of the line, however, was fair game. Flight Lieutenant Ron Dorey of 148 Squadron was puzzled at first:

We couldn't understand this because nobody said 'The battle is about to open'. When we turned from Wadi Natrun heading west, I have never ever seen a sight like it! Thirty miles of solid gunfire. At night. From the coast down to the Qattara Depression. We looked at this and said 'God Almighty, what's going on?!' And then as we flew closer, we thought it was flak at first, but miles of it! As we got nearer we suddenly realized what it was all about.[16]

The squadron was instructed to fly at 6,000 feet and target artillery gun flashes, which in Dorey's opinion in the darkness was 'a bit ridiculous really'. Consequently, his crew persuaded him to undertake a risky manoeuvre:

I said '6,000 feet. That's because there's British artillery shells going over.' They said 'Oh, Go on, have a go'. So we went up to the coast and came hurtling back down at 200 feet and let them blaze away with their guns! Whether we hit anything or not, I think is debatable. When we got back for debriefing, another crew were sitting on the next table to us and the Wing Commander walked in and he was going absolutely spare. This sergeant pilot had gone down like we had machine-gunning on the front line but unfortunately, on his way down, he got a British artillery shell right through the fuselage in one side and out the other. It left this gaping hole about 3 feet across! Right through, and all they did was patch it up.[17]

The attack of 9th Australian Division on the northern flank began well. Three battalions (2/24th, 2/17th and 2/15th) encountered little opposition or delay in taking their first objective. The 2/48th Battalion, commanded by the same Lieutenant-Colonel 'Tack' Hammer who had led them at Tel el Eisa, had practised long and hard at capturing and consolidating positions and was as efficient on the night as in rehearsals. Only one battalion (2/13th) did not take all its objectives. Its mine-clearing 'Scorpion' tanks broke down and supporting Valentines from 40th RTR were delayed in the minefields. Heavy casualties ensued before the tanks finally arrived to assist.

On the southern flank of the XXX Corps attack, 1st South African Division, although delayed, managed to reach 'Oxalic' – the final objective. The division was fundamentally weaker than its Eighth Army counterparts, but used machine-guns to good effect in support of its attack. Raids, demonstrations and 'Chinese attacks' were carried out by both 1st Greek Brigade and 4th Indian Division. These were necessary, but costly, diversions.

In the centre, success in the attacks of 51st and New Zealand Divisions was essential for an armoured breakthrough. The attack by 51st Division was modelled on methods used by the division's Great War antecedent and its controversial commander, 'Uncle' Harper, and witnessed first-hand by Wimberley.[18] Four lines coloured green, red, black and blue marked the divisional objectives. Defended localities were given the Scottish place names and the attack frontage split into six lanes. Wimberley's experience of the last war would probably have warned him of the likely problems arising from an attack frontage which widened as the advance went forward. On the flanks, therefore, units 'leapfrogged' each other in the attack to compensate for this.

In the northernmost lane, both 5th Black Watch and 1st Gordons suffered heavy casualties from machine-gun fire and several of their supporting tanks from 50th RTR were knocked out. Further south, Charles Barker, officially posted as a deserter having made an unauthorized return to his unit from a base camp in the Delta, was a liaison officer with 5/7th Gordons:

> The barrage was not far in front of us as we moved steadily forward and were soon in the fog of war. Grit and sand thrown up by thousands of exploding projectiles reduced what visibility existed, the clean air became foul with the smell of cordite as we paced out the distance we covered keeping direction by compass and the red tracer shells from bofors anti-aircraft guns. It was important that we kept pace with the barrage in order to give the enemy no time to recover before we were upon him It was equally important that we did not get casualties from our own guns. The Battalion Intelligence officer was the main check advancing alongside Lieutenant-Colonel Roscoe Saunders, the Commanding Officer. It was a fantastic experience going into such an action with such a splendid Division accompanied by the pipes.[19]

When 5/7th Gordons reached the black line, Barker was sent back to report progress before being sent on a thrillingly dangerous reconnaissance mission with Universal carriers to discover whether the lead companies of 1st Gordons had reached their final objective. Discovering a gap in the German minefield, Barker mounted his carrier and ordered the driver forward:

> Suddenly, above the general rumble of battle there was a shattering crash from our left as German 88mm anti-tank guns opened up on us. I tapped the driver's steel helmet. Signalling him to press on with all speed, we ran the gauntlet of fire

the whole length of the gap. Being carriers, we had a low silhouette and were unscathed. It was a very frightening experience being engaged by 88mm guns at close range. There was no warning, no whining of a shell's approach, just a mighty bang and an enormous flash. On reaching the end of the gap I turned the patrol right and kept along the wire searching for the two companies but there was no sign of them. We circled an oil drum which later I discovered to be located near the east end of the Kidney feature. Our tracks were visible in the sand as we retraced our route and we were soon in the thick of it once again. The noise was appalling as the Germans opened up on us as we returned through the minefield gap. I spotted a Gordon lying wounded in the minefield. I stopped the carrier, leapt out, grabbed him and bundled him into the carrier and pressed on. Through a hail of fire we arrived back at Battalion HQ. I reported where we had been, the existence and extent of the minefield and the unmined German gap. Also, that our search along the wire on the far side indicated that A and C Companies were not near 'Aberdeen'. Although I had failed in my task this was important information.[20]

Lieutenant-Colonel Murray therefore ordered his men to dig in on the black line. The apparent failure to take 'Aberdeen' was important as it would prevent 1st Armoured Division from getting on by dawn.

In the centre of 51st Division's attack were 1st Black Watch and 7th Argyll & Sutherland Highlanders. Lieutenant Hugh Samwell of 7th Argyll & Sutherland Highlanders recounted:

Oddly enough I don't remember the actual start – one moment I was lying on my stomach on the open rocky desert, the next I was walking steadily as if out for an evening stroll, on the right of a long line of men in extended order. To the right I could dimly see the tall thin figure of the major commanding the other forward company. He had a megaphone, and was shouting down the line, 'Keep up there on the left – straighten up the line.' I turned to my batman, who was walking beside me, and told him to run along the line and tell the sergeant in charge of the left-hand platoon to keep his direction from the right.[21]

Both battalions found the pace of the barrage at 100 yards every three minutes too slow for the eager infantry, as Private Frank Devaney remembered:

We worked to 100-yard lifts behind the guns. We were even curtailed to a certain walking pace for a hundred yards so the guns could be governed to this lift – so many minutes plus seconds of our walking time. They were adjusted to us. On the night, the Jocks were walking too quick – they were going too far, too fast. They had to slow down a bit so's the guns could lift and we wouldn't be suffering casualties from our own guns.[22]

After taking the red line, both battalions began to encounter fierce resistance, losing men to rifle machine-gun and mortar fire as well as the German anti-personnel 'S' mines and booby traps. Hugh Samwell recalled:

Mortar shells were landing right among us. I heard a man on my left say, 'Oh, God!' and I saw him stagger and fall. The major was shouting again. I couldn't hear what he said, but his company seemed to be already at grips with the enemy. At that moment I saw a single strand of wire ahead about breast high. I took a running jump at it and just cleared it. My sergeant, coming behind, started to climb over it, and immediately there was a blinding flash and a blast of air struck me on the back of the neck. I never saw that sergeant again. I remember wondering what instinct had made me jump that wire. Strange? I hadn't been thinking of booby-traps.[23]

Entering the German minefields, Frank Devaney recognized the extent to which his survival was a lottery:

You're in the minefield before you realize it. You know you're in the minefield because they've got forward markings. They've got wire of their own and once in it, you don't know the depth of it, you've got to keep going and you know within yourself that something's going to happen. If they're anti-personnel mines, you're going to go with it. You're hoping you're going to get to the other side of it before you go up.[24]

It was doubly unfortunate therefore that Devaney was in the vicinity of a carrier when disaster struck, but his good fortune to live to tell the tale:

I was alongside it. There was a terrific explosion and we were just scattered about like a pack of cards and the carrier was just thrown over on its side. It went over a Teller mine – one of these anti-vehicle mines – and by luck the ammunition in the carrier stayed intact, it didn't go off.[25]

Recovering and getting beyond the minefield, Devaney saw bloodlust descend on the attackers seeking revenge for friends killed alongside them in the attack.

With admirable candidness he described the mix of emotions, environment, training and basic instinct that defined men's actions in close combat:

> A lot of people changed. They went berserk. Generally, they [the enemy] do their best till you're on top of them and once they're exposed to it, well, they want to just 'hands up, it's all over', so to speak. They hate the moment it doesn't happen that way. A man goes down ... well, he's finished. You kill him – you've got to do that. *You've got to do that.* It's a pressure. It's him or you and that's it. You just shot or bayoneted the man who's in front of you. The man that's defying you from completing your task. Because while you were allowing him to survive, somebody beside him, or coming round, was going to take your life. So, in other words, you couldn't allow anybody to survive. You had to kill him. After all, it's in darkness. He's not just a person standing up when he jumps up out of his slit trench shouting 'Kamerad' or whatever. You can't stop to think because the quicker that you put him away, the better. He could have a revolver in his hand or anything and it is dark. All you see is the figure. To you, the silhouette there is the enemy to be destroyed and that's all that's in it. There are no second thoughts because if there are, that's that.[26]

What Devaney's training had taught him and others like him to guard against was precisely what happened to Hugh Samwell:

> Suddenly I heard a shout of 'Watch out!' and the next moment something hard hit the toe of my boot and bounced off. There was a blinding explosion, and I staggered back holding my arm over my eyes instinctively. Was I wounded? I looked down rather expecting to see blood pouring out, but there was nothing – a tremendous feeling of relief. I was unhurt. I looked for the sergeant who had been beside me. At first I couldn't see him, and then I saw him lying sprawled out on his back groaning. His leg was just a tangled mess. I realised all at once what had happened: one of the enemy in the trench had thrown a grenade at me as he came out with his hands up. It had bounced off my boot as the sergeant shouted his warning, and had exploded beside him. I suddenly felt furious; an absolute uncontrollable temper surged up inside me. I swore and cursed at the enemy now crouching in the corner of the trench; then I fired at them at point-blank range – one, two, three, and then click! I had forgotten to reload. I flung my pistol away in disgust and grabbed a rifle – the sergeant's I think – and rushed in. I believe two of the enemy were sprawled on the ground at the bottom of the square trench. I bayoneted two more and then came out again.[27]

Despite their slogging fight the two battalions did not reach and capture the blue line – the final objective. It was a similar story further south again where 51st Reconnaissance Regiment and 50th RTR tanks did manage to reach their final objective but were driven back. Only on the extreme left, next to the New Zealanders, did the combined efforts of 5th Cameron Highlanders and 7th Black Watch put one platoon of the latter on the blue line, where they remained until morning.

The 2nd New Zealand Division had an advance of between 5,000 and 6,800 yards from its start line. With 104 guns on a front that almost doubled between the start line and the final objective, a full creeping barrage was impossible, as Howard Kippenberger recorded:

> That meant that each gun would be firing on a lane 24 yards wide and increasing to 46 yards wide, far too few shells to the yard to be worth much as a barrage, for a barrage must saturate every yard of ground with shells to be effective. Accordingly, the artillery plan was for a fourth of the guns to fire on the barrage lines to help the infantry to keep direction and for the other three-quarters to fire concentrations on particular spots where the enemy was known to have defences. Therefore, by later standards, there was no real barrage. The divisional objective was equally divided between the two brigades, 5 Brigade having a little farther to go.[28]

Once again, the rate of advance was 100 yards in three minutes, which proved too slow for the infantry. Nevertheless, Kippenberger's brigade with 23rd Battalion leading and 21st and 22nd Battalions behind, pressed forward despite heavy fire and the minefields, amongst which were scattered many anti-personnel devices. Lieutenant Dick Wardell of 22nd Battalion described the scene:

> The enemy now opened up on us with everything they had and their fire was withering. They were obviously expecting us in spite of the utmost secrecy of our previous movements. It seemed impossible that anyone could advance into this fire, but we did. By now we were going through thick dust like fog caused by bursting shells and smoke from bursting shells; it was pinkish to look at as tracer bullets winging through all the time made it so. The enemy used tracer a lot and it was actually possible to avoid machine-gun tracer. You could see where it was going and walk beside it as they were firing mostly on fixed lines.[29]

Meanwhile, out in front, 23rd Battalion's commander, Lieutenant-Colonel Reg Romans, had stepped in when there was confusion over the location of his unit's final objective, which supposedly stood on rising ground. Sergeant Tom Hutchesson recalled:

> [The Colonel] looked in the direction we had been advancing, saw Miteiriya Ridge looming up ahead and decided that was the only distinct rise... Colonel Romans stopped the discussion with 'You see that rise ahead of you. That is your objective. Take it!'[30]

The passage of 23rd Battalion had so far been too easy for its commander who stated 'We haven't done any real fighting yet – let's get cracking.' It was only later realized they had advanced too far and the battalion withdrew back through the barrage to its correct objective.

Meanwhile, Dick Wardell had already had one lucky escape when a mortar shell had landed at his feet, blowing him into the air, and wounding his batman. In such a storm of fire as 22nd Battalion encountered, it was always likely his luck would run out:

> We pushed on all the time. The creeping barrage was crashing shells overhead and bursting about 200 yards in front of us. On we went and now right in front of us was a large German machine-gun pit with about 7 or 8 Germans firing with all they had; we charged them with Brens, Tommys and grenade and finished them off. Then on again. We had come a long way by this time and still the fire was terrific. Then we were going through a very heavy cloud of dust and smoke, and I got a most terrific whack on my shoulder and a burning pain. I was on the sand again with blood running down my arm onto my chest.[31]

Wardell's battle was over but his battalion had taken all its objectives by 0315hrs. In 6th New Zealand Brigade, 24th Battalion, assisted by 28th (Māori) Battalion which mopped up pockets of resistance, gained its objectives with relative ease but still suffered disproportionate casualties given that its rifle strength was about 180 down at the start.

The artillery resources allotted to XIII Corps, which used 136 field guns to neutralize Axis guns, but which by at least one estimate had almost 300 guns available, suggest that Montgomery may to some extent have been hedging his bets in case XIII Corps achieved more than expected, or XXX Corps less.[32] Ironically, the end result was to weaken support in the north without significant benefit in the south, where the wide front worked against counter-battery techniques.

Horrocks had only limited resources in infantry and armour to work with and settled on using 131st Lorried Infantry Brigade to form a bridgehead for 44th Reconnaissance Regiment, equipped with carriers, to be followed by 22nd Armoured Brigade, through the January and February minefields. Meanwhile, 44th and 50th Divisions remained on the defensive. In the event of success, 4th Armoured Brigade would be available for exploitation. However, the principal objective of XIII Corps was to ensure that 21. Panzer-Division and Divisione 'Ariete' remained pinned for as long as possible in the south.

Lance Corporal Laurie Phillips' narrative of events (and the criticism it contains) encapsulates all the fundamental elements of the XIII Corps action.

The gaps in the minefield were to be made by the sappers, covered by the carriers of the 44th Recce Regiment, with the new Scorpion flail tanks to help them lift the mines. Our Company was to go through the two left-hand gaps, and 'A' Company the two on the right; to form a bridgehead on the far side through which the armour could advance; the rest of the Brigade would follow. Having dealt with the first minefield (January) in this way, the second (February) would be similarly penetrated. I cannot believe that this was the best way to do it. The whole of the Brigade's vehicles were lined up nose to tail in four columns stretching from the German minefield back across no man's land, through the gaps in our own minefield and beyond... The troops facing us were an Italian parachute division – the Folgore – a fairly tough lot. As soon as they realised where the gaps were being made, their guns, machine-guns and mortars opened up; some vehicles were set on fire, lighting up the scene like daylight and making it even easier for them. Our Company had a difficult time getting through, and when they finally got through January they had to knock out a number of machine-gun nests and anti-tank guns; they had quite a lot of casualties with the company commander and two other officers wounded, and two of the sergeants in our platoon killed – Mac Mulford and Graham Bradbury; both were regulars and both had been awarded the MM shortly before. They were first class types who instilled great confidence in those serving under them, and we were all very depressed that they had gone.[33]

In the same battalion a fellow lance corporal, Douglas Waller, was not even sure of the purpose of his unit's attack:

> I think it was classified as a diversionary or feint attack. We were up against the Italian 'Folgore' Division which, contrary to the general opinion of Italian troops, were really tough nuts. We got through the first minefield. We were in the gap and our portee got hit in the engine – I think it must have been a solid shot because there wasn't a big explosion. We just heard 'BANG' and something hit the front of the truck and it just folded up. We were then useless because we couldn't manhandle or drag the anti-tank gun. So we left that and spent that first night as infantry attacking strongpoints. It was very hairy because they were well dug-in. I don't know whether it was deliberate or not in the confusion – but you would have some of them coming out to surrender and then suddenly somebody would open up and they would drop down ... we suffered quite a few casualties to that.[34]

Some tanks of 5th RTR and the Royal Scots Greys also got through the first minefield but attempts using the 'Scorpion' 'flail' tanks to go further were foiled by heavy fire and daylight. Captain B.E. Miles, the Royal Scots Greys' medical officer, was in the midst of the shambles on this first night.

> Our Sappers had been unable to penetrate the second minefield so we were stuck more or less in a gap in the first where we were forced to remain as wounded kept being brought to us, instead of siting our Aid Post between the two gaps in the first minefield as planned. Our petrol and ammunition lorries were close behind us. Jerry soon pinpointed the gap and I estimated that at least 25 shells landed within 50 yards. We could do no more than spend the night digging the wounded into slits in the sandy gravel, giving them morphine and attaching the appropriate label.[35]

Further to the south, Général Marie Pierre Koenig's 1ère Brigade Française Libre also failed to make progress in the vicinity of the Himeimat promontory. Horrocks was left, finally, to decide between trying to break through the February minefield or to indulge in 'crumbling'.[36]

———————

In the mine-clearing operations Leese's XXX Corps was responsible for making lanes in the British minefields but, forward of this, XXX Corps and X Corps were responsible for clearing their own. In the event, the efforts of both corps went more or less to plan, although the flail-equipped 'Scorpion' tanks allotted to infantry divisions proved unreliable. Approximately 500 mine-detector devices were available for the attack, but on many occasions the work still depended on care, the bayonet and a sapper's very cool nerve amidst a raging battle. Progress with the mine-detectors was about three yards a minute; without them, somewhat less. The engineers with each of the infantry divisions found the overall process much slower than expected.

The tank lanes for X Corps were in two separate one-mile wide 'corridors', one for 1st and one for 10th Armoured Divisions. Furthermore, these lanes had to continue beyond the limit of the infantry advance. Gaps sixteen yards wide were made first (to allow one vehicle to pass another if the latter was destroyed). These gaps were then to be broadened to forty yards. Peter Moore recalled:

> The great thing about our drill was that I never had to issue an order. Every member knew what to do and could go on doing it in his sleep. I was therefore able to reserve my energies for when something went seriously wrong. I was able to walk over to the Ink gap where 1 Troop under Jimmy Haig and Bernard Jarvis and a very business-like section of 573 Company under a Lieutenant Smith had everything under control.[37]

Moore's unit, in the New Zealand sector, found progress so slow that he watched each gap being cleared with rising concern. Because of low enemy fire, it was sometimes necessary to operate the detectors crouching or kneeling. This slowed matters further and Moore's attempts to contact his commander, Brigadier Gilbert McMeekan, to tell him this, failed. McMeekan's wireless was useless, forcing him to make face-to-face confirmation with Brigadier Neville Custance that 8th Armoured Brigade could get forward.

Conscious that time was running out before the leading units of the armoured brigades arrived, Moore recognized there was nothing for it but to press on.

> Eventually we found indications that we had reached the far side of the minefield. As Sergeant Stanton was hammering in the last of the mine markers in an eight-yard gap, I ran through the gap in a tearing hurry. There were, by my estimate, less than 20 minutes left before the dawn would break and then it would be like the 9th Lancers' casualties south of the El Meriya [sic] Depression in the July battles.[38]

The 8th Armoured Brigade's vanguard in this sector was the Sherwood Rangers.

> We found the leading squadron of the Sherwood Rangers all ready to go and we guided the leading tank up to and through the gap as first light was coming. Almost immediately the first tank was hit. I remember six tanks deploying left and right at the end of the gap and engaging some enemy anti-tank guns with their Besas, but by this time it was getting light. It was also becoming clear that the Sherwood Rangers could not get forward. Several tanks were hit and a crash action by an RHA battery in the open could not silence the enemy anti-tank guns. I decided that I must collect our men and get them behind the ridge. Leaving a party with the unenviable task of keeping the gap marking signs in order, we withdrew behind the crest and brewed up some breakfast.[39]

Moore felt that, despite their best efforts, he and his sappers had failed. They had done their part, but not in time.

> We had breached the minefields as ordered. But that first night had been just not long enough. Whether another hour would have given the armour a clear run, I don't honestly know. The cost in sapper casualties was considerable. We had 25 in my squadron on the first night alone out of the deployed strength of about 150. We were, though, wonderfully fortunate, for of these only five were fatal.[40]

This was unfair. A tremendous achievement had been accomplished under exceptionally trying circumstances. Eighth Army's plan and timings had always been over-ambitious since even under 'average operational conditions' a section of Royal Engineers required two hours to clear a sixteen-yard gap to a depth of 400 yards.[41]

However, the lanes cleared were narrow and did not go as far as hoped. At dawn all further attempts had to stop. The results were such that for 1st Armoured Division, only one lane had been cleared as far as the limit of the Australians' advance and the other lanes were considerably less advanced, whilst, despite Moore's pessimistic view, in 10th Armoured's sector greater progress was made and four lanes reached as far as the Miteirya Ridge. Now it was the armour's time.

At 0200hrs tanks of 1st and 10th Armoured commenced their final approach to the battle zone – a distance of between six and nine miles. Brigadier Frank Fisher's

2nd Armoured Brigade led Major-General Raymond Briggs' 1st Armoured Division and reached the German front line just after 0400hrs. The advance was in three regimental groups: The Queen's Bays (2nd Dragoon Guards) on 'Sun' track on the right, 9th Lancers on 'Moon' in the centre and 10th Hussars on 'Star'. Scout cars of the reconnaissance troop led, followed by two tank squadrons, regimental headquarters, the third tank squadron, a battery of 'Priest' self-propelled guns, motorized infantry, a battery each of anti-tank and anti-aircraft guns and finally the supply vehicles. Fisher and Briggs were both on 'Moon' track.

Following the tiny lights set up to mark the paths cleared through the Axis minefields, their progress gradually slowed until, as Major Anthony Wingfield remembered:

> John Brook Hunt, who was acting as a liaison officer with 1st Gordons, came 'on the air' to say that the Jocks were held up by an enemy strongpoint; that two of their companies were out of touch, and that they could go no further that night. The Recce Troop which was in touch with the rear of the Gordons confirmed that there was no forward movement.[42]

With the tanks strung out along the tracks in the midst of an enemy minefield and with dawn breaking, Jack Archer-Shee, 10th Hussars' commander, was faced with a difficult decision. Wingfield continued:

> To go on through the infantry into minefields which had not yet been gapped would certainly end in disaster. To remain where we were in situ strung out in single file along 'Star' Track in daylight would invite annihilation by 88mm anti-tank guns and enemy aircraft alike. A third course – that of dispersing in what appeared to be a minefield also seemed uninviting. Jack had just about made up his mind to press on in accordance with the original instructions when the Brigade Commander put him out of his agony by ordering the adoption of the third course.[43]

Fisher's decision and Archer-Shee's prompt action fortunately paid off, as 10th Hussars' Sergeant Douglas Covill recounted:

> He said 'Disperse!' but we said 'We can't – it's a minefield' and he said 'Bugger the mines! It's better to go in and get out. You're right in line. We've got to get off the track'. Well, luckily it was a dummy minefield – they weren't proper mines – so we then dispersed into the 'alleged minefield' and opened up.[44]

All three regiments did likewise. As daylight came they saw the ground ahead rising for almost two miles forming what became known as Kidney Ridge – from which the German 88mm guns now began to open fire. The Priest SP guns, Shermans and Grants with their ability to fire high explosive (HE) shells indirectly were all soon in action and remained so throughout the day in a slogging attritional fight.

In the southern 'corridor' it was the New Zealanders' own attached armour, 9th Armoured Brigade, with the Wiltshire Yeomanry out in front, that got into action on Miteirya Ridge first but suffered heavily when they went into an uncharted minefield. The remaining Wiltshires, the Warwickshire Yeomanry and 3rd Hussars with the New Zealand Divisional Cavalry Regiment all took up position behind the ridge crest in support of the infantry.

In the same divisional sector, Peter Moore had witnessed the immediate tank losses suffered by the Sherwood Rangers of 8th Armoured Brigade as they emerged from the 'Boat' minefield gap. When he and his men had withdrawn, the fight between tanks firing almost 'blind' at gun flashes and the anti-tank guns continued, as Arthur Reddish described:

> In a very short time, 16 tanks out of the original 44 had been lost. With dawn breaking and much of the armour still head to tail in the narrow lane of the minefield, orders came to withdraw. At daylight, the tanks in the minefield would have been sitting ducks. We withdrew in good order without further tank losses, but a gun-towing vehicle was lost. Evacuation of the wounded took some time.[45]

It was a similar story for the Staffordshire Yeomanry on 'Bottle' track. They too went into hull-down positions behind the ridge. 'Hat' track did not extend as far forward as 'Boat' and 'Bottle'. Consequently, 3rd RTR remained further back, whilst coming up behind them was 24th Armoured Brigade, including Alf Flatow's 45th RTR:

> The march along 'Hat' track was the same as all the other night marches we had done so many times before – the clouds of choking sand dust which got in the eyes and mouth, the difficulty of driving caused by this, the tanks getting spread out and losing touch and then catching up with each other again: wireless silence 'until first contact' (how often that expression had been used parrot-like on all exercises and schemes). According to orders we expected to push through the minefields that night and make a thrust at the enemy but the unexpected strength

of the enemy's defences foiled this plan. However we were all keyed up for this and I got out a 'Mills' bomb and put it on a ledge inside my cupola. Corporal Hudson my gunner was dozing inside the turret just under this ledge and the tank going over a ditch or hole caused the bomb to fall off the ledge and crack onto Hudson's head. Poor man it gave him a hell of a start and we had a few awkward seconds grovelling in the bottom of the turret trying to retrieve it and hoping the pin hadn't been knocked out en route![46]

Halting at the entrance to the last British minefields, 45th RTR soon heard news that the advance had been held up and that any further progress was impossible. Flatow continued:

Our introduction to war was therefore rather in the form of ringside spectators. We didn't know when we would be ordered to advance and we were all rather excited and jumping about. Apparently 'Hat' gap was now impassable due to enemy pressure and strength of defences – New Zealand wounded were coming through now and as we moved off the shelling – both ours and the enemy – increased. It was all rather depressing as by this time according to the orders the whole Brigade should have been through the enemy minefields chasing his armour – if any![47]

Dawn brought the fullest indication of the incredible congestion of tanks, guns, men and vehicles in the 'corridors' – particularly at Miteirya. Nevertheless, the ground gained needed to be held to precipitate the 'crumbling' operations envisaged by Montgomery. The 10th Armoured Division commander, Major-General Alec Gatehouse, an energetic, courageous and determined leader, surely had this in mind when he informed the New Zealand Division's headquarters of his plans to stay hull-down behind the ridge during daylight and only intervene if there was an Axis counter-attack. His decision was based on a personal reconnaissance witnessed by Brigadier McMeekan:

General Gatehouse roared by with his Tac. HQ in three Crusaders. The General, looking larger than ever in his white sheepskin coat and black beret, was sitting calmly on top of his tank. He went right up to the ridge, and toured round to see the situation. It was an encouraging sight, and a well-timed visit.[48]

This information did not reach Lieutenant-General Sir Bernard Freyberg immediately because there was no direct wireless link between their respective

Tactical Headquarters. Consequently, Freyberg whose experiences in two wars had undoubtedly conditioned him against inactivity and indecision in battle, spent much time urging his staff to energize 10th Armoured into attacks in broad daylight. On what grounds Freyberg could argue that such attacks should be attempted *with a realistic chance of success* is not clear. He believed he was executing Montgomery's orders, just as Gatehouse did. Eighth Army instructions for X Corps had been to 'bring on an armoured battle where full use could be made of British armour and armament to destroy the enemy' and, otherwise, to 'prevent the enemy's armour from interfering with XXX Corps' operations'.[49] Disputes sprang in part from the dichotomy between the quick, decisive breakthrough Montgomery originally conceived and the 'methodical destruction' of his revised plan.

Freyberg is often regarded as *sans peur et sans reproche* in the Desert War historiography – Montgomery's best divisional commander, the defender of Crete, several times wounded and a Victoria Cross winner in the Great War. On 24 October, he was definitely wrong in attempting to dictate to the armoured unit commanders (both Briggs and Lumsden had also decided to stand in readiness for counter-attack rather than press on). The difficulty for Lumsden *et al* was that his opinions carried weight with the Army Commander.

During the course of the morning, a series of meetings between various corps, divisional and brigade commanders took place. In these, the all-important role of Lieutenant-General Oliver Leese as a corps commander was well-demonstrated. Discussion with Freyberg, Briggs and Gatehouse produced an agreed plan for action by infantry, with support of tanks from three armoured brigades (9th, 8th and 24th). Crucially, Leese committed all his corps artillery to support the effort. He then secured Montgomery's backing for the scheme and prompted him to issue clear verbal orders regarding planned operations to get the armoured divisions out into the open as soon as possible. This, and a face-to-face meeting with Lumsden, clarified X Corps' role in operations. The result was that Briggs also chivvied Fisher to get into action and for his tanks to press on whatever the casualties. In the afternoon, this in turn led to a failed attempt by 9th Lancers to get forward.

The troops in the forward battle were certainly not inactive throughout the day. First the dawn allowed the anti-tank guns to get to work properly, as Anthony Wingfield observed:

The improvement of visibility inevitably produced anti-tank fire at a target of so many tanks herded together. Several 88mms opened up on A and C Squadrons; but both Douglas Kaye and George Errington were excellent at spotting which of their tanks was being 'ranged' upon and ordering it to move in time. The enemy anti-tank gunners were engaging us at very long range and had the rising sun in their eyes, so fortunately we received no casualties at this stage.[50]

Then two *Kampfgruppen* of 15. Panzer-Division with units of Divisione 'Littorio' made their counter-attacks. In the northern sector, the Bays and 10th Hussars of 2nd Armoured Brigade engaged approximately twenty tanks. This first combat involving the Shermans was a significant landmark in the Desert War, as Wingfield recorded.

A little later in the morning some German tanks appeared in front of us and halted about 3,000 yards away. I noted at least one of their new Mark IV 'Specials' with its long 75mm gun amongst them. It was now that our new gunnery methods and our new Sherman tanks showed their worth. For, when the German tanks moved forward, both A and C Squadron began to hit their targets and several of the German tanks went up in flames. This was indeed a morale-raising sight, and I felt the Germans were surprised as they turned northwards and moved across our front leaving several wrecks behind.[51]

The Sherman's ability (unlike the Grant) to occupy true hull-down positions, combined with the range of its 75mm guns, meant that German tanks standing off at long-range no longer enjoyed the considerable advantages that had defined their tactics previously.

The 88s were also more vulnerable now the Priests and Shermans could bring HE fire to bear on them. For the first time, the multi-role 88s were at a *disadvantage* because of their use as both anti-tank and anti-aircraft guns. Wingfield continued:

The next appearance on the scene was the RAF. A squadron of Bostons flew over us to decant their bombs accurately on the enemy's forward positions. Up went the barrels of the 88s to fire at the Bostons, for they are AA [anti-aircraft] as well as anti-tank guns. This gave our tank commanders an excellent chance of pin-pointing their targets. Squadrons of Bostons or Mitchells then arrived at twenty minute intervals for the rest of the morning and an ad hoc co-operation between them and our tanks in dealing with the 88s was built up.[52]

The Desert Air Force's contribution that day was immense with nearly 1,000 sorties, almost all in support of land operations, and despite two fighter airfields being put out of action by sandstorms.[53] Reg Crimp noted:

> Almost continually throughout the day the 'Boston Bus Service' – groups of 18 bombers escorted by fighters – is in the sky. Dog-fights develop: lazily swirling silver specks up in the sky, occasional peremptory, wrathful machine-gun burst, and long, deepening drones.[54]

To Martin Ranft and his fellow gunners the Bostons were the *Stur Achtzehn* – the 'Stubborn Eighteen'.[55]

In the southern 'corridor', the German and Italian armour also remained at long range, 'swanning about', but the exchanges of artillery and tank fire were continuous and death struck randomly and suddenly, as Arthur Reddish found:

> A young tank officer jumped on the side of the tank to converse with our commander. A heavy shell hit the tank, hurtling the officer in the air and depositing him some 20 metres ahead of us. He lay there like a rag doll, with arms and legs at grotesque angles. A sapper took one look at the body and covered it with a blanket. The tank turret was crimson with blood and bits of flesh, bone and clothing were splattered all over the right side of the vehicle. After we'd topped up with petrol and replenished the ammunition, the quartermaster-sergeant arrived with a special ration issue. He tried to wash the blood off the turret, using petrol and hessian rags. But a dirty brown stain remained with that tank for the rest of its days. 'These things will happen,' the SQMS said consolingly.[56]

Meanwhile, Wimberley's belief that the missing two companies of 1st Gordons had 'done their stuff' to the end, and were on the edge of 'Aberdeen', was borne out at noon when it was learnt that they actually were on the 'Kidney feature'. Charles Barker's reconnaissance had missed them. Nevertheless, the seeds of an important disagreement concerning this had been sown. Wimberley recorded:

> The [1st] Armoured Division HQ insisted that it was a thousand yards further on than the position of the 1st Gordons' foremost troops. We said the opposite, and in that waste of sand with few features, and a battle raging, it was not easy to be dogmatic. I felt, all the time, we were right, because we had gone there on foot with pacers on foot and compasses, and behind a timed barrage while the tanks

behind us had motored it, out of action. Over the next few days feelings ran high between myself and Fisher, and to a lesser degree with Briggs, as to who was right.[57]

In the midst of the British Army's most significant offensive effort of the war so far, a dispute like this was indicative of significant flaws in relations between infantry and armour and was deleterious to effective co-operation by the two arms. Montgomery's assumption of command had, seemingly, merely papered over Eighth Army's long-standing cracks.

At Panzerarmee Headquarters, Stumme had received fragmentary information piecemeal about the battle's progress. Initial losses in German and Italian units – three battalions of 62° Reggimento Fanteria 'Sicilia' from Divisione 'Trento' and a battalion from Panzergrenadier-Regiment 382 in 164. Infanterie-Division were overrun – suggested where the attack's main effort might be and, consequently, why Mitte and Süd Kampfgruppen of 15. Panzer-Division and Divisione 'Littorio' units were used in counter-attacks. With daylight, Stumme went forward accompanied only by his driver and Oberst Andreas Büchting, *Armeenachtrichtenführer* (army chief signals officer), to the headquarters of 90. leichte-Afrika-Division, to assess the threat to his left flank in the coastal sector. Further forward still, the car and occupants came under fire. Büchting was killed and Stumme suffered a fatal coronary whilst trying to escape. He was reported missing, presumed captured but his body was not found until the next day.

Without definite news of Stumme's fate, General der Panzertruppen Wilhelm von Thoma, the Afrika Korps commander, assumed overall command but there was inevitably a hiatus in which definite orders were lacking. Consequently, no other major counter-attacks were made during the day. Stumme and Thoma were both capable and experienced yet, when news of the attack reached OKW, Generalfeldmarschall Keitel promptly telephoned Rommel to ascertain if he was fit enough to return to Africa. Rommel travelled immediately to Wiener Neustadt and, after receiving a personal call that evening from Hitler requesting that he return to duty, set off via Rome on the morning of 25 October.[58]

Hitler and the OKW, therefore, demonstrated a rather irrational belief that a physically weak Rommel was a better option than his capable subordinates. However, the fundamental problems of the Panzerarmee were already far beyond anything that any commander, however forceful in personality, could fix simply by his presence. Hitler was prepared to dispatch a sick man to Africa immediately, but for too long both he and Mussolini had been unprepared to provide enough physically fit men and adequate resources for these men to sustain themselves and their weapons in the desert fighting. The Panzerarmee's severely depleted resources already threatened its survival. Rommel's return might boost morale but could not fuel tanks, supply gun batteries with ammunition or equip units with motor transport. These were what the Axis forces needed above all.

The attack by 2nd Seaforths of 51st Division on 24 October demonstrated why night-time was the right time for the infantry in the battle. In it, the advance without artillery or tank support got almost as far as the battalion's final objective 'Stirling'. However, the men then had to hang on under heavy fire throughout the rest of the next day, with excessive casualties as a consequence. This suggests that Wimberley was indulging in Great War 'line straightening'. Indeed, the division as a whole may have been tied too closely to 'established methods'. All three of its brigade commanders, whilst 'real fighting soldiers', were, like Wimberley, veterans of the 1914–18 conflict.[59] Given alternative ways of proceeding, namely night operations, this attack and attendant losses might have been avoided.

The second night's operations achieved some success but, overall, were a disappointment. On the right, two Australian infantry battalions reached their final *Lightfoot* objectives, although there were some losses to 'friendly fire' when the Valentines of 40th RTR mistook them for Axis troops. The Australians dug in to cover the clearing of four minefield gaps and a lateral track linking them. They were vexed, however, by the arrival of 7th Rifle Brigade and its 'A' Echelon vehicles, which could not be dispersed adequately and soon attracted attention from the 100/17 howitzers and 75/27 guns of 3° Reggimento Artiglieria. 'The enemy gunners were not too proud to shoot at sitting ducks.'[60] Having seen action in July, 7th Rifle Brigade was not a novice battalion, but its actions were tactically naïve and the result of poor co-ordination at the corps level.[61] Corporal Donald Main remembered:

> We were now told to dig in and, remembering the very apt saying 'dig or die', we did so. It took me little time to discover that I was on hard rock and I only managed to dig a trench two feet deep. When daylight came we found that we

were in an exposed position, being engaged not only from the front but also from the left flank.[62]

Despite this, the riflemen remained in position amongst the burning wrecks of their transport.

In the southern 'corridor' 10th Armoured Division's attempts to get beyond the Miteirya Ridge were ill-starred. The ridge minefields were especially dense and slowed 24th Armoured Brigade. There was greater misfortune for 8th Armoured Brigade on its way forward. Arthur Reddish told the story:

> Both Freyberg's armour and the Staffordshire Yeomanry got into battle order without hindrance; but not us. As we marshalled our column in the pitch-darkness with lorries in the centre and tanks on the outer, a German plane dropped flares over our positions. Within minutes, the bombers arrived. The first bomb landed on a lorry containing petrol and blazing fuel spewed over a wide area. Our other lorries caught fire and some exploded. The desert was lit up for kilometres around. The conflagration attracted enemy artillery, mortar and machine-gun fire and more bombers. That part of Miteiriya wasn't the best place to be. Our lorried infantry suffered heavy casualties; we lost our entire transport section and many of its drivers; and some tanks were disabled. Throughout the carnage, our padre and medical officer calmly went about their work, despite their aid post having been put out of action by a direct hit.[63]

The isolated Staffordshire Yeomanry pressed on through the second minefield gap and were joined later by 9th Armoured Brigade. The devastation on the ridge was now such that it prompted a determined and surprising choice by Trooper Ian King of 3rd Hussars, bringing up fuel for the brigade's tanks:

> On the way, shells were falling in the surrounding minefields which were erupting with numerous explosions. I felt vulnerable in a vehicle containing hundreds of gallons of high octane fuel. All round was the fresh debris of war silhouetted by fires and the flashes of guns and explosions. Some fallen bodies, burnt-out vehicles and some tanks which had gone astray on minefields. To our left were the burning remains of the Notts Sherwood Rangers convoy. There were some 15 vehicle skeletons, some still in flames and others smoking, each vehicle having held either fuel or ammunition. They had been caught on a minefield and shelled. It was then

I decided I would take the first chance to get back onto a tank crew; it seemed much less exposed.[64]

This devastation and disorganization prompted Brigadier Custance to ask Gatehouse, who also had grave doubts about the second night's operations, to call off the attack. As a consequence, whilst the infantry, engineers and armour continued struggling forward at Miteirya, a crisis conference was held at 0230hrs at Eighth Army's Tactical Headquarters. Leese, Lumsden, Guingand and Montgomery were all present.[65] Guingand's observation that such an hour was 'not a good time to hold a conference' perhaps hints at Montgomery's state of mind and demeanour after being disturbed in this way.[66]

Whether or not this conditioned his responses, Montgomery (through his Chief of Staff) had an extraordinarily accurate grasp of the current situation at Miteirya (which had improved since Custance first raised concerns). Consequently, no deviation from the original army plan was contemplated and the armoured commanders were ordered to remain determined and resolute. After an acrimonious telephone conversation with Gatehouse during this conference, Montgomery ensured that both corps commanders and Gatehouse were clear about his wishes.

The chief consequence of all this was not in the short term where, by the morning, 8th Armoured Brigade's tanks had withdrawn behind the ridge again, but in the longer term. Montgomery's telephonic instruction (by his own account) to Gatehouse to 'lead his division from in front and not from behind'[67] was an intentional slur on Gatehouse's undoubted courage and well-known command style which, like that of Currie, Briggs and Lumsden, had been *de rigueur* for Eighth Army's armoured commanders for at least two years. In addition, Lumsden via Guingand had brought the problem to Montgomery's door in the first place. Clearly, the tank generals lacked 'push' and determination. Their commander never forgave them. Meanwhile, Freyberg (who possessed the qualities Montgomery valued) insisted that 9th Armoured Brigade stay exposed beyond the minefield gaps for much of 25 October where the continual shelling took its toll and nothing was achieved. Ironically, Custance's brigade also stayed out, avoiding losses as far as possible by constant and skilful manoeuvring by its tank commanders.

In the northern 'corridor', 2nd Armoured Brigade also tried to progress but met an anti-tank screen containing significant numbers of 88mm guns. Further long-range duelling followed in the course of which a PzKpfw IV was hit and disabled at a distance of more than 4,000 yards by a Sherman gunner – perhaps the finest achievement of the day, feted as 9th Lancers' 'best shot of the whole war' and a definite augury of the armour's new state of tactical affairs.[68] The sparring at distance produced a disconcerting incident for Anthony Wingfield during an impromptu discussion with his regimental commander:

> At that moment the Brigadier drove up in his rather large 'Grant' tank and stopped about 20 yards away. There was then a noise like an express train and an object like a Rugby football bounced between us and sailed away into the distance, luckily without exploding. 'Old Fish' – Brigadier Fisher – leaned out of his turret and said: 'How very rude.'[67]

That afternoon, the dogged 7th Rifle Brigade had an opportunity to redeem itself when suddenly attacked by about forty PzKpfw IIIs and M13/41s. Corporal Donald Main recalled:

> At the same time a heavy barrage was brought down on our positions, also machine-gun and mortar fire. Since we were in the front with our machine-guns, as the tanks drew closer we had to stop firing and take cover in our slit trenches. Our sixteen six-pounders engaged the tanks, several firing at one particular tank, so that the closest was knocked out fifty yards in front. The Battalion were credited with fourteen tanks. As some of the enemy tanks were hit, the occupants tried to escape through the turrets. One Italian officer was hoisting himself out when a six-pounder hit him in the chest and he literally disintegrated. In front of the stationary tanks were two Italians sitting on the ground. From the right came cries of 'You rotten Pommie bastards!' The Australians strongly objected to our knocking out the tanks with six-pounders before they came within range of their two-pounders.[70]

The attackers drew off, the 6-pounder's capabilities clearly demonstrated. A late afternoon attack with the setting sun behind – a favourite tactic of the Afrika Korps – still resulted in heavier losses to the Axis tanks with as many as thirty-nine being claimed as knocked out by the British.

In the second attack of XIII Corps, 131st Brigade got through, but not beyond, the February minefield because of enemy fire. Dennis Gibbs was there with 1/6th Queen's Royal Regiment:

> My battalion and the 1/5th Queens on our Brigade front were ordered to 'try again'. This entailed a very long and noisy night advance and attack – noisy because of the creeping barrage ahead of us, the exploding of mines in the minefields set off by the barrage shells, and the shattering, explosions of the enemy defensive fire directed at us whilst we ploughed through the extensive minefields attempting to keep up with the barrage.[71]

Private Jack York was with the other battalion:

> We were well up now behind our barrage, and the ground started to slope towards the enemy. Several times we stumbled into new shell holes reeking with cordite. I could just see the company in front, looking like a black mass in the dim light, when suddenly several mortar bombs descended right among these extended groups, each leaving a large black cloud of smoke hanging above them. Many were the cries and shouts for stretcher bearers then. Still we struggled forward when without warning, the ground was swept like hail with heavy machine gun fire.[72]

Frantically, men dug themselves shallow 'scrapes' for protection. York continued:

> Unfortunately, the ground was hard and rocky, and at best we only managed to scrape very shallow holes – just enough to give us some protection. Shortly after we heard a sudden explosion behind us, and to our right in the minefield. Looking round I saw a Scorpion [tank] which was soon enveloped in flames. This vividly illuminated that area of the minefield for a time, and it also became the target for several enemy anti-tank guns. Evidently the sappers were working feverishly to clear a gap in the minefield, and we prayed earnestly for their success. We knew that if they completed a gap by first light, the heavy tanks of 7th Armoured Division would then pass through, and rove forward to clear up enemy positions between the two minefields. We would then be able to consolidate, and make our own positions much more secure.[73]

Two minefield gaps were cleared, mostly by hand, for Roberts' 22nd Armoured Brigade advance. York went on:

Slowly, the long hours of the night wore away, as we laid shivering in the bitter cold. Just before dawn, two soldiers nearby, who started to crawl towards the wire, were told by an officer that he would shoot them unless they returned to their positions. As the first faint light of dawn started to filter down, we heard the roar of tank engines from across the minefield behind us, and the noise gradually increased as four or five tanks approached and passed through the gap, which had been made by the sappers. They had almost made the passage safely – when 'thump', 'thump', 'thump', 'thump'; the ground shook as four thick black columns [of] smoke shot up near the gap – enemy 88mm anti-tank guns trying to get the range. They continued to fire at intervals, and their shooting soon became very accurate, nearly every shell landing in the gap. We heard some of the tanks turn left, and move across our front, and then start firing at enemy positions. Soon one or two explosions came from their direction and we never heard them moving again. No further tanks tried to force the gap, as the sun came up, and evidently the ones that got through had run onto unmarked mines, or been knocked out by anti-tank fire.[74]

The attack stalled. Tank losses alone were enough for 7th Armoured Division's commander, John Harding, to seek approval for his decision to stop the attack. However, Montgomery insisted that the attackers stay out between the two minefields. This was sheer bloody-mindedness by the Army Commander and hell for the men made to endure there, as York vividly described:

About 3 o'clock, when we were all feeling parched and constricted, we came under some very heavy machine-gun fire from our own tanks in position across the minefield. They were firing tracer, and the bullets came arching across in a solid sheet, passing above and about our slits with an awe inspiring hiss. As the afternoon hours dragged slowly by, and the relentless sun beat down from a brassy sky, our position seemed desperate. There would be no point in staying in our present position for another night, especially as the tanks could not force the gap. We would either have to attack and overcome the enemy positions that night, or withdraw across that dreadful minefield. An Officer from H.Q. Company then very gallantly and quickly ran across the minefield when one of our armoured cars came right up to the wire, and hastily clambering on to the turret, made good his escape under heavy machine-gun fire. As a result, he was able to put our Commander in the picture regarding our hopeless position.[75]

Meanwhile the men's sufferings would continue.

With tanks and infantry left occupying exposed positions as a consequence of the night's operations, and with 51st Division being responsible again for the main offensive endeavours by Eighth Army during the day with a two-battalion attack that finally secured the divisional objectives, the opportunity existed for Thoma to take back the initiative with determined action designed to seal off Eighth Army's bridgeheads in the Axis defences. The acting commander and his chief staff officer, Oberstleutnant Siegfried Westphal, after discussions with Generalfeldmarschall Albert Kesselring, drafted plans on 25 October for counter-attacks that would, by their nature, lose the Panzerarmee one of the few potential advantages it still had. So far, the Axis armour had largely stood off at long range in action against the British armour. Whilst they could no longer expect to win even these long-range duels they could, by prolonging the battle, weaken their opponents, preserve their own strength and buy time.

The three counter-attacks they launched that day produced disproportionate Axis tank casualties in which the 6-pounder anti-tank guns had their chance to shine. Tank loss rates in Divisione 'Littorio' and particularly 15. Panzer-Division (which had only thirty-two tanks left by 26 October) were unsustainable.[76] The beginnings of a real crisis for the Panzerarmee had, paradoxically, been prompted by the actions of the Axis commanders.

That same evening, the order was finally given for the withdrawal of 131st Brigade – but only after eighteen hours of being 'shot up' by Italian mortars and artillery. The 'Folgore' paratroops had proved too tough to crack and the Panzerarmee's desert flank remained intact. The unlucky Colonel Gibbs and some of his men were taken prisoner, and left contemplating what might have been:

> If only our armour had managed to follow us, the battle down on this Southern Flank would have been highly successful. Yet it was for us a most dispiriting experience and left one wondering about what had 'gone wrong'. At the same time, one was thankful to be alive when so many others were not, or were badly wounded, and I began to work out how to make the best of a poor situation.[77]

Conditions for the men in the exposed prisoner of war 'cage' were austere, and that evening news filtered through of a significant development in the battle. Gibbs continued:

The desert nights at the end of October are cold compared to the intense heat of the burning sun by day which we had experienced during those hours of daylight prior to our 'rounding up', as it were. On that first night one had only khaki shirt and shorts, and the one blanket provided by the Germans was not proof against the extreme chilliness of the night. The German sentries were fairly 'cock-a-hoop' because, they said, Rommel, who had been in Germany ill, was now back in the Desert in command of his Armies. Hence, they declared, the British would be once more and finally 'on the run'. So we pulled their legs as best we could in the kind of half guttural pigeon English with which they addressed us, and then we lay down on the sand again and gazed at the starry desert night, which seemed strange enough from inside a large wire enclosure.[78]

News of the Generalfeldmarschall's return on the evening of 25 October had travelled fast. Its effect on Axis morale was obvious.

How ironic, therefore, that among Rommel's first actions on his return was his decision to continue the armoured counter-attacks ordered by von Thoma. He also brought 90. leichte-Afrika-Division and Divisione 'Trieste' up to co-operate. This was in spite of the fact that he was acutely aware that sufficient supplies of fuel for his army's vehicles were still not getting through. By committing to further armoured attacks, he was using up vital fuel reserves for his tanks. His anger at his Italian allies over this situation should not disguise that he himself could have done more to reduce the effects of the fuel shortage. The first attacks at dawn once again involved Divisione 'Littorio' and 15. Panzer-Division, but supported by the concentrated fire of all available Axis artillery. Eighth Army countered with artillery DF concentrations which severely disrupted the preparations and delayed the attack, which was consequently broken up quite easily. More attempts were made and countered by artillery or tanks. Capitano Davide Beretta's unit, 554° Gruppo Semoventi da 75/18 from Divisione 'Littorio', equipped with the Semovente self-propelled gun, took part in a further, larger battle later that day.

In front of our *Semoventi* there were some tens of M14 tanks of Littorio Division that were firing their 47/32 guns against some enemy anti-tank positions. Suddenly on the horizon there appeared overwhelming formations of heavy British tanks, Shermans and Grants, aiming their 75mm guns like hunters. Sometimes they stopped their advance, and then continued forward. Our tiny M14/41s moved towards them to shorten the range – the shorter the range, the better the chances of penetrating their armour with their small guns. The British were about 1,500m from our tanks and began to put up a rapid fire. We observed this action with dismay, because the 47mm shells of the M14s were bouncing off the heavy armour of their tanks. We were confident, however, that our own 75mm guns would have a very different effect on the British. 'Watch out, they're advancing towards us!' 'Tally Ho!' We started to advance as well, and we reached our blazing M14s with guns ready! 'Range 700, 800, 900... Fire!'... We managed to destroy some Shermans and Grants, and the British halted their advance and tried to attack our flanks. We barely managed to stop their advance, and failed to force them to withdraw; but it was a miracle indeed that we stopped them. In the evening we counted twenty Shermans and Grants and some Valentines and Crusaders destroyed; but the price we paid in that uneven battle was far too high.[79]

Cold statistics explained why the Panzerarmee could not continue indefinitely, but the British High Command did not know with certainty whether or not the defenders were buying time until reinforcements and supplies were dispatched by Hitler and Mussolini – although nothing from Ultra suggested this.

During the night, Rommel's forces suffered a further blow when 2/48th Australian Infantry Battalion captured the tactically important Point 29 in a lightning-fast assault, strongly supported by six Field and two Medium artillery regiments, and which used the battalion's carriers in quickly seizing the final objective from Panzergrenadier-Regiment 125. The capture of sketch maps of the German minefield defences, the Panzergrenadier-Regiment commander and one of his battalion commanders, immediately prior to the attack was fortunate but, although the attacks of both 2/48th and 2/24th were successful, both suffered heavily in their attacks. On 26 October these battalions were under intense artillery fire for three hours but any attack on them was largely snuffed out by more British DF fire.

The pressure was building on Rommel's forces as the losses in men and tanks mounted. Bringing 21. Panzer-Division and Divisione 'Ariete' northwards looked an increasingly necessary, but perhaps (given his fuel reserves) irrevocable, option. On the other hand, for the time being Montgomery could maintain Horrocks' XIII Corps in the south without prejudice to his northern operation. Furthermore, even as the Axis armour was engaged in self-immolating attacks on the British tank units in, or beyond, the minefields, the Eighth Army's commander and chief of staff were contemplating a radical change in direction and tempo for operations. It was clear that the initiative still rested with Montgomery, despite the best efforts of Thoma and Rommel.

CHAPTER EIGHT

ATTRITION

On the morning of 26 October Eighth Army's lack of significant progress in the 'crumbling' operations after the initial assault was clear. The Army Commander used much of the day to assimilate information from Brigadier Freddie de Guingand, his Chief of Staff and others on the state of his forces. When he had done so, three important points were plain.

The first related to the armour. Whatever Montgomery's opinion of his armoured formations' performance in the fighting so far, it was clear that tank casualties had been higher than he might have assumed. Having begun the battle with 1,060 tanks of all types, he now had 754 available. But Guingand recognized that, crucially, the majority of tanks had suffered damage from mines rather than enemy shells. Damaged tracks and wheels could be repaired or replaced by the very efficient tank workshops in a relatively short period of time. Guingand estimated, consequently, that a daily flow of forty to fifty tanks might be expected to be returned for further use in the fighting. The arithmetic of attrition was not yet, therefore, suggesting that Eighth Army need terminate, or even limit, its offensive operations.

Of greater concern was the situation regarding casualties.[1] The Army's estimated casualties from the evening of 23 October until dawn on 26 October were about 6,140 killed, wounded and missing with 4,640 coming from XXX Corps. Of the last figure, nearly 2,000 were from 51st Division. Particular issues arose from those suffered by the Dominion infantry units with approximately 1,000 Australians, 1,000 New Zealanders and 600 South Africans.[2] The problem was that there were very few replacements for the New Zealand and South African formations. Montgomery, mindful that this was as much a political issue as a question of reserves, saw that 'he would have to go carefully with his infantry'.[3]

The third area of concern for Montgomery ought to have been the expenditure of artillery ammunition. Brigadier Sidney Kirkman, Eighth Army's Commander, Royal Artillery (CRA), had originally estimated that 150 rounds per gun per day would allow continuation of the battle for up to three weeks. However, the severe nature of the fighting now meant that Kirkman, when discussing the matter with Montgomery that day, needed to revise his calculations:

> I [Kirkman] said to him, 'I've been going into the ammunition situation and it's very difficult to find out how much ammunition there is in the Middle East. But as far as I can find out we can go on with this battle for ten days at the present rate – but we can't go on indefinitely.' Monty replied: 'Oh, it's quite all right, absolutely all right, don't worry about ammunition. This battle will be over in a week's time. There'll be no problem.' We argued a bit. I said, 'Well it wouldn't be a bad thing if we cut XIII Corps down to 40 rounds per gun per day anyway.' And he said, 'All right, we'll do that.'[4]

Later in the war, with his persona as a confident, assertive commander firmly established in Eighth Army's collective consciousness, Montgomery could not display doubts even to his immediate subordinates, but as an unproven army commander his decision-making on 26 October was a more collegiate process paying due attention to the views of his more senior staff officers.

Montgomery decided to regroup his army to create a reserve with which to resume the offensive in a different sector. This reserve would consist of the New Zealand and 10th Armoured Divisions and 9th Armoured Brigade. Guingand had also suggested that 7th Armoured Division might be available if 21. Panzer-Division was sent to the northern battle front. This reorganization was to be completed, with minor exceptions, by dawn on 28 October. The burden of operations between that date and the launch of his next major attack in the coastal sector was to fall on 9th Australian Division. These decisions were the origins of Operation *Supercharge* – which Montgomery hoped would 'bring about the disintegration of the whole enemy army'.[5]

In deciding on this course of action, Montgomery effectively abandoned the *corps de chasse* concept, falling back instead on the abilities of the man he considered to be his best divisional commander, Bernard Freyberg, and his

New Zealand Division staff to plan for, and effect, the breakthrough.[6] Montgomery's decision was probably precipitated by information received from Kirkman concerning Lumsden's X Corps, leading the Army Commander to believe that Lumsden was not maintaining good liaison with his Corps CRA and that, like other 'RAC [Royal Armoured Corps] Generals', he did 'not understand the co-operation of all arms in battle.'[7]

As a consequence of its low strength and lack of immediate reinforcements, the New Zealand Division was in no shape to conduct an operation of the type envisaged – a point Freyberg was keen to stress to Leese, his Corps Commander, even doing so in writing with statistical information in support of his assertions. Montgomery's solution placed two brigades of British infantry (151st and 152nd) under New Zealand command for the operations. This was both 'elegant and effective'[8] but went against Montgomery's 'earlier assertions that he would fight divisions as divisions and not piecemeal.'[9] Freyberg's staff needed time to prepare and the attack was scheduled for the night of 31 October–1 November.

For the Panzerarmee with Rommel now back in charge, decisions had to be made concerning Eighth Army's main focus. Clearly, it was not in the south where the efforts of XIII Corps were now recognized as a bluff. Rommel therefore ordered 21. Panzer-Division and half his artillery to what was obviously the offensive's *Schwerpunkt** in the north.[10] Here they would be used to make a major counter-attack in combination with units from 15. Panzer-Division, 164. Infanterie-Division and Divisione 'Littorio'.

Rommel indulged in *post facto* exaggeration of certain aspects of the Panzerarmee's situation after his return on 25 October.[11] Fuel was a case in point. His German tank forces had at least enough petrol for their immediate operational needs, thanks to an undisclosed reserve accumulated by the Afrika Korps quartermaster, Major Otto. The real shortage was fuel for transport for the wider Panzerarmee – especially the artillery and infantry. Rommel also claimed that his opponents had apparently inexhaustible stocks of ammunition (perhaps forgivable given the effectiveness of Eighth Army's artillery) and that the Sherman tank 'showed itself to be far superior to any of ours'.[12] This last remark contrasted sharply with the radically revised opinions of British tank crews. Ian King observed:

---

* 'Centre of gravity' i.e. focal point of the attack.

It had now been realised that the Sherman was not the super-tank it had been supposed to be. The armour was no protection against the German 88mm; and its high octane fuel meant that it caught fire readily and burned with a life-threatening ferocity and intensity.[13]

There is no doubt that the Panzerarmee now faced an exceptional crisis but its possible defeat was certainly not a study in inevitability yet.

Montgomery's plans did not affect operations already in train. On the night of 26–27 October 1st Armoured Division ordered 7th Motor Brigade to capture two positions approximately 3,000 yards west of the northern minefield corridor. The two locations (on the extreme right of 51st Division's front) were known as 'Woodcock' and 'Snipe' and were respectively about a mile north-west and a mile south-west of a kidney-shaped ring contour marked on Eighth Army maps and, consequently, termed 'Kidney Ridge'.[14] 'Approximately' and 'about' – there was complete disagreement between the two divisions over the location of all three positions. Nor was 'Kidney Ridge' a ridge; it was a slight depression with raised lips.

The dispute over 'Aberdeen' (or the 'Kidney feature') – 1st Gordons' final objective for the initial attack – which had first arisen on the morning of 24 October – had festered. In Wimberley's view it was a product of ingrained prejudice:

> I think the Armoured Commanders thought as we were new troops our map reading in the desert was sure to be wrong. Also, as they had not achieved the first night what was expected of them ... the wish that we were not on 'Aberdeen', to justify their halting so far short of their night's objective, may well have unconsciously affected their opinion.[15]

Two battalions – 2nd King's Royal Rifle Corps (KRRC) for 'Woodcock' and 2nd Rifle Brigade for 'Snipe'– would attack at 2300hrs. The artillery of two corps would support the attack. A feature of the battle which presaged the 'Montgomery method' throughout the remainder of the war was the heavy reliance placed on the Royal Artillery – which since late 1917 had attained the reputation of being the most tactically adept and technologically progressive branch of the British Army. At dawn on 27 October, 2nd and 24th Armoured Brigades would advance using the captured positions as 'pivots of manoeuvre'. Alf Flatow attended a briefing:

At about 11:00 hrs [26 October] we were called to RHQ where the Colonel had just returned from Brigade with new orders for a move. The gist of what the Colonel told us was the two Sherman squadrons were to advance to a feature called 'SNIPE' after the area had been recce'd by Squadron and Troop Commanders and the tanks were to be dug in and be sort of pill boxes.[16]

The tank crews, already fatigued from a combination of sleep deprivation and their heavy involvement in the *Lightfoot* fighting, were now experiencing side-effects from Benzedrine they had been given. Flatow continued:

By now we had taken our second and third doses of 'Pep' tablets and I was feeling very queer – I suffered in a slight way from hallucinations. I kept seeing things which didn't exist; others experienced the same thing. As for the Colonel he saw the sky all divided up by grid lines like a map. This lasted quite a time. Giving orders the next day the Colonel kept thinking 'Willie' Williamson was Bill Watson and at night I suddenly saw a man riding a bicycle coming straight for me – in the middle of the Desert! We all wished we hadn't taken the darned things.[17]

The night assembly of 41st and 47th RTR of 24th Armoured Brigade was chaotic:

During the small hours of the morning the Provost section of Brigade came forward and marked the centre line of the 41st and 47th Battalions but when first light came there was no sign of them and we got rather worried. However, they approached at last and in my opinion a greater military shambles was never before witnessed. Two separate lines of tanks went over the ridge, they lost the centre line, part of the 41st got mixed up with the 47th and I myself was responsible for dashing over to 'Tiger' Slater, a Squadron Leader of the 41st and put him on the right track.[18]

For the infantry attack, 2nd KRRC's commander, Lieutenant-Colonel William Heathcoat-Amory, chose to make a 'motorized' advance with carriers in front of lorries carrying infantry, machine guns and the anti-tank portees at the rear. The carriers 'bumped' a small German position before coming under small-arms and anti-tank gun fire from close range. Rather than dismounting, the lead company drove on to reach what was thought (in the darkness and under fire in an almost featureless landscape) to be 'Woodcock', capturing six anti-tank guns and almost a hundred prisoners in the process. They dug in to the south-east of

Pt 33, east of 'Woodcock'. The battalion's unorthodox approach had achieved a measure of success on which an armoured advance could develop and, during the day, they were largely untroubled by the Germans and Italians.

The 2nd Rifle Brigade, with Royal Engineers and 239 Anti-Tank Battery accompanying them, made a more conventional dismounted advance with their carriers moving in front. Supporting artillery fire seemed, however, to be falling on a different compass bearing i.e. further south than expected.[19] Lieutenant-Colonel Victor Turner decided to advance towards the shell fire. Meeting little opposition and having advanced sufficiently far to consider themselves on 'Snipe', they moved to consolidate for all-round defence in the undulating ground – as per their instructions. This included the deployment of the anti-tank guns by the anti-tank company commander. Major Tom Bird of the 2nd Rifle Brigade, recalled:

> I accompanied my Colonel in the attack so that I would be there to meet the guns when they arrived and allot them their fields of fire. After we had done the 2,000 yards, the Colonel called for a round of smoke which landed within 100 yards and I remember the Colonel saying 'Well, here we are and here we will stay'. We sent for the guns which were pulled behind their portees. We dug them in as best we could in the middle of the night and sent the portees away.[20]

The consolidation was covered by aggressive reconnaissance by the carrier platoon, as 2nd Rifle Brigade's Lieutenant Dick Flower described:

> Having attacked and occupied a position, it was quite normal for the Bren gun carriers to be sent forward – not only to reconnoitre forward of the position which we were defending but also to cover the digging-in of the guns and the riflemen in the position.[21]

Helped by bright moonlight, Flower and his men navigated through a minefield gap and, beyond it, took a number of prisoners before discovering a leaguer of what Flower estimated was fifty or more tanks:

> It became quite clear that these German tanks were in the process of being replenished and they had a number of lorries there. Quite clearly they were filling up with petrol and being replenished with food and water and ammunition. So we decided this was a super target in view of the fact that we could see about 200 or

300 yards. We started firing with our Bren guns at these replenishment lorries. Being soft-skinned vehicles with no armour round them, a number of them very soon caught fire, which was very satisfying. As a result of this, of course, the German tanks started to open up. They weren't quite sure where we were or who we were but they managed to locate us and started firing mainly high explosive shells at us but also machine-gun fire from the gun turrets.[22]

After this remarkable display of aggression, the carrier platoon hastily retired.

The events that followed should not obscure an important point regarding the infantry's continued faith in the armour. In disclosing its positions the battalion was *relying* on 1st Armoured Division's arrival at dawn.[23] This faith was by no means based on new tactical principles occasioned by Montgomery's arrival but lay in Eighth Army tactical doctrine that had existed under Auchinleck, Ritchie and even before. It remained to be seen whether it was misplaced.

The first counter-attack arrived in the shape of tanks of 15. Panzer-Division and Divisione 'Littorio' appearing approximately 200 yards from the battalion position. Flower continued:

Our anti-tank guns with their 6-pounder guns got their first shoot of the – I was going to say day – of course it was still night – and they let loose at very short range and managed to knock out I think it was three in that little action, three German tanks which caught fire. The German tank crews dived out of their turrets and, as they dived out of their turrets, the machine-gunners were able to train their guns on these turrets and, in many cases, kill the German crews as they bailed out.[24]

It was the first time the anti-tank gunners had used the 6-pounders in action and there had been doubts concerning their efficacy, but Sergeant Joe Swann felt these had been dispelled:

Well, as far as I could see, everybody was quite happy. The guns were scoring and stopping them. I think this was the biggest morale booster. I think if some of these tanks had come straight on after being clouted by two or three shells, we'd probably all have been saying 'Get back out of it'.[25]

This was another example of the morale-boosting effects of the new equipment Eighth Army units were now receiving. Another unexpected opportunity for the 6-pounders to wound their opponents arrived when, at first light, two groups of tanks emerging from the leaguer offered exposed flanks and prime targets. The British claimed six Panzers, eight M14s and two *Semoventi* destroyed and two other Panzers hit.[26]

There was an unfortunate 'friendly fire' incident at 0730hrs when the riflemen were shelled by tanks of 24th Armoured Brigade[27] whose cautious advance had been dictated by a lack of knowledge of the dispositions. Shermans and Crusaders from 41st RTR led the advance and found the ground 'very unfavourable for the Regiment to fight on and littered with anti-tank guns – 50mm, 7.62cm and 88mm. Heavy shelling made visibility difficult and our artillery was not able to silence the enemy guns.'[28] Alf Flatow observed 41st RTR's attack:

> The place was alive with A/T [anti-tank] guns including some 88mms and it certainly was no fit country for tanks to advance over. The 7th Motor Brigade had put in an attack on our right that morning and it was presumed that all A/T guns had been put out of action by them. This was certainly the case as far as the two which had been firing across our flanks were concerned but there were many others, and many a Lancashire lad was killed that day, many of them officers.[29]

Unable to gain close contact with the Rifle Brigade, and considering it 'useless to attempt to secure [their objective] – a feature which did not exist', the tank units withdrew to hull-down positions.[30] This caused some panic amongst 24th Armoured Brigade's reserve unit, as Alf Flatow remembered:

> And then the atmosphere changed – something happened that made our bowels cling and our mouths dry up – some Shermans appeared over the ridge in front of us, some reversing, some facing us, some in flames – they were odd tanks of the 41st and 47th Battalions retreating, coming out of it. Some stayed with us, blocking our view, getting in our way, others passed through us and went away. The shelling increased, the Colonel's voice boomed over the air, 'The Regiment will not retire one yard but will stand and fight where it is'. Cheerful words! How I cursed everything.[31]

German use of the unit's wireless frequencies compounded the demoralization:

> Then the wireless – my wireless – went loud and a voice talking a mixture of Lancs and Yorks started to pump out propaganda, in this form: 'Aye, it's the 45th, 41st and 47th Regiments, they came from Lancashire and Yorkshire. We'd be

much better at home in our gardens with our wives. We can't do anything against the German artillery. These 88mms are so accurate I don't know what we're fighting for.' It was all in that strain, two soldiers talking to each other. To make matters worse I got it over my I.C. as well as my 'A' set and I couldn't get hold of the RHQ at all – it just blotted the whole thing out. After stopping a little it came on again, much louder, obscene words were thick in the dialogue and believe me it was incredibly demoralising. I switched off my set so my crew couldn't hear it – as it was they were rather windy.[32]

In the face of seeming disaster, Flatow was fatalistic:

The horrible thing was we couldn't see why it was that the other two regiments had retreated and we expected German tanks to come into view at any moment. When the Colonel gave out his momentous speech before the propaganda started, I really felt it was the end and I just resigned myself to meet it. It was a most peculiar feeling and one I don't want to have again.[33]

But further disaster did not ensue and the tanks held firm against this major Axis counter-attack. Consequently, Lumsden decided to bring up 133rd Lorried Infantry Brigade to reinforce 7th Motor Brigade during the night and planned a further advance.

Meanwhile, 2nd Rifle Brigade was continually subjected to attacks from German and Italian armour and artillery. Now its war experience showed its significance, as Dick Flower described:

A lot of one's actions are automatic. I was lucky enough to be in a regular battalion of the Rifle Brigade largely composed at that stage of the war of regular soldiers who'd had extremely good training, had had a lot of experience in the desert. The battalion was in the desert from 1940 onwards so we'd had 2 years' experience of the desert and I think as a result of the splendid training we'd received a lot of these actions were automatic.[34]

Also of significance for morale was the feeling of 'winning', as Sergeant Joe Swann made clear:

We realized we were cut off because on two or three occasions our own Sherman tanks had come through from the rear – our rear – and on one occasion three

Sherman tanks more or less got to our position. I'm afraid the German 88s opened up and they were finished within about half a minute and three tanks had disappeared. Also our own wounded were lying about. The thing is the morale of the men, who knew we were fighting to the finish. But we were scoring and this is the big thing: we were winning.[35]

The fact that for much of the day many Axis units were unaware of 2nd Rifle Brigade's presence does not diminish its achievements. Nor did it prevent vigorous armoured assaults. The Italian *carristi* (tank crew men) demonstrated the incredible courage needed to fight with their inferior tanks and self-propelled guns. The regimental commander of 133° Reggimento Carri, Colonnello Amoroso, ordered an attack for 0700hrs in close collaboration with the Stiffelmaier Kampfgruppe. Capitano Costanzo Preve of XII Battaglione Carri, 133ª Divisione Corazzata 'Littorio', told the story:

The 12th Battalion attacks. In spite of the violent enemy fire and the resultant initial losses of tanks and men, the battalion advances firmly, keeping a certain distance from the anti-tank guns, which are extremely well dug-in and camouflaged. Suddenly there is violent fire from a further eight or ten anti-tank guns hidden on our left and located in depth. Their fire claims a number of victims and the battalion advance comes to a halt. Enemy fire becomes more and more violent. The survivors then give incredible proof of valour. Second-Lieutenant Camplani from the outside of his vehicle urges his tanks on to the attack, and at their head drives his own machine at full speed at the most advanced anti-tank gun. A belt of mines halts him and then a shell breaks its tracks. The vehicle commanded by Second-Lieutenant Stefanelli is hit and explodes; that of Lieutenant Pomoni is struck as he advances at the head of his company; Lieutenant Bucalossi's tank is hit and set on fire. At 11:30 hours Colonel Teege orders a withdrawal back to the start line. The vehicles that have been brought back are dispersed in a wadi and the damaged ones, except the burnt-out ones, recovered.[36]

The losses reported were: tanks – 9 burnt, 3 hit and immobilized but recovered. Personnel – 4 dead, 11 wounded.

Increasingly desperate, 2nd Rifle Brigade's defence depended on its 6-pounders and especially on its sergeants, the gun team leaders. According to Joe Swann:

There was three or four tanks coming through and no gun could engage them so I stood up and shouted out to Sergeant Miles to 'take on', but then I was told that Sgt Miles had been hit. I decided that I had better go across myself. So I stood up and started to run – I had about 50 yards to run – and as I did so, the German tank opened up – I expect with a machine-gun. I straight away went to ground and crawled 30 or 40 yards on my stomach. When I got to the gun, I found there was no available ammunition so I scouted around and found a box with 3 or 4 rounds in it. I then took one of these rounds out, put it up the gun – at the same time noticing that the German tank was searching for me. He'd seen me go down somewhere. And I thought 'Well, I'll go and move this gun quick before he can get one out at me. I swivelled the gun round and let him have one over open sights. It hit the tank and jammed his turret. I then put another gun [round] up the breach and put this into him, causing casualties because two or three chaps jumped out leaving one man in there badly wounded who was screaming out for help. I then got the rest of the crew up on to the gun at this stage and I went back to my own platoon.[37]

Prominent among the defenders was Colonel Vic Turner, who led by example, manning a gun himself at a critical point in the fighting and suffering a severe head wound in the process. At this time the 6-pounder's superior range over the Italian tanks' 47mm guns enabled it to account for five M14/41s and a Semovente da 75/18. However, the gun was only as good as the training of the men who operated it, and when coolness under fire was at a premium, it came from being well trained. Men like sergeants Charles Calistan (who destroyed three M14/41s with successive shots) and Joe Swann demonstrated this fact, whilst the whole action illustrated the excellent morale of this long-established and experienced Eighth Army battalion.

During the fight, Tom Bird was wounded whilst in the thick of the action:

I'd gone up to see one of the platoon commanders, Jack Toms, and we were discussing how to re-arrange his remaining men and guns when a shell landed just beside us. He was hit in the hand and I was hit in the head. I kept going for a bit but in due course with the heat and exhaustion I passed out. After dark, the Colonel and I were sent off in a jeep with a driver. Neither of us was up to much. After a bit we were both asleep and I remember being woken up by the driver who said 'I think we are in the middle of a minefield'. Not very welcome news.[38]

Fortunately, the driver was either mistaken or the jeep's occupants' luck still held out and the wounded colonel and major were treated at a New Zealand dressing station.

The battalion was mistakenly withdrawn but had now knocked out an estimated twenty-two German and ten Italian tanks. Sergeant Calistan's reaction on withdrawal epitomized that of many of the unit: '[I] did something you may think rather stupid – I went back and kissed my gun'.[39] Tom Bird was conscious of his unit's achievement but more acutely aware of its losses:

> I knew that we had knocked out a lot of enemy tanks and it was regarded as a great victory but at the time it didn't seem to me like much of a victory. All I could think of was that we had lost all our guns and all my officers had been killed or wounded.[40]

The sequel to the 'Snipe' action was unfortunate. Lumsden's decision to bring up 133rd Lorried Infantry Brigade as reinforcements was prejudiced from the beginning by the continuing problems with map locations. A description of the advance as 'ill-conceived'[41] was a masterly understatement. Private Eric Laker of 4th Royal Sussex Regiment, 133rd Lorried Infantry Brigade, recounted:

> Almost from the start the manoeuvre was a fiasco – unfortunately for us! We arrived at the appointed starting line at approximately 22:15 hrs, apparently 45 minutes late, for the preliminary barrage by the Corps Artillery had ceased at 21.15 hrs. Another barrage had started and been cut short again because we were still not there. Absolute chaos reigned. Officers were dashing here, there and all over the place, trying to put their men 'in the picture' but, owing to the rush, instructions were perforce of a very much abridged nature.[42]

Further mishap occurred in the advance, as Douglas Wimberley observed:

> Due to faulty map reading, as to where the 1st Gordons on 'Aberdeen' were in position, the 4th Sussex actually began to fire into them from the rear, thinking the Jocks were enemy... Luckily for us, little damage was done, but this incident did not enhance our opinion, at the time, of the Armoured Divisions.[43]

Eric Laker witnessed the scene soon after:

In the distance I could see a bright glow which as we approached turned out to be one of our English 3-tonners. It was the ration truck of the Gordon Highlanders, set on fire by our forward companies. Apparently the chaps had not been told to expect any of our own troops in front of them, in fact they had been told to shoot up anyone they came across. Consequently when they came up to a company of the Gordons they opened fire on them and inflicted severe casualties until the error was realised.[44]

Co-ordination between armour and infantry also broke down. Eric Laker continued:

Forward again, passing a derelict tank out of which I got a grand little automatic. We then came to some Italian trenches and stopped there. It was now about dawn and we heard the tanks warming up in the distance. (Wed 28 Oct). We then saw a couple of Crusaders come up and lay a perfect smoke screen, but when it had cleared all our tanks had WITHDRAWN under cover of it. We did not worry unduly, however, thinking they were perhaps going through in a different place, but concentrated on keeping well down as the stuff was now coming thick and fast. MG fire was singing about in goodly quantities also.[45]

Eventually the battalion occupied positions east of 'Woodcock' where their lack of desert (and combat) experience was soon cruelly exposed by the inevitable counter-attack of 15. Panzer-Division. Private 'Dusty' Ayling, also of 4th Royal Sussex Regiment, recalled:

Apart from lack of sleep in this rather noisy affair, all went well from our point of view, until 8.30 a.m. on the following Wednesday morning, when a German 50mm armour-piercing shell went through my bren-carrier, catching it on fire. We had to hop out quickly, as a carrier has two ten gallon petrol tanks, and sixteen gallons reserve. The two members of the crew, apart from getting burned badly, were both injured, one was shot through the foot, and the other in the stomach, by small-arms fire centred upon us as we baled out. Part of my clothing was on fire, but I managed to throw it off. I was most fortunate, being the driver, in also being the only one uninjured, but was however, put quickly and expeditiously, 'into the bag' just the same. So here we were, miles from anywhere, with no transport, and no chance of a getaway, for the German Mark IV tanks which had ranged upon us, were upon us in numbers, but they had ceased firing I am glad to say. They came up and took us prisoners.[46]

For Eric Laker, it was 'the shock of our lives':

> We were contentedly playing with our automatics when I looked up and saw
> some of the fellows climbing out of their slit trenches with their hands up! One
> even had a white handkerchief tied to his rifle. I blinked and then looked round.
> I saw a tank that had come over the ridge with others on the right of it. A fellow
> was sitting on the top with a nasty looking LMG which he was waving around in
> a most unfriendly manner, and walking beside the tank was another chap with
> a revolver. He was waving his hands around him indicating to our fellows that
> they were to come to him and surrender. Then to my horror I saw a black cross
> on the front of the tank.[47]

The rapid counter-attack was enough to overcome the battalion: forty-seven
were killed, 342 taken prisoner before any armour could intervene. This 'local'
reverse 'during a battle which is nevertheless being steadily won'[48] was startling
in being unique in Second Alamein. It was reminiscent of some of the July
losses when Auchinleck commanded. But the circumstances were very
different.[49]Although not possessing 2nd Rifle Brigade's considerable experience
of desert fighting, 4th Sussex had, like all 44th Division, had considerable
training in Montgomery's period as commander. Despite this, its performance
was almost naïve. The same could be said about some of the Territorial
armoured units (24th Armoured Brigade, for example, which demonstrated
great courage and endurance but was tactically raw) at this time. Taken as a
whole these were not ringing endorsements for the Army Commander's
'thorough' preparations.

———————

Doubts about Montgomery's abilities had existed in the minds of several British
politicians even prior to his appointment as Eighth Army commander.
Simmering beneath the surface, they suddenly re-emerged when news of his
abandonment of the *corps de chasse* and the reorganization of his reserves was
received by members of the Cabinet in London. On 29 October, Alan Brooke
awoke to a crisis occasioned by a late-night drink and conversation between
Churchill and Foreign Secretary Anthony Eden.

His subsequent meeting with Churchill showed the worst of the Prime
Minister's character. Brooke's handling of the matter equally illustrated the
latter's enormous importance in managing British politico-military relations:

I was met by a flow of abuse of Monty. What was *my* Monty doing now, allowing the battle to peter out (Monty was always *my* Monty when he was out of favour!). He had done nothing now for the last three days, and now he was withdrawing troops from the front. Why had he told us he would be through in seven days if all he intended to do was to fight a half-hearted battle? Had we not got a single general who could even win one single battle? etc. When he stopped to regain his breath I asked him what had suddenly influenced him to arrive at these conclusions. He said that Anthony Eden had been with him last night and that he was very worried with the course the battle was taking, and that neither Monty nor Alex was gripping the situation and showing a true offensive spirit.[50]

At a later meeting, Brooke defended *his* Monty (it cannot be denied that Montgomery *was* Brooke's *protégé*) with support from the South African Premier, Field Marshal Jan Smuts. He also made effective reference to Eden's own service in the Great War to support his somewhat off-the-cuff analysis of Montgomery's actions:

I said since the Foreign Secretary had been a Staff Captain* in the last war he must be familiar with administrative matters. (Winston was always drawing my attention to the fact that Eden had been a Staff Captain and therefore familiar with military matters!) Had he not observed that Monty's attack had advanced the front several thousand yards, did he not remember this entailed a forward move of artillery and the establishment of new stocks of ammunition before another attack could be staged? Finally the Foreign Secretary accused Monty of withdrawing formations. Had he forgotten that the fundamental principle of all strategy and tactics lay in immediately forming new reserves for the next blow? I then went on to say that I was satisfied with the course of the battle up to the present and that everything I saw convinced me that Monty was preparing for his next blow.[51]

Brooke's analysis combined an expounding of the principles of 'bite and hold' (a concept well understood by many of those present who had experience of warfare on the Western Front, especially in 1917) and a robust display of confidence in his subordinate general.

---

* Eden had been a Brigade Major in 198th Brigade, 66th Division in late 1918.

When Brooke and Churchill met again late that evening, the Prime Minister was charm personified, at pains to smooth over any ill-feeling that might remain from their earlier dispute:

> This forged one more link between him and me! He is the most difficult man I have ever served with, but thank God for having given me the opportunity of trying to serve such a man in a crisis such as the one this country is going through at present.[52]

After a year as Chief of the Imperial General Staff, Brooke was learning how to deal with confidence with the capricious and impetuous Churchill. He had struggled with his responsibility 'to enforce in stubborn argument the compulsion of strategic facts upon Churchill's restless genius without losing its astonishing impetus and fertility'[53] but was now mastering his role. His position was never again seriously under threat. It was not without cost. The arguments with Churchill and the Prime Minister's erratic hours were tremendously wearing. Regarding the battle in Egypt, Brooke remained dependent on Montgomery and Eighth Army achieving military success. His own doubts remained:

> On returning to my office I paced up and down, suffering from a desperate feeling of loneliness. I had, during that morning's discussion, tried to maintain an exterior of complete confidence. It had worked, confidence had been restored. I had then told them what I thought Monty must be doing, and I knew Monty well, but there was still just the possibility that I was wrong and that Monty was beat. The loneliness of those moments of anxiety, when there is no one one can turn to, have to be lived through to realize their intense bitterness.[54]

Despite tempering Churchill's ire, Brooke could not prevent Eden from contacting Richard Casey, the Minister of State responsible for the Middle East, and persuading him to visit Eighth Army Tactical Headquarters in company with Alexander and McCreery on the morning of 29 October. Once again, Montgomery's outward portrayal of confidence was important in reassuring his visitors but by now it was based on more concrete information that the Axis forces were struggling. The support of his Chief of Staff and the expectation of Brooke's support for their approach were of great assistance. Guingand practically threatened Casey if he interfered. Alexander and McCreery were also bullish. The crisis of confidence passed.

Whilst McCreery and Alexander were at Montgomery's Tactical Headquarters, an important meeting took place at which they, Montgomery, Guingand and Leese were all present. There is some controversy over the decision resulting from that meeting.[55] However, the outcome was that an initially unwilling Montgomery was persuaded to change the attack front for *Supercharge* from the coast road to a point further south believed to be a boundary between German and Italian units. Guingand's arguments with reference to the morning's intelligence reports were probably the decisive factors, but Alexander, McCreery, Guingand and Eighth Army's Intelligence staff all seem to have been in agreement about the virtues of the change. Brigadier Edgar 'Bill' Williams, Montgomery's Chief of Intelligence, even went so far as to observe that: 'It wasn't a specially brilliant idea because I mean it was a fairly obvious thing to do.'[56]

Most importantly, the change of plan negated Rommel's efforts (known to Williams and his team) in reorganizing his forces so that 90. leichte-Afrika-Division was responsible for the coastal sector, with 21. Panzer-Division in reserve north of Tell el Aqqaqir and Divisione 'Trieste' occupying the positions previously held by the Panzer division. To Rommel, however, the *obvious* thing for the British to do was attack north-westwards along the coast towards Sidi Abd el Rahman and he had deployed his few remaining reserves accordingly.

Of crucial importance to the success of *Supercharge* were the continued efforts of the Australians at the northern end of the line. It was essential to keep up pressure on the Axis forces and allow them no respite. Accordingly, on the nights of 28–29 October and 30–31 October ambitious attacks threatening to turn Rommel's left flank or cut off part of Panzergrenadier-Regiment 125 were launched. In the first, originally intended as a precursor to Montgomery's planned thrust along the coast road, 2/13th and 2/15th Battalions attacked under what the Germans described as 'the heaviest artillery fire which had so far been experienced'[57] and 'reminiscent of Great War days'.[58] This was a consequence of the use of 360 guns from four divisions and three medium regiments.

The attack started at 2200hrs when the Australian battalions, which were both already considerably depleted and tired by their involvement in the previous fighting,[59] went forward supported by 40th RTR's Valentines. Both took casualties from artillery and machine-gun fire but reached their objectives. Local opposition was subdued and the battalions dug in. Both battalion commanders were wounded, whilst 2/13th's headquarters staff were almost all killed or wounded.[60] Yet even with their leaders gone and very weak in numbers – there were about 100 men left in 2/13th's rifle companies – the Australians mounted a gritty and determined resistance in the face of counter-attacks and shelling.[61] Already true of the fighting since July, this was to be their story for the next four days.

In the next phase, 2/23rd Battalion and 46th RTR were to establish a base for a further advance by 2/32nd, 2/48th and 2/24th Battalions. The infantry and tank units had previously trained together – usually an important factor in effective co-operation in battle. It could not counter an alert opponent and inadequate opportunities for proper prior reconnaissance. When the attack did commence, some of the infantry rode on the Valentine tanks or in carriers but both vehicles and men were soon under fire. The infantry disembarked and all co-operation broke down when the tank regimental commander and most of his squadron commanders were wounded.

As the Australian official account pithily observed: 'The operation was developing into the type of muddle for which there were several derisive epithets in common army parlance.'[62] The decisive action of 2/23rd Battalion's commander in leading about sixty to seventy men in the capture of the key German position that were holding out, snatched some success from the chaos. The Australians had suffered over 200 casualties whilst only eight tanks of 46th RTR remained in running order and these were withdrawn.[63]

The defence of the captured ground throughout the next day was facilitated by the Germans having no clear idea of the Australian positions; some strayed into these and were consequently captured. One thing was certain and of great concern; the Germans still held the dominating strongpoint known as 'Thompson's Post'. Four successive attacks were made by 90. leichte-Afrika-Division against the dogged Australian defenders but all were defeated. This gave 9th Australian Division's staff breathing space to prepare the next attack, scheduled for the night of 30–31 October.

Although this next assault featured very thorough preparatory work from the Desert Air Force with a total of 150 aircraft participating and eighty-five tons of bombs being dropped on the Axis forces and defences,[64] otherwise the attack's misfortunes and complications were of a type frequently encountered in the Great War. Despite concentrated artillery support from the same 360 guns which had been available for the previous attack, overcrowding in the assembly areas and a delay in moving off meant that the lead battalion (2/32nd) 'lost' the

-pdr anti-tank guns firing portee. (Imperial War Museum, E 11223)

Winston Churchill with General Harold Alexander and Lieutenant-General Bernard Montgomery during his second visit to the Western Desert, 23 August 1942. (Imperial War Museum, E 15905)

Montgomery with Brigadier Philip 'Pip' Roberts and Major-General Alec Gatehouse. (Imperial War Museum, E 16484)

Rommel with (from left) Oberst Fritz Bayerlein, Oberstleutnant Friederich von Mellenthin and Generalleutnant Walther Nehring, commander of the Afrika Korps. (Bundesarchive Bild, 1011-784-0203-14A)

Sherman tanks of the Queen's Bays (2nd Dragoon Guards) moving up to the Alamein line, 24 October 1942. (Imperial War Museum, E 18380)

Captured Panzer III 'Special' with long-barrel 50mm gun. (Imperial War Museum, E 16567)

Italian crew of a 149/40 Modello 35 gun. The Italian artillery was generally well-respected by both enemy and ally alike. (Private Collection)

Italian Semovente da 75/18 self-propelled gun. Capable of tackling both the Grant and Sherman tanks. (Private Collection)

Panzer IV Ausf F1 from Panzer-Regiment 8 of 15. Panzer-Division with short 75mm gun. (Bundesarchive Bild, 1011-439-1276-12)

German signals post near Tel el Eisa, close to where wireless intercept unit, NFAK 621, was lost. (Imperial War Museum, MG 5581)

88mm Flak being used in an anti-tank role. The gun's high silhouette made it vulnerable in the flat, featureless desert unless well dug-in. (Bundesarchive Bild, 1011-443-1574-24)

Rommel with Generalmajor Georg von Bismarck at the headquarters of 21. Panzer-Division. (Bundesarchive Bild, 1011-785-0286-31)

Sappers of the Royal Engineers using a mine-detector, 28 August 1942. (Imperial War Museum, E 16226)

A 25-pdr gun firing during the British night artillery barrage which opened Second Battle of El Alamein, 23 October 1942. (Imperial War Museum, E 18467)

A British 5.5-inch gun in action in the desert. A plentiful supply of 100lb shells lie to hand, 14 September 1942. (Imperial War Museum, E 16776

artillery barrage. These 'traditional' difficulties aside, a bulldozer intended for use in clearing a gap in the railway embankment that ran across the line of advance also failed to appear.[65] For this task the Australians fell back on their own resources, using their entrenching tools instead. The work took three hours but was eventually completed and sufficient progress was made to allow the next stage of the attack.

The 2/48th Battalion was simply too weak in numbers and its 'tremendous' task (a four-phase operation with three sequential advances in different directions and the whole advance totalling 6,600 yards) too much for a battalion whose total strength in its four rifle companies was 213 men. The battalion had already 'been fighting strenuously for six days during which it has launched two major attacks and withstood several strong counter attacks.' Its commander, Lieutenant-Colonel Heathcote Hammer, described how:

> At Zero (01:00 hrs) our artillery barrage began and many shells fell on and near the start line, causing slight disorganization and some casualties. Our artillery fire seemed to lack the accuracy which characterized its previous support for the battalion in the earlier attack – this was due to the difficult task of firing a receding barrage with guns at all angles to the task.[66]

The 'receding barrage' in which the gunners were *reducing* the range at each lift was necessitated by the direction of the infantry advance which was *towards* their own gunners i.e. eastwards along the coastal highway into the rear of the defenders. Much of the artillery support's benefit was lost because the advancing infantry had to keep 600 yards back from the fire-beaten zone.[67]

In spite of these early problems, considerable progress was made by both 2/48th and 2/24th Battalions though they could summon only about 450 men between them. They succeeded in trapping elements of Panzergrenadier-Regiment 125 in the vicinity of Thompson's Post but could not capture the strongpoint itself. A subsidiary action by 2/3rd Australian Pioneer Battalion was also unsuccessful. All three units were left so weak that a German–Italian breakthrough was considered a serious possibility.

To counter this threat on 31 October the Desert Air Force made vigorous efforts in support of the Australians throughout the day, repelling Stuka attacks and bombing Axis troop concentrations. In the late morning thirty-two Valentines of 40th RTR took up hull-down positions just in time to meet an attack by Kampfgruppe Pfeiffer – a typical *ad hoc* armoured formation formed by the Afrika Korps for the specific task. It comprised approximately half of 21. Panzer-Division's tanks and self-propelled anti-tank guns with Flak, medium and heavy artillery support. The Valentines would be no match for Mark III and Mark IV tanks; hence their deployment hull-down. A Rhodesian anti-tank battery bolstered the defence further.[68] They and 2/3rd Anti-Tank Regiment were equipped with 6-pounders which could tackle these tanks (given favourable circumstances).

Rommel personally ordered this counter-attack but, puzzlingly (not least to the man chosen), put Thoma in charge, though it meant he 'had to leave his main front ... to direct a counter-attack on an unfamiliar front some distance away'.[69] Thoma used Kampfgruppe 361 in support of the tanks.[70] The courage of both Australian infantry and Valentine crews cannot be underestimated in this, and subsequent, counter-attacks delivered that day. Equally important were the efforts of what the Australians termed the 'football teams'* of Desert Air Force bombers. However, for Rommel the crucial factor in the successful defence was 'concentrated artillery fire'.[71] Again and again the Australian 'bite and hold' attacks were perfect opportunities for 7th Medium Regiment (RA) to use the 'stonk' against 'targets of opportunity'. Lieutenant Robert Foulds of 107 Battery recalled:

> We had much more idea at Alamein as to what was going off in front of [us] than we had previously during the war. We kept on getting nice things said about us – how true they were I don't know because there was so much firing but I suspect it did break up a lot of the German counter-attacks – especially the 'stonk' – that tremendous weight of material brought down on one spot. It must have been terrifying to have been underneath it.[72]

From their coastal positions, the regiment's 5.5-inch guns were in an ideal situation to influence the Australians' dogfight. Lieutenant Charles Laborde, from 107 Battery, describes their use:

> The one that affected us most of course was the 'stonk' because if that came through, whatever you were doing you had to stop and fire it. The same of course applied to the DF lines that were put down in front of the infantry. Defensive Fire could be very efficient. The Germans assaulted the Australians just in front

---

* Australian Rules 'Footy' team have eighteen players on the field.

of us and we got wireless back to battery to put down this Defensive Fire and ten rounds gunfire from the eight guns completely destroyed the attack.[73]

Naturally, because of the numbers deployed and their superiority in armour and weaponry, German tank losses were significantly less than the twenty-one Valentines eventually destroyed.[74] However, what mattered to the numerically superior Eighth Army was the result of the actions: steadily weakened Axis forces forced to make continual local attacks on unfavourable terms in what was, by this time, a mistaken belief that this was the critical sector.

Giving up the ground gained was anathema to Morshead, the Australian commander.[75] Orders were issued for the surviving infantry to be relieved by 2/28th and 2/43rd Battalions. The 2/28th had been rebuilt in strength and morale after its July disaster. Amongst its numbers was Lieutenant Leo Lyon:

> We went over the railway line about Tel el Eisa station. We went south driving along at very low speed. We turned west. We came into where apparently there had been a breakout attempt by armoured formations. Unsuccessful. There were burning tanks, burning vehicles, exploding ammunition – all very eerie and rather depressing for us. We skirted that. We weren't in any way fired on. We turned north and we moved into a position replacing the 24th Battalion.[76]

There were immediate problems trying to get about 450 men under cover in positions previously held by less than 150 men:

> We only had about 3–4 hours to get dug in and in co-operation with the other two battalions it was finally worked out that each battalion would have two companies north of the line and two companies south of the line. We just hoped that when daylight came we'd be able to put up some sort of co-ordinated fireplan to hold onto what was obviously a very important bit of ground. This area of ground was known as the 'Saucer'.[77]

The Germans and Italians lost little time in launching their first attack and contact with Panzergrenadier-Regiment 125 was re-established:

> Soon after first light, the German tanks appeared along the desert road. They appeared in the dead ground beyond the desert road and they would come

along turret high and observe what was going on. They then commenced to shell us and machine-gun us. This went on all day. They had the opportunity to move along the desert road along the whole of the Saucer which was about 600 metres long. So at various times during the day they would appear at various points, engage us, disappear and appear again a few hundred metres further along. They were far out beyond our range. They generally only gave us a turret to fire at – it's quite useless firing at a turret of a tank which is completely armoured – and so all we could do was lay low and hope. They also kept a continual barrage along the railway line. I went forward to the railway line to see if I could get across there only to find the area was covered by machine-gun fire. So this was hopeless.[78]

Once again, for the Australian infantry it was a matter of grimly holding on to their positions and 'sticking it'. Throughout the day they endured attacks by tanks, self-propelled guns and field artillery, Stukas and mortars, small-arms fire and 88mm guns – the last firing the much-feared and dreaded airburst. The value of this determined defence in laying the basis for Eighth Army's eventual success cannot be overstated, although it remains insufficiently appreciated. Night brought little respite although the defenders did get a hot meal. From about 0230hrs to the south an intense artillery barrage raged throughout the rest of the night. No one was under illusions concerning what the next day might bring in their own battered sector.

———————

Throughout this fighting, Rommel had had insufficient fuel for his tanks and transport to make any attempt at breaking through the Australian front. The losses to shipping bringing his vital fuel supplies had grown increasingly significant since Alam Halfa. Now the sinking on 26 October of the *Prosperina* carrying 3,000 tons of fuel and the *Tergestea* with a further 1,000 tons assumed their most deadly import for the front-line units. However, it was receipt of news of the loss of the *Louisiano* with its 1,459 tons of petrol that shattered Rommel's own morale on 29 October.[79] This was followed later by information (which subsequently proved false) that two British divisions had advanced through the Qattara Depression to positions south of Mersa Matruh.[80] The full consequences of his personal ambition in attempting to seize Alexandria and Cairo by a *coup de main* and, most particularly, the failure to overcome Malta must now have been obvious. Those who praise Rommel's 'genius' cannot ignore his responsibilities in this regard. For all the plaudits Rommel has received as a military commander, committing his forces to this offensive without securing his supply lines was military suicide. It was precisely the type of situation against which, in the British High Command, Alan Brooke worked as a bastion.

————————

Meanwhile 2nd New Zealand Division's preparations for *Supercharge* proceeded rapidly. The changes agreed by Montgomery and Guingand meant an attack front of about 4,000 yards, with an equivalent depth of advance.[81] The infantry would assault first with powerful artillery support and the Valentine tanks of 8th and 50th RTR of 23rd Armoured Brigade. Routes would once again be cleared through the minefields. Then 9th Armoured Brigade would break through the enemy gun line advancing a further 2,000 yards beyond it. The Durham Light Infantry and Highland infantry brigades (151st and 152nd under Brigadiers George Murray and Jocelyn Percy respectively) were told of their task on 30 October. Freyberg was to reserve his New Zealand infantry for the pursuit which would follow. Except for the initial twenty minutes of counter-battery fire, the New Zealand CRA, Brigadier 'Steve' Weir, was responsible for preparing and controlling the artillery plan. Once again, he turned to the creeping barrage – an old technique perhaps but an entirely appropriate methodology for the circumstances of *Supercharge*.[82]

On 30 October details of the attack plan were explained to officers at a 151st Brigade conference. For one experienced, though perhaps biased critic, Lieutenant-Colonel Fred Baker of 28th (Māori) Battalion, 5th New Zealand Infantry Brigade, the brigade planning was well below the standards of the New Zealanders:

> This conference was the most unsatisfactory Brigade or other conference I have ever attended. There was no orderly presentation (as we had been used to) of either information or of the job that had to be done, or who was to do what. My recollection of the conference was that it commenced with a discussion of whether hot tea should be supplied to the men at the start line, recognition signals, success signals and a password (finally resolved by adopting the word 'Joss' which we were given to understand was the Brigade Commander's name). On matters of more concern to unit commanders the orders were very indefinite and the only definite information given, viz., the means of getting to the Brigade start line proved later to be inaccurate.[83]

Baker subsequently discovered that the Australians occupying the area of the start line knew nothing of the attack.[84] Nevertheless, according to Lieutenant-Colonel William Watson of 6th DLI, 151st Brigade, key details were explained:

> The objectives would be the Sidi Abd El Rahman track which was way ahead in the enemy's positions. That track was very conspicuous because it was on sight lines and it had telephone poles running all the way down it. It ran from the sea or from the coast road, down towards the Qattara Depression.[85]

Captain Ian English of 8th DLI was also present:

> It was thought that if we could get onto that then we would have got through the last of the German defences and the tanks would be able to get out into open country... We were all issued with maps and we were told that the artillery support was going to be on a scale which was greater than anything so far in the war. Two brigades were to be supported by a barrage provided by thirteen field regiments and four medium regiments* and this was of course in addition to preliminary counter-battery work and concentrations elsewhere. The barrage was to move forward a hundred yards in two and a half minutes. So it was going to go on for several hours. Having reached our objective, 9th Armoured Brigade which was also under the command of the New Zealand Division was to pass through.[86]

The narrower front meant a greater concentration of artillery fire. There would be nearly one 25-pounder to every twenty yards of front; the medium regiments would add further weight.[87]

The advance required an unusual change of direction at the halfway point. For 6th DLI, the turning point was a line of seven disabled Italian armoured vehicles, as William Watson described:

> Bofors guns were to fire tracer down each flank to guide us. There were to be twenty-two lifts before you might say 'half-time'. At half-time, there'd be a lull for half an hour, after we'd got about halfway. The role of the 6th Battalion was in reserve. The 8th and 9th were to be the leading battalions and when we got to the line of seven dug-in self-propelled guns or tanks we were to do a right-hand swing and face northwards and we were to be the north side – facing northwards – of this

---

*   The two (not four) medium regiments available were 64th and 69th Medium, R.A.

bridgehead. The guns had been imposed on our maps so we could see where they were and when we got to them we were to do this quite remarkable swing northwards. Then the whole of the artillery barrage would restart after half an hour to help the 8th and 9th battalions to get onto the Sid Abd el Rahman track.[88]

Similar briefings were conducted in 152nd Brigade and Brigadier Currie's 9th Armoured Brigade. The latter would clear the way for 1st Armoured Division, which now included 2nd and 8th Armoured Brigades and 7th Motor Brigade, and which would lead the breakout. Currie's brigade had past experience of the New Zealanders' thoroughness in planning and executing operations, which was reassuring to Lance-Corporal Mick Collins of the Wiltshire Yeomanry:

We learned that the regiment was to be attached as armoured support to our old friends of the first 'do', the 2nd New Zealand Infantry Division under everyone's hero, General Freyberg. On hearing this news I think everyone was a lot happier especially as we were all put into the picture and knew beforehand down to the last man exactly what we were supposed to do and when. It helps an enormous lot when one is aware of the general picture and not left stumbling along in the metaphorical dark, as had happened so many times in the past.[89]

Nevertheless, the task to which the brigade was assigned was not made less daunting by this knowledge, as Collins was well aware:

The role of the armour was to push through to just beyond Tell El Aqqaqir and this was just fine in view of the fact that we would be travelling in the dark, through our own minefields, through a Jerry anti-tank gun screen, through uncharted Jerry minefields plus anything else they planned to throw at us for good measure. As it later transpired we met all these obstacles and I don't think any of our lads enjoyed it one little bit.[90]

When the combination of engineers, tanks and infantry had opened a channel, 9th Armoured Brigade's task was to break the strong crescent of German anti-tank guns and defended positions along the Rahman track. One thing was obvious to all based on experience of the fighting since July: sending armour without adequate infantry support against dug-in anti-tank guns was a recipe for heavy casualties and potential disaster. As Major Anthony Wingfield of 10th Hussars observed:

In retrospect it seemed to be a Balaclava charge to expect that brigade to drive through a dug-in anti-tank screen in the dark without further infantry support – particularly after our experience of the deadliness of the 88s and the depth of the German anti-tank screens.[91]

Currie initially estimated his potential brigade losses as fifty per cent. However, Montgomery told both Freyberg and Lieutenant-Colonel Sir Peter Farquhar of 3rd Hussars that he was prepared to accept considerably higher casualties: 'It's got to be done and, if necessary, I am prepared to accept 100 per cent casualties in both personnel and tanks.'[92] Nevertheless, responding to Freyberg, he deprecated the risk of such high losses because of the immediate follow through of 1st Armoured Division.

On the night of 30 October, Freyberg returned from touring the various units due to take part in the attack and, shortly after midnight, contacted Leese to ask for a postponement of 24 hours. He had encountered fatigue amongst many units and chaotic congestion immediately to the rear of the proposed attack front. Leese accepted Freyberg's judgement and, subsequently, the attack was rescheduled for the night of 1–2 November.[93]

In preparation for the attack, the infantry had been drilled in a skill familiar to their Great War forebears. Ernie Kerans remembered:

> The battalion moved up north to await its turn for the big battle. Here, camped by the side of the 'Boat track' we rested and waited, away from the shelling. We had a mobile canteen and were near enough to the sea to swim. To get ready for our part every man had to practice walking a 100 yards in exactly 2½ minutes, which was to be between 'lifts' in the 'creeping barrage'.[94]

When told of their role in the forthcoming attack, most of the men were canny enough to dismiss the suggestion that powerful artillery support would make this 'a piece of cake'. Kerans continued:

> The men could see it was not going to be so easy. Could see the officers were 'chain smoking', noticed one or two unsteady on their pins with drink taken for unsteady nerves. One officer, accidentally (?) shot his toe off. Anyway front line 'squaddies' lived for the moment and made good use of the swimming parties and the goods

from the mobile NAAFI. Enemy planes broke up an odd swimming party, but no one was hurt. We spent a couple of nice days there but soon it was time to leave.[95]

With the delay in operations, it was the afternoon of 1 November when they moved up to their forming-up positions. The Durhams' seven-mile approach march – 'a bloody long way'[96] – with equipment was especially galling, as Kerans described:

At 16:00 hours we halted for the evening meal – a tin of M and V* – not much to die off. An hour later we continued not so much as a column as an untidy 'Crocodile'. Thick layers of sand clung to our skin rags wrapped round the bolts of our weapons, to ensure they would work when needed.[97]

The final approach was through Australian positions:

The last few yards were through a wired-off gap in a minefield. It was lined with Aussies, who watched us in silence or quietly cheered us on in half-whispers. One slapped me on the back and whispered 'Sic em for me, Limey'. I got the queer feeling we were going to a dangerous sort of football match. The continuous growling of the guns and the whining of the shells seemed unreal.[98]

The men themselves were generally quiet, realizing the importance of the occasion and that they were going to have a fight on their hands. Private Jackson Browne of 8th DLI remembered:

We were going in about 1 o'clock in the morning. You just get your kit off and lie down. They give you plenty of warning. You sit and talk and one thing and another. A lot of tension. Everybody's tense. You've got to be to a certain degree – wondering what tomorrow's going to bring.[99]

The atmosphere on the eve of *Supercharge* was redolent of infantry attacks in the Great War. Private John Drew, another member of 8th DLI, wrote that:

We lay there for quite a while and after the sweat of the march we were beginning to shiver. We only had KD [Khaki Drill] on, so we cuddled up together to keep

---

*   Meat and vegetable stew, aka 'Maconachie'.

warm, and you believe me 'Sardines' had nothing on us. It was here we had an issue of rum and nothing was ever more welcome. In fact, we felt ten times better for it.[100]

With rum giving the illusion, if not the reality, of warmth – 'the body glowed even if it was so much goose-flesh outside'[101] – the men who had had 'a pretty shitty wait'[102] were now as prepared as they could be for their moment to arrive.

————————

Even whilst the infantry were getting into position, sixty-eight Wellington bombers led by nineteen flare-dropping Albacores began attacking targets about the Rahman Track and Tell el Aqqaqir. These attacks continued for seven hours. Night-flying Hurricanes attacked the Stukas' base and Royal Navy Motor Torpedo Boats made demonstration attacks along the coast. *Supercharge* would be no surprise, although its focal point might be.

CHAPTER NINE
'LA CADUTA DEGLI DEI'

For the watching Bernard Freyberg the barrage for Operation *Supercharge* was disappointing. He had envisaged something more spectacular than *Lightfoot*. The anti-climax was almost certainly because, despite the barrage's use of 192 field guns with 168 further guns employed on other tasks like counter-battery fire, the attack front was considerably narrower than before. Consequently, the artillery flashes were much more concentrated.[1] It was rather different for the attacking infantry, as Private Jackson Browne of 8th DLI observed:

> 'Get your kit on'. And then when the time comes, everybody's just waiting. Half a dozen guns opened up – pop, pop, pop, pop ssshhhhhwwww!! Then all of a sudden you hear – Bugger! The earth starts to shake. Well, you looked back and saw that lot. God Almighty! Hell!
>
> It was well organized. On each flank – on the battalion flanks – they had Bofors guns firing tracer every two or three minutes so that you could keep on line. The barrage was going now for about two minutes then they'd drop two or three smoke bombs – they were a bloody nuisance... But when they dropped you knew the barrage was lifting. You just moved in.[2]

Never before had British infantry received such artillery support in the Desert War.[3] The tried and trusted techniques from the Great War (as during *Lightfoot*) were again applicable, as Captain Ian English described:

We realized that [the barrage] in fact was our armour. That was our protection. The barrage stood on the opening line for twenty minutes while we closed up. This was the first attack behind a barrage we'd done and it was emphasized that one should always be within a hundred yards of it so one can arrive on the enemy position within a few moments of the barrage passing over.[4]

Among 9th DLI, it was Lieutenant Wilfred White's first action:

The noise was terrific, gunfire, shell bursts, mortars, rifle fire, machine-gun fire, the skirl of the bagpipes, the shouts of our charging infantry all combining in an incredible and unbelievable cacophony of sound. And above this noise we could hear from time to time the call of our Company Commander's hunting horn. It made us feel rather special and somehow comforted us.[5]

Major Teddy Worrall's hunting horn – another example of the eccentricities of British officers in combat throughout the Second World War.

The barrage rolled forwards, battering a path, until pausing at 0220hrs on the first objective. Both infantry brigades advanced to time behind it, as English recalled:

Promptly at 0105hrs we crossed the start line in formation with bayonets fixed. At that time it was a pretty dark night because the moon was well past full and ten minutes later the barrage started. We had been expecting a lot of noise. We heard the guns behind us and the flashes we could see and the whistle of the shells going over our heads and then an enormous crash and clouds of dust in front of them.[6]

The terrain, seemingly flat, did little to assist the advance. English described the scene:

It wasn't flat, but it was extremely open. There were little bits of scrub. When you got down on the ground you could see in fact there were undulations and little crests. If you took a quick look at it, standing on your feet, you'd say they weren't there at all. But in fact these little crests and pieces of dead ground were extremely useful.[7]

Dead ground, however, could conceal Italian and German defenders whilst the absence of any features, except the line of telegraph poles marking the

Rahman track, made it especially hard for any officer or sergeant with compass and map 'trying to walk a straight course through the inferno for more than two miles to an objective which was only a pencil line on a map'.[8] Jackson Browne remembered:

> The company commander had a bloke – his batman. He had to pace this out all
> the way. He had a hell of a job. He had to count the paces. Somewhere along the
> line – it was about 5–6,000 yards we had to do – I think when we got to about
> three and a half thousand yards we had to stop for consolidation. Find out what
> was happening.[9]

Despite assistance from 28th New Zealand (Māori) Battalion, which was to deal with a strongpoint on the right flank, it was the three DLI battalions who encountered the greatest problems. Initially, however, their advance met little opposition, as Jackson Browne recalled:

> The first thing I knew was some of the Germans were coming out hysterical. What
> a bloody state they were in. God Almighty! There was dozens of them coming out.
> Some of them was cradling and crying and one thing and another. It must've been
> bad then right under that barrage. But his machine-gunners were still having a
> go – the diehards, y'know. Odd mortars and that coming over.[10]

The Māori battalion had a tough fight in fulfilling its task and suffered almost 100 casualties, including its inspirational commander, Fred Baker, who was seriously wounded. The attack was conducted wholly in the spirit of its warrior heritage, as one of its officers, Major Charles Moihi Te Arawaka Bennett, made clear:

> We had to fight almost every inch of the way. We were never far behind the
> barrage which gave us good protection and did some damage too... At one spot
> we were opposed by a wall of enemy firing at us with all they had. We all broke
> into the haka 'Ka mate! ka mate!' and charged straight in with the bayonet... It was
> the most spirited attack that I myself had taken part in.[11]

The advance of 151st Brigade was led by 8th and 9th DLI. Ernie Kerans was with the latter's Headquarters Company when they first met determined resistance:

The barrage was literally raising the dust and through it I could see the single explosions of shells and grenades and multiples from scores of Spandaus and other machine-guns. My Alamein was in full swing. I realised I still had my rifle slung. Bullets were now plucking at our clothes in large numbers. The bullets and bits of shrapnel came like a shower of deadly hailstones and we had to throw ourselves down to live. On the right a vehicle burst into flames and by the light I could see A Company men trying to advance. We were ahead of them but some of them were still on their feet, others were falling or had done. There were tracers amongst them and explosions all around them. Over the sounds of the barrage and the small-arms could be heard curses and the cries of the wounded. Someone in a pitiful voice was crying for his mother.[12]

Kerans, surrounded by the terrifying sights and sounds of battle, did what the 'poor bloody infantry' always did in such circumstances: buried his nose in the dirt and hoped not to get hit:

From everywhere 'Stretcher Bearer, Stretcher BEARER!' Whatever had been on fire went out and we were just left with noise. Sight had gone but the screams and curses mixed with the chatter of the machine-guns and explosions of shells continued. We hugged the ground and bullets skimmed our heads. Ken took a bullet in his shoulder.[13]

Similar resistance was met by 8th DLI. Men were helpless as they saw mates killed by their side.

Private John Drew's memories were bitter:

Though we had to keep apart Joe and I kept in touch with one another till we were held down by machine-gun fire... Things here looked pretty grim and it was only the audacity of an NCO that got us out of it and which cost him an arm. By this time Joe and I had got our Gun going again and we began to advance with the section. The next thing I knew was a tremendous crash behind us. As I fell forward I caught a glimpse of Joe going down. Picking myself up, I discovered that, except for a few scratches, I was OK. I then walked over to Joe and found much to my regret that there was nothing I could do for him. Looking round I found what had been the cause of it all, one of the Jerrys had feigned dead. I then picked up the Gun. I must admit I was pretty mad by this time and let him have a full magazine. I am pretty certain he never lived to tell the tale.[14]

As the attack fragmented, control by officers and NCOs became difficult to exercise. Lieutenant Jamie Kennedy of 9th DLI, describing his experiences in the third person, admitted his helplessness:

> The company came to tanks, some dug into the ground, and here the fear of the power of the tanks seemed to make Jamie's men crazed; he realised that they were beyond accepting any orders other than his finger pointing out targets. If a German tried to get out of his tank no one waited to see if he was surrendering; two men jumped on the tank, pushed the German back in, dropped a grenade in and closed the lid.[15]

From a variety of motivations, men in this extreme environment of savage violence and fear committed acts that defied justification by rational explanations of revenge, orders or conditioning. The most basic instinct of survival – kill or be killed – overwhelmed them. Clear concepts of 'combat' and 'atrocity' were lost, as is evident from Jackson Browne's account:

> Quite a few went back as prisoners but there was a hell of a lot got their come-uppance. You see that list of Montgomery's – the last list we got, the final one about what he was going to do – he said the watchword is 'Kill Germans'. So that's what they did. They were shooting the buggers down like they was flies. Blokes who'd never shot any bugger before were having a go. They certainly were. I don't know if that's good or bad. It was good from our point of view![16]

Browne witnessed further callous and brutal actions, some committed in cold blood:

> We were having casualties what with one thing and another but we had no problems with mines or anything like that. We found two blokes – one was dead with the barrage and the other was typical German with his blond hair and that. They had a tin box. I think they'd been going to lay booby traps and they'd been caught in the barrage. So, he's lying there and Phil Thompson from Bishop Auckland shot the bugger. He said: '____ !' (Bad Language – you know). 'Laying so-and-so booby traps!'[17]

Distasteful as it may be to citizens of the modern democracies, such acts were committed in the defeat of fascism, giving the lie to the myth of '*Krieg Ohne*

Hass'.* Moreover, these actions were exceptional neither in the desert nor in the war in general.

Lieutenant-Colonel William Watson's 6th DLI followed the lead battalions. The necessity of adequate 'mopping up' of resistance after the first advance (another Great War principle that was still applicable) was brought painfully home to Watson:

> The tragedy was that in our enthusiasm we must have walked over some of these Italians – single chaps or ones or twos – who lay 'doggo' as we passed. Undoubtedly one of them killed my RSM, [Arthur] Page, killed my doctor who was tending [the wounded] and also Sergeant Fairley, who ... played cricket for Crook and for the battalion down in Dorset. They all three were killed together and it was a great blow. I also think young Vickers, who had just come to the battalion, who was a splendid junior officer from a well-known Durham family and whose father farmed and was an auctioneer and valuer, he too was killed.[18]

Watson, a true County Durham man, felt these losses of his 'neighbours' keenly. His men sought out the line of dug-in Italian armour marking the point at which they swung to form a north-facing flank for the bridgehead:

> Sure enough, we came across this group of dug-in tanks. It was almost too good to be true that we should find them there. Practically every one of the crews was still inside and I remember walking up to one and the corporal shouting 'Stand back, sir, stand back!' after planting a limpet mine that sticks onto the armour plating. It just blew inwards and killed the crew. I saw A Company having great fun trying to set one alight. But we did the turn and we got into these positions. The positions that we held were absolutely in the right place. Then the guns opened up again for the 8th and 9th Battalions to continue their advance.[19]

When the advance resumed, it was inexorable, as Browne described:

> The barrage had stopped for that time and then, when it started, it was time to start moving forwards. You weren't charging forward. I mean, you weren't more

---

*   'War Without Hate' – the title Rommel chose for his account of the North African Campaign.

than a bloody stroll, y'know. There were dugouts and such as that and, whether there was anybody in or not, you either fired a burst in or threw a grenade in. A lot of these Germans, they didn't know how to give themselves up they were in such a bad state and blokes were just shooting the lot of them down.[20]

Private Corley, Ian English's batman, still paced out the distance:

After we'd gone about 35 minutes from the first objective, Corley said that by his reckoning we were just about on the objective. So I said 'Right, we'll go on about another 200 yards to make certain we are there.' We realized we must be because the barrage had halted and we came up to it and started to consolidate the position. This was at 0340hrs and the barrage went on till 4 o'clock. The silence when it stopped was absolutely amazing. One thought one had almost got used to this deafening noise. Then it stopped and you could see the stars and the moon and it was a different world.[21]

On their objective, perhaps even a little beyond it, the Durhams attempted to dig in. Their survival until the tanks' arrival depended upon it.

The advance of 152nd Brigade met less opposition. The men, dressed (unlike the Durhams) in full battledress and each wearing a St Andrew's Cross made from strips of 'four-by-two'* on their backs for recognition purposes, went forwards to the sound of bagpipes.[22] Douglas Wimberley recounted:

It was not an easy attack, and George Murray and his Brigade did splendidly. Casualties were by no means light. For instance, 5 Seaforth, whose first attack it was, as they had held the whole start line on the night of the 23rd, lost 12 officers and 165 men. The whole Brigade reached its objective up to time on the instant and began to dig in on the hard ground.[23]

In its wake, two squadrons of armoured cars from the Royal Dragoons succeeded in breaking out to the west to attack supply lines and installations. With 133rd Lorried Infantry Brigade also completing its task on the left of the attack and with heavy losses inflicted on Panzergrenadier-Regiment 115 and 65° Reggimento Fanteria Motorizzata, the infantry awaited 9th Armoured Brigade's 'Balaclava charge'. 9th DLI's Jamie Kennedy wrote:

---

*   Rifle cleaning cloth.

SECOND ALAMEIN: OPERATION *SUPERCHARGE*

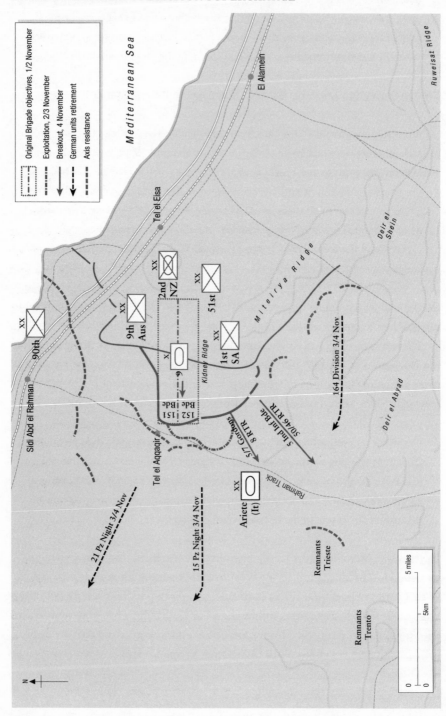

Legend:
- Original Brigade objectives, 1/2 November
- Exploitation, 2/3 November
- Breakout, 4 November
- German units retirement
- Axis resistance

Mediterranean Sea

El Alamein

Tel el Eisa

Ruweisat Ridge

Deir el Shein

90th

9th Aus

2nd NZ

51st

1st SA

152 151 Bde i Bde

Kidney Ridge

Miteirya Ridge

164 Division 3/4 Nov

Deir el Abyad

Sidi Abd el Rahman

Tel el Aqqaqir

5/7 Gordons

8 RTR

5 Ind Inf Bde

50/46 RTR

Rahman Track

Ariete (It)

21 Pz Night 3/4 Nov

15 Pz Night 3/4 Nov

Remnants Trieste

Remnants Trento

N

5 miles

5km

0

So there in their holes they hid, eyes looking around as the sun rose; and then from behind them came the rumble of tanks advancing, widely spaced, and guns at the ready. Jamie thought how cold they had been in their desert uniform at midnight a few hours earlier; now they awaited a roasting while the tanks did their fighting.[24]

The armoured might of Brigadier John Currie's three regiments was something of a façade. Montgomery had ordered on 29 October that it be brought up to full strength, but this was accomplished by supplying repaired and reconditioned tanks as imagined by Guingand. The process had been too rushed and many had mechanical faults. Of seventy-nine Shermans and Grants and fifty-three Crusaders, only a total of ninety-four tanks reached the start line.[25]

The eccentric use of fox hunting terminology was again in evidence, with the brigade assembly and advance referred to as 'The Meeting of the Grafton Hounds'.[26] The tanks encountered various problems in 'attending the meet'. For one regiment, the approach march was 'painful' as 'the track was narrow and the dust appalling'.[27] At 0500hrs Currie requested a half-hour postponement of the attack and supporting barrage because the Warwickshire Yeomanry's passage of a minefield was delayed. Nevertheless, this regiment, like the Wiltshire Yeomanry and 3rd Hussars, was ready at the original 'Zero'. However, the revised artillery arrangements meant the attack started at 0615hrs. Len Flanakin, with the Warwickshire Yeomanry, met a horrific sight:

We were in the vanguard of the armour and as we came out of the minefields we fanned out to form a line. I had just witnessed the most gruesome sight I had ever seen in my life. Where the infantry had passed by they had left a tangle of bodies from both sides but the most pathetic sight was that of a Pipe Major in kilt and bagpipes hanging on the barbed wire. We had lost a few tanks in the mines but the remainder of us reached the start line and waited for the signal to advance.[28]

The three regiments used Crusader tanks in front of Grants and Shermans but on the right 3rd Hussars had only three still running. They and the Wiltshires, in the centre, met only slight opposition initially but the Warwickshire Yeomanry, whose path of advance diverged from the other regiments, was engaged early, as Flanakin recounted:

We charged in with dawn not too far off and were soon in action against dug-in tanks and anti-tank guns including the nasty sort, the dreaded 88s. All the tanks by now were fighting their own individual battles and I was too busy to notice anything. The turret was filled full of acrid smoke each time the 75mm ejected a spent cartridge case and another shell had to be pushed in.[29]

Since the battle opened, Lance-Corporal Mick Collins and his team of 'flying fitters' had worked flat out to give the Wiltshire Yeomanry tank crews every conceivable combat advantage. Collins described how:

We were doing our damnedest to keep the old Crusaders mobile and in fighting condition. When the crews asked us if we could give them a bit more pep for their engines we were only too glad to oblige. The Nuffield Liberty engine on the Crusaders was fuelled through a 'Solex' carburettor that was sealed to limit the speed and revolutions. To appease the tank drivers we broke the seals and adjusted the carburettors to allow maximum revs and the speed increased noticeably. After all, we agreed with the drivers that a good turn of speed is vitally essential when you know there is a distinct possibility of an 88mm shell chasing you with the sole intention of blowing you and your tank apart.[30]

Now the value of applying learning from previous combat experience was revealed:

Our Squadron of Crusaders were able to travel quite smartly when conditions permitted and it was becoming fashionable with some of the lads to indulge in what was termed 'beetle crushing'. If a Jerry 88mm was being troublesome and was within range the Crusader was driven straight at the gun emplacement and straight over it, thereby inflicting considerable damage to the gun and its crew. This manoeuvre depended entirely on getting in quick before Jerry could loose one off at the Crusader. Now you can appreciate why the drivers wished to have the governors removed from their carburettors. The six-pounders on the Crusaders were a definite improvement on the two-pounder on their previous tanks but even so it is a pity they were not fitted with 75s as on the Shermans.[31]

In fact, some Crusaders in the attack were armed only with the 2-pounder gun. More significantly for their crews' chances of survival, the artillery barrage, advancing at 100 yards every three minutes, was too slow for these tanks, which depended on speed and manoeuvrability in the absence of thicker armour.[32] Those from the Wiltshires, therefore, drove rapidly through the barrage to get onto the Rahman track ahead of the heavy squadrons.

At first light, the attacking tanks came under fire from the arc of anti-tank guns. These were engaged by all three regiments and the 6-pounder of 7th New Zealand and 73rd Anti-Tank Regiments. Nevertheless, tank casualties climbed rapidly. Len Flanakin's Sherman was hit:

> The first enemy shell to hit us knocked off a track and without mobility our chances of survival were nil. We continued firing away knowing that sat amongst all the metal flying about we had to catch another one sometime. When it eventually happened it was, thank God, in the rear quarters. Our driver's voice came over the intercom informing us we were on fire. I don't think I heard the order 'Bale Out'. I was on my way up between the commander's legs and hitting ground level while he was still trying to unravel his ear phones.[33]

Having baled out, the crew were vulnerable witnesses to scenes of chaos:

> When I looked around, what a sight. There must have been over a hundred tanks in various stages of burning, while the ones left intact were either still fighting or carrying the injured to safety. Our driver and co-driver bailed out through their escape hatch in the bottom of the tank but unfortunately the co-driver got drenched in high octane petrol and was suffering temporary blindness. Apart from that all the crew were in one piece, but we were not too sure of the safest place to go. Our minds were made up for us. A passing tank spotted our injured comrade. It stopped and we hauled him aboard together with our driver to hold him on. They were driven off and deposited at a spot where a dug-in tank had previously been parked. We followed along on foot.[34]

The Grant tank of Captain John Mills of C Squadron, Warwickshire Yeomanry, was more fortunate, as its driver, Nevill Warner, recalled:

> We kept on the move and belted away at the dug-in 75s and 88s. Tanks were brewing up all around us but we didn't get hit that morning. There were flashes from guns on all sides and it wasn't until the sun came up that we knew which direction we were facing. We picked up two survivors from a 1st Troop tank which was hit and dropped them off by a gun pit near another tank. Then the Colonel came on the air 'For God's sake, get those bloody guns before they get the lot of us'.[35]

The shortcomings of the reconditioned tanks further hampered the units as they grimly endeavoured to hold the ground taken. The 3rd Hussars in particular found their wirelesses so useless that Lieutenant-Colonel Peter Farquhar and B Squadron commander, Major Mike Everleigh, had to go from tank to tank issuing orders to individual commanders.[36] Frustration under fire sometimes compounded the problem – as the Wiltshire Yeomanry tank fitters, always close at hand despite the raging battle, found. Mick Collins remembered:

> A common request was to fit a replacement radio hand-set as apparently when they failed to work immediately the irate user would knock the offending thing against the turret and this sort of treatment was not conducive to a quick repair job.[37]

In the tumult of shot and shell, men worked courageously to offer medical assistance to the casualties. The 'Heavenly Twins' of the Wiltshire Yeomanry were much admired, by Mick Collins for one:

> They were the drivers of two Austin ambulances attached to our Squadron who were forever getting stuck in the sand and having to be yanked out by the nearest available tank or four-wheel drive vehicle. Unfortunately for them, their vehicles were only equipped with rear-wheel drive and in soft sand they just dug themselves in. Those two lads did sterling work ferrying the injured back to forward dressing stations irrespective of conditions and it was not until much later that we discovered they were both conscientious objectors. They were averse to carrying any arms whatsoever but that did not deter them from being up in the thick of battle and there were probably many more out there doing similar jobs. Although their consciences barred them from killing their fellow human beings, they had the guts to go into battle areas with soft-skinned vehicles and their faith in God.[38]

Losses mounted alarmingly. The plan called for 1st Armoured Division to come through 9th Armoured Brigade and expand the funnel but Currie's anxiety must have been great as, well forward in the battle, he watched tank after tank being knocked out. The brigade's situation might have become untenable had a co-ordinated counter-attack at the gap between the Warwickshires and Wiltshires by the remaining tanks of 15. and 21. Panzer-Divisionen taken place. The Afrika Korps' confusion over the position of both Axis and British forces was a good illustration of how far tactical intelligence had declined in the Panzerarmee. When the error was finally resolved, the opportunity had passed.

The vanguard of 1st Armoured Division was 2nd Armoured Brigade, consisting of 10th Hussars, 9th Lancers and The Queen's Bays (2nd Dragoon Guards). Shortly after 0200hrs they started forwards. It was a nightmare drive, as Anthony Wingfield recalled:

> On this occasion the stage-management was not so easy, nor so good, for we had to move from track to track on our approach. Starting on Star, we changed first to Moon and then to the Australian Two Bars track.
>
> Our Recce Troop, under command of Grant Singer, led the column, but was unfortunately misdirected by a military policeman at one of the track junctions which caused a serious delay. Furthermore the sand was so soft – no watering this time – that tank drivers could not see the vehicle in front of them for dust; and often tank commanders had to shine torches to their rear to prevent collisions.[39]

As a consequence, they were delayed by approximately twenty minutes but cleared the minefields at about 0700hrs – just prior to dawn.

The hammering taken by 9th Armoured Brigade was obvious and, according to one account, led to a difficult meeting between Currie and Lieutenant-Colonel Gerald Grosvenor of 9th Lancers amidst the raging battle.[40] Anthony Wingfield accepted it was 'more than a misfortune that we were late coming to the aid of 9th Armoured Brigade' and that Currie had 'every excuse for his disparaging accusations'.[41]

Tanks from 2nd Armoured Brigade were already getting into action. Wingfield described the scene:

> As the 10th Hussars deployed into the open, the situation seemed to be one of chaos; for the enemy was putting down smoke as well as firing rather too accurately at the end of Two Bars Track. As RHQ cleared the end of that track I remember seeing some tanks several hundred yards away on our right front. Jack Archer-Shee thought they belonged to our B Squadron and drove off towards them. Fortunately I held back the rest of RHQ for a few minutes; and then saw Jack's tank go up in flames. Those tanks belonged to 15th Panzers and not to B Squadron.[42]

Archer-Shee and his crew were lucky to escape unharmed but now the newly arrived regiments knew the type of opposition they were facing and recent combat experience, together with the arrival of dawn, probably conditioned the brigade's subsequent response.

The decision taken at this stage by Fisher, the brigade's commander, and supported by his divisional commander, Briggs, although subsequently criticized for excessive caution, was certainly appropriate for a force with a considerable advantage in available assets over its opponent. With the support of Priest self-propelled 105mm howitzers from 11th (Honourable Artillery Company) Regiment, Royal Horse Artillery, and the Desert Air Force, and using the indirect-fire capability of the Shermans, 2nd Armoured Brigade could retain a hold on the positions gained, allowing the Germans to be the architects of their own destruction through their counter-attacks, whilst making careful forward movement themselves. According to Wingfield:

> By 8.00 a.m. the whole of 2nd Armoured Brigade was deployed clear of the minefield. The German tanks had withdrawn from our front leaving four knocked out behind them. The Bays on our right and in touch with what was left of the 3rd Hussars were being heavily counter-attacked. We were ordered to be ready to go and support them. But before we moved another tank counter-attack appeared over the crest of the Aqqaqir Ridge to our front. A and C squadrons held their fire till the enemy tanks were on the forward slope then 'let them have it,' reaping a fine harvest before the remainder retired to hull-down positions behind the crest.
>
> Using these tactics, the British armour gradually prevailed. Numerous columns of smoke on the enemy side signified many tank brew-ups. The enemy's tactics had been to launch concentrated panzer attacks through his anti-tank screen and on a narrow front. We allowed the panzers to come onto our guns, rather than sally forth to meet them. That way, their 88mm anti-tank guns could not assume a decisive role. When rising casualties forced withdrawal, the panzers would reassemble and probe elsewhere. We met them head-on. Although numbers overall were in our favour, it wasn't always so at the point of contact.[43]

Ironically, the armoured unit commanders were delivering on Montgomery's *Lightfoot* attritional aims, rather than the goals envisaged for *Supercharge*.

In this fighting, it was the turn of the Germans to find their wireless communications disrupted – as Alfons Selmayr, the regiment's medical officer, discovered:

We were constantly subjected to jamming on the radios. Tommy had captured the signals operating instructions of Panzer-Regiment 8 and attempted to confuse us and yap his way into our radio traffic.[44]

The doctor was in the thick of the fighting throughout the day, caring for the mounting numbers of casualties:

As I had moved up, *Oberleutnant* Dübois had waved to me. Now they were also bringing him back with a head wound. It was said he looked so terrible that his crew did not even want to show him to me. We tried to eject Tommy twice, but we were deflected each time. An 8.8-centimetre *Flak* moved up to support us, but it was blown apart as it unlimbered. The forward lines were hit by mortar fire. A 2-centimetre *Flak* was hit; two of the crew lay on the ground, badly wounded. I took off! We placed them on our tank despite the fire; one up front, the other to the rear. I knelt on the side of the turret and held on to them so that they did not fall off during the movement. Then the tank took off as fast as it could. All of a sudden, Tommy took notice of us and engaged us with a battery. Always four shells at a time; sometimes to the left of us, sometimes to the right. Thank god they were really firing poorly. Of course I still thought we were moving too slowly. I pressed myself against the turret, held on to my wounded and yelled at Krause to move faster.[45]

Having evacuated these wounded in ambulances, Selmayr returned immediately to the fray.

Rommel was well aware of what was happening to his forces. Above all, he needed to prevent a breakthrough. In his own words:

It was only by the desperate fire of all available artillery and anti-aircraft guns, regardless of the ammunition shortage, that a further British penetration was prevented.

It was now extremely difficult to obtain any clear picture of the situation, as all our communication lines had been shot to pieces and most of our wireless channels were being jammed by the enemy. Complete chaos existed at many points on the front.[46]

British tactical intelligence via the 'Y' Service, on the other hand, ensured that XXX Corps was aware of Rommel's counter-attack plans by 0935hrs. The attack would use those elements of 15. and 21. Panzer-Divisionen together with Kampfgruppe Pfeiffer to attack from the north and south of the incursion. Rommel continued:

> Violent tank fighting followed. The British air force and artillery hammered away at our troops without let-up. Inside an hour at about midday seven formations, each of 18 bombers, unloaded their bombs on my troops. More and more of our 88mm guns, which were our only really effective weapons against the heavy British tanks, were going out of action.[47]

This ignored the armour and firepower of the PzKpfw IV Ausf F2 and G 'Specials', but these were now too few in number to turn the tide.[48] Nevertheless, the British armour could not make even cautious progress and, with the arrival of 8th Armoured Brigade, the attack salient became very congested, as Arthur Reddish observed:

> The 2nd Armoured Brigade adopted the role of static defence and 8th Armoured that of the fire brigade, responding to threats to the salient as they emerged. We were first in action facing north-west, then were directed south. On one occasion, a column of enemy tanks came down the Rahman Track completely side-on to us. It was like shooting tin ducks at a shooting gallery.[49]

However, despite this success, Reddish, like other Sherman crewmen, was learning of the tank's shortcomings through the experience of combat:

> The high-explosive shell we used against the 88mm guns had no tracer and it was necessary to observe the fall of shot to determine accuracy. With the desert shimmering in a heat haze, this was by no means easy. And the gunsight of the Sherman didn't help. For such a good tank, the sights were disappointing.[50]

A tremendous battle between the armour of both sides now raged throughout the rest of the day. Reddish's descriptions capture the spirit of the day's fighting:

> The day was hot. High temperatures, aircraft active on both sides, shelling very heavy and sniper-fire also. Armour-piercing shot came from right, left and centre. A blazing Grant tank exploded as we passed by, its side flattening and the turret hurling some 50 metres into the air. The explosion was tremendous, even when wearing earphones. Each member of the crew had a set of earphones

and a microphone. We could talk within the crew and the commander with other commanders. All could hear the talk on the regimental radio network, so knew the score...

We in the heavies kept the battle at long range when possible to exploit our [ad]vantage in that area. The Italian tanks were hopelessly outranged and the German Mk IIIs also. But the German Mk IV and Mk III Specials fought us on equal terms.[51]

This wasting fight was something the already-depleted Panzer units could ill afford and approximately seventy tanks were destroyed or damaged.[52] Equally important was the loss of experienced Panzer commanders such as Oberst Willi Teege and Hauptmann Otto Stiefelmayer – both *Ritterkreuzträger* (Knight's Cross holders) of Panzer-Regiment 8. The situation was so serious that Divisione 'Ariete' – the last remaining intact armoured formation – was already being drawn piecemeal into the fighting.

In the north, the arrival of the British tanks, and especially 8th Armoured Brigade, had finally relieved the pressure on Leo Lyon and the hard-pressed Australian battalions in the 'Saucer'. Lyon recounted:

I remember about midday attempts by the Germans to wheel up an 88mm gun to our front. We had excellent observation both to the right and the left as we faced. I could see the silhouette of this gun behind the road. I could see the tractor bring it up, the tractor disengage, and then the gun crew manhandling it up to where it could be brought in to fire. But as soon as it came into position to fire, the machine-gunners mounted their guns on them and destroyed the gun crew.

At almost the same time, to our left flank I could see our armour attack appearing and I could see a larger number of tanks – it would be about thirty or forty I would have thought – with their smoke dischargers – on the turret of each tank there's a smoke discharger – and they were firing these as they went forward to try and cover the fire against them. This was a most spectacular scene and apparently they were making progress because the attack on our front seemed to disappear.[53]

The exhausted Australians, finally given respite, still managed to launch aggressive fighting patrols later in attempts to prevent Panzergrenadier-Regiment 125 extricating itself from the coastal sector.

***

At 2015hrs that evening, Thoma told Rommel the Afrika Korps would have, at most, thirty-five tanks available for action the following day.[54] Nevertheless, the British advance, which Thoma considered cautious and deliberate, had been contained.[55] However, there was further bad news from the Panzerarmee's Higher Artillery Commander (*Arko*), Generalmajor Fritz Krause, who reported that 450 tons of ammunition had been fired that day, but only 190 tons had arrived. Three hundred tons had been lost when the *Brioni* was sunk by allied bombers whilst unloading in Tobruk harbour that afternoon.[56]

With this information, Rommel recognized that in order to avoid annihilation of his forces, it was essential to make a withdrawal to positions previously reconnoitred at Fuka. In informing the Oberkommando der Wehrmacht (OKW) of this decision, Rommel spared nothing in painting a realistic and bleak picture. The ten days' fighting had been 'extremely hard' and had left the Panzerarmee no longer able to prevent the next breakthrough attempt:

> An orderly withdrawal of the six Italian and two German non-motorized divisions and brigades is impossible for lack of MT [Motorized Transport]. A large part of these formations will probably fall into the hands of the enemy who is fully motorized. Even the mobile troops are so closely involved in the battle that only elements will be able to disengage from the enemy. The stocks of ammunition which are still available are at the front but no more than nominal stocks are at our disposal in rear. The shortage of fuel will not allow of a withdrawal to any great distance. There is only one road available and the Army, as it passes along it, will almost certainly be attacked day and night by the enemy air force.
>
> In these circumstances we must therefore expect the gradual destruction of the Army in spite of the heroic resistance and exceptionally high morale of the troops.[57]

In a narrow sense, the initial *Supercharge* assault can be portrayed as a failure.[58] But the critical outcome – Rommel's acceptance of the Panzerarmee's defeat – was accomplished by the evening of 2 November. Irrespective of what happened subsequently, 9th Armoured Brigade's sacrifice had helped achieve a significant success. It remained for Eighth Army and its commander to turn this into a complete victory.

In London, the Chief of the Imperial General Staff, anxiously awaiting each fragment of news of the battle, experienced a tremendous fillip from Ultra. In Brooke's own words:

Whilst at lunch I was called up by DMI [Director of Military Intelligence] and informed of two recent intercepts of Rommel's messages to GHQ and Hitler in which he practically stated that his army was faced with a desperate defeat from which he could extract only remnants![59]

This was a remarkable and early indication of the possibility of imminent victory.

Rommel now formally confirmed the move of Divisione 'Ariete' northwards to join with the Italian XX Corpo d'Armata. Together with the Afrika Korps, they would cover the withdrawal of the other two Italian corps which consisted essentially of infantry, as well as Fallschirmjäger-Brigade Ramcke and 164. leichte Afrika-Division. The infantry formations began pulling out that night.

That evening, 51st Division was tasked with broadening and strengthening the corridor now created. Successful attacks with strong artillery support were made against objectives on the south-west edge of the salient by 2nd Seaforth Highlanders and 5th Royal Sussex. To X Corps' commander, General Herbert Lumsden, at 2030hrs it seemed that the opportunity of smashing through the remnants of the anti-tank screen that night was too good to miss. Consequently, 7th Motor Brigade, consisting of 2nd and 7th Rifle Brigades and 2nd King's Royal Rifle Corps (KRRC), was given orders to attack on a front of two miles, to make a passage for 1st, followed by 7th, Armoured Division. Corporal Donald Main of 7th Rifle Brigade remembered:

In the early evening we were told that [we] would attack at midnight to force a gap for our tanks. It was considered that the area of the Rahman Track was lightly held, although we never found out who was responsible for this view. As we had motored into the line we had heard shouts for stretcher bearers, presumably from the Sherwood Foresters and Green Howards, who were survivors of the previous attack. In view of the barrage, it would have been suicide to attempt to reach them. It was, therefore, decided that we would make a silent attack i.e. without a barrage from our guns, although the 2nd KRRC on our left and the 2nd Battalion Rifle Brigade on our right were to receive artillery support.[60]

The attack commenced at 0115hrs on 3 November.[61] In fact, whilst 2nd KRRC had strong artillery support, 2nd Rifle Brigade did not. In Main's attack with 7th Rifle Brigade, all was quiet until the battalion was about fifty yards from the

German positions. Suddenly, all hell was let loose when the Germans opened fire from the flanks with machine guns, together with flares and mortar bombs:

> Above the noise of explosions I heard the Company Commander, Major Trappes-Lomax, shout 'Up the Rifle Brigade! Charge!' Major Trappes-Lomax disappeared through a hail of tracer bullets. I felt that he could not go in by himself and gave the order to charge. I went through the enfilade fire and felt my body as I could not understand how I had not been hit. I was shouting 'Brino, where are you?' It was like daylight with the flares and mortar explosions. Before I could reach Sgt Brine, Major Trappes-Lomax said 'Go to your right'. Sgt Brine had run straight on and into a German machine-gun. He was hit all over and asked another member of the platoon to put his tin hat back on and to be put facing the enemy. His last message was 'Give my love to my wife'[62]

Upon reaching the rear of the German positions, Main and the remnants of his company had to deal with one of the guns that formed an important part of the Axis defence:

> From where we lay I could see an 88mm gun and I told Sandy that I was going for this. It was at least 50 yards away. As I ran with my rifle and bayonet the tracer from a German machine-gun was going all around me. However, I considered that if I continued running I would not be hit and eventually reached the gun followed by several riflemen.[63]

Both Rifle Brigade battalions destroyed German anti-tank and machine-gun posts and killed the occupants. However, several posts still survived and, in each battalion's case, it was necessary to withdraw because they could not bring up sufficient numbers of anti-tank guns in time for defence in the morning against what was assumed would be the inevitable counter-attacks. The KRRC did, however, retain its gains. Main's account continued:

> We met Major Trappes-Lomax and found that only twenty-two of the Company were left. We also met up with the surviving KRRC and our 2nd Battalion. We now received the order to withdraw and I was asked which way we should fight our way out. I was in favour of another route, but it was decided that we should go back the same way as we had come, also we were under no circumstances to stop for any wounded. My rifle by this time had jammed with sand and I could

not move the rifle bolt. We ran back and I would frequently look over my shoulder to watch the tracer fire which followed us from the German positions.[64]

It was an ignominious end to 7th Motor Brigade's efforts but at least these units escaped in time. A hastily planned and executed and poorly supported improvised operation had failed once again. Fortunately, the consequences were less serious in their effect than 4th Sussex's attack on 27–28 October, although for a survivor like Donald Main, the experience was no less painful. On his return the roll-call revealed that his company had only fourteen men left and his platoon consisted of only three men – himself included.[65] Many of those killed were friends from Main's pre-war Territorial days. Another such friend was Colour Sergeant Eric Kealsey, whose attempts to cheer up the survivors on the evening of 3 November when they were out of the line, led to an unfortunate misunderstanding, as Main recounted:

Later that afternoon we were relieved by a battalion of the Black Watch, and we were taken by our vehicles to an area behind the line, to obtain reinforcements and replace equipment lost during the battle. When we arrived at what appeared to us to be an unreal world, free of explosions, we went for our evening meal presided over by Colour Sergeant Kealsey. Kealsey was a great character from Territorial days and he was very fond of impersonating a queer. He and the cooks were very upset to find that D Company now consisted of only fourteen men, as they had cooked a meal for one hundred and twenty. Colour Sergeant Kealsey said to me in an effeminate voice 'What can I get for you, ducks?' I replied 'Some stew please, Eric'. Unfortunately the person next to me was a reinforcement and when asked the same question replied 'Stew, darling'. This caused a major explosion as Kealsey shouted 'Colour Sergeant to you, you little worm!'[66]

This was the postscript to a 'trifling, inconsequent, nameless battle'[67] within a battle. A failed attack and a heavy toll of casualties – soon lost in the bigger picture of general success for the British, Imperial and Dominion forces and decline of the German and Italians.[68]

The mixed fortunes of the infantry operations meant that Lumsden revised Briggs' orders; at 0530hrs. 2nd KRRC was to be supported by 2nd Armoured Brigade whilst 8th Armoured Brigade worked south-westwards. The poet Keith Douglas was a lieutenant with the Sherwood Rangers and wonderfully evoked the atmosphere of this (and perhaps another) armoured move at dawn:

The moment I was wakeful I had to be busy. We were to move at five; before that, engines and sets had to be warmed up, orders to be given through the whole hierarchy from the Colonel to the tank crews. In the half-light the tanks seemed to crouch, still, but alive and like toads. I touched the cold metal shell of my tank, my fingers amazed for a moment at its hardness, and swung myself into the turret to get out my map case. Of course, it had fallen down on the small circular steel floor of the turret. In getting down after it, I contrived to hit my head on the base of the six-pounder and scratched open both my hands; inside the turret there is less room even than in an aircraft, and it requires experience to move about. By the time I came up, a general activity had begun to warm the appearance of the place, if not the air of it. The tanks were now half-hidden in clouds of blue smoke as their engines began one after another to grumble, and the stagnant oil burnt away. This scene with the silhouettes of men and turrets interrupted by swirls of smoke and the sky lightening behind them was to be made familiar to me by many repetitions. Out of each turret, like the voices of dwarfs, thin and cracked and bodyless, the voices of the operators and of the control set come; they speak to the usual accompaniment of 'mush,' morse, odd squeals, and peculiar jangling, like a barrel-organ, of an enemy jamming station.[69]

The tank units were straight into action that morning. Arthur Reddish recalled:

At first light on November 3, the Sherwood Rangers tanks were on the left flank of an attack by the 1st Armoured Division on the remnants of the Panzerarmee's anti-tank gun screen dug-in before and behind the Rahman Track. The day started propitiously for our crew. As the regiment assembled behind the infantry line prior to advancing, a young Highlander officer left his slit-trench and jumped onto the back of the tank. He'd spotted an enemy anti-tank gun, he said. It was in the scrub only 200 metres [approximately 220 yards] away and was right in front of our position. John quickly got him into the tank and into the gunner's seat. His first shot missed but not the second. The third caused an explosion. Presumably, he'd hit the ammunition.[70]

Major Anthony Wingfield was concerned by the ammunition shortages his unit was suffering, but was soon temporarily bolstered by the arrival of another new weapon in the Eighth Army's armoury:

At first light our Recce Troop and the Crusaders of B Squadron moved out to make contact with [the] KRRC, and support them against any tank counter-attack.

The situation had become grave because the replenishment of 75mm ammunition to the Shermans of A and C Squadrons had not arrived during the night. However 4 or 5 new Churchill tanks, as an experimental detached troop, now arrived between ourselves and The Bays. These heavy tanks had been sent out to the Middle East for battle trials; whether it was the sight of these new monsters which scared the German tanks I did not know, but they withdrew behind a screen of 88mm anti-tank guns. The latter then promptly halted the Churchill tanks whose crews were possibly concussed if their tanks were not actually 'brewed up'.[71]

There were too few Churchills – a heavy 'infantry' tank for close-support work designed to replace the Valentine – for losses to these tanks to be significant at this time. Nevertheless, this British-built tank 'made a favourable impression on their crews, and also on the co-operating troops'.[72] On a more personal level, it was Wingfield's misfortune that day to be caught quite literally with his trousers down by the Germans:

It was while we were withdrawing a short way to find hull-down battle positions that Nature gave me her morning call. I dismounted but stayed close to my tank for protection. Just at 'le moment critique' an HE shell burst underneath my tank and a red flame shot between my bare legs. A momentary thought of my ancestor at 'the singeing of the King of Spain's beard' passed through my mind. Motion – in every sense – was quick and I was back in my tank in a flash and before there was another one.[73]

Throughout the day, the British armour was held up by the continued resistance offered by the screen of anti-tank guns and by the remaining tanks covering the slow withdrawal of the Axis forces on foot or in vehicles. The work of the remaining elements of Panzerjäger-Abteilungen 605 and 33 and Flak-Division 19 was especially noted by the British.[74] Nevertheless, the Axis withdrawal was observed by the Desert Air Force and the coastal road consequently came under almost-constant attack from the air.[75]

The Panzerarmee and its commander suffered another significant blow to morale in the early afternoon with Hitler's response to Rommel's plans for withdrawal, which constituted a direct order to stand and fight and, if necessary, die. In Hitler's view, this was a battle in which the commander with the strongest will to fight would ultimately win through.[76] If that was indeed the case (which it was not, of course, given the attritional effects of the last ten days' fighting), it was already too late. Alamein was lost in the mind of Rommel. A characteristically magniloquent message from Mussolini only served to compound the Panzerarmee's confusion as Rommel ordered all units to defend their present positions till the last although permitting Thoma to withdraw the Afrika Korps ten miles east of El Daba.[77] This, in effect, abandoned infantry without motor transport – almost exclusively Italians and Fallschirmjäger-Brigade Ramcke – to their fate.[78]

Meanwhile, the continued resistance of the Panzerjäger units and the Luftwaffe 88mm gun teams, combined with Freyberg's perception of the imminent collapse of the Panzerarmee as a whole, led him to suggest to Leese that a breakout through the salient's south side should be attempted. This would avoid the screening anti-tank positions. An attack by 5/7th Gordon Highlanders of Wimberley's division supported by 8th RTR was decided upon. The events of this attack were especially tragic and another indication of the problems beneath the veneer of Eighth Army's ruthless efficiency. Wimberley described them as follows:

> On the afternoon of 3rd November I was ordered to attack again, and selected the 5/7 Gordons as the freshest battalion available. With the help of George Elliot, we laid on a heavy barrage to take them forward on to the Rahman Track. Shortly before the attack was due to go in, I was amazed to be rung up by Oliver Leese to be told that our Armour was already on the objective, that the Gordons had been ordered by me to capture, and it was only a question of their moving forward. This was not my information at all, and I pleaded hard for the Tanks, if there were any there, to clear out and let my attack go in properly under a Barrage. I was told, No. It was only with difficulty that I could get leave to let, at least, a smoke barrage be fired to guide the Jocks. So, late in the afternoon they were launched in a divisional attack under Saunders with smoke only. As in the case of the 'Kidney' feature, we were again right and the Armour's Intelligence was all wrong. This time it had even more tragic consequences on many lives.[79]

Wimberley took no pleasure in being right where Leese and Briggs, whose 1st Armoured Division's headquarters was the source of the erroneous information,[80] were mistaken:

> The position was, as we had reported, strongly held. Not a sign of our tanks was to be seen, but plenty of enemy ones. To move forward in daylight, under smoke only, was impossible. The Gordons made little progress, and lost a lot of men, and

I felt it had been sheer waste of life and was sick at heart. Worst of all, thinking that it was an advance rather than an attack, the Gordons put a number of their Jocks on the top of the tanks to be carried on them forward to the objective. I saw those tanks, later, coming out of action, and they were covered with the dead bodies of my Highlanders. It was an unpleasant sight and bad for any troops' morale.[81]

The two units suffered ninety-four casualties, including sixteen officers; nine Valentines were destroyed and a further eleven damaged from about thirty-two starters.[82]

Two further attacks were planned for 4 November. The first involved 5th Indian Brigade which, according to Major-General Francis 'Gertie' Tuker:

after struggling and buffeting its way through the choked corridor, was eased forward by over 350 guns, and punched a narrow hole four miles deep through a few pickets covering the retreat, out into the open desert.[83]

The number of guns mentioned by the division's commander was important. After the debacle over the 5/7th Gordons attack, Wimberley was insistent that 1/4th Essex and 4/6th Rajputana Rifles should have the support of a fully constituted and effective artillery programme of counter-battery fire, concentrations and creeping barrage. This was all organized in a short time by the combined efforts of the staffs of 51st and 4th Indian Divisions, 5th Indian Brigade and Brigadier Weir's 2nd New Zealand Divisional artillery – a remarkable example of the maintenance of operational tempo. As a consequence, the two battalions encountered only sporadic opposition.

Before 1st Armoured Division's tanks could break out into the open desert, however, a dawn attack by 7th Argyll & Sutherland Highlanders went in. The attack of the Argylls – 'almost the last reasonably fresh infantry available' – was, as Wingfield described:

directed onto Tel el Aqqaqir, the top of the whole ridge to our front. They found the enemy gone. 2nd Armoured Brigade was ordered to advance immediately, with 10th Hussars leading (always their rightful place!), with The Bays on the right and 9th Lancers on the left. But it was not till 9.00 a.m. that we got under way.[84]

As a consequence of this action, more armoured cars were also able to break out to the south and into the open desert.

The sight of the armour passing through 5th Indian Brigade moved one overawed Havildar, Nila Kanten, to hyperbole:

> Our role was something less than a participant and more than a spectator... We were asked to break through at Ruweisat Ridge and allow all the armoured divisions to pass through and trap him. When we captured our objectives, then came the thunder of these armoured divisions passing through us. I remember that. I had never seen so many tanks going in one go. Two divisions, I think, passed through. If the head of the column of an armoured division was in Bangalore, the tail would be in Madras – so many vehicles there were and they were all racing. So many tanks, so many armoured vehicles, so many personnel carriers. Oh, the dust cloud! We created dust, we ate dust, we drank dust... Then the whole Eighth Army started moving.[85]

However, after 4,000 yards, the tanks met the Panzerarmee's rearguard of 90. leichte-Afrika-Division and the Afrika Korps under Thoma's personal command. The Afrika Korps commander and *Kampfstaffel* were in the midst of the fighting throughout the morning before the battle group was destroyed and the courageous Thoma surrendered. Fittingly, as the armour was let loose to pursue its quarry, the officer who took the general prisoner was Master of Foxhounds with the Hursley Hunt. Wingfield recalled:

> One of our tanks had 'brewed up' a German tank at considerable range and I could see a man waving a red cross flag near it. Grant Singer – the Recce Troop leader, went forward to investigate and found a highly decorated General coming towards him. Grant returned with this prize to the Colonel who decided that Grant should take him at once to Brigade HQ. On arrival there Grant was told to take him straight to Monty at Army HQ as quickly as possible, for it transpired that he was Rommel's deputy who had been on a forward reconnaissance to convince Rommel of the British breakthrough when he had been captured.[86]

At Army Headquarters, liaison officer Carol Mather described the meeting of Montgomery and Thoma:

> Well, of course, I couldn't judge him [Thoma] as a commander at all, although he was deputizing for Rommel at the time. What he had to face at Alamein was something quite new as far as the Germans were concerned, which was a set-piece attack. As a man he seemed rather a charming fellow actually. Very civilized and

you couldn't help thinking he was quite a decent one. The meeting was so short it was difficult to judge. Montgomery was tickled to death at the idea of having the commander of the opposing forces in his tent having dinner and questioning him and discussing the progress of the battle. This was a great feather in his cap really. It was just the kind of situation he enjoyed. And it was a very amusing meeting.[87]

Whilst 1st Armoured Division was engaged in this action, Major-General John Harding's 7th Armoured, led by Brigadier 'Pip' Roberts of 22nd Armoured Brigade, was out in the open desert from 0830hrs. But it too encountered strong resistance from the remaining Italian armour, XX Corps' artillery and some 88mm guns. Despite Roberts' urgings by radio to his units to 'Brush them aside, we have bigger fish to fry!',[88] the opposition proved a tough nut to crack. A long-range artillery duel in which the excellent Italian guns, under centralized control, performed well, went on all day and there were frequent clashes between Roberts' brigade and the inferior Italian armour of Divisione 'Ariete', 'Littorio' and 'Trieste'. Soldato Antonio Tomba of 'Ariete' remembered:

Our poor M13s with their 47mm guns could never be effective against them – we could only hope to hit their tracks in order to immobilize them at least; our shells just bounced off when we hit their armour. In addition, while they numbered sixty, we had little over half of that. We did everything possible, giving our very best… We had no chance, but we proved a difficult opponent for the English: the secret lay in manoeuvring the tank properly. Our tactics were simple: always keep moving, never expose your flank to their guns, and don't let them fire first. All the crew must act as a single unit: everyone must know what to do and when to do it, in complete harmony with each other. We managed to hold off the enemy that day, but they replaced their losses again while we could only count how many of us were left alive. We could never have resisted for another day… Everyone fought an unequal battle without complaint and without yielding, even when there was no water and no food. We were lucky when it started to rain as this slowed the English advance, and we, the last survivors of the Ariete Division, were able to escape their pursuit.[89]

The Germans were grudgingly admiring of their allies' bravery, which undoubtedly made possible the escape of many remaining German units. Doctor Alfons Selmayr saw assault guns of Divisione 'Ariete' conduct an attack. 'Despite their poor armour, they advanced boldly. Of course, they were blown to bits in a miserable fashion.'[90]
Major Hans von Luck was more generous:

It was heart-rending to have to witness how the Ariete Division (our most loyal allies) and the remains of the Trieste and Littorio Divisions, fought with death-defying courage; how their tanks (the 'sardine tins' so often mocked by us) were shot up and left burning on the battlefield. Although I was engaged in actions myself, I kept in contact with the XX Italian Corps until it was almost surrounded. At about 1530 hours, the commander of the Ariete Division sent his last radio message to Rommel: 'We are encircled, the Ariete tanks still in action.' By evening, the XX Italian Corps had been destroyed. We lost good, brave friends, from whom we demanded more than they were in a position to give.[91]

The Italians' resistance was finally overcome when 4th Armoured Brigade tanks attempted to complete their encirclement from the south. Roberts described the day as 'very good battle practice for the brigade!'[92] but 7th Armoured's momentum had been arrested and night intervened shortly after the advance started again. Jack York remembered the scene:

As we carried on in the direction our tanks had taken, we could see, reaching up into the sky, great columns of black smoke, and enormous dust clouds. This was the funeral pyre of the Italian Armoured Corps (Ariete, and remnants of Littorio and Trieste Divisions), who had been engaged for several hours by nearly 100 tanks of the 22nd Armoured Brigade. Nearly all their tanks had been knocked out, and a large number of field and anti-tank guns were destroyed or abandoned. The Italians had fought with exemplary courage in this action, and although nearly surrounded, had held their positions to the last. During this day also, our 1st Armoured Division to the north of us, had severely battered the weakened Afrika Korps, giving them no choice but to retreat. We spent the night concentrated behind the tanks of the 22nd Armoured.[93]

Churchill had seen an intercept of Hitler's 'victory or death' message at 1020hrs on the morning of 4 November. Ever cautious, Brooke had implored him not to order the ringing of church bells in celebration until 'we were quite certain that we should have no cause for regretting ringing them'.[94] Alexander, whose statement confirming that the Panzerarmee was breaking reached the Prime Minister in the afternoon, was contacted with Churchill's arbitrary figure of 'at least 20,000 prisoners' as 'proof' of victory. That night, in his diary, even Brooke, with his knowledge of the imminent landings in Algeria, was prepared to see the possibilities victory at Alamein offered for the future direction of the war. It was the culmination of many of his hopes and his constant toil:

> The Middle East news has the making of the vast victory I have been praying and hoping for! A great deal depends on it as one of the main moves in this winter's campaign in North Africa. Success in Libya should put Spaniards and French in better frame of mind to make Torch a success. And if Torch succeeds we are beginning to stop losing this war and working towards winning it! However, after my visit to Cairo and the work I had done to put things straight, if we had failed again I should have had little else to suggest beyond my relief by someone with fresh and new ideas! It is very encouraging at last to begin to see results from a year's hard labour.[95]

Only on the evening of 4 November, with the remnants of the forces that once stood on the brink of capturing Alexandria and Cairo in tatters, did Hitler offer vague promises of significant numbers of reinforcements for the North African theatre and, finally, give Rommel permission to act as necessary in the light of events. This was prompted by the arrival at his headquarters of Rommel's aide, Alfred-Ingemar Berndt, with full details of the crisis. However, Rommel had already been forced to act. At 1530hrs he had ordered a general retreat to positions near Fuka. This decision, essentially confirming the instructions of his chief of staff, Oberstleutnant Siegfried Westphal, to the Afrika Korps the previous evening was the Panzerarmee's official sanction for the mobile units to abandon the Italian infantry and the parachute units of both nations in the south.[96] Many Italians never forgave their allies; others, like Tenente Emilio Pulini, were restrained in their response:

> We were slightly uncomfortable about the idea of being left there without no transport. Our division had very little transport. Because we were paratroops we had very little transport of our own. But as far as I know the majority of the German troops withdrew before us and not too much transport was left to us.[97]

As Eighth Army's advance recommenced on 5 November, the victorious troops encountered similar scenes throughout the day, as Gervase Markham observed:

> We were able to advance. My first experience of advancing across a battlefield and seeing a defeated army with all the relics that they'd left behind, and their

dugouts still there with meals half eaten and Italian troops standing there waiting to be captured because the Germans had taken all the transport and had driven away, leaving the Italians to look after themselves without food or water or transport, begging to be taken into captivity.[98]

The sight of large numbers of Italian troops walking towards captivity seemed confirmation of the widely held view that Mussolini's forces were a liability to their ally. Sergeant Neville Howell of the 73rd Anti-Tank Regiment was struck by what he saw:

There were just hundreds and hundreds of Italians walking in groups and we were passing through them. Literally hundreds of them... They were asking for water. The Italians. That was the one thing they were asking for. Water. Hundreds of them. How long it took them to reach somewhere where they were given water, I don't know. Of course, we couldn't give them water. We only had a limited amount. You'd got to look after it. If you stopped – which you weren't allowed to do of course – you'd have been surrounded by them in no time.[99]

The sacrifice of the 'Ariete', 'Littorio' and 'Trieste' and the tough 'Folgore' was quickly forgotten. Yet without them the Afrika Korps could not have garnered the laurels it had, survived at Alamein as long as it had, or escaped in the manner it did.

Only one 'infantry' unit of significant size managed to escape, despite its lack of transport. Hans von Luck recounted:

On 7 November, in the depths of the desert, a patrol putting out a long feeler to the east, discovered General Ramcke, the commander of the paratroop division, which had been in action on the right wing south of Alamein. General Ramcke was brought to us in a scout car. He looked emaciated and asked to be taken, at once, to Rommel. His paratroops – an elite unit – had been through an adventurous time. I at once sent a radio message to Rommel: 'General Ramcke, with 700 men and all weapons, has been discovered by us; he himself is with me at the command post.'[100]

The exhausted paratroops had nothing except their weapons and water. They had captured a small British convoy on 5 November and used this to reach the Axis lines. It was small comfort to Rommel, given that on 5 November Eighth Army had easily exceeded Churchill's target for prisoners of war. Alexander had duly signalled: 'Ring out the bells!'[101]

The battle was over. It was theoretically time for the victors to pursue and annihilate their opponents. It did not happen. There was no single reason why not, but many could be laid at the door of Eighth Army's commander. To the amazement of their enemy, the British remained cautious in their operations. Ambitious plans to cut off the retreating Axis forces were not attempted. Proper reserves for pursuit had not been prepared. Congestion prevented units from getting forward. Personal animosity between Montgomery and several subordinates – especially Lumsden, Briggs and Gatehouse – stood in the way of effective use of the armoured formations they commanded.[102] Poor staff work was the cause of at least one brigadier's subsequent dismissal.[103] Tanks worn out by continuous action and needing overhaul consumed so much fuel they outran their supplies.[104] Bad weather – something outside the control of any commander – played a part as heavy rain fell on 6 November hampering movement and preventing air reconnaissance. However one informed critic felt 'this was a very thin excuse, seen through by all who had known the desert dry out in a few hours after rain the previous November.'[105]

Nevertheless, as the *Official History* rightly points out, the fact that a small part of Rommel's command managed to break away probably seems more of an anti-climax in retrospect than it did at the time to the men of Eighth Army.[106] The remarkable Charles Potts – 'The Fighting Parson' – writing on 12 November summarized the experience of Second Alamein for many of the survivors:

The shelling was terrific for the first 13 days of the battle while we struggled through the rows of enemy minefields. All day and all night the noise was deafening, gun flashes and explosions all round us. It was horrible, and very frightening. Some men lost their nerve altogether and shivered and chattered with terror. It was a job to keep some of them going. I was lucky in that I managed to keep pretty cheerful all the time, except for such ghastly moments as when my best corporal, of whom I was extremely fond, had his head blown clean off; I had to cover him up so that the others shouldn't see him. And now everywhere there is wreckage, vehicles, including huge tanks, blown to smithereens. Thank God the dead are mostly burned. It was not an easy victory – at least not at first. We had a bitter struggle and a taste of bloody hell. It must have been even worse for the Germans. Our artillery pounded them mercilessly and our bombers strafed them continuously (Damn these b___ flies – they are all over me).[107]

CONCLUSION
THE END OF THE BEGINNING

This is not the story of victory against the odds. During the entire period from late June until early November 1942 the British, Commonwealth and Dominion forces in North Africa together with those of their allies retained a numerical superiority over the Germans and Italians in men and equipment with nothing less than temporary parity in statistical terms in a few specific areas for short periods of time. It is, rather, a story of victory won through an arrest in the decline and retreat of an army and the defeat in turn of its chief protagonist's ambitious designs for glory. The subsequent introduction of fresh troops as reinforcements and the development of appropriate tactics for the use of new and improved technologies available in increasing numbers contributed to a final and irrevocable success.

In June 1942, Eighth Army's greatest enemy was the effect on morale of the two previous years of desert warfare. After an initial major success against an opponent whose troops were subsequently, and wrongly, universally dismissed as being of doubtful military value, the advent of a relatively small, new force, which was more tactically skilful and better equipped, led by a dynamic and tactically adept military commander had produced a 'see-saw' of fighting with advance and counter-attack back and forth along the many miles of desert roughly parallel with the North African coast. In this fighting, men at all levels of Eighth Army had been painfully aware of the limitations of their leaders and the increasingly obvious shortcomings of *some* of their equipment (particularly tanks). With fundamental flaws in the organization and tactics of its armoured formations, but without sufficient opportunity to address these weaknesses adequately, events on the battlefield had undermined their belief in the possibility of securing victory. These events also encouraged them to magnify the achievements of their enemy's most celebrated commander, who was credited with almost superhuman qualities. 'Rommel' became the personification of the German-Italian Panzerarmee in North Africa, although it actually comprised tens of thousands of men.

Morale, however, is a most amorphous element of warfare, indicated by the broad and various terminologies it frequently encompasses. These include 'fighting spirit', 'the will to combat/win', 'combat motivation', 'belief' (in war aims, leaders, the possibility of victory or success, etc). The term is often partnered by 'combat performance' or 'combat effectiveness'. Most recently, in connection with the Desert War, it has been defined as 'the willingness of an individual or group to prepare for and engage in an action required by an authority or institution'. This willingness 'may be engendered by a positive desire for action and/or by the discipline to accept orders to take such action'.[1] In the story of the Desert War, it is often the arrival of Bernard Montgomery to command Eighth Army that is taken as the point at which that force's decline in morale was stopped and turned around; the point at which 'belief in victory' was re-engendered. This very connection demonstrates the multi-faceted nature of morale and the difficulty in understanding how each facet relates to the others.

As this account of the battles around El Alamein clearly shows, Eighth Army had most emphatically not lost its 'will to combat' in late June and early July 1942 – the nadir of its military fortunes. Undoubtedly, however, there were those at that time (and, indeed, it is possible to suggest later) who had lost their 'belief in victory'. Nevertheless, just as in connection with the British Expeditionary Force of 1917 there was a tendency to place too much store on the 'grousings' and complaints of the ordinary 'Tommy' and to suggest they were not really committed to the task in hand, so there has been a desire to over-stress the depth of any 'morale crisis' in Eighth Army in July 1942. This is in order to emphasize Lieutenant-General Bernard Montgomery's undoubted understanding of the importance of morale and his success in re-instilling a belief in victory in the minds of the men he commanded. The over-emphasis on the chronological divide around Montgomery's assumption of command would be less significant if it were not for the fact that this split is then used to differentiate between the relative combat *effectiveness* of the force when commanded by General Sir Claude Auchinleck and by Montgomery.

In fact, as this account has shown, Eighth Army under Auchinleck became an increasingly effective fighting force in defence in the first half of July 1942.

A victory was assuredly secured when Rommel was forced to admit failure in his drive on Alexandria and cease his attacks on 4 July. Crucially, however, this was not a decisive victory, obvious to all. It would take several more days before this decision became widely recognized and, even then, the part played by most men in securing that victory was not clear to them. Precisely why Rommel's forces ceased offensive operations was not understood.

Nevertheless, a success had been accomplished by men fighting and dying. Even the 'local' or 'tactical' defeats such as the loss of 18th Indian Brigade at Deir-el-Shein after being effectively besieged offered important contributions to the overall success. There was no better way for Eighth Army to demonstrate that it had retained its fighting spirit, or 'combat motivation' than in fighting. An expression popular amongst Luftwaffe pilots during the Desert War was '*Der Geist machts!*' ('It is the spirit which counts!'). This correctly emphasized the importance of combat will as the most important facet of morale. In regard to 'Auchinleck's' Eighth Army in July 1942 the spirit was not only intact but could even be considered reasonably healthy. This point is reinforced by the fact that, during the second half of July, an almost, but not quite, unbroken sequence of failures in Eighth Army's offensive operations did not produce an overall crisis in the army's morale, which remained sufficiently good to weather these setbacks.

Conversely, this should also not be taken as an attempt to diminish Montgomery's contribution in terms of morale to Eighth Army's ultimate success at Alamein. Montgomery had an extremely good understanding of the importance of morale. It is principally he who is responsible for the Alamein story which centres on his assumption of command as critical to the turn round in morale that, in turn, inspired victory. What Montgomery did do was to engender in the minds of the men he came to command a belief in the genuine *possibility* of victory. His confident portrayal of the manner in which 'Rommel' would be defeated by his army carried much weight with the majority of his command. There were undoubtedly 'old sweats' who saw his published proclamations to this effect for just what they undoubtedly were. Until they were proved by action, they were just words. Nevertheless, for every occasion when men at whatever level responded with cynicism to his references to the Almighty and his 'With God's help' exhortations, there were others – such as his appearances at the Amariya cinema prior to the start of *Lightfoot* – which won for him the infinite loyalty of almost all those he addressed. In the latter circumstance, it was the regimental commanders and senior officers who returned to their units keen, in turn, to instil this new-found belief in their own commands.

On 30 June Auchinleck had issued a message to the army he commanded to encourage them in the forthcoming fighting. His urging to his men to show Rommel 'where he gets off' seemingly had little effect on its intended audience since no reference appears to it in censorship reports based on soldiers' correspondence with home at the time. It may well be that this was, to a large extent, because it was unnecessary. Men knew and understood the predicament that the British cause was in after Gazala and the fall of Tobruk. The opportunity to stand and fight was welcomed. The men were already hoping to tell Rommel where to get off. By contrast, in October 1942, when men could witness for themselves the preparations being made for a large offensive against the Axis forces and the extent to which reinforcements and new equipment had arrived for use in this attack, they needed to believe that victory was really possible. Those who had fought Rommel before wanted to believe that this time an attack was being prepared with thoroughness and due regard to their opponents' abilities. Those for whom this was their first time in battle needed to believe that their commander would not squander their lives in vain. Montgomery's oratory duly delivered. Victory, however, was secured by the side with the bigger battalions, with weapons greatly improved in quality and quantity.

In a letter to *The Times* newspaper published on 27 September 2001, the veteran of 2nd Rifle Brigade's epic stand at 'Snipe', Major Tom Bird DSO, MC and Bar, most effectively summarized the views of many Eighth Army veterans who had served under both Auchinleck and Montgomery. He began by taking the historian Alastair Horne to task concerning Horne's 'miracle' by which Montgomery 'in a matter of weeks turned a defeated horde into a victorious army'. In Tom Bird's view, 'a lot of us who were there when he arrived didn't regard it as the miracle it has since been made out to be'. By way of explanation, he wrote that 'Although we were dismayed that we had withdrawn so far, we did not at all look upon ourselves as a *demoralised** army in need of a miracle.' Whilst Montgomery was initially regarded as 'a funny little man in an Australian hat with a nasal voice who spoke in excruciating clichés which embarrassed rather than uplifted us', the real encouragement came from new, greatly improved weapons and the fact that 'these were for the first time in plentiful supply'. 'We could at last penetrate enemy tanks at an acceptable range,' Bird

---

*   My emphasis.

wrote. Finally, regarding Montgomery, he observed that 'when Monty had won battles and proved himself to be a great commander we came to trust and admire him – but not in those early days'.[2]

––––––––––

The circumstances in which the three battles around Alamein came to be fought all suited the acknowledged tactical strengths of the British forces. In the defence in prepared positions, tactical responses were to an extent obviously conditioned by the enemy's decisions and actions. In the attack, considerable experience from the Great War was still applicable in the battlefield situation now encountered and many techniques of positional warfare were once again applied – particularly in 'First' and 'Second Alamein'. Concentrated artillery fire – whether in the form of a bombardment, barrage or an updated variant such as the 'stonk' – had increased effect and validity in these circumstances. There are numerous examples of attacks by infantry preceded by artillery preparation being remarked on by observers with some reference to similar attacks witnessed in the Great War. So, for example, on 22 July Howard Kippenberger watched as 161st Indian Motor Brigade attacked along Ruweisat Ridge:

> From 21 Battalion Headquarters I had a grandstand view at less than a mile. They had strong artillery support: either a ragged barrage or a series of heavy concentrations, probably the latter. The advance went forward smoothly for about a mile. It reminded me of a battle of 1916, waves following one another in good alinement [sic].[3]

The supporting techniques of flash-spotting, sound-ranging, gun calibration, survey and meteorological observation therefore resumed their Great War position of importance for the work of counter-battery fire, for which Eighth Army now received a boon in the shape of the remarkably accurate and reliable 5.5-inch guns which saw service from mid-July 1942.

In addition, the introduction of 'Priest' 105mm self-propelled guns improved the capability of the army to provide barrage fire further forward in support of armoured formations, whilst the Shermans and Grants of these units were also able to fire HE and, thereby stand off from targets in the manner that the German PzKpfw IV 'Special' had previously been able to do. This new combination of tank main armament and other guns freed up the 25-pounder field guns for more effective work in developing barrage and area fire, whilst the introduction of the 6-pounder anti-tank gun further assisted this liberation of the artillery's 'workhorse'. In noting the contribution of the 6-pounder, however, it would be wrong to dismiss completely the 2-pounder anti-tank gun with which many infantry formations were still equipped throughout the Alamein battles. Given the right circumstances, these could still make an effective battlefield contribution – albeit chiefly in close defence and against tanks with poorer armoured protection.

The Germans and Italians, by comparison, also received some new equipment or already possessed better equipment for particular roles than their opponents. In this regard, the 88mm dual-purpose anti-tank and anti-aircraft gun was especially important and Eighth Army never possessed a weapon to match it despite suggestions for using the 3.7-inch anti-aircraft guns defending Alexandria and Cairo and installations in the Delta. However, even these much-dreaded German weapons had their shortcomings and numbers were destroyed in the late October fighting in particular because of their high profile and attempts to use them as anti-aircraft weapons when occupying positions designed to support their deployment as anti-tank guns.

Armoured vehicles such as the Italian Semovente da 75/18 had a low silhouette ideal for the desert and were welcomed. Also highly regarded were the self-propelled anti-tank guns with which some *Panzerjäger* units were equipped and, of course, the PzKpfw Mark IV 'Special' tanks. Italian heavy artillery remained of consistently good quality throughout the campaign – a valuable contribution too infrequently recognized. However, all these weapons were available in limited numbers, by contrast with the 6-pounder, for example, of which over 800 were in service with Eighth Army units by 23 October 1942. Nor can it be said for the British that quantity replaced quality since both the 6-pounder and Sherman tank were to see considerable service, with the latter remaining in use by front-line units until the end of the war.

New weapons and equipment became available to Eighth Army throughout the entire period of the Alamein battles and not just with the arrival of the Alexander–Montgomery command team. Those available for Second Alamein were in greater numbers than at First Alamein or at Alam Halfa but, given the nature of the fighting in October 1942, it was the arrival of the Sherman/Priest combination that gave Montgomery's Eighth Army a significant advantage over the army Auchinleck had led, as opposed to any other weapons.

Rommel made much of the quantitative differences in strengths between his German forces and Eighth Army in explaining away his defeat at Alamein, but his doing so should not marginalize the important fact that he received both German and Italian reinforcements of good quality in mid-1942 in the shape of Fallschirmjäger-Brigade Ramcke and 164. leichte Afrika-Division as well as Divisione Paracadutisti 'Folgore'. The equipment establishments of these formations were admittedly never at full strength. They were especially lacking in vehicles. Still, as combat proved, in the case of the parachute units they were at least a match for experienced desert divisions like 50th and 7th Armoured and their performance in Operation *Beresford* showed them in considerably better light than 44th Division.

These reinforcements did good service for the Panzerarmee, as did the Italian armoured formations 'Ariete' and 'Littorio' and the motorized 'Trieste' divisions. Rommel's acknowledgement that, with the former's destruction in November 1942, 'we lost our oldest Italian comrades, from whom we had probably always demanded more than they, with their poor armament, had been capable of performing'[4] went some way towards recognizing the important contribution Italian units made to the Axis cause but still fell short of making clear the fact that the forces he commanded *needed* the Italian units. Focus on the performance of Italian formations of all types in disadvantageous circumstances, such as that of the 'Sabratha' on 9–10 July or the 'Trento' and 'Bologna' formations under the 23 October barrage, has created an unbalanced and misleading picture of the Italian contribution. Their high command and strategic leadership were confused and weak but the battlefield performance of what was, after all, the greater part of the Panzerarmee was admirable given these factors and the inferior quality of most of their tanks and personal weapons. Howard Kippenberger would rail against how an attack by two infantry and two armoured brigades had been 'easily dealt with' by a single small Panzer unit of twenty or thirty tanks and a 'fifth-rate Italian infantry division'[5] but, in doing so, unwittingly credited even the much-derided Italians with better fighting qualities than their Eighth Army opponents.

———————

Regarding the question of the conduct of military operations under the two Eighth Army commanders and the supposedly clear differentiation between Auchinleck's command and Montgomery's, researching this account has revealed that, on the contrary, there was considerable continuity in terms of tactical, technological and organizational changes and innovations that straddled the periods of command of both men. Indeed, these are so extensive as to suggest that, rather than Eighth Army being continually shaped and transformed by the two senior commanders to be weapons of their will, the army was actually an organic entity that was constantly revising and reinventing itself in small or more significant ways in response to the changing situation in the war. To take one example, artillery techniques that were appropriate to the concentration of artillery effect only assumed greater importance and received new impetus in the situation at Alamein in June–July 1942, even though Brigadier 'Steve' Weir may have been practising some of these techniques in exercises before that date. The means to perform these tasks more effectively arrived in the form of new weaponry which could actively contribute to this work or free up 25-pounders for the role by reducing the burden of their anti-tank role. All this, in turn, was helped by opportunities to give infantry the necessary training required to operate effectively behind a creeping barrage, etc.

Similarly, the rapid British response in developing means to deal with deep minefield defences was catalysed by the introduction of extensive Axis minefields as a key element of their defensive positions in early July 1942. The means to clear mines already existed. The imperative to do this quickly and efficiently developed from the necessity of employing armour to break down the Panzerarmee defences in such positions.

Similar continuities existed in the failure of both commanders to address with any success the operational problems encountered. A specific example was obviously infantry co-operation with armour concerning which Auchinleck began to grope towards a solution in a clumsily managed process soon after he assumed army command and which Montgomery equally did not completely resolve. The 'accidental' necessity of twinning New Zealand infantry with 9th Armoured Brigade indicated where the solution might lie. Credit should go to the commanders of both these units for the work they did in creating a climate in which effective liaison and co-operation could flourish, based on prior discussions, training and broader activities designed to create a bond between the infantry and the men *inside* the tanks (as opposed to the impossible i.e. bonding with the tank itself).

The contribution of men at the level of brigadier and below in tactical and technological innovation has also been recognized in this account. Too much attention is given to the senior commanders and too much credit/criticism is attributed to them for the successes and failures in battle. Men like Colonel 'Toc' Elton, Major Henri Le Grand and Major Peter Moore were the tactical and technological innovators whose contribution to ultimate victory is immeasurable but 'personalities' or senior commanders are frequently credited with the success their subordinates accomplished. Brigadiers Kirkman, Weir and Kisch in particular are the names associated with the innovations introduced, when more appropriately they might be seen as sponsors of the innovators.

Other continuities existed in the continual problems with wireless communication and security that plagued British operations at Alamein and, indeed, which had done so for most of the Desert War. It remained all too often the case that at critical junctures in the battle, British commanders could not communicate or be contacted. An example from Montgomery's Alamein battle was Brigadier Gilbert McMeekan, Commander Royal Engineers of 10th Armoured Division. In July, Lieutenant-General William Gott was regularly 'missing' and uncontactable by radio. This did not facilitate clear and timely operational decision-making. Meanwhile, in the same month, the destruction of Nachrichten Fernaufklärungs Kompanie 621 was an important intelligence coup but it did not stop the problems associated with British units continuing to communicate using inadequate wireless security procedures. Furthermore, there was another radio intercept company attached to 15. Panzer-Division and NFAK 621 was subsequently reconstituted – although it did not achieve the successes its predecessor had enjoyed.

The issues regarding the employment of Commonwealth, Empire and Dominion troops plagued both army commanders. Montgomery's chief blessing was that he had more infantry options to turn to, somewhat diminishing (although not by much) the power of the Australian, New Zealand and South African divisional commanders. Montgomery did not have the stand-up row that Auchinleck experienced with Morshead over the deployment of Australian troops, chiefly because these issues were now dealt with at a lower level of the command structure and because Montgomery, after initially upsetting Freyberg, Morshead and Pienaar over the appointment of Leese as his XXX Corps commander, recognized the need in a coalition force like Eighth Army, to maintain good relations with the commanders and troops of all the nations represented. He and Leese worked hard in this respect in the weeks before the battle.

Another area of continuity was in senior commanders and Eighth Army staff. Guingand, whilst always depicted as a 'Montgomery man', was an Auchinleck appointment brought in as BGS to replace Whiteley. Guingand was previously on the GHQ staff at Middle East Command as Director of Military Intelligence, from where he 'head hunted' Captain 'Bill' Williams, who subsequently became Montgomery's intelligence 'guru'. Brigadier Frederick Kisch was already on Eighth Army staff, as was Brigadier Brian Robertson. John Harding, Montgomery's protégé, may not have chosen to acknowledge his debt to Auchinleck for his time as Director of Military Training and in other posts on Middle East GHQ staff, but he certainly owed one. There was definitely a period of 'Monty purges' after Alamein (in which men like Lumsden, Gatehouse, Fisher and others were removed from command), but these men from his headquarters staff were not amongst those 'degummed' and all had served the 'Auk' – by subsequent reputation a 'bad picker'.

The chief criticism of Auchinleck from amongst those in close proximity to him as a military commander appears to be that, at a critical time in the First Alamein battle, he brought in Eric Dorman-Smith as his Chief of Staff. The role was unfamiliar at this stage to the men already at Eighth Army HQ. They grew to understand it when Guingand took the post and it was correctly framed by Montgomery, but much of the criticism of the admittedly 'awkward' Dorman-Smith can be sourced to those who did not like this sudden imposition of a fine mind with the army commander's ear in their midst. Dorman-Smith, like John Frederick Charles Fuller, partly through his own personality, remained an unrealized talent whose climb in the army was abruptly halted and his career never recovered.

Auchinleck's other key 'appointment' was to empower his deputy, Tom Corbett, to act in his stead on all matters relating to Middle East Command, a role in which he was competent but massively over-worked. It was Corbett's misfortune to be the target of General Sir Alan Brooke, the Chief of the Imperial General Staff. From that point forward, he was doomed. Brooke's judgement was demonstrably good in most matters relating to his single-minded pursuit of his plans for victory. His assessment may have been fair regarding Corbett; it was less so in connection with Auchinleck, who was ultimately dismissed from Middle East Command because he was unlikely to work well with Montgomery, for whom Brooke was determined to secure command of Eighth Army. Churchill's caprice and misunderstanding of the command structure in the Middle East only confused the issue.

One aspect of the Desert War this book has addressed is the myth of the *Krieg Ohne Hass* or 'War Without Hate'. This concept was introduced by Rommel in his written memoirs at a time when Germany's victory in the war was, at best, by no means certain and her defeat much more likely. Rommel's personal disenchantment with Hitler's leadership was growing. It seems a convenient device to position his own military conduct away from that of others in operations on the Eastern Front, for example. In drawing attention to the fact that there were no significant numerical losses amongst the sparse civilian populations of Egypt and Cyrenaica and that both the Panzerarmee forces and Eighth Army had behaved largely with dignity and respect for their opponents in victory or defeat, Rommel was suggesting that he was in some way a more decent commander than his fellow German commanders – something that might form the basis of a post-war negotiating position perhaps.

Rommel undoubtedly *did* behave personally with correctness towards prisoners and non-combatants. This was acknowledged by high-ranking officers who encountered him as prisoners of war. In doing so, he was not exceptional in the desert or in the war in general. Nor was this type of good conduct limited to one side or the other in the desert fighting. But it was not the universal experience either. Men did kill, wound, rob and wantonly destroy at any opportunity in the desert fighting, as elsewhere. Unarmed prisoners in the act of surrendering were shot or otherwise executed without a moment's hesitation; tank crews trapped in their armour were easy targets for 'revenge' attacks by infantry at close quarters where a few grenades or some small arms fire might be directed into the tank interior. Dugouts would be routinely bombed when known to contain occupants perhaps prepared to surrender. Very real atrocities were committed that participants attributed to 'blood lust', 'battle fury' or simply the heat of battle.

More importantly still, and with Rommel's definite knowledge (although not necessarily his support), there were lurking behind the Axis forces in this supposed 'War without Hate' the same instruments and forces of repression and hatred that had already been employed throughout areas occupied by the German forces in Europe. Arab nationalism had been recognized as a possible avenue of support for Germany in the Middle East and Hitler had communicated his plans for the destruction of Jewish communities in Arab countries to the Grand Mufti of Jerusalem in November 1941. Eighth Army stood as a bulwark against this threat and against definite plans made in this regard. The *Krieg Ohne Hass* would very quickly have been unmasked as the sham it was, had the Panzerarmee triumphed in early July 1942.

So the Americans have landed in Algiers and Tunis. Good luck to them. I expect they will claim that they have won the war for us in North Africa – but who cares who gets the credit so long as we get the damned thing over. We may get sent home soon. We are hoping so – Or we may be kept for further fighting in the Mediterranean area.[6]

Sometimes after struggling to find adequate words to describe a complex aspect of this superficially simple, but complex in detail, sequence of battles, it has proved better to let the words of the participants themselves do all that is necessary. Charles Potts, known as 'The Fighting Parson' was one of many in Eighth Army with a fascinating and remarkable background. When war began he was helping to run a settlement for dockland boys in Canning Town. He had been a chaplain to the forces until April 1942 when he had resigned to serve as an infantry officer. He received the Military Cross at the end of the Second Battle of El Alamein for silencing snipers who were using derelict tanks in no man's land as cover. He appears several times in this account because of his unique and insightful views on the war. However, he also had the ability in some of his letters to capture the mood and feeling of an entire army. His remarks concerning Operation *Torch*, the Anglo-American landings in North Africa which took place on 8 November 1942, days after the victory at Alamein sum up the feelings of the Eighth Army soldier. There was almost an expectation that their victory would soon be marginalized as events elsewhere took over.

Thankfully this did not occur. In fact, the opposite has sometimes happened. The importance of overall victory at Alamein has been exaggerated and, in particular, this has happened in connection with the victory of Montgomery's Eighth Army which, in turn, has produced depreciation in the perception of the battle's conduct under Auchinleck. Alamein was in fact a victory achieved over several months by many of the same men under two very different army commanders. It marked a turning point in Britain's fortunes in the war. It was *not* the point at which the war was won or even a victory in the most important theatre of that global conflict. But it was a definite victory and one achieved by a force that was, in the main, composed of men from Britain, the Commonwealth and Dominions and the Empire. From the moment American troops in significant numbers landed in North Africa, the nature of Britain's role in the conflict changed and it became a minority partner in an American-led coalition in the West, whilst the forces of the Soviet Union dominated the war in the East where the sacrifice of the Red Army's soldiers ultimately achieved victory over Fascism.

Charles Potts' words, with the hope of home but the expectation of further fighting, say so much for the ordinary Eighth Army soldier. But Potts was not alone and this book ends with the words of others who experienced the critical events of five months in mid- to late-1942, beginning first with the observations of Potts once more from soon after the final battle at Alamein had been won:

> This experience that we have been through has changed us all a bit. We know each other better. Some of the most unlikely men have shown themselves to be heroes and some of the plausible ones have been discredited. We have found a greater comradeship. There is a more general geniality and friendliness everywhere.[7]

Canon Gervase Markham's birthday celebrations took place on 7 November 1942 amidst the aftermath of the battle:

> There was great excitement when we finally discovered that the battle had been won. I remember having a little sort of birthday party. In the afternoon, I buried a sapper who had been shot by a comrade playing with an Italian revolver. Side by side we buried an Italian prisoner of war. About 500 of them were standing half a mile away. They had no food or water. We had none to spare for so many, we had no transport to take them away in, they were too tired to walk. Another thousand were reported a few miles away and more to come in. They needed no capturing.[8]

It would be invidious not to include the thoughts of Frank Devaney, a private soldier who experienced the barrage and battle on 23 October 1942:

> People at home didn't understand. They didn't realize what it was about. They pictured that El Alamein was ... the mere fact that there was a big barrage, they thought that everything was drenched out and finished. But that wasn't the case at all. Although we'd a lot of guns, we'd a lot of opposition from the German guns too. We met a lot of their defensive fire, but we went through it. Generally the Germans were in sound positions. There was bayonet fighting and that sort of thing at El Alamein. Plenty of it. People that think there wasn't, well, the whole point is this – they probably picture El Alamein and wrongly project it to people at home.[9]

Devaney's understanding of what motivated the Germans and their Italian allies was simple but incisive:

The Jerries wouldn't come out of their slit trenches unless they were forced to. That's all there was in it. They were there to stay. To think that they had come all the way down to be sitting just on the edge of the delta for one attack that would've seen them open up the whole of Africa and then have all the necessary things in life. The German Army knew that. Was he going to forego all that and go way back up the desert where he'd come from without putting up a good fight? This was the psychological effect. When he was pushed out, he was pushed out because he was *made* to go.[10]

Finally, on behalf of the men of Eighth Army, consider a heartfelt complaint by Gunner James Brooks of 211 Battery, 64th Medium Regiment (RA), in a letter home sent some months after the battle:

That brings us to the Battle of Alamein and to the end of my story. I can't tell you anymore, as we can only tell you about our experiences up to Oct 23rd. But I will tell you this as I've told lots of times before. I'm sick and tired of this bloody desert and the sooner I get out of it the better I shall like it. I think I've done more than my share in this war and it's about time somebody took my place.[11]

ORDER OF BATTLE

EIGHTH ARMY ORDER OF BATTLE, 23 OCTOBER 1942
(excluding signals, medical, supply, police and workshop units)

Lieutenant-General B.L. Montgomery

(BGS: F.W. de Guingand)

HQ EIGHTH ARMY

Army Troops and Formations under command included:

1st Army Tank Brigade (42 and 44 RTR) – Matilda 'Scorpions'; 2nd and 12th AA
 Brigades

X CORPS

(Lieutenant-General Herbert Lumsden)

(BGS: Ralph Cooney)

1st ARMOURED DIVISION (Major-General Raymond Briggs)

2nd Armoured Brigade (A.F. Fisher): The Queen's Bays, 9th Lancers,
 10th Hussars and Yorkshire Dragoons (motor battalion)

7th Motor Brigade (T.J.B. Bosvile): 2nd and 7th Bns, the Rifle Brigade and
 2nd KRRC (60th Rifles)

Divisional Troops

12th Lancers (armoured cars)

RA: (CRA, B.J. Fowler): 2nd and 4th RHA, 11th RHA (HAC), 78th Field Regt
 (less Troops with other divisions), 76th Anti-Tank Regt and 42 Light AA Regt

RE: 1st and 7th Field Sqns, 1st Field Park Sqn. *Attached*: 9th Field Sqn and
 572 Field Park Coy

Others: Two companies R. Northumberland Fusiliers

10th ARMOURED DIVISION (Major-General A.H. Gatehouse)

8th Armoured Brigade (E.C.N. Custance): 3rd RTR, Nottinghamshire
Yeomanry (Sherwood Rangers), Staffordshire Yeomanry, 1st Buffs
(motor battalion)

24th Armoured Brigade (A.G. Kenchington): 41st, 45th and 47th RTR and
11th KRRC (motor battalion)

133 Lorried Infantry Brigade (A.W. Lee), added from 44th Division: 2nd, 4th
and 5th Royal Sussex Regt and one company R Northumberland Fusiliers.

Divisional Troops:

The Royal Dragoons (armoured cars)

RA: (CRA, W.A. Ebbels): 1st, 5th and 104th RHA, 98th Field Regt,
84th Anti-Tank Regt, 53rd Light AA Regt

RE: 2nd and 3rd Field Sqns, 141st Field Park Sqn; *attached*: 6th Field Sqn,
571st and 573rd Army Field Coys

XII CORPS

(Lieutenant-General B.G. Horrocks)

(BGS: George Erskine)

7th ARMOURED DIVISION (Major-General A.F. Harding):

4th Light Armoured Brigade (M.G. Roddick): 4/8th Hussars, The Scots Greys
and 1st KRRC (motor battalion)

22nd Armoured Brigade (G.P.B; Roberts): 1st and 5th RTR, 4th City of London
Yeomanry and 1st Rifle Brigade (motor battalion)

131 Lorried Infantry Brigade. See under 44th Infantry Division

Divisional Troops:

Household Cavalry Regt, 11th Hussars and 2nd Derbyshire Yeomanry
(armoured cars)

RA: (CRA, Roy Mews): 3rd RHA, 4th and 97th Field Regts, 65th Anti-Tank Regt,
15 Light AA Regt

RE: 4th and 21st Field Sqns, 143rd Field Park Sqn

Under command: *1ère* and *2ème Brigade Française Libre* (*Général* Pierre
Koenig)

44th Reconnaissance Regt (from 44th Division)

44th (HOME COUNTIES) INFANTRY DIVISION (Major-General I.T.P. Hughes):

131 Infantry Brigade (W.D. Stainer): 1/5th, 1/6th and 1/7th The Queen's
(became incorporated in 7th Armoured Division on 1 November)

132 Infantry Brigade (L G. Whistler): 2nd Buffs, 4th and 5th Royal West
Kent Regt

133 Infantry Brigade. See under 10th Armoured Division

Divisional Troops:

RA: (CRA, H.R. Hall): 57th, 58th, 65th and 53rd Field Regts, 57th Anti-Tank
Regt, 30th Light AA Regt

RE: 11th, 209th and 210th Field Coys, 211th Field Park Coy and 577th Army
Field Park Coy

Others: 6th Cheshire Regt (machine-gun battalion)

50th (NORTHUMBRIAN) INFANTRY DIVISION (Major-General J.S. Nichols):

69th Infantry Brigade (E.C. Cooke-Collie): 5th East Yorkshire Regt, 6th and
7th Green Howards

151 Infantry Brigade (J.E.S. Percy): 6th, 8th and 9th Durham Light Infantry

1st Greek Infantry Brigade Group (Col Katsotas)

Divisional Troops:

RA: (CRA, Claude Eastman): 74th, 111th, 124th and 154th Field Regts,
102nd (Northumberland Hussars) Anti-Tank Regt, 34th Light AA Regt

RE: 233rd and 505th Field Coys, 235th Field Park Coy

Others: 2nd Cheshire Regt (machine guns)

XXX CORPS

(Lieutenant-General Sir Oliver Leese, Bt)

(BGS: G.P. Walsh)

51st (HIGHLAND) INFANTRY DIVISION (Major-General D.N. Wimberley):

152 Infantry Brigade (G. Murray): 2nd and 5th Seaforth Highlanders, 5th
Cameron Highlanders

153 Infantry Brigade (D.A.H. Graham): 5th Black Watch, 1st and 5/7th Gordon
Highlanders

154 Infantry Brigade (H.W. Houldsworth): 1st and 7th Black Watch, 7th Argyll
and Sutherland Highlanders

Divisional Troops:

RA (CRA, G.M. Elliot): 126th, 127th, and 128th Field Regts, 61st Anti-Tank
Regt, 40th Light AA Regt

RE: 274th, 275th and 276th Field Coys, 239th Field Coy

Others: 1/7th Middlesex Regt (machine guns), 51st Reconnaissance Regt

2nd NEW ZEALAND DIVISION (Major-General B.C. Freyberg, VC):

9th Armoured Brigade (*United Kingdom*) (John Currie): 3rd Hussars,
Royal Wiltshire Yeomanry, Warwickshire Yeomanry and 14th Sherwood
Foresters (motor infantry)

5 NZ Infantry Brigade (Howard Kippenberger): 21, 22 and 23 NZ Battalions,
28 Māori Bn

6 NZ Infantry Brigade (William Gentry): 24, 25 and 26 NZ Bns

Divisional Troops:

2nd NZ Divisional Cavalry Regt (light tanks)

NZA (CRA, C.E. 'Steve' Weir): 4th, 5th and 6th Field Regts, 7th NZ Anti-Tank Regt, 14th NZ Light AA Regt

NZE: 6th, 7th and 8th NZ Field Coys, 5th NZ Field Park Coy

Others: 27 NZ Bn (machine guns)

9th AUSTRALIAN DIVISION (Major-General L.J. Morshead)

20th Australian Infantry Brigade (W.J.V. Windeyer) 2/13th, 2/15th and 2/17th Australian Infantry Bns

24th Australian Infantry Brigade (Arthur Godfrey): 2/28th, 2/32nd and 2/43rd Australian Infantry Bns

26th Australian Infantry Brigade (D.A. Whitehead): 2/23rd, 2/24th and 2/48th Australian Infantry Bns

Divisional Troops:

RAA (CRA, A.H. Ramsay): 2/7th, 2/8th and 2/12th Australian Field Regts, 3rd Australian Anti-Tank Regt, 4th Australian Light AA Regt

Engineers: 2/3rd, 2/7th, 2/13th Australian Field Coys, 2/4th Australian Field Park Coy, 2/3rd Australian Pioneer Bn

Others: 2/2nd Australian Bn (machine guns)

4th INDIAN DIVISION (Major-General F.S. Tuker):

5th Indian Infantry Brigade (D. Russell): 1/4th Essex Regt, 4/6th Rajputana Rifles, 3/10th Baluch

7th Indian Infantry Brigade (A.W.W. Holworthy): 1st Royal Sussex Regt, 4/16th Punjabi Regt, 1/2nd Ghurka Rifles

161st Indian Infantry Brigade (F.E.C. Hughes): 1st Argyll and Sutherland Highlanders, 1/1st Punjabi Regt, 4/7th Rajputs

Divisional Troops:

RA (CRA, H.K. Dimoline): 1st, 11th and 32nd Field Regts, 149th Anti-Tank Regt, 57th Light AA Regt

RE: 2nd, 4th and 12th Field Coys, 11th Field Park Coy

Others: 6th Rajputana Rifles (machine guns)

1st SOUTH AFRICAN DIVISION (Major-General D.H. Pienaar)

1st SA Infantry Brigade (C.L. de W du Toit) 1st Royal Natal Carabiniers, 1st Duke of Edinburgh's Own Rifles, 1st Transvaal Scottish

2nd SA Infantry Brigade (W.H.E. Poole): 1/2nd Field Force En, 1st Natal Mounted Rifles, Cape Town Highlanders

3rd SA Infantry Brigade (R.J. Palmer): 1st Imperial Light Horse, 1st Durban Light Infantry, 1st Rand Light Infantry

Divisional Troops:

SA Artillery (CRA, F Theron) 1st, 4th and 7th SA Field Regts, 1st SA Anti-Tank Regt, 1st SA Light AA Regt

SA Engineers: 1st, 2nd, 3rd and 5th SA Field Coys, 19th SA Field Park Coy

Others: Regiment President Steyn and one coy Die Middelandse Regt (machine guns)

30th CORPS TROOPS and Troops in Corps Reserve

23rd Armoured Brigade Group (G.W. Richards): 8th, 40th, 46th and 50th RTR, 121st Field Regt RA, 168 Light AA Battery, RA, 295th Army Field Coy, RE, 7th Light Field Ambulance

Armoured Cars: 4/8th South African Armoured Car Regt

RA: 7th, 64th and 69th Medium Regts

RE: 66th Mortar Company

WESTERN DESERT AIR FORCE ORDER OF BATTLE

Air Headquarters Western Desert (Air Vice-Marshal Arthur Coningham)

No. 1 Air Ambulance Unit (DH86)

No. 3 (South African Air Force) Wing

Squadrons:

Nos. 12 and 24 (SAAF) (Bostons)

No. 21 (SAAF) (Baltimores)

No. 232 Wing

Squadrons:

Nos. 55 and 223 (Baltimores)

US 12th Bombardment Group

Squadrons:

81st, 82nd, 83rd and 434th (Mitchells)

No. 285 Wing

Squadrons:

No. 40 (SAAF) and No. 208 (Hurricanes)

No. 60 (SAAF) (Baltimores)

Flights, Other units:

No. 1437 Strategic Reconnaissance Flight (Baltimores)

No. 2 Photographic Reconnaissance Flight detachment (Various)

211 GROUP

Squadrons

Nos. 6 and 7 (SAAF) (Hurricanes)

No. 233 Wing.

Squadrons

Nos. 2 and 4 (SAAF) and No. 260 (Kittyhawks)

No. 5 (SAAF) (Tomahawks)

No. 239 Wing

Squadrons

Nos. 3 and 450 (Royal Australian Air Force) and Nos. 112 and 250
(Kittyhawks)

No. 244 Wing

Nos. 92, 145 and 601 Squadrons (Spitfires)

No. 73 (Hurricanes)

United States 57th Fighter Group

Squadrons

64th, 65th and 66th (Warhawks)

212 GROUP

No. 7 (SAAF) Wing

Squadrons

Nos. 80, 127, 274 and 335 (Hurricanes)

No. 243 Wing

Squadrons

Nos. 1 (SAAF), 33, 213 and 238 (Hurricanes)

ITALIAN ARMY ORDER OF BATTLE

C-in-C: Maresciallo d'Italia Ettore Bastico

X Corpo d'Armata

(Generale di Corpo d'Armata Edoardo Nebba; Generale di divisione Enrico
Frattini in temporary command until 26 October)

9° Reggimento bersaglieri

16° Reggimento artiglieria d'armata

27ª Divisione Autotrasportabile 'Brescia' (Generale di divisione Brunetto
Brunetti):

19° Reggimento fanteria 'Brescia'

20° Reggimento fanteria 'Brescia'

55° Reggimento artiglieria

27° Battaglione misto Genio.

185ª Divisione paracadutisti 'Folgore' (Generale di divisione Enrico Frattini):

186° Reggimento fanteria paracadutisti

187° Reggimento fanteria paracadutisti

185° Reggimento artiglieria paracadutisti

17ª Divisione Autotrasportabile 'Pavia' (Generale Nazzareno Scattaglia):

    27° Reggimento fanteria 'Pavia'

    28° Reggimento fanteria 'Pavia'

    26° Reggimento artiglieria 'Rubicone'

    17° Battaglione misto Genio.

XX Corpo d'Armata (Generale di Divisione Giuseppe de Stephanis)

    132ª Divisione Corazzata 'Ariete' (Generale di Divisione Adolfo Infante):

    132° Reggimento Carristi

    8° Reggimento Bersaglieri

    132° Reggimento Artiglieria Corazzata

    V (DLI) e VI (DLII) Gruppo Semoventi

    RECO Ariete (Reparto Esplorante Corazzato):

    LII Battaglione Carri

    III Gruppo Corazzato Nizza (cavalleria Corazzata)

    CXXXII Battaglione misto Genio.

133ª Divisione Corazzata 'Littorio' (Generale di divisione Gervasio Bitossi):

    133° Reggimento Carri

    12° Reggimento Bersaglieri

    III Battaglione (gruppo squadroni)'Lancieri di Novara'

    III Reggimento Artiglieria Celere

        133° Reggimento Artiglieria Corazzata

    CCCII Gruppo Artiglieria

    DLIV Gruppo Semoventi

    DLVI Gruppo Semoventi

101ª Divisione motorizzata 'Trieste'

(Generale di divisione Francesco La Ferla):

    65° Reggimento fanteria motorizzata 'Valtellina'

    66° Reggimento fanteria motorizzata 'Valtellina'

    8° Battaglione bersaglieri autoblindo

    21° Reggimento artiglieria motorizzata 'Po'

    32° Battaglione misto del genio motorizzato

    XI Battaglione carri

XXI Corpo d'Armata (Generale di Corpo d'Armata Enea Navarini; Generale di divisione Alessandro Gloria in temporary command until 26 October)

7° Reggimento bersaglieri

8° Reggimento artiglieria d'armata

102ª Divisione Motorizzata 'Trento' (Generale di brigata Giorgio Masina):

    61° Reggimento Fanteria 'Sicilia'

    62° Reggimento Fanteria 'Sicilia'

7° Reggimento bersaglieri
46° Reggimento Artiglieria motorizzata 'Trento'
LI Battaglione misto Genio
25ª Divisione fanteria 'Bologna' (Generale di divisione Alessandro Gloria):
    39° Reggimento fanteria 'Bologna'
    40° Reggimento fanteria 'Bologna'
    205° Reggimento artiglieria
    25° Battaglione misto Genio
IN ARMY RESERVE
16ª Divisione fanteria 'Pistoia' (Generale di divisione Giuseppe Falugi)
    35° Reggimento fanteria 'Pistoia'
    36° Reggimento fanteria 'Pistoia'
    3° Reggimento artiglieria 'Fossalta'
    51° Battagione del Genio
136ª Divisione fanteria 'Giovani Fascisti' (Generale di divisione Ismaele di Nisio)
    136° Reggimento fanteria 'Giovani Fascisti'
    136° Reggimento artiglieria semovente

GERMAN ARMY ORDER OF BATTLE

PANZERGRUPPE AFRIKA

GOC (and C-in-C Deutsch-Italienische Panzerarmee):
General der Kavallerie Georg Stumme
(Chief of Staff: Generalmajor Alfred Gause)
19. Flak-Division (General Heinrich Burchard): Stab/Flak-Regiment 102, Stab/Flak-Regiment 135, Stab/Flak-Regiment 66.

DEUTSCHES AFRIKA KORPS ('DAK')

(General der Panzertruppen Wilhelm von Thoma)
15. Panzer-Division (Generalmajor Gustav von Vaerst):
    Stab der Division
      Divisions-Kartenstelle (mot) 33
      Kradmelder-Zug
      Panzer-Regiment 8
      Panzerjäger-Abteilung (mot) 33
    Schützen-Brigade (mot) 15
      Infanterie-Regiment (mot) 115
      Maschinengewehr-Bataillon (mot) 8
      Kradschützen-Bataillon (mot) 15

Aufklärungs-Abteilung (mot) 33

Nachrichten-Abteilung (mot) 33

Artillerie-Regiment (mot) 33

Pionier-Bataillon (mot) 33

Feldersatz-Bataillon 33

21. Panzer-Division (Generalmajor Heinz von Randow)

Stab der Division

Divisions-Kartenstelle (mot) 200

Kradmelder-Zug

Panzer-Regiment 5

Panzerjäger-Abteilung (mot) 39

Schützen-Regiment (mot) 104

Artillerie-Regiment (mot) 155

Aufklärungs-Abteilung (mot) 3

Nachrichten-Abteilung (mot) 200

Pionier-Bataillon (mot) 200

Feldersatz-Bataillon 200

Panzer-Nachrichten-Kompanie

Panzer-Funk-Kompanie

leichte Nachrichten-Kolonne

90. leichte Division (Generalmajor Theodor Graf von Sponeck):

Stab der Division

Divisions-Kartenstelle (mot) 259

Infanterie-Regiment (mot) 200

Panzer-Grenadier Regiment 155

Infanterie-Regiment Afrika 361

Sonderverband 288

Kolbeck-Bataillon

schwere Infanteriegeschütz-Kompanie 707

schwere Infanteriegeschütz-Kompanie 708

Panzerjäger-Abteilung (mot) 190

Artillerie-Regiment (mot) 190

Aufklärungskompanie (mot) 580

Nachrichten-Abteilung (mot)

Pionier-Bataillon (mot) 900

Feldersatz-Bataillon

164. leichte Division (Generalleutnant Carl-Hans Lungershausen) :

Stab der Division

Panzer-Grenadier Regiment 125

Panzergrenadier-Regiment 382
Panzergrenadier-Regiment 433
schwere Infanteriegeschütz-Kompanie 707 (von der 90. leichten Div)
schwere Infanteriegeschütz-Kompanie 708 (von der 90. leichten Div)
Flak-Abteilung (mot) 609
Artillerie-Regiment (mot) 220
Aufklärungs-Abteilung (mot) 220
Nachrichten-Kompanie (mot) 220
Panzerpionier-Bataillon (mot) 220

AUFKLÄRUNGSGRUPPE:

Aufklärungs-Abteilung 3
Aufklärungs-Abteilung 33
Aufklärungs-Abteilung 580
Flak-Abteilung 612 (- 1./612)
Fallschirmjäger-Brigade 1 (Ramcke) (Generalmajor Hermann Bernhard
    Ramcke):
      I./Fallschirmjäger-Regiment 2
      I./Fallschirmjäger-Regiment 3
      II./Fallschirmjäger-Battalion 5
      Fallschirmjäger-Lehr-Battalion/ XI.Flieger-Korps
      II./Fallschirm-Artillerie-Regiment
      Panzerjäger-Kompanie

GRUPPE AND KAMPFGRUPPE AT ALAMEIN

AFRIKAKORPS STAB KAMPFGRUPPE

This Gruppe was formed in April 1942.
2./Flak-Abteilung 606
1 Zug/Panzerjäger-Abteilung 39 (4 x 47mm Panzerjäger I self-propelled
    guns)
1 Panzer-Zug (5 PzKpfw IIs)
1 Zug, 1./Pioniere-Bataillon 33
1 Panzerspähwagen-Zug/Aufklärungs-Abteilung 3 (Armoured Cars)

AUFKLÄRUNGSGRUPPE

This Gruppe was formed on 22 August 1942, and put under the command of
Schützen-Brigade 15. The Italian XX Corpo Reconnaissance Group was
instructed to co-operate with this Gruppe.
Aufklärungs-Abteilung 3

Aufklärungs-Abteilung 33
Aufklärungs-Abteilung 580
Flak-Abteilung 612 (12 x 20mm self-propelled Flak)
Commander: Oberst Erwin Menny

GRUPPE BAADE

This Gruppe was formed on 17 July 1942.
Stab Panzergrenadier-Regiment 115
1 Bataillon/Panzergrenadier-Regiment 115
1 Panzer-Zug/Panzer-Regiment 5
1 Artillerie-Batterie
Commander: Oberst Ernst-Günther Baade

GRUPPE BESDE

This Gruppe, also known as Abschnitt Mitte, was formed on 25 June 1942, from units of the 15. Panzer-Division. The Gruppe, along with Gruppe Warrelmann and Gruppe Dedekind, was under the overall command of Oberst Baade.
Panzerjäger-Abteilung 33
Panzer-Pionier-Bataillon 33
III. /Artillerie-Regiment 33
Commander: Major Besde

GRUPPE DEDEKIND

This Gruppe, also known as Abschnitt West, was formed on 25 June 1942, from units of the 15. Panzer-Division. The Gruppe, along with Gruppe Warrelmann and Gruppe Besde, was under the overall command of Oberst Baade.
Infanterie-Regiment 115 (III. /115 and two Kompanien, I. /115)
I. /Artillerie-Regiment 33
leichte Flak-Abteilung
Commander: Major Dedekind

KAMPFGRUPPE FISCHER

Formed on 3 November 1942, to cover the 15. Panzer-Division while it withdrew to new positions.
Panzerjäger-Abteilung 605
III. /Artillerie-Regiment 33
I./Flak-Regiment 33
II. /33 Luftwaffe
Commander: Hauptmann Fischer

GRUPPE HAIN

On 16 September 1942, the Panzerarmee informed DAK that Feldersatz-Bataillon 33, Feldersatz-Bataillon 200 and the 90. leichte Division Versorgungsführungs-Bataillon was to be tactically subordinated to the Armee as Gruppe Hain; under the command of Major Hain.

Feldersatz-Bataillon 33

Feldersatz-Bataillon 200

90. leichte-Division Versorgungsführungs-Bataillon

12. Küsten Artillerie-Batterie

Commander: Major Hain

RESERVE-GRUPPE MILDEBRATH

On 27 July 1942, 15. Panzer-Division received orders from Afrika Korps to hold in readiness a reserve Gruppe under the command of Oberstleutnant Mildebrath. This Gruppe consisted of:

I. /Infanterie-Regiment 115

one leichte Artillerie-Abteilung (less one Batterie)

one schwerste Flak-Batterie

one Panzer-Zug

Commander: Oberstleutnant Werner Mildebrath

KAMPFGRUPPE MITTE

This Gruppe was formed on 23 October 1942, along with two other Gruppen, for defensive operations during the British offensive. The other Gruppen were Nord and Süd. The following day, the units assigned to Kampfgruppe Nord were attached to this Gruppe.

11. /Panzer-Regiment 8

Stab/Panzer-Grenadier-Regiment 115

III /Panzer-Grenadier-Regiment 115

13. /Panzer-Grenadier- Regiment 115 (Sturmgeschütz)

15. /Panzer-Grenadier-Regiment 115 (captured guns)

III /Artillerie-Regiment 33

HQ/133º Reggimento Carri

IV/133º Reggimento Carri

23. /12º Reggimento Bersaglieri

29. /Artillerie-Regiment 3

DLVI Gruppo Semoventi

Commander: Major Schemmel

KAMPFGRUPPE NORD

Formed on 23 October 1942, as one of three Gruppen of 15. Panzer-Division, for defensive operations during the British offensive. The other Gruppen were Mitte and Süd. This Gruppe was disbanded on 24 October 1942, and its units attached to Kampfgruppe Mitte.

1. /Panzer-Grenadier-Regiment 115
Stab, Stabsbatterie/Artillerie-Regiment 33
3. /Flak-Abteilung 617
51./133º Reggimento Carri
Commander: Oberst Eduard Crasemann

KAMPFGRUPPE NORD (3 NOVEMBER 1942)

Formed on 3 November 1942, the Gruppe was to operate alongside Kampfgruppe Süd during the retreat from El Alamein.

Remnants of Panzer-Regiment 8
Panzer-Pionier-Bataillon 33
1. /Artillerie-Regiment 33
1. and 2. /Flak-Abteilung 43 (Luftwaffe)
Commander: Hauptmann Siemens

KAMPFGRUPPE PFEIFFER

On 31 October 1942, DAK informed 21. Panzer-Division that it was to form a Kampfgruppe comprising approximately half of its tanks, anti-tank guns (self-propelled), medium howitzers (self-propelled) and 2 cm Flak guns. 21. Panzer-Division designated Major Pfeiffer, commander of Panzerjäger-Abteilung 39, as commander of the Kampfgruppe.

Since the Division had no serviceable medium field howitzers available, it was ordered to incorporate one light and one heavy battery into the Kampfgruppe.

Pfeiffer Kampfgruppe was to launch a counter-attack north of the El Alamein railway line in an attempt to relieve the encircled Panzer-Grenadier-Regiment 125.

KAMPFGRUPPE SIEMENS

Formed on 3 November 1942, for operations during the withdrawal of the 15. Panzer-Division to new positions.

Panzer-Regiment 8
Panzer-Pionier-Bataillon 33
1. /Artillerie-Regiment 33
1. /Flak-Regiment 43 (Luftwaffe)
II. /Flak-Regiment 43

plus an unknown number of Italian tanks.

Commander: Hauptmann Siemens

KAMPFGRUPPE SÜD

This Gruppe, formed on 23 October 1942, was one of three formed by 15. Panzer-Division for defensive operations during the British offensive. The other Gruppen were Mitte and Nord.

II. /Panzer-Grenadier-Regiment 115

II. /Artillerie-Regiment 3

Stab/Artillerie-Regiment 33

II. /Artillerie-Regiment 33

HQ/12º Reggimento Bersaglieri

DLIV Gruppo Semoventi

Commander: Oberst Willi Teege

KAMPFGRUPPE SÜD (3 NOVEMBER 1942)

Formed on 3 November 1942, this Gruppe was to operate alongside Kampfgruppe Nord and set up new defensive positions during the retreat from El Alamein.

GRUPPE WARRELMANN

This Gruppe, also known as Abschnitt Ost; was formed on 25 June 1942 from units of 15. Panzer-Division. The Gruppe, along with Gruppe Baade and Gruppe Dedekind, was under the overall command of Oberst Baade.

GRUPPE WERNEYER

This Gruppe was formed on 25 June 1942, from units of 15. Panzer-Division. Its task was to act as divisional reserve for Gruppe Warrelmann, Besde and Dedekind.

one Zug/Panzer-Pionier-Bataillon 33

1. /Infanterie-Regiment 115 (two Kompanien)

one leichte Batterie/Artillerie-Regiment 33

Commander: Major Werneyer

KAMPFGRUPPE 155

Formed on 5 September 1942 for defensive operations in the El Alamein area.

Panzer-Grenadier-Regiment 155 (less two Kompanien)

Stab/Panzerjäger-Abteilung 190

2. /Panzerjäger-Abteilung 190

one Batterie/Artillerie-Regiment 190

Flak-Batterie 190

Commander: Major Kost

KAMPFGRUPPE 200

Formed on 5 September 1942 for defensive operations in the El Alamein area.
two Kompanien/ Panzer-Grenadier-Regiment 155
Stab/Panzer-Grenadier-Regiment 200
1. /Panzerjäger-Abteilung 190
7. /Flak-Regiment 25 (Luftwaffe)
Commander: Major Georg Briel

KAMPFGRUPPE 361

Formed on 5 September 1942 for defensive operations in the El Alamein area.
I /Panzer-Grenadier-Regiment 200
Panzer-Grenadier-Regiment 361
I./Artillerie-Regiment 190 (one Batterie)
9./Flak-Abteilung 25
Commander: Oberstleutnant Albert Panzenhagen

GLOSSARY OF TERMS AND ABBREVIATIONS

AAR	After-Action Report
ADC	aide-de-camp
AIF	Australian Infantry Force
Alam	a cairn or rock (Arabic)
AP	armour-piercing ammunition
Armata	army (Italian)
Armeenachtrichtenführer	army chief signals officer (German)
Arztpanzer	light tank used by a German medical officer
ASC	Army Service Corps
A/T	anti-tank
Aufklärungs-Abteilung	reconnaissance battalion (German)
Aufklärungsgeschwader	a Luftwaffe unit. Reconnaissance wing (German)
Battaglione Carri	tank battalion (Italian)
BEF	British Expeditionary Force
	The title given to the forces of the British army sent to fight in France and Belgium in the opening months of the First World War. This remained the official title for British forces serving on the Western Front until the end of the war.
Begleitkommando	senior commander's personal escort group (German)
BGS	Brigadier General Staff
BHQ	Battalion Headquarters
Brigade Française Libre	Free French Brigade
CGS	Chief of the General Staff
Chef der Operationsabteilung	Chief of Operations Section (Staff) (German)
CIGS	Chief of the Imperial General Staff

C-in-C	Commander-in-Chief
CO	Commanding Officer
Comando Supremo	Italian High Command
Corpo d'Armata	Army Corps (Italian)
Corpo di Spedizione Italiano	Italian Expeditionary Corps which fought on the Eastern Front
CRA	Commander, Royal Artillery (the usual term for a divisional artillery commander)
CSM	Company Sergeant-Major
Deir	a depression (Arabic)
Deutsches Afrika Korps	German Africa Corps – the distinct principal component of the Panzerarmee
Divisione Corazzata	armoured division (Italian)
Divisione di Fanteria	infantry division (Italian)
Divisione Motorizzata	motorized division (Italian)
Divisione Autotrasportabile	'Division that can be transported by motorized means' (Italian)
DLI	Durham Light Infantry
DSO	Distinguished Service Order
Echelon	unit transport was divided into these groups. F Echelon vehicles are the fighting vehicles such as command vehicles and armoured troop carriers which go into battle as part of the action. A Echelon vehicles have the immediate needs of the unit after the battle such as rations, extra ammunition, packs and cooking equipment. B Echelon is further back with the longer-term stores, administrative headquarters and workshops.
Einsatzkommando	company-sized mobile killing units of the Security Police and SS Security Service (German)
Flak	variously claimed to stand for *Flugzeugabwehrkanone* or *Flugabwehrkanone* – both meaning 'anti-aircraft gun'
Fliegerkorps	Air Force Corps (Luftwaffe subordinate operational command of a *Luftflotte* – which itself was the equivalent to an army group)
Fliegerführer Afrika	Air Force commander (Luftwaffe commander of a *Luftflotte* or of an area of air operations i.e. North Africa in this case)
Freie Jagd	'Freelance air sortie' – A Luftwaffe fighter tactic
Gefechtsstaffel	combat echelon i.e. a commander's tactical operations force (German)
Generale d'Armata	Italian military rank equating to [full] general

General der Panzertruppen	General of Armoured Forces (German)
Generale di Corpo Armata	Italian military rank equivalent to lieutenant-general
Generale di Divisione	Italian military rank equivalent to major-general
Generalfeldmarschall	Field Marshal (German)
GHQ	General Headquarters, Middle East Command
GOC	General Officer Commanding
Gruppe	(two meanings – German): (1) Luftwaffe operational unit of three *Staffeln*, about twenty-seven aircraft (2) Army tactical unit or groupment
GSO1, 2, 3 (I)/(O)	General Staff Officer, Grade 1, 2 or 3, belonging to the (Intelligence) or (Operations) branch of the Staff.
HE	high explosive
Hochseeflotte	Imperial German Navy
HQ	headquarters
IWM	Imperial War Museum
Jagdgeschwader	Luftwaffe unit – a fighter wing (German)
Kampfgruppe	Task Force (German)
Kampfstaffel	German Army combat formation
KRRC	King's Royal Rifle Corps
LHCMA	Liddell Hart Centre for Military Archives
Luftwaffe	German Air Force
Maggiore	Major (Italian rank)
Maresciallo d'Italia	Marshal of Italy (Italian rank)
MC	Military Cross
MG	machine gun (LMG = Light machine gun)
MO	Medical Officer
Naqb or *Bab*	a pass or cutting (Arabic)
NCO	Non-Commissioned Officer
Oberbefehlshaber Süd	Luftwaffe Commander-in-Chief South
Oberkommando der Wehrmacht (OKW)	German High Command
Oberarzt	First Lieutenant, Medical Services (German)
OC	Officer Commanding (like 'CO')
OH	British *Official History*
OP	observation post
Ordonnanzoffizier	a German staff officer who assisted a commanding officer or another staff officer in a variety of duties
Panzerarmee Afrika	German–Italian formation which succeeded the Panzergruppe Afrika

Panzergruppe Afrika	German–Italian formation which controlled all German army formations in North Africa plus two Italian army corps
Panzerbefehlswagen	Armoured command vehicle (German)
Panzerjäger-Abteilung	anti-tank battalion (German)
Panzerkampfwagen	(abbrev. *PzKpfw*) A tank. Often abbreviated to Panzer (German)
Qaret	a low hill (Arabic)
QF	'Quick Firing' (artillery)
RA	Royal Artillery
RAMC	Royal Army Medical Corps
RE	Royal Engineers
Regia Aeronautica	Italian Royal Air Force
Regio Esercito	Italian Royal Army
Regia Marina	Italian Royal Navy
RHA	Royal Horse Artillery
Ritterkreuzträger	holder of the *Ritterkreuz des Eisernen Kreuzes* (Knight's Cross of the Iron Cross) – Nazi Germany's highest award for battlefield courage or skilful leadership
RTR	Royal Tank Regiment
Sanyet	a deep well (Arabic)
Soldato	Private soldier (Italian)
Sonderverband	special unit (German)
Sperrverband	'Blocking force' (German) – An advanced force sent before arrival of the main unit(s).
SQMS	Squadron Quartermaster Sergeant
Staffel	Luftwaffe formation. The equivalent of a squadron
Tenente	Second Lieutenant (Italian)
TEWT	Tactical Exercise Without Troops
Zerstörergeschwader	destroyer wing (German) – Luftwaffe formation

ENDNOTES

CHAPTER ONE

1. Paolo Colacicchi interview, 2951, IWM Sound Archive.
2. Paolo Colacicchi interview, 2951, IWM Sound Archive.
3. Richard O'Connor interview, 12, IWM Sound Archive.
4. Richard O'Connor interview, 12, IWM Sound Archive.
5. Richard O'Connor interview, 12, IWM Sound Archive.
6. [Wavell's dispatch] *Operations in the Western Desert from December 7th, 1940 to February 7th, 1941* in Supplement to *The London Gazette*, 26 June 1946.
7. Richard O'Connor interview, 12, IWM Sound Archive.
8. Paddy Griffith, *World War II Desert Tactics* (Oxford: Osprey, 2008), pp.12–14.
9. Heinz Werner Schmidt, *With Rommel in the Desert* (London: Panther, 1955), p.11.
10. Peter Caddick Adams, *Monty and Rommel: Parallel Lives* (London: Random House, 2011).
11. Hans-Otto Behrendt interview, 2793, IWM Sound Archive.
12. Heinz Werner Schmidt, *With Rommel in the Desert*, p.16.
13. Martin Kitchen, *Rommel's Desert War: Waging World War II in North Africa, 1941–1943* (Cambridge: Cambridge University Press, 2009), p.58.
14. 'Flak' is variously claimed to stand for *Flugzeugabwehrkanone* or *Flugabwehrkanone* – both meaning 'anti-aircraft gun'.
15. Ian W. Walker, *Iron Hulls, Iron Hearts: Mussolini's Elite Armoured Divisions in North Africa* (Marlborough: The Crowood Press, 2006), pp.58–59.
16. Hans-Otto Behrendt interview, 2793, IWM Sound Archive and Hans-Otto Behrendt, *Rommel's Intelligence in the Desert Campaign, 1941–1943* (London: William Kimber, 1985), p.227.
17. David French, *Raising Churchill's Army: The British Army and the War against Germany, 1919–1945* (Oxford: Oxford University Press, 2000), p.228.
18. The film was *Ice Cold in Alex* (1958) starring John Mills, Sylvia Syms, Anthony Quayle and Harry Andrews. The line was delivered by Quayle's character 'Captain van der Poel' (actually a German officer, Hauptman Otto Lutz).
19. Nila Kanten interview, 18391, IWM Sound Archive.
20. 'A PERSONAL NARRATIVE OF EL ALAMEIN by Major A.F. Flatow, TD, OC, A Sqdn, 45 (Leeds Rifles) Royal Tank Regiment', 99/16/1, IWM Documents.

21. Nila Kanten interview, 18391, IWM Sound Archive.

22. Cyril Mount interview, 13123, IWM Sound Archive.

23. Cyril Mount interview, 13123, IWM Sound Archive.

24. Cyril Mount interview, 13123, IWM Sound Archive.

25. Private papers of I.D. King, 96/12/1, IWM Documents.

26. Private papers of C.W.K. Potts, Con Shelf & 92/28/1, IWM Documents.

27. Martin Ranft interview, 23210, IWM Sound Archive.

28. Frederick Hunn interview, 19898, IWM Sound Archive.

29. Cyril Mount interview, 13123, IWM Sound Archive.

30. Gervase Markham interview, 16716, IWM Sound Archive.

31. Heinz Werner Schmidt, *With Rommel in the Desert*, p.169.

32. Quoted in John Connell, *Auchinleck: A Critical Biography* (London: Cassell, 1959), p.445.

33. Billy Drake interview, 27073, IWM Sound Archive.

34. Billy Drake interview, 27073, IWM Sound Archive.

35. Billy Drake interview, 27073, IWM Sound Archive.

36. I.S.O. Playfair, *The Mediterranean and Middle East, Volume III: British Fortunes Reach Their Lowest Ebb* (London: HMSO, 1960 [Repr. Naval & Military Press, 2004]) (henceforth '*OH, Vol. III*'), pp.199–200.

37. *OH, Vol. III*, pp.285–86.

38. F.W. von Mellenthin, *Panzer Battles* (London: Futura, 1977), p.123.

39. Klaus Michaelse interview, 2798, IWM Sound Archive.

40. Thomas Russ interview, 14979, IWM Sound Archive.

41. Mellenthin, *Panzer Battles*, pp.149–50.

42. B.H. Liddell Hart [ed.], *The Rommel Papers* (New York: Da Capo Press, 1953), p.232.

43. Mellenthin, *Panzer Battles*, p.150.

44. Kitchen, *Rommel's Desert War*, p.247.

45. Albert Kesselring, *The Memoirs of Field-Marshal Kesselring* (London: Greenhill, 2007), pp.124–25.

CHAPTER TWO

1. Private papers of C.T. Witherby, 78/61/1, IWM Documents.

2. John Connell, *Auchinleck: A Critical Biography* (London: Cassell, 1959), pp.617–18.

3. The officer was Major Michael Carver, at that time a GSO3 (General Staff Officer Grade 3) at 'Strafer' Gott's XIII Corps Headquarters. Quoted in Adrian Stewart, *The Early Battles of Eighth Army: Crusader to the Alamein Line, 1941–42* (Mechanicsburg, PA: Stackpole, 2010), p.117.

4. Sir Charles Richardson, *Flashback: A Soldier's Story* (London: Kimber, 1985), p.104.

5. New arrivals to the Middle East theatre of operations were likely at an early stage to be given the advice, 'Put some time in and get yer knees brown!' by desert veterans.

6. Quoted in J.A.I. Agar-Hamilton & L.C.F. Turner, *Crisis in the Desert May–July 1942* (Cape Town: Oxford University Press, 1952), p.248.

7. Quoted in Agar-Hamilton & Turner, *Crisis in the Desert*, p.263.

8. Quoted in Agar-Hamilton & Turner, *Crisis in the Desert*, p.263.

9. Private papers of J.E. Brooks, 84/13/1, IWM Documents.

10. Douglas Waller interview, 23447, IWM Sound Archive.

11. Vincent Orange, *Coningham: A Biography of Air Marshal Sir Arthur Coningham KCB, KBE, DSO, MC, DFC, AFC* (Washington: Center for Air Force History, 1992), p.96.

12. Orange, *Coningham*, p.101.

13. Connell, *Auchinleck*, p.622.

14. Corelli Barnett, *The Desert Generals* (London: Phoenix, 2007), p.199.

15. Howard Kippenberger, *Infantry Brigadier* (London: Geoffrey Cumberledge, 1949), p.139.

16. Kippenberger, *Infantry Brigadier*, p.139.

17. Quoted in Agar-Hamilton & Turner, *Crisis in the Desert*, p.276.

18. Kippenberger, *Infantry Brigadier*, p.138.

19. Private papers of G.M.O. Davy, PP/MCR/143, IWM Documents.

20. Martin Kitchen, *Rommel's Desert War: Waging World War II in North Africa, 1941–1943* (Cambridge: Cambridge University Press, 2009), pp. 276–82 details Nazi preparations for the extermination of the Jews in Egypt and Palestine. See also Klaus-Michael Mallmann and Martin Cüppers, *Nazi Palestine: The Plans for the Extermination of the Jews of Palestine* (Washington, DC: Enigma and United States Holocaust Memorial Museum, 2010).

21. Private papers of A. Page, 02/46/1, IWM Documents.

22. Eric Watts interview, 21555, IWM Sound Archive.

23. Ray Middleton interview, 20996, IWM Sound Archive.

24. Quoted in Agar-Hamilton & Turner, *Crisis in the Desert*, p.285.

25. These figures are taken from Agar-Hamilton & Turner, *Crisis in the Desert*, p.288. The infantry strengths of the two German armoured formations seem very low given the overall numbers of German troops in the theatre of operations. However, Rommel subsequently described the low fighting strength of his [Panzer?] divisions on 2 July 'which amounted to no more than 1,200 to 1,500 men...' Liddell Hart [ed.], *The Rommel Papers*, pp. 248–49. He also suggested (p.248) that 90. leichte-Afrika-Division's strength was 1,300 men.

26. Niall Barr, *Pendulum of War: The Three Battles of El Alamein* (London: Pimlico 2005), pp.73–74.

27. Agar-Hamilton & Turner, *Crisis in the Desert*, p.292.

28. Quoted in Agar-Hamilton & Turner, *Crisis in the Desert*, p.293.

29. Private papers of A. Page, 02/46/1, IWM Documents.

30. F.W. von Mellenthin, *Panzer Battles* (London: Futura, 1977), p.161.

31. Mellenthin, *Panzer Battles*, p.161.

32. B.H. Liddell Hart [ed.], *The Rommel Papers* (New York: Da Capo Press, 1953), p.246. Kampfgruppe Kiehl was also known as Kampfstaffel des Oberbefehlshabers der Pz.Armee Afrika.

33. The Afrika Korps was still complaining that 'nothing is to be seen of our own fighter defence' on the evening of 2 July. See Agar-Hamilton & Turner, *Crisis in the Desert*, p.309, quoting the unit's War Diary.

34. Charles Westlake interview, 11048, IWM Sound Archive. Westlake only joined 7th Medium when 107 Battery (formerly South Notts Hussars) was transferred a little later in July, but he was soon familiar with Elton's aims and tactical principles.

35. Quoted in I.S.O. Playfair, *The Mediterranean and Middle East, Volume III: British Fortunes Reach Their Lowest Ebb* (London: HMSO, 1960 [Repr. Naval & Military Press, 2004]) (henceforth '*OH, Vol. III*'), p.342.

36. Waller was the Commander, Royal Artillery (CRA) of 10th Indian Division.

37.   Cyril Mount interview, 13123, IWM Sound Archive. In fact, 'Robcol' consisted of two companies of 1/4th Essex, three platoons of Northumberland Fusiliers, two batteries from 11th (HAC) Regiment, Royal Horse Artillery and 11th Field Regiment, Royal Artillery.

38.   Cyril Mount interview, 13123, IWM Sound Archive.

39.   See Peter Hart, *To the Last Round: the South Notts Hussars, 1939–1942* (Barnsley: Leo Cooper, 1996) for an excellent use of oral history accounts in describing this action and the events leading up to it.

40.   Cyril Mount interview, 13123, IWM Sound Archive.

41.   Private papers of K.L. Phillips, 06/2/3, IWM Documents.

42.   Douglas Waller interview, 23447, IWM Sound Archive.

43.   *OH, Vol. III*, p.343.

44.   This was the opinion of Sergeant Walter Jones, 95th Anti-Tank Regiment, Royal Artillery, 150th Brigade, 50th Division. See Walter Jones interview, 15474, IWM Sound Archive.

45.   Armando Luciano, *Guerra dei corazzati in Africa settentrionale: battaglie e ricordi (1942–1943)* (Modena: STEM Mucchi, 1980)

46.   Luciano, *Guerra dei corazzati in Africa settentrionale.*

47.   Figures from Walker, *Iron Hulls, Iron Heart*, pp.140–41.

CHAPTER THREE

1.   F.W. von Mellenthin, *Panzer Battles* (London: Futura, 1977), p.163.

2.   J.A.I. Agar-Hamilton & L.C.F. Turner, *Crisis in the Desert May–July 1942* (Cape Town: Oxford University Press, 1952), pp.317–18.

3.   See, for example, [General] Sir Charles Richardson, *Flashback: A Soldier's Story* (London: Kimber, 1985). Richardson condemned attempts to use the term 'The First Battle of Alamein' for Auchinleck's 'piecemeal', 'chaotic series of attacks scraped together' – a comment which suggests that Richardson perceived a battle as an offensive operation 'teed-up' by a commander on his own terms in the Montgomery style.
      Richardson's comments are refuted in Corelli Barnett, *The Desert Generals*, p.242.

4.   Barton Maughan, *Australia in the War of 1939–1945: Volume III – Tobruk and El Alamein* (Canberra: Australian War Memorial, 1966) (henceforth *AOH, Vol.III*,) p.552.

5.   Phil Loffman interview, 21614, IWM Sound Archive.

6.   Peter Salmon interview, 21613, IWM Sound Archive.

7.   Alex Danchev and Daniel Todman (eds), *Field Marshal Lord Alanbrooke: War Diaries, 1939–1945* (London: Weidenfeld and Nicholson, 2001), *p.278.*

8.   Billy Drake interview, 27073, IWM Sound Archive.

0.   Christopher Shores and Hans Ring, *Fighters over the Desert: The Air Battles in the Western Desert, June 1940 to December 1942* (London: Neville Spearman, 1969), p.141.

10.   Cyril Mount interview, 13123, IWM Sound Archive.

11.   Private papers of L. Challoner, P479, IWM Documents.

12.   Shores and Ring, *Fighters over the Desert*, p.140.

13.   A.J. Hill, 'Hammer, Heathcote Howard (1905–1961)', Australian Dictionary of Biography, National Centre of Biography, Australian National University, http://adb.anu.edu.au/biography/hammer-heathcote-howard-10405/text18439, accessed 21 August 2011.

14.   Stuart Hamilton, MC, *Armoured Odyssey: 8th Royal Tank Regiment in the Western Desert, 1941–42, Palestine, Syria, Egypt, 1943–44, Italy, 1944–45* (London: Tom Donovan, 1995), pp. 68–69.

15.   Quoted in Agar-Hamilton & Turner, *Crisis in the Desert*, p.328.

16. Mellenthin, *Panzer Battles*, pp.164–65.

17. Mellenthin, *Panzer Battles*, p.165.

18. Quoted in Craig Tibbetts, 'Australians in the first battle of El Alamein July 1942' in *Sabretache* (Journal of the Military Historical Society of Australia), 2004, I, pp.5–20.

19. See Niall Barr, *Pendulum of War: The Three Battles of El Alamein* (London: Pimlico 2005), pp. 109–11 for an explanation of this attack as an attritional one, and therefore an anathema to Liddell Hart.

20. Barr quotes Eric Dorman-Smith's description of the attack as 'a shattering, and almost decisive blow'. See Barr, *Pendulum of War*, p.109.

21. Private Papers of A.D.R. Wingfield, PP/MCR/353, IWM Documents.

22. Hans-Otto Behrendt, *Rommel's Intelligence in the Desert Campaign, 1941–1943* (London: William Kimber, 1985), p.170.

23. Behrendt, *Rommel's Intelligence in the Desert Campaign*, p.170.

24. B.H. Liddell Hart [ed.], *The Rommel Papers* (New York: Da Capo Press, 1953), p.254.

25. Charles Laborde interview, 15103, IWM Sound Archive.

26. Charles Westlake interview, 11048, IWM Sound Archive.

27. David Tickle interview, 14794, IWM Sound Archive.

28. J L. Scoullar, *Battle for Egypt: The Summer of 1942* (Wellington: New Zealand Historical Publications Department, 1955), p.221.

29. Howard Kippenberger, *Infantry Brigadier* (London: Geoffrey Cumberledge, 1949), pp. 156–57.

30. Kippenberger, *Infantry Brigadier*, p.159.

31. Scoullar, *Battle for Egypt*, p.221.

32. Kippenberger, *Infantry Brigadier*, p.157.

33. Kippenberger, *Infantry Brigadier*, pp.159–60.

34. Kippenberger, *Infantry Brigadier*, pp.160–61.

35. Kippenberger, *Infantry Brigadier*, pp.159–60.

36. Quoted in Jim Henderson, *The Official History of New Zealand in the Second World War 1939–1945: 22 Battalion* (Wellington: New Zealand Historical Publications Department, 1958), p.173.

37. Quoted in Jim Henderson, *22 Battalion*, p.175.

38. Quoted in Jim Henderson, *22 Battalion*, p.176.

39. Quoted in Jim Henderson, *22 Battalion*, p.176.

40. Quoted in Jim Henderson, *22 Battalion*, pp.176–77.

41. Kippenberger, *Infantry Brigadier*, p.169.

42. Kippenberger, *Infantry Brigadier*, pp.169–70.

43. Consisting of the staff and one battalion of Schützen-Regiment 115, a detachment from Panzer-Regiment 5 and one artillery battery.

44. Sir Francis Tuker, *Approach to Battle: A Commentary – Eighth Army, November 1941 to May 1943* ((London: Cassell, 1963), p.169.

45. Tuker, *Approach to Battle*, p.169.

46. Tuker, *Approach to Battle*, p.172.

47. Private papers of C.T. Witherby, 78/61/1, IWM Documents.

48. Private papers of C.T. Witherby, 78/61/1, IWM Documents.

49. Kippenberger, *Infantry Brigadier*, pp.169–70.

50. Dawyck Haig interview, 32636, IWM Sound Archive.

51. Kippenberger, *Infantry Brigadier*, pp.169–70.

52. Dawyck Haig interview, 32636, IWM Sound Archive.

53. Dawyck Haig interview, 32636, IWM Sound Archive.

54. Private papers of C.T. Witherby, 78/61/1, IWM Documents.

55. Geoffrey Bays interview, 17610, IWM Sound Archive.

56. Private papers of G.P. Jackson, PP/MCR/350, IWM Documents.

57. Alan Potter interview, 22084, IWM Sound Archive.

58. Phil Loffman interview, 21614, IWM Sound Archive.

59. Phil Loffman interview, 21614, IWM Sound Archive.

60. Phil Loffman interview, 21614, IWM Sound Archive.

61. Patrick Toovey interview, 22393, IWM Sound Archive.

62. Phil Loffman interview, 21614, IWM Sound Archive.

63. Vernon Northwood interview, 18383, IWM Sound Archive.

64. Vernon Northwood interview, 18383, IWM Sound Archive.

65. Vernon Northwood interview, 18383, IWM Sound Archive.

66. Vernon Northwood interview, 18383, IWM Sound Archive.

67. Vernon Northwood interview, 18383, IWM Sound Archive.

68. Vernon Northwood interview, 18383, IWM Sound Archive.

69. Alan Potter interview, 22084, IWM Sound Archive.

70. Ray Middleton interview, 20996, IWM Sound Archive.

CHAPTER FOUR

1. Alex Danchev and Daniel Todman (eds), *Field Marshal Lord Alanbrooke: War Diaries, 1939–1945* (London: Weidenfeld and Nicholson, 2001) [henceforth *Alanbrooke War Diaries*], p.280.

2. I.S.O. Playfair, *The Mediterranean and Middle East, Volume III: British Fortunes Reach Their Lowest Ebb* (London: HMSO, 1960 [Repr. Naval & Military Press, 2004]) (henceforth '*OH, Vol. III*'), p.361.

3. Danchev and Todman, *Alanbrooke War Diaries,* pp.281–82.

4. CIGS to General Auchinleck, 17 July 1942. Quoted in John Connell, *Auchinleck: A Critical Biography* (London: Cassell, 1959), p.676.

5. CIGS to General Auchinleck, 17 July 1942. Quoted in Connell, *Auchinleck*, p.676.

6. Auchinleck to CIGS, 25 July 1942. Quoted in Connell, *Auchinleck*, pp.677–78.

7. Auchinleck to CIGS, 25 July 1942. Quoted in Connell, *Auchinleck*, pp.679–80.

8. Danchev and Todman, *Alanbrooke War Diaries, p.*286.

9. Sir Arthur Bryant, *The Turn of the Tide*, p.433, quoted in Connell, *Auchinleck*, p.687.

10. Danchev and Todman, *Alanbrooke War Diaries, p.*286.

11. Auchinleck to CIGS, 25 July 1942. Quoted in Connell, *Auchinleck*, p.678.

12. C.S. Nicholls, 'Williams, Sir Edgar Trevor [Bill] (1912–1995)', *Oxford Dictionary of National Biography*, Oxford University Press, 2004; online edn, May 2011 [http://www.oxforddnb.com/view/article/57959, accessed 21 Oct 2011] and *Daily Telegraph* obituary.

13. Auchinleck to CIGS, 25 July 1942 in Connell, *Auchinleck*, p.679.

14. Whilst Guingand's appointment is often credited to Montgomery, Auchinleck's assessment of Whiteley was spot on and the latter subsequently saw successful service at Supreme Headquarters Allied Expeditionary Force (SHAEF) and later became Deputy Chief of the Imperial General Staff.

15. [Auchinleck's Official Dispatch] *Operations in the Middle East, 1st November 1941 – 15th August 1942*, issued as a supplement to *The London Gazette*, 15 January 1948.

16. Sir Francis Tuker, *Approach to Battle: A Commentary – Eighth Army, November 1941 to May 1943* (London: Cassell, 1963), p.224.

17. John Harding interview, 8736, IWM Sound Archive.

18. John Harding interview, 8736, IWM Sound Archive.

19. Eric Dorman-Smith's account of the meeting quoted in Niall Barr, *Pendulum of War: The Three Battles of El Alamein* (London: Pimlico 2005), p.187.

20. Private papers of D.N. Wimberley, PP/MCR/182, IWM Documents.

21. Private papers of D.N. Wimberley, PP/MCR/182, IWM Documents.

22. Bryant, *The Turn of the Tide*, p.433.

23. 'APPRECIATION OF THE SITUATION IN THE WESTERN DESERT – El Alamein, 1445 hours, 27th July 1942' in Corelli Barnett, *The Desert Generals* (London: Phoenix, 2007 [reprint of 1960 edition]), pp.339–45.

24. Private papers of Brigadier D.M.O. Davy, PP/MCR/143, IWM Documents.

25. John Harding interview, 8736, IWM Sound Archive.

26. Private papers of Brigadier D.M.O. Davy, PP/MCR/143, IWM Documents.

27. Brian Wyldbore-Smith interview, 19956, IWM Sound Archive.

28. 'Appreciation by C-in-C ME at Eighth Army at 0800hrs 1st August 1942', in Barr, *Pendulum of War*, p.188.

29. Barr, *Pendulum of War*, p.189.

30. Connell, *Auchinleck*, pp.621–23.

31. Auchinleck's 'Western Front – Appreciation of the Situation', 2 August 1942, in Barr, *Pendulum of War*, pp.192–93.

32. Danchev and Todman, *Alanbrooke War Diaries*, p.288.

33. Danchev and Todman, *Alanbrooke War Diaries*, pp.288–289.

34. Danchev and Todman, *Alanbrooke War Diaries*, p.289.

35. Danchev and Todman, *Alanbrooke War Diaries*, p.290.

36. Danchev and Todman, *Alanbrooke War Diaries*, p.291.

37. Private papers of G.M.O. Davy, PP/MCR/143, IWM Documents.

38. Private papers of G.M.O. Davy, PP/MCR/143, IWM Documents.

39. Winston S. Churchill, *The Hinge of Fate* (London: Cassell, 1954), p.458.

40. Dorman-Smith's account quoted in Barr, *Pendulum of War*, p.201.

41. Danchev and Todman, *Alanbrooke War Diaries*, p.293.

42. Danchev and Todman, *Alanbrooke War Diaries*, p.295.

43. Connell, *Auchinleck*, p.706; Danchev and Todman, *Alanbrooke War Diaries*, p.295.

44. Connell, *Auchinleck*, pp.708–09.

45. Danchev and Todman, *Alanbrooke War Diaries*, p.296.

46. This error, which has remained unchallenged since in the writings of many of Montgomery's admirers, appears to be based on Montgomery's signature as Staff Captain appearing on a document circulated by IX Corps prior to the first of the attritional attacks conducted in September and October 1917 by General Sir Herbert Plumer's Second Army. The document in question was actually the August 1917 version of *SS 135 'Instructions for the Training of Divisions for Offensive Action'*, first produced in December 1916.

    The battle of the Menin Road Ridge, which took place on 20 September 1917, was the epitome of Plumer's 'bite and hold' tactics and sought to make modest gains in advance before inflicting heavy casualties on the counter-attacking Germans. For more on this important battle, see John Lee, 'Command and Control in Battle: British Divisions on the

Menin Road Ridge, 20 September 1917' in Gary Sheffield and Dan Todman [eds], *Command and Control of the Western Front: The British Army's Experience 1914–18* (Staplehurst: Spellmount, 2004), pp. 119–39.

47. Private papers of G.M.O. Davy, PP/MCR/143, IWM Documents.

48. Quoted in Nigel Hamilton, *Monty: The Making of a General, 1887–1942* (Feltham, Middlesex: Hamlyn, 1981), pp.622–25.

49. Churchill, *The Hinge of Fate*, p.522.

50. Jonathan Fennell, *Combat and Morale in the North African Campaign: The Eighth Army and the Path to El Alamein* (Cambridge: Cambridge University Press, 2011), pp 206–07.

51. Quoted in Nigel Hamilton, *Monty: The Making of a General, 1887–1942* (Feltham, Middlesex: Hamlyn, 1981), pp.622–25.

52. Quoted in Hamilton, *Monty: The Making of a General, 1887–1942*, p.626.

53. John Harding interview, 8736, IWM Sound Archive.

54. B.H. Liddell Hart, [Generalleutnant] Fritz Bayerlein and G.P.B. Roberts, *A Battle Report: Alam Halfa* (Quantico, Virginia: US Marine Corps Association, 1956), p.9.

55. Eric Watts interview, 21555, IWM Sound Archive.

56. Cyril Mount interview, 13123, IWM Sound Archive.

57. Carol Mather interview, 19629, IWM Sound Archive.

58. Cyril Mount interview, 13123, IWM Sound Archive.

59. Private papers of J. Anderson Smith, Con Shelf, IWM Documents.

60. Private papers of I.D. King, 96/12/1, IWM Documents.

61. Carol Mather interview, 19629, IWM Sound Archive.

62. Private papers of K.L. Phillips, 06/2/3, IWM Documents.

63. Private papers of E. Kerans, 86/61/1, IWM Documents.

64. Mick Collins, 'One Man's War', 92/1/1, IWM Documents.

65. Private papers of D.N. Wimberley, PP/MCR/182, IWM Documents.

66. David Elliott interview, 16706, IWM Sound Archive.

67. Cyril Mount interview, 13123, IWM Sound Archive.

68. Private papers of G.F. Bartle, 85/27/1, IWM Documents.

69. Private papers of E. Kerans, 86/61/1, IWM Documents.

70. Private papers of L. Challoner, P479, IWM Documents.

71. Private papers of C.W.K. Potts, Con Shelf & 92/28/1, IWM Documents.

CHAPTER FIVE

1. Unless otherwise stated all statistics listed in this chapter are from I.S.O. Playfair, *The Mediterranean and Middle East, Volume III: British Fortunes Reach Their Lowest Ebb* (London: HMSO, 1960 [Repr. Naval & Military Press, 2004]) (henceforth '*OH, Vol. III*').

2. Douglas Austin, *Malta and British Strategic Policy, 1925–1943* (London: Frank Cass, 2004), p.158 suggests that Malta-based submarines and aircraft accounted for half (six from twelve) Axis supply vessels sunk between 17 August and 6 September 1942.

3. Martin L. van Creveld, *Supplying War: Logistics from Wallenstein to Patton* (Cambridge: Cambridge University Press, 2004), p.197.

4. These figures are for the period June 1940 and January 1943 and are in Giuseppe Fioravanzo, *La Marina Italiana nella Seconda Guerra Mondiale – vol. I – Dati Statistici* (Rome: Ufficio Storico della Marina Militare, 1950).

5. B.H. Liddell Hart, Fritz Bayerlein and G.P.B. Roberts, *A Battle Report: Alam Halfa* (Quantico, Virginia: US Marine Corps Association, 1956), p.19.

6. F.W. von Mellenthin, *Panzer Battles* (London: Futura, 1977), pp.171–72.

7. Mellenthin, *Panzer Battles*, p.172.

8. Martin Kitchen, *Rommel's Desert War: Waging World War II in North Africa, 1941–1943* (Cambridge: Cambridge University Press, 2009), p.294. Contrast this with the gloomy picture in B. H. Liddell Hart [ed.], *The Rommel Papers* (New York: Da Capo Press, 1953), pp. 265–70: '… German forces were below strength … Rations were miserable and so monotonous we were sick of the sight of them … petrol and ammunition situation was as serious as ever'.

9. Emilio Pulini interview, 2924, IWM Sound Archive.

10. Ian English interview, 10599, IWM Sound Archive.

11. This remark was made at a meeting of the Dardanelles Committee, 20 August 1915.

12. Few military units are ever at full strength, even when not in combat.

13. Figures taken from Pier Paolo Battistelli, *Rommel's Afrika Korps: Tobruk to El Alamein* (Oxford: Osprey, 2006), p.87. The breakdown was ninety-three PzKpfw III, seventy-three PzKpfw III Ausf L 'Specials', ten PzKpfw IV Ausf F and twenty-seven PzKpfw IV 'Specials' (with long high-velocity 75mm gun, and designated Ausf F2).These figures exclude PzKpfw IIs and self-propelled guns.

14. Hans-Otto Behrendt, *Rommel's Intelligence in the Desert Campaign, 1941–1943* (London: William Kimber), p.189.

15. Kitchen, *Rommel's Desert War*, p.295. Kitchen quotes documents in the *Bundesarchiv* (RH/19/VIII/26) in support of his analysis.

16. Behrendt, *Rommel's Intelligence in the Desert Campaign*, p.189.

17. Mellenthin, *Panzer Battles*, p.172. Mellenthin claims that the general staff advised against an offensive and *exaggerated* Eighth Army's tank superiority. This is not supported by available evidence.

18. B.H. Liddell Hart [ed.], *The Rommel Papers* (New York: Da Capo Press, 1953), p.318.

19. Liddell Hart, Bayerlein and Roberts, *A Battle Report: Alam Halfa*, p.20.

20. Albert Kesselring, *The Memoirs of Field-Marshal Kesselring* (London: Greenhill, 2007), p.130.

21. Mellenthin, *Panzer Battles*, p.174. For consistency, I have removed the anglicized version of the German unit names.

22. John Harding interview, 8736, IWM Sound Archive.

23. John Harding interview, 8736, IWM Sound Archive.

24. Freyberg's address to New Zealand Divisional Headquarters Conference, 16 August 1942, quoted in Jonathan Fennell, *Combat and Morale in the North African Campaign: The Eighth Army and the Path to El Alamein* (Cambridge: Cambridge University Press, 2011), pp. 205–06.

25. Private papers of J. Anderson Smith, Con Shelf, IWM Documents.

26. Quoted in Brigadier-General Sir James E. Edmonds, *History of the Great War Based on Official Documents by Direction of the Historical Section of the Committee of Imperial Defence: Military Operations France and Belgium, 1918. Vol. 1. The German March Offensive and its Preliminaries* (Nashville, Tennessee: Imperial War Museum and Battery Press, 1995 (repr. of 1935 edition)), p.258.

27. Private papers of T. Witherby, 78/61/1, IWM Documents.

28. Private papers of J. Anderson Smith, Con Shelf, IWM Documents.

29. Private papers of C.T. Witherby, 78/61/1, IWM Documents.

30. Douglas Waller interview, 23447, IWM Sound Archive.

31. Private papers of C.T. Witherby, 78/61/1, IWM Documents.

32. Winston S. Churchill, *The Hinge of Fate* (London: Cassell, 1954), p.522.

33. Private papers of R.L. Crimp, 96/50/1 & Con Shelf, IWM Documents.

34. Mellenthin, *Panzer Battles* (London: Futura, 1977), p.174.

35. Frederick Hunn interview, 19898, IWM Sound Archive.

36. Liddell Hart, Bayerlein and Roberts, *A Battle Report: Alam Halfa*, p.9.

37. Private papers of R.L. Crimp, 96/50/1 & Con Shelf, IWM Documents.

38. Mellenthin, *Panzer Battles*, p.175.

39. For more on the 'going map' deception see Sir David Hunt, *A Don at War* (London: Routledge, 1990), pp.123–25.

40. Frederick Hunn interview, 19898, IWM Sound Archive.

41. Liddell Hart, Bayerlein and Roberts, *A Battle Report: Alam Halfa*, p.10.

42. Liddell Hart, Bayerlein and Roberts, *A Battle Report: Alam Halfa*, p.10.

43. Liddell Hart, Bayerlein and Roberts, *A Battle Report: Alam Halfa*, p.11.

44. Douglas Waller interview, 23447, IWM Sound Archive.

45. Quoted in Bernd Hartmann, *Panzers in the Sand Volume Two 1942–45: The History of the Panzer-Regiment 5* (Barnsley: Pen & Sword, 2011), p.49.

46. Liddell Hart, Bayerlein and Roberts, *A Battle Report: Alam Halfa*, p.11.

47. Private papers of K.L. Phillips, 06/2/3, IWM Documents.

48. Stephen Kennedy interview, 19089, IWM Sound Archive.

49. Private papers of K.L. Phillips, 06/2/3, IWM Documents.

50. Quoted in Hartmann, *Panzers in the Sand Volume Two 1942–45*, p.50.

51. Liddell Hart [ed.], *The Rommel Papers*, pp.279–80.

52. Liddell Hart, Bayerlein and Roberts, *A Battle Report: Alam Halfa*, p.20.

53. Christopher Shores and Hans Ring, *Fighters over the Desert: The Air Battles in the Western Desert, June 1940 to December 1942* (London: Neville Spearman, 1969), pp.168–70.

54. *OH, Vol. III*, p.382 [fn].

55. Heinz Werner Schmidt, *With Rommel in the Desert* (London: Panther, 1955), p.171.

56. Niall Barr, *Pendulum of War: The Three Battles of El Alamein* (London: Pimlico 2005), p.239.

57. Ronald Walker, *The Official History of New Zealand in the Second World War 1939–1945: Alam Halfa and Alamein* (Wellington: NZ Historical Publications Branch, 1967), p.123.

58. Harry Crispin Smith interview, 19090, IWM Sound Archive.

59. Harry Crispin Smith interview, 19090, IWM Sound Archive.

60. Howard Kippenberger, *Infantry Brigadier* (London: Geoffrey Cumberledge, 1949), p.215.

61. Kippenberger, *Infantry Brigadier*, p.215.

62. Kippenberger, *Infantry Brigadier*, p.216.

63. Harry Crispin Smith interview, 19090, IWM Sound Archive.

64. Quoted in Barr, *Pendulum of War*, pp.239–40.

65. Private papers of J.W. York, PP/MCR/97, IWM Documents.

66. Private papers of F.W. Daniels, PP/MCR/159, IWM Documents.

67. Private papers of E. Norris, 80/18/1, IWM Documents.

68. Private papers of J.W. York, PP/MCR/97, IWM Documents.

69. Private papers of E. Norris, 80/18/1, IWM Documents.

70. Private papers of E. Norris, 80/18/1, IWM Documents.

71. Private papers of E. Norris, 80/18/1, IWM Documents.

72. Private papers of E. Norris, 80/18/1, IWM Documents.

73. Private papers of E. Norris, 80/18/1, IWM Documents.

74.   Private papers of E. Norris, 80/18/1, IWM Documents.

75.   Private papers of F.W. Daniels, PP/MCR/159, IWM Documents.

76.   Private papers of J.W. York, PP/MCR/97, IWM Documents.

77.   Private papers of D.L.A. Gibbs, P470, IWM Documents.

78.   Private papers of D.L.A. Gibbs, P470, IWM Documents.

79.   Shores and Ring, *Fighters over the Desert*, p.181.

80.   Quoted in Shores and Ring, *Fighters over the Desert*, p.231.

CHAPTER SIX

1.   It was, for example, Rommel's opinion that the 'ultra-conservative structure' of the British Army meant that 'although excellently suited for fighting on fixed fronts, [it] was far from suitable for war in the open desert'. B.H. Liddell Hart [ed.], *The Rommel Papers* (New York: Da Capo Press, 1953), p.298. Mellenthin believed 'The British excelled at static warfare, while in mobile operations Rommel had proved himself master of the field'.   F.W. von Mellenthin, *Panzer Leader* (London: Futura, 1977), p.172.

2.   'LIGHTFOOT: *General Plan of Eighth Army*', 14 September 1942, BLM28/3, Montgomery Papers, IWM Documents.

3.   John Harding interview, 8736, IWM Sound Archive.

4   This included Alexander and Montgomery as well as Lumsden, Leese and Horrocks (the latter albeit briefly before being made a prisoner of war). Amongst the divisional commanders, Gatehouse, Wimberley, Freyberg, Morshead, Briggs, Hughes and Nichols had all seen action in France and Belgium. This meant that only Harding, Tuker and Pienaar amongst those of General rank had not.

5.   Carol Mather interview, 19629, IWM Sound Archive. Montgomery's much-praised use of liaison officers like Mather actually resembled a similar practice employed by Field Marshal Sir Douglas Haig as the British Expeditionary Force commander in the First World War.

6.   Brian Wyldbore-Smith interview, 19956, IWM Sound Archive.

7.   Brian Wyldbore-Smith interview, 19956, IWM Sound Archive.

8.   Brian Wyldbore-Smith interview, 19956, IWM Sound Archive.

9.   Quoted in Jonathan B.A. Bailey, *Field Artillery and Firepower* (London: Routledge, 1989), p.182.

10.   Meteorological reports in the desert were notoriously unreliable.

11.   Private papers of V.L. Bosazza, 80/2/1, IWM Documents.

12.   Private papers of J.B. Scollen, 80/38/1, IWM Documents.

13.   Private papers of V.L. Bosazza, 80/2/1, IWM Documents.

14.   Private papers of V.L. Bosazza, 80/2/1, IWM Documents.

15.   I.S.O. Playfair, *The Mediterranean and Middle East, Volume IV: The Destruction of the Axis Forces in Africa (London: HMSO, 1966* [Repr. Naval & Military Press, 2004]) (henceforth '*OH, Vol. IV*'), p.5.

16.   'A Dour Soldier Takes Over In Germany', *The Sydney Morning Herald*, 27 September 1947. Robertson was the eldest son of Field Marshal Sir William 'Wully' Robertson, the Chief of the Imperial General Staff for much of the First World War.

17.   Francis Tuker, *Approach to Battle: A Commentary – Eighth Army, November 1941 to May 1943* (London: Cassell, 1963), p.16.

18.   Jon Latimer, *Alamein* (Harvard, Connecticut: Harvard University Press, 2002), p.126. For more on Robertson, see D.G. Williamson, *A Most Diplomatic General: the Life of General*

Lord Robertson of Oakridge Bt, GCB, GBE, KCMG, KCVO, DSO, MC, 1896–1974 (London: Brassey's, 1996).

19. Stephen Kennedy interview, 19089, IWM Sound Archive.

20. Stephen Kennedy interview, 19089, IWM Sound Archive.

21. Private papers of F. Hunn, PP/MCR/420, IWM Documents.

22. Private papers of R.L. Crimp, 96/50/1 & Con Shelf, IWM Documents. According to Michael Carver, as a result of this change 'some curious hybrid animals were seen painted on vehicle mudguards for a long time after'.

23. Mick Collins, 'One Man's War', 92/1/1, IWM Documents.

24. Stuart Hamilton MC, *Armoured Odyssey – 8th Royal Tank Regiment in The Western Desert 1941–1942, Palestine, Syria, Egypt 1943–1944, Italy 1944–1945* (London: Tom Donovan, 1995), p.70.

25. Carol Mather interview, 19629, IWM Sound Archive.

26. Carol Mather interview, 19629, IWM Sound Archive.

27. Quoted in Niall Barr, *Pendulum of War: The Three Battles of El Alamein* (London: Pimlico 2005), p.267.

28. Ronald Walker, *The Official History of New Zealand in the Second World War 1939–1945: Alam Halfa and Alamein* (Wellington: NZ Historical Publications Branch, 1967), p.194.

29. 'The Teddy Bear Lancers', private papers of L. Flanakin, 07/13/1, IWM Documents.

30. Howard Kippenberger, *Infantry Brigadier* (London: Geoffrey Cumberledge, 1949), p.223.

31. See Bryn Hammond, *The Theory and Practice of British Tank Warfare on the Western Front during the First World War* (Farnham, Surrey: Ashgate, forthcoming), *passim*.

32. Kippenberger, *Infantry Brigadier*, p.223.

33. Walker, *Alam Halfa and Alamein*, p.194.

34. Private papers of D.N. Wimberley, PP/MCR/182, IWM Documents.

35. Private papers of D.N. Wimberley, PP/MCR/182, IWM Documents.

36. Private papers of D.N. Wimberley, PP/MCR/182, IWM Documents.

37. Frank Devaney interview, 2699, IWM Sound Archive.

38. '*LIGHTFOOT: Memorandum No. 2 by Army Commander*, 6 October 1942, BLM28/5, Montgomery Papers, IWM Documents.

39. '*LIGHTFOOT: Memorandum No. 2 by Army Commander*', 6 October 1942, BLM28/5, Montgomery Papers, IWM Documents.

40. Kippenberger, *Infantry Brigadier*, p.224.

41. Lieut. Col. J.H. Boraston [ed.], *Sir Douglas Haig's Despatches (December 1915–April 1919)* (London: J.M. Dent & Sons, 1979 (reprint of 1919 edition)), Final Dispatch, March 1919, p.319.

42. Montgomery may have consciously amended this model after the battle, reducing it to three stages, in an attempt to distance himself from his Great War influences. See '*The Battle of Egypt 23 Oct – 7 Nov 1942: Some Notes by Lt. Gen. B.L. Montgomery*' 'Main Lessons of the Battle', BLM28/1 Montgomery Papers, IWM Documents.

43. Carol Mather interview, 19629, IWM Sound Archive.

44. Peter Moore interview, 11890, IWM Sound Archive.

45. Peter Moore interview, 11890, IWM Sound Archive.

46. Peter Moore interview, 11890, IWM Sound Archive.

47. Peter Moore interview, 11890, IWM Sound Archive.

48. Private papers of K.E.A. Wilson, 83/25/1, IWM Documents.

49. Peter Moore interview, 11890, IWM Sound Archive.

50. Tuker, *Approach to Battle*, pp.208–09.

51. Frank Devaney interview, 2699, IWM Sound Archive.

52. Private papers of J.W. York, PP/MCR/97, IWM Documents.

53. Private papers of R.L. Crimp, 96/50/1 & Con Shelf, IWM Documents.

54. 'The Teddy Bear Lancers', private papers of L. Flanakin, 07/13/1, IWM Documents.

55. Douglas Covill interview, 18023, IWM Sound Archive.

56. Arthur Reddish, *El Alamein: A Tank Soldier's Story* (Wanganui, New Zealand: Wanganui Newspapers, 1992), p.20.

57. *OH, Vol. IV.* p.10.

58. James Lucas, *War in the Desert: The Eighth Army at El Alamein* (London: Arms & Armour, 1982), p.110.

59. Kippenberger, *Infantry Brigadier*, pp.215–216.

60. 'Fly With Me', private papers of C.M.S. Gardner, 99/23/1, IWM Documents.

61. Billy Drake interview, 27073, IWM Sound Archive.

62. Billy Drake interview, 27073, IWM Sound Archive.

63. Private papers of G.M.O. Davy, PP/MCR/143, IWM Documents.

64. Later in the war, Clarke was the man behind Operation *Copperhead* – the use of a Montgomery lookalike – subsequently celebrated in the film *I Was Monty's Double*.

65. Heinz Werner Schmidt, *With Rommel in the Desert* (London: Panther, 1955), p.173.

66. Barr, *Pendulum of War*, p.270.

67. C.E. Lucas Phillips, *Alamein* (London: Pan Books, 1965), p.112.

68. Hamilton, *Armoured Odyssey*, p.70.

69. Alex Danchev and Daniel Todman (eds), *Field Marshal Lord Alanbrooke: War Diaries, 1939–1945* (London: Weidenfeld and Nicholson, 2001), p.329.

70. Danchev and Todman, *Alanbrooke War Diaries*, p.332.

71. Private papers of G.M.O. Davy, PP/MCR/143, IWM Documents.

72. Private papers of D.N. Wimberley, PP/MCR/182, IWM Documents.

73. Private papers of J.R. Harris, 86/5/1, IWM Documents.

74. Reddish, *El Alamein: A Tank Soldier's Story*, p.12.

75. Private papers of R.L. Angel, 88/46/1, IWM Documents.

76. Danchev and Todman, *Alanbrooke War Diaries*, p.332.

CHAPTER SEVEN

1. Gervase Markham interview, 16716, IWM Sound Archive.

2. Although Eighth Army had 892 guns of all calibres under command, a good proportion were with X Corps waiting to deploy after the breakthrough or, in the case of a sizeable percentage of the total, in a similar state with XIII Corps.

3. Sir Francis Tuker, *Approach to Battle: A Commentary – Eighth Army, November 1941 to May 1943* (London: Cassell, 1963), p.233.

4. Cyril Mount interview, 13123, IWM Sound Archive.

5. Gervase Markham interview, 16716, IWM Sound Archive.

6. B.L. Montgomery, *The Memoirs of Field-Marshal Montgomery* (London: Fontana, 1960), p.129.

7. 'The Battle of Egypt 23 Oct – 7 Nov 1942: Some Notes by Lt. Gen. B.L. Montgomery', BLM28/1 Montgomery Papers, IWM Documents.

8. Douglas Waller interview, 23447, IWM Sound Archive.

9.   According to the British *Official History*, the Germans and Italians had 200 field-, forty medium- and fourteen heavy guns to oppose XXX Corps. I.S.O. Playfair, *The Mediterranean and Middle East, Volume IV: The Destruction of the Axis Forces in Africa (London: HMSO, 1966* [Repr. Naval & Military Press, 2004]) (henceforth '*OH, Vol. IV*'). p.36.

10. Martin Ranft interview, 23210, IWM Sound Archive.

11. On this day, Panzerarmee Afrika was renamed Deutsch–Italienische Panzerarmee or Armata Corazzata Italo-Tedesca. For consistency, I have continued to use the term Panzerarmee throughout.

12. Private papers of R.L. Crimp, 96/50/1 & Con Shelf, IWM Documents.

13. 'The Teddy Bear Lancers', private papers of L. Flanakin, 07/13/1, IWM Documents.

14. Jonathan B.A. Bailey, *Field Artillery and Firepower* (London: Routledge, 1989), p.180.

15. Alan Newson interview, 2499, IWM Sound Archive.

16. Ron Dorey interview, 19572, IWM Sound Archive.

17. Ron Dorey interview, 19572, IWM Sound Archive.

18. Some of Wimberley's Great War experiences in 51st (Highland) Division are described in Bryn Hammond, *Cambrai 1917: The Myth of the First Great Tank Battle* (London: Weidenfeld & Nicolson, 2008).

19. C.N.Barker, 'Wielding the Sword: An Autobiography', 96/12/1, IWM Documents.

20. Barker, 'Wielding the Sword', 96/12/1, IWM Documents.

21. H.P. Samwell MC, *An Infantry Officer with the Eighth Army* (Edinburgh: William Blackwood, 1945), p.28.

22. Frank Devaney interview, 2699, IWM Sound Archive.

23. Samwell, *An Infantry Officer with the Eighth Army*, p.31.

24. Frank Devaney interview, 2699, IWM Sound Archive.

25. Frank Devaney interview, 2699, IWM Sound Archive.

26. Frank Devaney interview, 2699, IWM Sound Archive.

27. Samwell, *An Infantry Officer with the Eighth Army*, pp.31–32.

28. Howard Kippenberger, *Infantry Brigadier* (London: Geoffrey Cumberledge, 1949), p.226.

29. Quoted in Jim H. Henderson, *The Official History of New Zealand in the Second World War 1939–1945: 22 Battalion* (Wellington: NZ Historical Publications Branch, 1958), p.205.

30. Quoted in Angus Ross, *The Official History of New Zealand in the Second World War 1939–1945: 23 Battalion* (Wellington: NZ Historical Publications Branch, 1959), p.204.

31. Quoted in Henderson, *22 Battalion*, p.205.

32. Figures are from *OH, Vol. IV*. p.36. The estimate of XIII Corps' total artillery strength is in Tuker, *Approach to Battle*, pp. 241–42.

33. Private papers of K.L. Phillips, 06/2/3, IWM Documents.

34. Douglas Waller interview, 23447, IWM Sound Archive.

35. Private papers of B.E. Miles, 86/25/1, IWM Documents.

36. Michael Carver, *El Alamein* (London: Wordsworth Editions, 2000), p.121.

37. Peter Moore interview, 11890, IWM Sound Archive.

38. Peter Moore interview, 11890, IWM Sound Archive.

39. Peter Moore interview, 11890, IWM Sound Archive.

40. Peter Moore interview, 11890, IWM Sound Archive.

41. *OH, Vol. IV*. p.39 [fn] quoting Eighth Army's after-action 'Lessons' from the operations. It was ironic that two critics of the timings, Brigadiers Kippenberger and Gentry, were both in 2nd New Zealand Division where mine-clearing operations were mostly successful.

42. Private papers of A.D.R. Wingfield, PP/MCR/353, IWM Documents.

43. Private papers of A.D.R. Wingfield, PP/MCR/353, IWM Documents.

44. Douglas Covill interview, 18023, IWM Sound Archive.

45. Arthur Reddish, *El Alamein: A Tank Soldier's Story* (Wanganui, New Zealand: Wanganui Newspapers, 1992), p.16.

46. 'A PERSONAL NARRATIVE OF EL ALAMEIN by Major A.F. Flatow, TD, OC, A Sqdn, 45 (Leeds Rifles) Royal Tank Regiment', 99/16/1, IWM Documents.

47. Flatow, 'PERSONAL NARRATIVE OF EL ALAMEIN', 99/16/1, IWM Documents.

48. Brigadier G. R. McMeekan DSO, OBE, 'The Assault at Alamein', *The Royal Engineers Journal*, Volume LXIII, December 1949, p.341.

49. *OH, Vol. IV.* p.34.

50. Private papers of A.D.R. Wingfield, PP/MCR/353, IWM Documents.

51. Private papers of A.D.R. Wingfield, PP/MCR/353, IWM Documents.

52. Private papers of A.D.R. Wingfield, PP/MCR/353, IWM Documents.

53. *OH, Vol. IV.* p.44.

54. Private papers of R.L. Crimp, 96/50/1 & Con Shelf, IWM Documents.

55. Martin Ranft interview, 23210, IWM Sound Archive.

56. Reddish, *El Alamein: A Tank Soldier's Story*, p.17.

57. Private papers of D.N. Wimberley, PP/MCR/182, IWM Documents.

58. B.H. Liddell Hart [ed.], *The Rommel Papers* (New York: Da Capo Press, 1953), p.304.

59. Private papers of D.N. Wimberley, PP/MCR/182, IWM Documents.

60. G.H. Fearnside, *Bayonets Abroad : A History of the 2/13 Battalion, A.I.F. in the Second World War*, (Sydney: Waite & Bull, 1953), p.274.

61. Niall Barr, *Pendulum of War: The Three Battles of El Alamein* (London: Pimlico 2005), p.334. Barr is mistaken in portraying this unit as a recent arrival in Egypt.

62. Private papers of D.A. Main, 87/35/1, IWM Documents.

63. Reddish, *El Alamein: A Tank Soldier's Story*, pp.17–18.

64. Private papers of I.D. King, 87/35/1, IWM Documents.

65. I have accepted Niall Barr's analysis and conclusions regarding the correct time of this meeting.

66. Francis de Guingand, *Operation Victory* (London: Hodder & Stoughton, 1947), p.199.

67. Montgomery, *Memoirs*, p.130.

68. Joan Bright [ed.], *The Ninth Queen's Royal Lancers, 1936-1945: The Story of an Armoured Regiment in Battle* (Aldershot: Gale & Polden, 1951), p.113.

69. Private papers of A.D.R. Wingfield, PP/MCR/353, IWM Documents.

70. Private papers of D.A. Main, 87/35/1, IWM Documents.

71. Private papers of D.L.A. Gibbs, P470, IWM Documents.

72. Private papers of J.W. York, PP/MCR/97, IWM Documents.

73. Private papers of J.W. York, PP/MCR/97, IWM Documents.

74. Private papers of J.W. York, PP/MCR/97, IWM Documents.

75. Private Papers of J.W. York, PP/MCR/97, IWM Documents.

76. Barr, *Pendulum of War*, p.343.

77. Private papers of D.L.A. Gibbs, P470, IWM Documents.

78. Private papers of D.L.A. Gibbs, P470, IWM Documents.

79. Davide Beretta, *Batterie Semoventi, alzo zero: Quelli di El Alamein* (Milan: Ugo Mursia Editore, 1970)

CHAPTER EIGHT

1. There was general concern about *infantry* casualties in British, Imperial and Dominion forces throughout the war. See David French, *Raising Churchill's Army: The British Army and the War Against Germany 1919–1945* (Oxford: Oxford University Press, 2000), *passim*.

2. Unless otherwise stated all battle statistics listed in this chapter are from I.S.O. Playfair, *The Mediterranean and Middle East, Volume IV: The Destruction of the Axis Forces in Africa* (London: HMSO, 1966 [Repr. Naval & Military Press, 2004]) (henceforth '*OH, Vol. IV*'), pp.51–52.

3. *OH, Vol. IV*, pp.51–52.

4. Quoted in Nigel Hamilton, *Monty* (London: Hamish Hamilton, 1981 [Hamlyn Paperbacks, 1982]), p.809.

5. *OH, Vol. IV*, p.60.

6. 'The Battle of Egypt 23 Oct – 7 Nov 1942: Some Notes by Lt. Gen. B.L. Montgomery', BLM28/1 Montgomery Papers, IWM.

7. Montgomery's diary entry for 1700hrs, 26 October, quoted in Hamilton, *Monty*, p.810.

8. Barr, *Pendulum of War*, p.365.

9. Ronald Walker, *The Official History of New Zealand in the Second World War 1939–1945: Alam Halfa and Alamein* (Wellington: NZ Historical Publications Branch, 1967), p.355 [fn].

10. B.H. Liddell Hart [ed.], *The Rommel Papers* (New York: Da Capo Press, 1953), p.308.

11. Liddell Hart [ed.], *Rommel Papers*, pp. 306–09. It should not be forgotten that much of what he wrote concerning the North African campaign was an attempt by Rommel to explain and justify his actions there.

12. Liddell Hart [ed.], *Rommel Papers*, p.309.

13. Private papers of I.D. King, 96/12/1, IWM Documents.

14. *OH, Vol. IV*, p.53.

15. Private papers of D.N. Wimberley, PP/MCR/182, IWM Documents.

16. 'A PERSONAL NARRATIVE OF EL ALAMEIN by Major A.F. Flatow, TD, OC, A Sqdn, 45 (Leeds Rifles) Royal Tank Regiment', 99/16/1, IWM Documents.

17. Flatow, 'PERSONAL NARRATIVE OF EL ALAMEIN', 99/16/1, IWM Documents.

18. Flatow, 'PERSONAL NARRATIVE OF EL ALAMEIN', 99/16/1, IWM Documents.

19. *OH, Vol. IV*, p.54 says the bombardment fell 'unexpectedly far to the *north*' but Barr, *Pendulum of War*, p.353 correctly states 'south'. As the *OH* map suggests, the position they eventually occupied was to the south and east of 'Snipe'. Lucas Phillips, *Alamein*, p.218 suggests they 'finished up 900 yards approximately SSE of it'.

20. Tom Bird interview, 16303, IWM Sound Archive.

21. Dick Flower interview, 27439, IWM Sound Archive.

22. Dick Flower interview, 27439, IWM Sound Archive.

23. Walker, *Alam Halfa and Alamein*, p.341.

24. Dick Flower interview, 27439, IWM Sound Archive.

25. Joe Swann interview, 27438, IWM Sound Archive.

26. Ian W. Walker, *Iron Hulls, Iron Hearts: Mussolini's Elite Armoured Divisions in North Africa* (Marlborough: The Crowood Press, 2006), p.162.

27. This Brigade of Territorials had transferred from the disbanded 8th to 10th Armoured Division and then to 1st Armoured.

28. '41st (Oldham) Royal Tank Regiment (TA). An account of operations 19th to 29th October 1942 written by Lieutenant-Colonel J.B. Whitehead MC TD, Commanding Officer', (henceforth '41st RTR account of operations'),

[http://homepage.ntlworld.com/tankeddy/new_page_2.htm accessed online 25 August 2011].

29. Flatow, 'PERSONAL NARRATIVE OF EL ALAMEIN', 99/16/1, IWM Documents.

30. '41st RTR account of operations'.

31. Flatow, 'PERSONAL NARRATIVE OF EL ALAMEIN', 99/16/1, IWM Documents.

32. Flatow, 'PERSONAL NARRATIVE OF EL ALAMEIN', 99/16/1, IWM Documents.

33. Flatow, 'PERSONAL NARRATIVE OF EL ALAMEIN', 99/16/1, IWM Documents.

34. Dick Flower interview, 27439, IWM Sound Archive.

35. Joe Swann interview, 27438, IWM Sound Archive.

36. War Diary of XII Battaglione Carri quoted in James Lucas, *War in the Desert: The Eighth Army at El Alamein* (London: Arms & Armour, 1982), pp.217–218.

37. Joe Swann interview, 27438, IWM Sound Archive.

38. Tom Bird interview, 16303, IWM Sound Archive.

39. Quoted in H.G.Parkyn, The Rifle Brigade Chronicle for 1942 (London: The Rifle Brigade Club and Association, 1943)

40. Tom Bird interview, 16303, IWM Sound Archive.

41. G.D.Martineau, *A History of the Royal Sussex Regiment. A History of the Old Belfast Regiment and the Regiment of Sussex 1701–1953* (Chichester: Moore & Tillyer, 1955), p.258.

42. Private papers of E.G. Laker, 85/18/1, IWM Documents.

43. Private papers of D.N.Wimberley, PP/MCR/182, IWM Documents.

44. Private papers of E.G. Laker, 85/18/1, IWM Documents.

45. Private papers of E.G. Laker, 85/18/1, IWM Documents.

46. Private papers of E. Ayling, 78/35/1, IWM Documents.

47. Private papers of E.G. Laker, 85/18/1, IWM Documents.

48. *OH, Vol. IV*, p.57.

49. Barr, *Pendulum of War*, p.361.

50. Alex Danchev and Daniel Todman (eds.) *Field Marshal Lord Alanbrooke: War Diaries, 1939≠1945* (London: Weidenfeld and Nicholson, 2001) [henceforth *Alanbrooke War Diaries*], p.335.

51. Danchev and Todman, *Alanbrooke War Diaries, p.*336.

52. Danchev and Todman, *Alanbrooke War Diaries, p.*335.

53. D.W. Fraser, 'Brooke, Alan Francis, first Viscount Alanbrooke (1883–1963)', rev. *Oxford Dictionary of National Biography*, Oxford University Press, 2004; online edn, Jan 2011 [http:// www.oxforddnb.com/view/article/32091, accessed 15 Aug 2011]

54. Danchev and Todman, *Alanbrooke War Diaries*, p.336.

55. This chiefly derives from an inability on the part of Montgomery's biographer, Hamilton, to accept that Montgomery himself was, initially, the chief point of resistance to a change in plan. See Hamilton, *Monty*, pp.827–30.

56. Quoted in Hamilton, *Monty*, p.828.

57. *OH, Vol. IV*, p.58.

58. Jon Latimer, *Alamein* (Harvard, Connecticut: Harvard University Press, 2002), p.261, quoting the War Diary of 15. Panzer-Division.

59. The 2/13th had 'companies barely stronger than platoons' according to Barton Maughan, *Australia in the War of 1939–1945: Volume III – Tobruk and El Alamein* (Canberra: Australian War Memorial, 1966) (henceforth *AOH, Vol. III*,) p.701.

60. Lieutenant-Colonel Keith Magno (2/15th) subsequently died.

61. *AOH, Vol. III*, p.700.

62. *AOH*, p.702.

63. *AOH*, p.703.

64. *OH, Vol. IV*, p.61.

65. The bulldozer had been lost on a mine. See '26th Aust Infantry Brigade Report on Operation 'Lightfoot'', AWM54 527/6/9, Australian War Memorial (AWM).

66. 'War Diary of 2/48th Aust Inf Bn, 29-30 Oct 1942', AWM52 8/3/36, AWM [online version http://www.awm.gov.au/cms_images/AWM52/8/AWM52-8-3-36-034.pdf, accessed 21 August 2011].

67. *AOH, Vol. III*, p.711.

68. C.E. Lucas Phillips, *Alamein* (London: Pan Books, 1965), pp. 253–56. Lucas Phillips commanded the battery's parent unit, 102nd (Northumberland Hussars) Anti-Tank Regiment.

69. War Diary of Deutsches Afrika Korps quoted in Walker, *Alam Halfa and Alamein*, p.372.

70. Kampfgruppe 361 comprised Panzergrenadier-Regiment I/200, Panzergrenadier-Regiment 361, one battery from Artillerie-Regiment 190 and elements of Flak-Abteilung 25.

71. Liddell Hart [ed.], *Rommel Papers*, p.315.

72. Robert Foulds interview, 12715, IWM Sound Archive.

73. Charles Laborde interview, 15103, IWM Sound Archive.

74. Lucas Phillips, *Alamein*, p.252.

75. *AOH, Vol. III*, p.723.

76. Leo Harry Lyon interview, 22335, IWM Sound Archive.

77. Leo Harry Lyon interview, 22335, IWM Sound Archive.

78. Leo Harry Lyon interview, 22335, IWM Sound Archive.

79. *OH, Vol. IV*, pp. 59 and 63; Liddell Hart [ed.], *Rommel Papers*, p.313.

80. This was probably the fruit of the work of Lieutenant-Colonel Dudley Clarke, which had formed part of the deception plan.

81. Walker, *Alam Halfa and Alamein*, p.365.

82. The unit history of the New Zealand artillery credits Freyberg with suggesting the employment of a creeping barrage for night attacks with infantry but Weir championed its use for *Lightfoot* and *Supercharge*. W.E. Murphy, *2nd New Zealand Divisional Artillery* (Wellington: NZ Historical Publications Branch, 1966), p.373.

83. Quoted in J.F. Cody, *28 Maori Battalion* (Wellington: NZ Historical Publications Branch, 1956), p.236.

84. Cody, *28 Maori Battalion*, p.236.

85. William Watson interview, 10420, IWM Sound Archive.

86. Ian English interview, 10599, IWM Sound Archive.

87. Murphy, *2nd New Zealand Divisional Artillery*, p.403.

88. William Watson interview, 10420, IWM Sound Archive.

89. Mick Collins, 'One Man's War', 92/1/1, IWM Documents.

90. Mick Collins, 'One Man's War', 92/1/1, IWM Documents.

91. Private papers of A.D.R. Wingfield, PP/MCR/353, IWM Documents.

92. H. Bolitho, *The Galloping Third, The Story of The 3rd The King's Own Hussars* (London: John Murray, 1963), p.277.

93. Walker, *Alam Halfa and Alamein*, p.368.

94. Private papers of E. Kerans, 86/61/1, IWM Documents.

95. Private papers of E. Kerans, 86/61/1, IWM Documents.

96. Jackson Browne interview, 14982, IWM Sound Archive.

97. Private papers of E. Kerans, 86/61/1, IWM Documents.

98. Private papers of E. Kerans, 86/61/1, IWM Documents.

99. Jackson Browne interview, 14982, IWM Sound Archive.

100. 'Letter describing the first few hours of the Battle of El Alamein', Misc 93 Item 1410, IWM Documents.

101. Private papers of E. Kerans, 86/61/1, IWM Documents.

102. William Watson interview, 10420, IWM Sound Archive.

CHAPTER NINE

1. W.E. Murphy, *Official History of New Zealand in the Second World War 1939–1945: 2nd New Zealand Divisional Artillery* (Wellington: NZ Historical Publications Branch, 1966), p.405.

2. Jackson Browne interview, 14982, IWM Sound Archive.

3. Murphy, *2nd New Zealand Divisional Artillery*, p.405.

4. Ian English interview, 10599, IWM Sound Archive.

5. 'War Experiences with the 9th Battalion DLI, June 1942 – December 1943' by Lieutenant Wilfred Scott White, Durham County Record Office, D/DLI 2/9/350.

6. Ian English interview, 10599, IWM Sound Archive.

7. Ian English interview, 10599, IWM Sound Archive.

8. Alistair Borthwick, *Battalion: A British Infantry Unit's Actions from El Alamein to the Elbe 1942–1945* (London: Bâton Wicks, 1994), p.28.

9. Jackson Browne interview, 14982, IWM Sound Archive.

10. Jackson Browne interview, 14982, IWM Sound Archive.

11. J.F. Cody, *The Official History of New Zealand in the Second World War 1939–1945: 28 Maori Battalion* (Wellington: NZ Historical Publications Branch, 1956), p.238.

12. Private papers of E. Kerans, 86/61/1, IWM Documents.

13. Private papers of E. Kerans, 86/61/1, IWM Documents.

14. 'Letter describing the first few hours of the Battle of El Alamein', Misc 93 Item 1410, IWM Documents.

15. Jim 'Jamie' Kennedy, 'Alamein: The Battle', Durham County Record Office, D/DLI/2/9/335.

16. Jackson Browne interview, 14982, IWM Sound Archive.

17. Jackson Browne interview, 14982, IWM Sound Archive.

18. William Watson interview, 10420, IWM Sound Archive.

19. William Watson interview, 10420, IWM Sound Archive.

20. Jackson Browne interview, 14982, IWM Sound Archive.

21. Ian English interview, 10599, IWM Sound Archive.

22. Ronald Walker, *The Official History of New Zealand in the Second World War 1939–1945: Alam Halfa and Alamein* (Wellington: NZ Historical Publications Branch, 1967), p.385. Full battledress was worn but not kilts – except in the case of the pipers.

23. Private papers of D.N. Wimberley, PP/MCR/182, IWM Documents.

24. Jim 'Jamie' Kennedy, 'Alamein: The Battle', Durham County Record Office, D/DLI/2/9/335.

25. I.S.O. Playfair, *The Mediterranean and Middle East, Volume IV: The Destruction of the Axis Forces in Africa (London: HMSO, 1966* [Repr. Naval & Military Press, 2004]) (henceforth '*OH, Vol. IV*'). p.66.

26. H. Bolitho, *The Galloping Third, The Story of The 3rd The King's Own Hussars* (London: John Murray, 1963), p.278. 'Grafton' was the codename given to the attack start line.

27.   'The Teddy Bear Lancers', private papers of L. Flanakin, 07/13/1, IWM Documents.

28.   Flanakin, 'The Teddy Bear Lancers', 07/13/1, IWM Documents.

29.   Flanakin, 'The Teddy Bear Lancers', 07/13/1, IWM Documents.

30.   Mick Collins, 'One Man's War', 92/1/1, IWM Documents.

31.   Mick Collins, 'One Man's War', 92/1/1, IWM Documents.

32.   This was actually a slower rate than that for the assault by infantry of 151st and 152nd Brigades.

33.   Flanakin, 'The Teddy Bear Lancers', 07/13/1, IWM Documents.

34.   Flanakin, 'The Teddy Bear Lancers', 07/13/1, IWM Documents.

35.   Quoted in Paul B. Baker, *Yeoman Yeoman: The Warwickshire Yeomanry, 1920–1956* (Birmingham: Regimental Association, 1971), pp.56–57.

36.   Bolitho, *The Galloping Third*, p.278.

37.   Mick Collins, 'One Man's War', 92/1/1, IWM Documents.

38.   Mick Collins, 'One Man's War', 92/1/1, IWM Documents.

39.   Private papers of A.D.R. Wingfield, PP/MCR/353, IWM Documents.

40.   Currie, disregarding the risk, was sat on top of his tank. Calling Grosvenor to join him, he informed him, 'Well, we've made a gap in the enemy anti-tank screen, and your brigade has to pass through, and pass through bloody quick'. Grosvenor replied, 'I have never seen anything, sir, that looks less like a gap'. This story appears in C.E. Lucas Phillips, *Alamein* (London: Pan Books, 1965), p.293. However, it does not claim to be based on a personal experience account and may well be an imagined conversation. Nevertheless, it's a good story!

41.   Private papers of A.D.R. Wingfield, PP/MCR/353, IWM Documents.

42.   Private papers of A.D.R. Wingfield, PP/MCR/353, IWM Documents.

43.   Private papers of A.D.R. Wingfield, PP/MCR/353, IWM Documents.

44.   Quoted in Bernd Hartmann, *Panzers in the Sand Volume Two 1942–45: The History of the Panzer-Regiment 5* (Barnsley: Pen & Sword, 2011), p.62.

45.   Quoted in Hartmann, *Panzers in the Sand Volume Two*, p.62.

46.   B.H. Liddell Hart [ed.], *The Rommel Papers* (New York: Da Capo Press, 1953), p.318.

47.   Liddell Hart [ed.], *The Rommel Papers*, p.318.

48.   Figures quoted on the Axis History Forum http://forum.axishistory.com/ and transcribed from records held by the US National Archives and Records Administration (from National Archives Microfilm Publication T313 Records of German Field Commands: Panzer Armies, Reels 467, 470, 471) suggest the two armoured divisions had a total of only eleven Mark IVs of this type available on 1 November. My thanks to the members of this forum for the very useful material they have published across various threads.

49.   Arthur Reddish, *El Alamein: A Tank Soldier's Story* (Wanganui, New Zealand: Wanganui Newspapers, 1992), p.27.

50.   Reddish, *El Alamein: A Tank Soldier's Story*, p.23.

51.   Reddish, *El Alamein: A Tank Soldier's Story*, pp.27–28.

52.   *OH, Vol. IV*, p.67.

53.   Leo Harry Lyon interview, 22335, IWM Sound Archive.

54.   *OH, Vol. IV*, p.69.

55.   Martin Kitchen, *Rommel's Desert War: Waging World War II in North Africa, 1941–1943* (Cambridge: Cambridge University Press, 2009), pp. 339–40; Liddell Hart [ed.], *The Rommel Papers*, pp.318–19.

56.   Kitchen, *Rommel's Desert War*, p.341; *OH, Vol. IV*, p.68 [fn] and p.69; Niall Barr, *Pendulum of War: The Three Battles of El Alamein* (London: Pimlico 2005), p.392.

57. *OH, Vol. IV*, Appendix 3(a) Rommel to OKW, No. 135/42, 19.50 [German Time], 2 November.

58. Barr, *Pendulum of War*, p.391 and Ronald Lewin, *The Life and Death of the Afrika Korps: A Biography* (Barnsley: Pen and Sword, 2003), p.173.

59. Alex Danchev and Daniel Todman (eds) *Field Marshal Lord Alanbrooke: War Diaries, 1939–1945* (London: Weidenfeld and Nicholson, 2001) [henceforth *Alanbrooke War Diaries*], p.332. By 'GHQ', Brooke was referring to the German High Command.

60. Private papers of D.A. Main, 87/35/1, IWM Documents.

61. *OH, Vol. IV*, p.70.

62. Private papers of D.A. Main, 87/35/1, IWM Documents.

63. Private papers of D.A. Main, 87/35/1, IWM Documents.

64. Private papers of D.A. Main, 87/35/1, IWM Documents.

65. Private papers of D.A. Main, 87/35/1, IWM Documents.

66. Private papers of D.A. Main, 87/35/1, IWM Documents.

67. R.H.W.S. Hastings, *The Rifle Brigade In The Second World War 1939–1945* (Aldershot: Gale & Polden, 1950), p.160.

68. Barr makes the valuable point that losses were almost as heavy as those in the action at 'Snipe' on 27–28 October. Barr, *Pendulum of War*, p.394.

69. Keith Douglas, *Alamein to Zem Zem* (Oxford: Oxford University Press, 1979), p.26.

70. Reddish, *El Alamein: A Tank Soldier's Story*, pp.27–28.

71. Private papers of A.D.R. Wingfield, PP/MCR/353, IWM Documents.

72. Lieutenant A.L. Deans, RTR, 'Report on Special Tank Squadron attached to 7th Motor Brigade from 20th Oct to 4th Nov 1942', 8 December 1942, in private papers of Lieutenant A. L. Deans, 73/211/1, IWM Documents.

73. Private papers of A.D.R. Wingfield, PP/MCR/353, IWM Documents.

74. *OH, Vol. IV*, p.71.

75. Liddell Hart [ed.], *The Rommel Papers*, pp.320–21.

76. The full text of Hitler's order is in Liddell Hart [ed.], *The Rommel Papers*, p.321 [fn].

77. Barr, *Pendulum of War*, p.399. Mussolini's message is in *OH, Vol. IV*, Appendix 3, p.476.

78. Arrangements had previously been made for 90. leichte-Afrika-Division to assist in the withdrawal of 164. leichte Afrika-Division.

79. Private papers of D.N. Wimberley, PP/MCR/182, IWM Documents.

80. *OH, Vol. IV*, p.75.

81. Private papers of D.N. Wimberley, PP/MCR/182, IWM Documents.

82. *OH, Vol. IV*, p.75.

83. Sir Francis Tuker, *Approach to Battle: A Commentary – Eighth Army, November 1941 to May 1943* (London: Cassell, 1963), p.254.

84. Private papers of A.D.R. Wingfield, PP/MCR/353, IWM Documents.

85. Nila Kanten interview, 18391, IWM Sound Archive.

86. Private papers of A.D.R. Wingfield, PP/MCR/353, IWM Documents. Captain Allen Grant Singer was the adopted son of the philanthropist Washington Singer, and Master of Foxhounds with the Hursley Hunt in Hampshire between 1936 and 1940. Sadly, he was killed on 5 November. This account contradicts suggestions that Thoma was cowering in a foxhole when captured. Wolf Heckmann, *Rommel's War in Africa* (London: Granada, 1981), pp. 480–81.

87. Carol Mather interview, 19629, IWM Sound Archive.

88. Private papers of M.E. Parker, 88/4/1, IWM Documents. Parker commanded 257 Anti-Tank Battery, 65th (Norfolk Yeomanry) Anti-Tank Regiment, RA.

89.   Antonio Tomba, *Sabbia e reticolati. Dal diario di un carrista dell'Ariete in Africa settentrionale* (Roma: Italia Editrice New, 2008).

90.   Quoted in Hartmann, *Panzers in the Sand Volume Two*, p.63. Selmayr became *Regimentsarzt* on 3 November.

91.   Hans von Luck, *Panzer Commander: The Memoirs of Colonel Hans von Luck* (London: Cassell, 2002), p.118.

92.   G.P.B. Roberts, *From the Desert to the Baltic* (London: William Kimber, 1987), p.119.

93.   Private papers of J.W. York, PP/MCR/97, IWM Documents.

94.   Danchev and Todman (eds) *Alanbrooke War Diaries*, p.338.

95.   Danchev and Todman (eds) *Alanbrooke War Diaries*, p.338.

96.   This analysis draws on Kitchen, *Rommel's Desert War*, pp.344–51.

97.   Emilio Pulini interview, 2924, IWM Sound Archive.

98.   Gervase Markham interview, 16716, IWM Sound Archive.

99.   Nevill Howell interview, 20937, IWM Sound Archive.

100. Hans von Luck, *Panzer Commander: The Memoirs of Colonel Hans von Luck* (London: Cassell, 2002), p.119.

101. Barr, *Pendulum of War*, p.407.

102. Barr, *Pendulum of War*, pp.402–03.

103. According to Lieutenant-Colonel William Watson of 6 DLI, Brigadier Jocelyn Percy of 151st Brigade was dismissed by Lieutenant-General Oliver Leese shortly after the battle for failing to provide adequate motor transport for his brigade in the pursuit.

104. *OH, Vol. IV*, p.89.

105. Private papers of Brigadier G.M.O. Davy CBE DSO, PP/MCR/143, IWM Documents. Brigadier George Davy was Director of Military Operations, Middle East General Headquarters and strongly critical of Montgomery for his caution in operation immediately after Alamein.

106. *OH, Vol. IV*, p.95.

107. Private papers of C.W.K. Potts, Con Shelf & 92/28/1, IWM Documents.

CONCLUSION

1.   Jonathan Fennell, *Combat and Morale in the North African Campaign: The Eighth Army and the Path to El Alamein* (Cambridge: Cambridge University Press, 2011), p.9.

2.   Tom Bird to *The Times*, 27 September 2001. I am extremely grateful to Tom's son, Nicky Bird, for bringing this letter to my attention and to Tom and Nicky for permission to quote from it.

3.   Howard Kippenberger, *Infantry Brigadier* (London: Geoffrey Cumberledge, 1949), p.190.

4.   B.H. Liddell Hart [ed.], *The Rommel Papers* (New York: Da Capo Press, 1953), p.325.

5.   Kippenberger, *Infantry Brigadier*, p.190.

6.   Private papers of C.W.K. Potts, Con Shelf & 92/28/1, IWM Documents.

7.   Private papers of C.W.K. Potts, Con Shelf & 92/28/1, IWM Documents.

8.   Gervase Markham interview, 16716, IWM Sound Archive.

9.   Frank Devaney interview, 2699, IWM Sound Archive.

10.   Frank Devaney interview, 2699, IWM Sound Archive.

11.   Private Papers of J E Brooks, 84/13/1, IWM Documents.

SELECT BIBLIOGRAPHY

Agar-Hamilton, J.A.I., and L.C.F. Turner, *Crisis in the Desert May–July 1942* (Cape Town: Oxford University Press, 1952)

Barr, Niall, *Pendulum of War: The Three Battles of El Alamein* (London: Pimlico 2005)

Barnett, Corelli, *The Desert Generals* (London: Phoenix, 1999)

Behrendt, Hans-Otto, *Rommel's Intelligence in the Desert Campaign, 1941–1943* (London: William Kimber, 1985)

Churchill, Winston S., *The Hinge of Fate* (London: Cassell, 1954)

John Connell, *Auchinleck: A Critical Biography* (London: Cassell, 1959)

van Creveld, Martin L., *Supplying War: Logistics from Wallenstein to Patton* (Cambridge: Cambridge University Press, 2004)

Danchev, Alex and Daniel Todman (eds), *Field Marshal Lord Alanbrooke: War Diaries, 1939–1945* (London: Weidenfeld and Nicholson, 2001)

Fennell, Jonathan, *Combat and Morale in the North African Campaign: The Eighth Army and the Path to El Alamein* (Cambridge: Cambridge University Press, 2011)

French, David, *Raising Churchill's Army: The British Army and the War Against Germany 1919–1945* (Oxford: Oxford University Press, 2000)

Hamilton, Nigel, *Monty: The Making of a General, 1887–1942* (Feltham, Middlesex: Hamlyn, 1981)

Hamilton, Stuart MC, *Armoured Odyssey: 8th Royal Tank Regiment in the Western Desert, 1941–42, Palestine, Syria, Egypt, 1943–44, Italy, 1944–45* (London: Tom Donovan, 1995)

Hartmann, Bernd, *Panzers in the Sand Volume Two 1942–45: The History of the Panzer-Regiment 5* (Barnsley: Pen & Sword, 2011)

Kesselring, Albert, *The Memoirs of Field-Marshal Kesselring* (London: Greenhill, 2007)

Kippenberger, Howard, *Infantry Brigadier* (London: Geoffrey Cumberledge, 1949)

Kitchen, Martin, *Rommel's Desert War: Waging World War II in North Africa, 1941–1943* (Cambridge: Cambridge University Press, 2009)

Liddell Hart, Basil (ed.), *The Rommel Papers* (New York: Da Capo Press, 1953)

Liddell Hart, Basil, Fritz Bayerlein and G.P.B. Roberts, *A Battle Report: Alam Halfa* (Quantico, Virginia: US Marine Corps Association, 1956)

Lucas, James, *War in the Desert: The Eighth Army at El Alamein* (London: Arms & Armour, 1982)

Maughan, Barton, *Australia in the War of 1939–1945: Volume III – Tobruk and El Alamein* (Canberra: Australian War Memorial, 1966)

von Mellenthin, F.W., *Panzer Battles* (London: Futura, 1977)

Montgomery, B.L., *The Memoirs of Field-Marshal Montgomery* (London: Fontana, 1960)

Murphy, W.E., *Official History of New Zealand in the Second World War 1939–1945: 2nd New Zealand Divisional Artillery* (Wellington: NZ Historical Publications Branch, 1966)

Orange, Vincent, *Coningham: A Biography of Air Marshal Sir Arthur Coningham KCB, KBE, DSO, MC, DFC, AFC* (Washington: Center for Air Force History, 1992)

Phillips, C.E. Lucas, *Alamein* (London: Pan Books, 1965)

Playfair, I.S.O., *The Mediterranean and Middle East, Volume III: British Fortunes Reach Their Lowest Ebb* (London: HMSO, 1960 [Repr. Naval & Military Press, 2004])

Playfair, I.S.O., *The Mediterranean and Middle East, Volume IV: The Destruction of the Axis Forces in Africa* (London: HMSO, 1966 [Repr. Naval & Military Press, 2004])

Reddish, Arthur, *El Alamein: A Tank Soldier's Story* (Wanganui, New Zealand: Wanganui Newspapers, 1992)

Richardson, Sir Charles, *Flashback: A Soldier's Story* (London: Kimber, 1985)

Schmidt, Heinz Werner, *With Rommel in the Desert* (London: Panther, 1955)

Scoullar, J.L., *Battle for Egypt: The Summer of 1942* (Wellington: New Zealand Historical Publications Department, 1955)

Shores, Christopher and Hans Ring, *Fighters over the Desert: The Air Battles in the Western Desert, June 1940 to December 1942* (London: Neville Spearman, 1969)

Stewart, Adrian, *The Early Battles of Eighth Army: Crusader to the Alamein Line, 1941–42* (Mechanicsburg, PA: Stackpole, 2010)

Tuker, Sir Francis, *Approach to Battle: A Commentary – Eighth Army, November 1941 to May 1943* (London: Cassell, 1963)

Walker, Ian W., *Iron Hulls, Iron Hearts: Mussolini's Elite Armoured Divisions in North Africa* (Marlborough: The Crowood Press, 2006)

Walker, Ronald, *The Official History of New Zealand in the Second World War 1939–1945: Alam Halfa and Alamein* (Wellington: NZ Historical Publications Branch, 1967)

INDEX